More than a Job
Securing Satisfying Careers for People with Disabilities

edited by

Paul Wehman, Ph.D.

and

John Kregel, Ed.D.

Rehabilitation Research and
Training Center on Supported Employment
Virginia Commonwealth University
Richmond

·P·A·U·L·H·
BROOKES
PUBLISHING CO

Baltimore • London • Toronto • Sydney

Paul H. Brookes Publishing Co., Inc.
Post Office Box 10624
Baltimore, Maryland 21285-0624
www.pbrookes.com

Typeset by Barton Matheson Willse & Worthington, Baltimore, Maryland.
Manufactured in the United States of America by
The Maple Press Company, York, Pennsylvania.

All of the vignettes in this book are based on real people and their actual
experiences. In most cases, names and identifying information have been
changed to protect confidentiality; in other cases, the subjects of vignettes
have been listed as chapter authors.

Permission to reprint the following materials is gratefully acknowledged:
Excerpts from COUNT US IN, GROWING UP WITH DOWN SYNDROME,
copyright © 1994 by Jason Kingsley and Mitchell Levitz, reprinted by
permission of Harcourt Brace & Company.

Library of Congress Cataloging-in-Publication Data

More than a job : securing satisfying careers for people with disabilities /
    edited by Paul Wehman and John Kregel.
        p.   cm.
    Includes bibliographical references and index.
    ISBN 1-55766-328-9
    1. Vocational rehabilitation—United States.   2. Handicapped—Employ-
ment—United States.   3. Handicapped—Services for—United States.
    I. Wehman, Paul.   II. Kregel, John.
HD7256.U5M666   1998   97-53075
331.5'9'0973–dc21   CIP

British Library Cataloguing in Publication data are available from the British
Library.

Contents

About the Authors

About the Editors

Paul Wehman, Ph.D., Professor, Department of Physical Medicine and Rehabilitation, Medical College of Virginia, and Director, Rehabilitation Research and Training Center on Supported Employment at Virginia Commonwealth University, 1314 West Main Street, Richmond, Virginia 23284. Dr. Wehman is recognized internationally for his service and scholarly contributions in the fields of special education, psychology, and vocational rehabilitation. He is the recipient of the 1990 Joseph P. Kennedy, Jr., Foundation Award in Mental Retardation, and he received the Distinguished Service Award from the President's Committee on Employment for Persons with Disabilities in October 1992. He is the author or editor of more than 100 research monographs, journal articles, chapters, and books in the areas of traumatic brain injury, mental retardation, supported employment, and special education. He also is Editor of the *Journal of Vocational Rehabilitation*, an international journal published by Elsevier. His research interests include transition from school to work, supported employment, developmental disabilities, and brain injury.

John Kregel Ed.D., Professor of Special Education, Virginia Commonwealth University, and Associate Director and Research Director, Rehabilitation Research and Training Center on Supported Employment at Virginia Commonwealth University (VCU-RRTC), 1314 West Main Street, Richmond, Virginia 23284. Dr. Kregel is Associate Director and Research Director at the VCU-RRTC. He is a Professor of Special Education at VCU and coordinates the Urban Services Leadership track in the School of Education doctoral program. His professional interests include supported employment and transition from school to work for individuals with disabilities. He is the author of more than 75 articles, chapters, monographs, and books on the employment of individuals with disabilities. He also serves as Co-editor of the journal *Focus on Autism and Other Developmental Disabilities.*

About the Contributors

Jennifer H. Aaron, B.A., Facilities Use Assistant, Ohio Historical Society, 1982 Velma Avenue, Columbus, Ohio 43211-2497. Ms. Aaron is a 1991 graduate of The Ohio University with a bachelor's degree in public and human relations. Having been told that she would never be successful in college, she pursued her dream despite the lack of support provided by her high school. Ms. Aaron speaks across the United States to parents of children with learning disabilities, to secondary education students, and to employers. She states that despite "always being the 'round peg in the square hole,'" she has "still managed to own a catering business and be a national speaker for alcohol and drug prevention programs." Ms. Aaron is employed as an Assistant Facilities Coordinator with the Ohio Historical Society and Village in Columbus, Ohio.

Amy J. Armstrong, M.A., Collateral Faculty on Supported Employment, Rehabilitation Research and Training Center on Supported Employment at Virginia Commonwealth University (VCU-RRTC), 1314 West Main Street, Richmond, Virginia 23284. Ms. Armstrong is collateral faculty on supported employment at the VCU-RRTC. In this capacity she produces, markets, and moderates live satellite training opportunities and coordinates courses offered through the Internet. Ms. Armstrong also has co-produced CD-ROM modules for personnel training. Ms. Armstrong has presented and/or trained nationally on supported employment and distance education. Prior to her current position at VCU, she worked as an employment specialist, a supervisor of a developmental day program, and an independent living skills instructor in a center for independent living. She received a master's degree in counseling educational psychology from Michigan State University.

John C. Barrett, Office Services Specialist, Rehabilitation Research and Training Center on Supported Employment at Virginia Commonwealth University (VCU-RRTC), 1314 West Main Street, Richmond, Virginia 23284. Mr. Barrett is an Office Services Specialist at the VCU-RRTC and has been involved in the disability rights field since the mid-1980s. Mr. Barrett has served as personal and administrative assistant to Ed Turner since 1990. He has taken several courses in word processing to improve his abilities to assist Mr. Turner. He has served as an administrative assistant in state government for 3 years and is currently using his word-processing skills in developing training materials for self-advocacy curriculum. He is familiar with federal laws and polices that affect the lives of people with disabilities and has accompanied Mr. Turner to all Americans with Disabilities Act training. He has been a member of and advocate for local and statewide disability organizations.

Alicia A. Cone, Ph.D., Instructor, DeSoto Center, University of Mississippi, 137 Education, University, Mississippi 38677. Dr. Cone graduated from Vanderbilt University in 1989 with a bachelor's degree in psychology and sociology. She began work at the North Mississippi Retardation Center in 1990 and in 1991, and she received a master's degree in education psychology with an emphasis in counseling at the University of Mississippi. Previous employment experiences include work as an employment specialist, an assistant director of a sheltered workshop, a human resources management specialist with the federal government, and a research assistant at the Rehabilitation Research and Training Center on Supported Employment at Virginia Commonwealth University.

Victoria Z. Dowdy, M.Ed., Teacher, Henrico County Public Schools, 4211 Hill Crest Road, Richmond, Virginia 23225. Ms. Dowdy is a teacher who received both her bachelor's and master's degrees in education from Virginia Commonwealth University and holds endorsements in mental retardation, severe and profound handicaps, and vocational special needs. She began her teaching career in the Williamsburg–James City County School system working with adolescents and adults at Eastern State Hospital. Since 1990, Ms. Dowdy has taught in Henrico County and is currently teaching secondary-level students at Virginia Randolph Special Education Center.

Shirley S. Ferguson, M.S., CRC, LPC, Vocational Rehabilitation Counselor, State Department of Rehabilitative Services, 1510 Willow Lawn Drive, Richmond, Virginia 23230. Ms. Ferguson is a certified Vocational Rehabilitation Counselor and is employed by the Department of Rehabilitative Services in Richmond, Virginia. She works with adults and high school students with severe disabilities. She also works part time as a mental health counselor specializing in youth and family issues.

Karen E. Gibson, M.S., Employment Specialist, Natural Supports Transition Project, Rehabilitation Research and Training Center on Supported Employment at Virginia Commonwealth University (VCU-RRTC), 1314 West Main Street, Richmond, Virginia 23284. Ms. Gibson is a technical assistance coordinator and an employment specialist with the Natural Supports Transition Project at the VCU-RRTC. Ms. Gibson has a master's degree in rehabilitation counseling, and she has worked with individuals with severe disabilities since the mid-1980s.

Beth Bader Gilson, M.S.W., Research Associate, Rehabilitation Research and Training Center on Supported Employment at Virginia Commonwealth University (VCU-RRTC), 1314 West Main Street, Post Office Box 842011, Richmond, Virginia 23284. Ms. Gilson has worked since the early 1970s in a variety of capacities within the disability services field. By combining her professional background of social work and physical therapy, she offers a blended perspective of that of a direct services provider, administrator, consultant, researcher, and trainer. Ms. Gilson acknowledges that it has been her life experiences as friend, sister, and wife that have taught her more about disability issues than any of her professional roles. Besides collaborating with her husband, Stephen French Gilson, Ms. Gilson is a Research Associate at the VCU-RRTC.

Stephen French Gilson, Ph.D., Assistant Professor, School of Social Work, Virginia Commonwealth University (VCU), Post Office Box 842077, 1001 West Franklin Street, Richmond, Virginia 23284. Dr. Gilson identifies proudly as a disabled man who is active in self-advocacy efforts and cross-disability coalition building. As an assistant professor in the School of Social Work at VCU, his primary research areas are the development of disability identity, the practice of self-determination, and the politics of community. He is also Beth Bader Gilson's partner; husband; and, most of all, friend.

Teresa A. Grossi, Ph.D., Assistant Professor, Department of Education, University of Toledo, 5004 Gillham Hall, Toledo, Ohio 43606. Dr. Grossi is an assistant professor of special education at the University of Toledo. She oversees the teacher certification areas of developmental and multiple disabilities and teaches courses in transition from school to adult life and supported employment. Prior to receiving her doctorate in special education from The Ohio State University in 1991, Dr. Grossi worked for a number of years as both a community-based instructor and an employment specialist. She has provided supported employment services for transition-age youth and adults with severe disabilities. She is especially interested in improving quality supported employment outcomes, enhancing the quality of employment specialists, and systems change.

Thomas Hock, B.S., Programmer/Analyst, Rehabilitation Research and Training Center on Supported Employment at Virginia Commonwealth University (VCU-RRTC), Post Office Box 842011, Richmond, Virginia 23284. Mr. Hock has cerebral palsy. He graduated from VCU School of Business in 1986. His degree is in information systems, and he is employed as a programmer/analyst at the VCU-RRTC.

Margo Vreeburg Izzo, M.A., Program Manager, School-to-Work and Transition to Adult Life, The Nisonger Center, The Ohio State University, 1581 Dodd Drive, Columbus, Ohio 43210-1296. Ms. Izzo is the Program Manager of the School-to-Work and Transition to Adult Life program at the Nisonger Center, a university affiliated program located at The Ohio State University. She directs a federally funded demonstration grant entitled "Making it Work: Improving Transitional Services for Youth with Disabilities" in Ohio. Ms. Izzo is also the Regional Vice President of Ohio's Association for Persons in Supported Employment and is past president of Ohio's Division of Career Development and Transition. She was a Mary E. Switzer Fellow in the 1997–1998 academic year. Previously, she worked as the Project Coordinator of Ohio Systems Change Grant to Improve Transition Services for Youth with Disabilities at the Ohio Department of Education. Her professional interests have focused on student involvement in individualized education program process and in meaningful career and vocational training opportunities for youth with disabilities as part of the secondary program.

John R. Johnson, Ph.D., Visiting Assistant Professor, National Transition Alliance at University of Illinois, Children's Research Center, 51 Gerty Drive, Champaign, Illinois 61820. Dr. Johnson is a Visiting Assistant Professor at the University of Illinois at Urbana–Champaign Transition Research Institute. He directs evaluation activities for the National Transition Alliance, which focuses on the transition of high school students from school to work and to adult life. Dr. Johnson is also chair of the Executive Committee and co-chair of the Consumer-Family Advocacy Committee for Self-Determination, which focuses on promoting the self-determination of adolescents and adults with disabilities. His professional interests primarily have focused on the self-determination, leadership, and employment of adolescents and adults with disabilities.

Kelly Kane-Johnston, B.A., Employment Specialist, Natural Supports Transition Project, Rehabilitation Research and Training Center on Supported Employment at Virginia Commonwealth University (VCU-RRTC), Richmond, Virginia 23284. Ms. Kane-Johnston is an employment specialist who provides supported employment services for individuals referred to the Natural Supports Transition Grant at the VCU-RRTC. She has had extensive experience identifying and developing supports within the community and workplace to address both work- and non–work-related issues as they pertain to individuals referred to the Natural Supports Project. She has a bachelor's degree in psychology.

Mitchell Levitz, Regents Diploma, Self Advocacy Coordinator, Capabilities Unlimited, Inc., 2495 Erie Avenue, Cincinnati, Ohio 45208. Mr. Levitz has co-authored a book entitled *Count Us In: Growing Up with Down Syndrome* (Harcourt Brace, 1994). Mr. Levitz graduated from high school in 1991 and is active in politics, has worked for two state assembly members, lives independently, and works full time. Mr. Levitz speaks on the state and national levels for people with disabilities. He believes in empowering people with disabilities to make informed choices.

Jay McLaughlin, B.S., Rehabilitation Research and Training Center on Supported Employment at Virginia Commonwealth University (VCU-RRTC), 1314 West Main Street, Post Office Box 842011, Richmond, Virginia 23284. Mr. McLaughlin survived a traumatic brain injury in 1988. Since that time, he has been an employment specialist at the Employment Services Division of the VCU-RRTC. He has a bachelor's degree in psychology and is working on a master's degree in rehabilitation counseling. He owns a business called Healthy Connections, which performs community involvement work with people with disabilities.

Wendy S. Parent, Ph.D., Assistant Professor, Department of Counseling and Human Developmental Services, 402 Aderhold Hall, University of Georgia, Athens, Georgia 30602. Dr. Parent is an assistant professor in the Department of Counseling and Human Development Services at the University of Georgia. She is responsible for teaching, performing research, and coordinating community services aimed at improving employment and independent living for individuals with severe disabilities. Prior to this position, she was associated with the Rehabilitation Research and Training Center on Supported Employment at Virginia Commonwealth University (VCU) for 10 years and was an assistant professor in the School of Education at VCU. Her research focuses on consumer empowerment, vocational integration, job satisfaction, natural supports, and other consumer issues related to supported employment implementation. Dr. Parent has written numerous articles and book chapters on supported employment, transition, and rehabilitation.

Julie Ann Racino, MAPA, President and Principal, Community and Policy Studies, 208 Henry Street, Rome, New York 13440. Ms. Racino is Principal and President of Community and Policy Studies and previous Associate Director of the National Research and Training Center at the Center on Human Policy of Syracuse University. A nominee selected for *Who's Who of Women in the World* and a graduate of Maxwell's School of International and Public Affairs, Ms. Racino has 20 years of experience in the policy, management, and development of community services. She is lead editor of the book, *Housing, Support, and Community: Choices and Strategies for Adults with Disabilities* (Paul H. Brookes Publishing Co., 1993), and her research publications include social policy and disability, organizational studies, and community services and systems change. She has taught at the undergraduate and graduate levels and has lectured throughout the United States, Canada, and the United Kingdom.

Beth Regan, 7724 South Grape Court, Littleton, Colorado 80122. Ms. Regan is the parent of four children. Her eldest daughter, Jenny, has developmental disabilities. Ms. Regan previously served as a parent mentor for the Sylvania School District and was active on the Local Interagency Transition Council. As Jenny makes the transition to being served by adult agencies, Ms. Regan continually advocates not only for Jenny but also for a number of consumers and families to ensure quality services.

Jennifer Regan, 7724 South Grape Court, Littleton, Colorado 80122. Miss Regan, at the time of this writing, was a high school student at Southview High School in Sylvania, Ohio. She was involved in a number of transition activities including community-based instruction, participated in a variety of work experiences during the school day, and had a part-time job after school. She also assisted with the girl's basketball team and was active on the yearbook staff.

Pamela Sherron Targett, M.Ed., Program Manager, Rehabilitation Research and Training Center on Supported Employment at Virginia Commonwealth University (VCU-RRTC), 1314 West Main Street, Richmond, Virginia 23284. Ms. Sherron Targett is Program Manager of the Employment Services Division of the VCU-RRTC. She has been involved with supported employment direct services since 1986. She has also co-authored a number of journal articles and book chapters on supported employment and other disability-related issues.

Ed Turner, Training Associate, Rehabilitation Research and Training Center on Supported Employment at Virginia Commonwealth University (VCU-RRTC), 1314 West Main Street, Richmond, Virginia 23284. Mr. Turner has 28 years of experience in the disability rights field. He has been an instructor in special education, a counselor for independent living, and an assistant administrator for a governor-appointed board that advocates for the rights of people with disabilities. Mr. Turner serves as a training associate at the VCU-RRTC. In this role, he has developed a Self-Advocacy Training Institute to inform consumers of their rights and how to use self-advocacy to get the full benefits of those rights.

Darlene D. Unger, M.Ed., Project Coordinator, School Based Supported Employment Project, Rehabilitation Research and Training Center on Supported Employment at Virginia Commonwealth University (VCU-RRTC), 1314 West Main Street, Richmond, Virginia 23284. Ms. Unger has been employed with the VCU-RRTC since the late 1980s. She is Project Coordinator for the School Based Supported Employment Project, which provides training and technical assistance to localities in developing school- and community-based employment programs for transition-age youth with disabilities. Previously, she coordinated demonstration projects that focused on the use of natural supports to assist transition-age youth with severe disabilities in becoming competitively employed. She also has worked as an employment counselor at the VCU-RRTC. Ms. Unger holds a master's degree in special education and is pursuing her doctoral degree in education.

Mary-Kay Webster, B.A., Systems Administrator, Chesapeake Corporation, James Center 2, 22nd Floor, 1021 East Cary Street, Richmond, Virginia 23219. Ms. Webster was 24 years old in 1985 and was thoroughly enjoying life. Secure in the early stages of her career, yet unencumbered by the responsibilities of a family, she felt invincible. It was also the time of major decision making. Should she make a career move, change her place of residence, or change marital status? Anything was possible. But suddenly, a spinal cord injury narrowed those options tremendously. Fortunately, her career in accounting could be continued with or without paralysis. She continues to work full time, owns and maintains a home, and pursues musical and gourmet interests with friends.

Michael West, Ph.D., Research Associate, Rehabilitation Research and Training Center on Supported Employment at Virginia Commonwealth University (VCU-RRTC), Post Office Box 842011, Richmond, Virginia 23284. Dr. West is a Research Associate at Virginia Commonwealth University, where he is affiliated with the VCU-RRTC and the Department of Physical Medicine and Rehabilitation. He has 20 years of direct services experiences, primarily in employment programs for individuals with developmental and acquired disabilities. Dr. West's research includes a study of students with disabilities in higher education in Virginia to determine needs and satisfaction with disability-related services and accommodation and a study of the use of Medicaid home- and community-based waivers to fund employment services.

Perry Whittico, Self-Advocate, 550 South Clinton Street, Syracuse, New York 13202. Mr. Whittico is a strong advocate for people with civil rights issues and a member of the Self Advocacy Association of Central New York. He has served as President of the organization and as a member of the Center on Human Policy's Advocacy Board at Syracuse University. Mr. Whittico has spoken at the National Council on Independent Living's annual conference and at state events, such as the Ohio Community Living Conference. He also has served as an independent consultant with Community and Policy Studies on its personal contract with the World Institute on Disability, California.

Mary R. Wilkinson, Information and Referral Specialist, Virginia Assistive Technology, 8004 Franklin Farms Drive, Richmond, Virginia 23288. Ms. Wilkinson supervised the Cash Management Department and managed the short-term investment portfolio of a Fortune 500 manufacturing company until 1988. She left this position because of disability. Between 1988 and 1993, she participated in a variety of community and statewide disability organizations, one of which was instrumental in establishing the first postpolio clinic in Virginia. She also has served as peer counselor at a local rehabilitation facility and chaired the Middle Peninsula Disability Services Board. When ready to pursue a second career, she found that her volunteer experiences had been so rewarding that she wanted to work in the disability field. In 1994, she went to work for the Virginia Board for People with Disabilities to coordinate an education program. In 1995, she began a job as an Information and Referral Specialist for the Virginia Assistive Technology System, which continues to provide an opportunity to work for people with disabilities.

Katherine Mullaney Wittig, M.Ed., Education for Employment Work Coordinator, Henrico County Public Schools, 2206 Mountain Road, Glen Allen, Virginia 23060. Ms. Wittig received her bachelor's degree in art/elementary education at the University of Rhode Island and received her master's in education degree in severe/profound handicaps at Rhode Island College. Ms. Wittig has worked in the fields of rehabilitation, supported employment, and special education since the late 1970s as a teacher and/or administrator. Ms. Wittig co-authored a grant to develop Project Transition, which she directed, in Bangor, Maine, until 1992. She is the Work/Transition Coordinator at Virginia Randolph Education Complex in Henrico County, Virginia.

Preface

Since the 1970s, there have been a number of books that have focused on the vocational rehabilitation of people with disabilities. These books have made important contributions to the formulation of training technology and service delivery issues such as implementation, evaluation, staff training, and technical assistance. Relatively few books, however, specifically address what we think is one of the most pressing needs in the vocational rehabilitation area—that is, consumer choice that leads to a career path. We acknowledge that, for many individuals with disabilities, their first job is just that—a job. It is not a well–thought-out or carefully planned blueprint for a career. Furthermore, a major impediment to people with disabilities becoming competitively employed is the lack of consumer choice, consumer participation, and consumer involvement in the vocational process. These impediments directly block the broader vision of establishing a long-term career path for people with disabilities. The direct involvement of individuals with disabilities in the specifics of job planning include choosing the type of job, the mode of transportation, and type of living situation in which they are comfortable. These all are factors that can play a significant role in gaining competitive employment. With the unemployment rate for people with disabilities continuing at a staggeringly high rate of more than 60% (Louis Harris and Associates, 1994), consumer satisfaction with a chosen career path is essential. The introduction of concepts such as person-centered planning (e.g., Mount & Zwernik, 1988) and self-determination (e.g. Wehmeyer, Agran, & Hughes, 1998) into the employment search process, however, can greatly enhance competitive employment opportunities and level of job satisfaction for people with disabilities.

The chapters in this book, therefore, focus on the individual in his or her search for competitive employment. Strategies that use vocational training, supported employment, and assistive technologies are just some of the key methods explored. Although the focus is squarely on the individual and his or her needs and desires, this is not to say that we conceptualize that all people with disabilities can solve all problems by themselves. After all, as Condeluci (1996) pointed out, all human beings are interdependent on each other for help, support, and accomplishment in society. We believe that people with disabilities have not been treated as equal partners by society and in their search for employment too often have been viewed as "units of service." This type of philosophy works directly in opposition to the attainment of long-term competitive employment and meaningful career paths.

More important than the attainment of an initial job for people with disabilities is their strong feeling of involvement and participation in the employment process. Employment, in general, is a function of the different cycles in the economy as well as other variables that are often outside of one's direct control. What is within one's control, however, is to have a say on the best way to go about the job hunt, participate in the interview process directly, have veto power over unattractive aspects of a job, and have direct involvement with the agency or counselor who has been assigned to help. The authors visualize career planning as an important means to an end: competitive employment. Without careful planning, individuals too frequently are shunted into low-paying, unsatisfying jobs that offer little hope for advancement. Once again, the best way to eliminate this practice is to ensure that consumers direct job-planning activities as opposed to having individuals be pushed into poorly planned, "dead-end" positions.

Work is a critically important part of everyone's lives, and this is no different for people with disabilities who tend to be less self-confident, have less money, and are often out of the mainstream of society. Furthermore, work demonstrates competence and the capacity for independence to others in society who may have a negative or patronizing perception of people with disabilities. As noted previously, almost two thirds of all people with disabilities are unemployed, so the ability to gain employment in the competitive workforce and maintain employment for an extended period of time is a major accomplishment for many people with disabilities. Obviously, those who are able to maintain employment and establish a career path are successful, indeed, and have found the right mix of motivation, training, and support.

It is essential for those who work in the disability field to understand that, just because one uses a wheelchair or sometimes is guided across the street or is helped to read a passage or is assisted with special technical tools, this does not mean that the person is unable to direct his or her own future. These supports may be more prominent for people with disabilities than for people without, but the same philosophy is in place for everyone: Help should be given only on an as-needed and as-requested basis, depending on what the individual wants and on the best professional advice of the person being consulted. We believe that successful, productive work is an important therapy that goes beyond the ability to earn a regular paycheck. There is a heavy emphasis in this book on the meritorious value of productive employment. Work offers the ability to show competence, make friends, and increase one's sense of self-worth. Successful day-to-day performance of a job leads to regular compensation; and this is an ongoing, positive reminder to many individuals with disabilities of their ability to contribute to their families and communities. In the chapters that follow, there is a pronounced emphasis on consumer choice and self-determination in the context selecting a job, networking with a variety of different types of friends, and expanding the capability to be successful in and around the community.

To help fulfill the objectives put forth in the National Council on Disabilities' (1996) call to improve the lives of Americans with disabilities, there is a need to provide a greater community orientation to the way services are provided and supports are arranged. There continues to be a perception that professionals know better than the individuals seeking their help and that people with disabilities are "sick" with needs that can be "cured," "fixed," or "taken care of." More than ever, we need to adopt a philosophy of supporting people and helping them to follow the path that they set for themselves.

One of our major goals in recruiting authors and editing this book is to show the human potential of people with disabilities, especially when supports are designed with the individual's help to meet personal vocational, residential, and community needs. In the absence of collaboration between support personnel and individuals with disabilities, people with disabilities will be doomed to continued stagnation and will be unable to achieve their full potential.

The majority of the authors have disabilities themselves or have close family members with disabilities. These authors live "disability" everyday. It is our hope that this book can touch thousands of people with disabilities and the professionals who work to support them.

REFERENCES

Condeluci, A. (1996). *Beyond difference.* Delray Beach, FL: St. Lucie Press.

Louis Harris and Associates. (1994). *The ICD Survey II: Employing disabled Americans* (pp. 6–8). Washington, DC: National Organization on Disability.

Mount, B., & Zwernik, K. (1988). *It's never too early, it's never too late: A booklet about personal futures planning.* St. Paul, MN: Metropolitan Council.

National Council on Disabilities. (1996, April 26). *Improving the implementation of the Individuals with Disabilities Education Act: Making schools work for all of America's children.* Washington, DC: Author.

Wehmeyer, M.L., Agran, M., & Hughes, C. (1998). *Teaching self-determination to students with disabilities: Basic skills for successful transition.* Baltimore: Paul H. Brookes Publishing Co.

Acknowledgments

It is a pleasure to acknowledge the many people who have helped us bring this unique project to fruition. *More than a Job: Securing Satisfying Careers for People with Disabilities* has been an unusual undertaking in the sense that it is one of the few employment-oriented books of which we know that is totally focused on a consumer perspective on disability and employment. We have had the good fortune of assembling a group of contributors who have been closely involved with or experienced disability from a personal perspective. By gaining the participation of contributors who have disabilities themselves, we have been able to develop content that more richly reflects traditional vocational rehabilitation materials.

We would like to specifically identify Stephen French Gilson as a major driving force behind this project and thank him for his willingness to contribute and for his creativity. Dr. Gilson, who is an assistant professor of social work at Virginia Commonwealth University (VCU) is an outstanding professional with a strong personality and clear values. He also happens to have a significant physical disability; this disability experience has helped him illuminate the challenges faced by many others with disabilities in Virginia. We think that his influence on *More than a Job* has been significant indeed.

We also are indebted to all of the other contributors—each of whom has taken time from his or her busy schedule to formulate a thoughtful perspective on how people with disabilities can be directly involved in arranging their own employment and careers.

We also are grateful for the excellent staff at the VCU Rehabilitation Research and Training Center on Supported Employment as well as for the faculty in the Department of Physical Medicine and Rehabilitation. Both of these groups of colleagues have directly influenced much of our work over the last few years and have helped us to understand many of the disability employment and functional assessment issues. We also want to recognize the positive influence of people like Paul Bates, Gary Bond, Lou Brown, John Butterworth, Susan Daniels, Tamara Freeman, Cary Griffin, Mark Hill, Katina Karoulis, Bill Kiernan, Rich Luecking, David Mank, Joe Marrone, Rebecca McDonald, Adelle Renzaglia, Marie Strahan, Michael Wehmeyer, Tony

Young, and many others too numerous to mention who have influenced the shape of our work in this book.

We also are grateful for the continuing federal and state support of our research and training activities. This external support partially helps us in writing efforts such as ones like *More than a Job*. We want to specifically thank and recognize the support of Dr. Bill Halloran, Dr. Judy Heumann, Dr. Richard Melia, Dr. Howard Moses, Dr. Kate Seelman, Dr. Fred Schroeder, and Delores Watkins, for their ongoing support of our research and training efforts on employment for people with disability. This support is critical to our ongoing efforts to learn more about people with disabilities as they overcome these complex challenges of entering the labor force.

Finally, we want to acknowledge the love and support of our families who are always these for us. Specifically, we acknowledge our wives, Le Le and Rhonda, and our children, Blake, Cara, Brody, Ragan, and Peyton, and Michael and Emily, for whom we hope that we are able to return the joy and happiness that they provide us.

We truly hope that this material will be of use and inspiration to others with disabilities and advocates who work on their behalf.

More than a Job

Issues

Consumer choice. Self-determination. Clients' rights. Self-advocacy. Consumerism. Person centered. These are all terms that have guided the disability advocacy movement in the 1990s. With the signing of the Americans with Disabilities Act (ADA) in July of 1990 (PL 101-336), a new era was ushered into the disability world. In the decades leading up to the passage of the ADA, great strides had been made in professional training, technology, community integration, financing of public school education programs, and deinstitutionalization. The emphasis rested, however, on the service provider, the system, and the funding agency rather than on the individual with the disability. The ADA helped to shift the focus of service provision to emphasize the wants, needs, and goals of the person with the disability.

The chapter authors in Section I address the continuing need to enhance self-determination opportunities for people with disabilities in the United States. Each of the authors—Gilson, Cone, Racino, and Kregel—provides a strong emphasis on consumer choice and self-advocacy. In the opening chapter, for example, Dr. Gilson provides a highly provocative and insightful look into the issues of choice and self-advocacy from a personal perspective. He talks passionately about the need for communities to drop barriers and to increase access for citizens with disabilities. Whereas Dr. Gilson provides a personal and moving reflection on the challenges of gaining full employment for people with disabilities, the ensuing chapters make liberal use of personal case studies to explore the issues of job attainment and retention by and for people with a variety of disabilities. The text draws its strength from these cases, many of which are true stories of self-advocacy and self-determination in practice, straight from some of the

1

very people who this book is designed to help. Professionals can draw invaluable insights from these cases.

Dr. Gilson's comments are reinforced and expanded by Dr. Cone and Ms. Racino, who write more directly about building self-advocacy programs and establishing community networks. Employment, careers, and acceptance into the mainstream of society begin in the community; hence, the mechanism for implementing the ADA is the development of community support networks. These two chapters focus on the fact that self-determination can be facilitated by proactive community support networks for people with disabilities who desire a chance to pursue fulfilling careers. These chapters demonstrate that with the help of just a few key supports, an individual with a disability can live in his or her own apartment and hold a meaningful and satisfying job.

A key tenet, which provides the foundation for this book, is that the focus must always be on the *individual*. Dr. Kregel elucidates the importance of person-centered planning, which concentrates on the individual in planning programs and determining the right path for vocational success. The best way to achieve job success is to find satisfying work, both for people with and without disabilities. Person-centered planning can facilitate vocational success.

CHAPTER

Choice and Self-Advocacy

A Consumer's Perspective

Stephen French Gilson

DIMITRI

As a single male, Dimitri, like many people in their mid-20s, was struggling to find his place in life. With a college degree and many interests, he had moved frequently, trying to find the perfect location—city or town, mountain community or seaside village—in which he could settle down, make friends, and begin a career that would not only be satisfying to him but would be a statement of worth to his family and to himself. But this never happened. Dimitri, who had a history of short hospitalizations while living in other communities, was admitted to a psychiatric inpatient hospital after months of participating in community outpatient mental health services, therapy, and medication prescription and management for the treatment of hallucinations, periods of depression, intense anxiety, and what seemed to be psychotic episodes. During this

---

The author of this chapter identifies as being disabled. It is recognized that the language of disability used in this chapter may differ from that suggested by professional organizations. Also, unlike other chapters in this book, the author uses a first-person narrative. The words "we," "our," and "us" are used throughout the chapter to mean the community of disabled people. Acceptance of the right to select terminology is essential to recognizing and understanding the needs of disabled people and is vital to appreciating their community. For a more complete discussion of this issue, please see Heumann (1993).

hospitalization, Dimitri was referred to a psychosocial clubhouse program. The psychosocial program was set up on a milieu-based model, in which there were regularly scheduled group treatments, medication prescriptions, recreation, and meal preparation training. Dimitri had been employed full time as a chef in an upscale bar/restaurant during the course of his outpatient treatment. And because he worked primarily in the late afternoon, he was able to participate in the program while maintaining his job at the restaurant.

Dimitri, however, was unhappy at work and felt as if this job reinforced the sentiment that he would never really be able to have a "career" as his parents had and as his siblings seemed well on their way to having. He thought that some of his disappointment in himself and his depression were related to feeling out of place at work and feeling as if he had no options. Fortunately, in addition to the mental health therapists and psychiatrists associated with the program, occupational therapists, recreational therapists, and vocational rehabilitation professionals also were part of the treatment team. During one of the group therapy sessions, Dimitri was informed about the existence of vocational rehabilitation counseling. Because he was new to psychosocial treatment and rehabilitation, however, he was not certain of the nature of the services that were available nor was he aware of his full range of community living and work options.

Following one of the group therapy sessions, Dimitri made an appointment with a vocational rehabilitation counselor, hoping that this person could administer a career aptitude evaluation and assist him in pursuing a graduate degree, which might help him find professional employment. The appointment with the vocational rehabilitation counselor was a disappointment. Dimitri was not given a skill and career aptitude evaluation. He was not encouraged to continue his education, despite having made very good grades as an undergraduate. Dimitri left the appointment still unsure about just what vocational services were or which options and opportunities might be possible. He did not make a follow-up appointment nor was one scheduled by the counselor.

At about the same time, Dimitri's mental health therapist told him that she was surprised that he could do as well as he seemed to be doing at his current job, considering all of the medications that he took. Dimitri was not aware that the staff at the psychosocial program knew anything about his work or even where he worked until the day of his vocational services appointment.

Self-determination, choice, empowerment, and *self-advocacy* have become the terms used to reflect the progressive work of professionals with disabled people. The terms also are found in statements made by disabled people about how we wish to define our services, programs, and organizations. How these terms are defined and who defines them is critical to the development and functioning of services, programs, and organizations. Furthermore, because the multiple dimensions of our lives, education, community living, and work are intertwined, it is important that the issues of self-determination, choice, empowerment, and self-advocacy be considered in the context in which they are learned, practiced, and reinforced within and between each dimension.

It is critical that I make clear how I define disability and how I understand the determination of "who is disabled." If an individual identifies as having a disability or as being disabled—whether that disability is visually apparent or not—that individual is disabled. Identifying as disabled, for many, is a complex phenomenon (Zola, 1993). The recognition and embracing of disability is often a process. For some, it is moving away from rejecting or denying one's disability toward acknowledging and affirming one's identity as being disabled. Within this context there may be several levels on which a disabled person "identifies," all of which are interrelated. As disabled people, we are a part of the larger disability community, which includes individuals with visible and invisible disabilities. This is a definition of *pan-disability* (a point to which the discussion will return shortly). As such, this definition includes people with orthopedic disabilities, neuromuscular disabilities, developmental disabilities, sensory disabilities, mental disabilities, cognitive disabilities, learning disabilities, congenital disabilities, acquired disabilities, disabilities due to trauma or illness, or disabilities that accompany the aging process. This is by no means intended to be an exhaustive list, nor is it a list that is limited to a professional's qualifications or determinations. If you say you are disabled, then you are disabled.

Identifying on this level does not necessarily mean that as disabled people we reveal our diagnoses or present our conditions; instead, those are subtexts within a much larger discussion. As an interesting note, it is quite possible to have a disability and not identify as being disabled. Identifying as disabled within this framework is linked to embracing self-determination and is tied to having a confident and positive sense of self (Gilson, Tusler, & Gill, 1997). If, however, disabled people are going to seek accommodation in educational settings or work environments, identifying as disabled may require that we disclose our mental health histories, learning disabilities, sensory and communication impairments, and physical restrictions. Disclosing our diagnoses to seek accommodation can be done without "embracing" disability. In this chapter, identification signifies a public acknowledgment of and affiliation with disability. It is within this public context that we experience both the negative consequences of oppression and discrimination, as well as the positive rewards of being linked to others with disabilities. It is within this public context that we also may begin to appreciate our history, our art, our music, our words and phrases, our literature, and our culture (Shaw, 1994). This identification helps to provide us with resources and supports.

THE EMERGING PAN-DISABILITY MOVEMENT

Far from being a monolithic entity, the disability community often has found itself split into factions, divided by—among other issues—types of disability, age at which the disability presented, degree of disability visibility, and level of disability severity (see Grobe, 1995; Shapiro, 1993; Zola, 1982). These divisions have had significant public policy implications, affecting, for example, which disabilities are provided support and assistance under federal legislation (see Percy, 1989; Scotch, 1984). Furthermore, these divisions have served to isolate and separate us, which has decreased our capability as a community to come together in a cohesive coalition to develop and shape policies, services, and programs to meet our needs. The advocacy leading up to issuance of Section 504 of the Rehabilitation Act of 1973 (PL 93-112) and the passage of the Americans with Disabilities Act (ADA) of 1990 (PL 101-336) began a process whereby we have been forced to examine the divisions that have existed within our community. For example, Mayerson (1993) described the passage of the ADA as a reflection of the commitment of the disability community and of the movement toward a "solidarity among people of different disabilities" (1993, p. 18). Within this context we must ask ourselves questions such as the following: Are the experiences of someone living with a physical disability different from someone living with a mental illness? Are some of us "disabled enough" to be considered "disabled?" Who is "correctly disabled?" What is the impact on people with hidden disabilities when terms such as "able bodied" are used to provide distinction from disability? Do different experiences, based on the visibility of the disability, limit the shared meaning of disability in a social movement? It is clear that a full discussion of these very important questions is beyond the scope of this chapter.

Breaking Down Barriers

Barriers are breaking down among disabled people as we find that although there is considerable diversity within our community, there are many shared or common experiences. Shared experiences for disabled people include lack of accommodations, denial of physical or communication access to educational or vocational opportunities, and denial of services through more covert practices such as failing to provide adequate medical insurance coverage. Nearly 1 in 5 Americans has a disability—the nation's largest minority. Forty-nine million Americans, including 29,000,000 Americans between the ages of 15 and 64, or more than 1 in 6 people of working age, have disabilities (National Organization on Disability [N.O.D.], 1994). Forty percent of individuals with disabilities, as compared with 18% of nondisabled individuals, live in households with an annual income of $15,000 or less (N.O.D., 1994). As of 1994, more than two thirds (68%) of people with disabilities between the ages of 16 and 64 were unemployed. According to the N.O.D.,

> Fully 47% [of people with disabilities] said [that] they were unemployed or unable to work because of a disability or health problem, while 9% were retired, 6% were homemakers, 6% were students, and 1% were full time volunteers. Of the 31% of people with disabilities who *were* working, only two thirds were employed full-time, and one-third were employed part time. (1994, pp. 9–10)

Of those of us with disabilities between the ages of 16 and 64 who are not employed, 79% (including 84% of those between ages 16 and 44) report that we want to work. Even among individuals with disabilities who feel that they are completely unable to work, two thirds report that they want a job (N.O.D., 1994).

Access to adequate health care coverage is a primary consideration for many people with disabilities in deciding whether to accept employment (N.O.D., 1994). In the late 1990s, many more individuals with disabilities are deterred from changing employment because of problems associated with health care policies and programs (President's Committee, 1993).

In the United States, in addition to the impact of attitudes and economic and sociocultural determinations on the lives of individuals with disabilities and their families, specific federal legislation can be identified that has sought to extend opportunities and support to disabled people for more inclusive participation in our communities, beginning with the Smith-Hughes Vocational Education Act of 1917—which established the Board of Vocational Education and that later became the basis for vocational rehabilitation—through and including the Mental Retardation Facilities and Community Mental Health Centers Construction Act of 1963 (PL 88-164). A major breakthrough occurred with the passage of the Education of the Handicapped Act (EHA) of 1970 (PL 91-230), which guaranteed a free and appropriate public education for all students in the least restrictive environment. Its many amendments have continued to secure rights for disabled schoolchildren; these amendments include the following:

- The Education for All Handicapped Children Act of 1975 (PL 94-142)

- The Education of the Handicapped Act Amendments of 1983 (PL 98-199)
- The Education of the Handicapped Act Amendments of 1986 (PL 99-457)
- The Individuals with Disabilities Education Act (IDEA) of 1990 (PL 101-476)
- The Individuals with Disabilities Education Act Amendments of 1997 (PL 105-17)

Other laws of great importance are the Rehabilitation Act of 1973 (PL 93-112) and its amendments of 1974 (PL 93-661), 1986 (PL 99-506), 1992 (PL 102-569), and 1993 (PL 103-73); the Developmentally Disabled Assistance and Bill of Rights Act of 1975 (PL 94-103) and its amendments of 1976 (PL 94-278), 1987 (PL 100-146), 1990 (PL 101-496), and 1994 (PL 103-230); the Technology-Related Assistance for Individuals with Disabilities Act of 1988; and the ADA of 1990 (Bryan, 1996; Percy, 1989; Weber, 1994). It is through the enactment of such legislation, the growth of a disability social movement (Scotch, 1989), the development of a positive perspective about disability among people with disabilities (Gilson et al., 1997), and the increasing political acumen of organizations such as American Disabled for Attendant Programs Today (ADAPT) (Tower, 1994) and Not Dead Yet (Byzek & Ehman, 1996) that the push for self-determination, choice, empowerment, and self-advocacy is squarely grounded.

For Dimitri, as with many people with disabilities, the policies and procedures of agencies and the behaviors and decisions of human services and health professionals can be confusing and mysterious. Dimitri had a right to request a full vocational evaluation, and as a consumer, he had the right to request that the counselor work with him in the areas that he had identified as important. However, unless someone told Dimitri of his rights and responsibilities as a consumer, it would have been exceedingly difficult for him to make honest choices, to determine goals, to appreciate his power as a member of the survivor-recovery community, and to initiate the services and supports that he wanted. For many people, regardless of whether their disabilities are visible or invisible, identifying as part of the disability community and soliciting support and guidance can be difficult; it is an ongoing and frequently time-consuming process. Being referred to a psychosocial rehabilitation program, without also being referred to a consumer-run clubhouse or peer support group, can only serve to make the process of identifying as disabled and of connecting with the disability community more difficult. If Dimitri had been referred to such a consumer group, it is likely that he would have more easily identified his rights within the rehabilitation services system as well as within the community in general. However, the professionals working with Dimitri also failed him by neglecting to realize and act on their obligations and provide him with the full range of services and supports that he might need to more fully participate in all aspects of community living, recreation, and work. This chapter discusses the issues of choice making; consumer-determined, directed, and controlled services and supports; the development of personal and community power; and the role and place of self-advocacy in seeking to end discrimination and securing the full measure of civil rights for disabled people. See Table 1 for definitions of terms used throughout this chapter.

DUANE: DEFINITION OF CHOICE

Since 1990, Duane has worked in the laundry room of the city's largest hotel. He has missed only one unscheduled week of work in all of his years at the hotel, and that was the week that he went to his grandmother's funeral in another state. Duane has received a small raise each year and has health care benefits associated with his job. There are not many people who come in contact with Duane during his 11 P.M. to 7 A.M. shift, but those co-workers who do consider him to be one who keeps to himself and who does not want to associate with others. He does not talk with others because he has a severe expressive language disability that is the result of a hearing impairment. Because of the noise in the laundry room, Duane does not wear his hearing aids at work, and

Table 1. Definitions of terms that are key to understanding self-advocacy issues

Choice is having more than one option from which to make a selection, and it must be linked to the development of skills and capabilities that will serve to further extend one's possibilities. Choice is more than offering what is available; it involves working to develop what should be available.

Self-determination can be experienced only by those who share a specific commonality. It is about setting one's own agenda; about being able to decide what one needs and wants; and about controlling how, where, and by whom the services are provided. It is a recognition by disabled people as well as an acceptance by nondisabled professionals of their capabilities, skills, and rights.

Advocacy is a process, group of actions, and set of activities that disabled people may do with others, or on behalf of others, to create opportunities or to implement, develop, or modify programs and/or services.

Self-advocacy occurs when disabled people identify issues by themselves and initiate and carry out actions and activities. As a form of advocacy, self-advocacy occurs on both individual and community levels. It involves decisions that disabled people make to create, implement, develop, or modify opportunities as individuals and as a community. Self-advocacy also involves efforts made by people to fight discrimination and oppression.

he depends on reading lips to respond to others' requests. What no one at work knows is that Duane hates his job, especially because he has so little contact with other people. Every Sunday he reads the want ads in the newspaper, and when there is a job that interests him, he tries to make an appointment with the rehabilitation counselor who handled his "case" before it was successfully closed. The counselor has met with Duane but has cautioned against changing jobs because a different job may not have similar stability or health benefits. In fact, the counselor has found a reason for Duane not to pursue each of the job ads that he has found. Duane did not realize that he did not have to have a rehab counselor involved to change jobs until he met an old friend from his special education class in high school who never was involved in the vocational rehabilitation system. Duane was surprised that he could choose not to use a rehab counselor and still be able to find a job of his choice.

O'Shea and Kennelly asserted that "people with disabilities are routinely denied the exercise of choice in their daily lives" (1996, p. 13). Family, friends, and health and social care professionals commonly make decisions on behalf of disabled people. In addition to such direct decision making, the preferences and needs of disabled people are commonly mediated through these individuals (O'Shea & Kennelly, 1996), denying disabled people the freedom of choice.

> What tends to happen is that people with disabilities, who are systematically denied a meaningful role in economic and social life, learn not to want what they have not got. Their well-being is consequently low because their preferences have been adapted and distorted in order to fit the needs and wants of others. (O'Shea & Kennelly, 1996, pp. 14–16)

If the concept of "choice" has been altered by some of the relationships that disabled people have had with nondisabled people, then how is this concept to be redefined? Certainly, possessing the ability and power to choose requires learned skills and behaviors. In general, people are able to make choices as adults because they learned to make choices as children and adolescents. People practice and reinforce vocational choice making by making decisions about where and how they live in the community and where and how they find employment. One of the challenges for disabled people, their families, friends, and health and social care professionals will be to develop responsive educational programs for children and adolescents as well as to institute policies and practices that support true choice for adults with disabilities. For many people with and for those without disabilities, this means unlearning how they have interacted in the past and evaluating current practices in terms of independent living. "Regardless of disability, people should have the opportunity to control their own life and should be able to pursue personally chosen activities" (O'Shea & Kennelly, 1996, p. 15). Disabled people must seek to avoid preferences that have been adapted and distorted to fit a pattern of structured dependency, conformity, and obedience. In the same light, it is important to avoid people who assert that disabled people should do everything for ourselves, by becoming super-achievers, without additional resources. Neither position will facilitate the practice of true choice.

What Does Choice Mean?

So, what do we really mean by the term *choice*? Grady defines *choice* as "having alternatives from which to make a selection" (1995, p. 302). Choice must be about exploring opportunities and a full range of options. However, because "making choices is another way of exploring personal values about daily living, relationships, roles, and the physical, psychological, social, and spiritual communities" (Grady, 1995, p. 302) in which we live; choice is more than having a limited list of alternatives from which to choose. Choice is linked to the removal of physical, environmental, communication, and attitudinal barriers to living and working in the community. Barriers to participation, and therefore to choice, take many forms (e.g., failing to build ramps or provide automatic doors; failing to provide text telephones or telecommunications devices for the deaf; failing to provide sign language interpreters for events and meetings; failing to provide computer disks, audiotapes, or enlarged-print translations of written material; refusing to interview or hire individuals for jobs for which they are capable). Choice means acknowledging and supporting the assertions by people with disabilities that we can and should have control over our own destinies. Furthermore, the determination of what constitutes a barrier, what accommodations must be made, and whether access exists must rest with disabled people. For services providers, including vocational services, this means adopting a *consumer-driven approach* (Brooke, Wehman, Inge, & Parent, 1995). Brooke et al., in referring to choice and supported employment, suggested that the consumer must be "presented with a variety of experiences, options and supports to achieve career goals" (1995, p. 310). To offer scaled-back options, limited opportunities, or inadequate support is not choice; it is a continuation of practices of domination and paternalism. Disabled people must have the opportunity to select options that are high risk and that may run counter to the opinions and beliefs of professionals. Choice is about turning away from the "professionals know best" attitude (Brooke et al., 1995; Chumbley et al., 1992; Kregel, 1992; Turner et al., 1995). Choice is about our practicing true self-determination.

SELF-DETERMINATION

As with the term choice, it is often difficult to arrive at an agreed-on definition of *self-determination*. Is it possible to have true self-determination in isolated and exclusionary environments? Is inclusion necessary? If disabled people do not have access to personal assistance services or to assistive technology (AT), can we honestly experience self-determination? Individuals with disabilities have identified that a major goal for independent living and quality of life is self-determination (Brotherson, Cook, Cunconan-Lahr, & Wehmeyer, 1995). Self-determination places the disabled person at the "center of decision making and control" (Tower, 1994, p. 101). But what is necessary if we are to move human services from being principally directive and prescriptive to being determined by the consumers of those services?

Disabled people must be willing to declare that "clients of the human services are consumers in the same way as are customers who acquire the services and products of a grocery store. Their consumption bears an actual cost that consumers pay either directly or through third-party payers, means-tested transfers, or charitable funding" (Tower, 1994, p. 102). Interpreting the relationship between human services and disabled people necessitates that providers reconceptualize the services delivery process and that individuals with disabilities recognize their rights and responsibilities in determining the direction and focus of their lives. For human services workers to adopt a true practice of consumer self-determination, they must adjust their relationships with individuals with disabilities and recognize that agency policies and procedures commonly serve to maintain control of services and of the consumer (Freedberg, 1989). Change in the relationship must occur on multiple levels, micro through macro. On a micro level, this may simply take the form of the professional listening to and following the direction of the consumer, whether the focus of the discussion is about which classes to take, which job or career offers the best opportunities, or the type and amount of personal assistance services that are needed. For an agency, this may take the form of ensuring that a full range of options and opportunities are made available and that programs are adjusted to the needs of individuals. Moving away from a micro perspective, services providers begin to recognize that more than one consumer has identified similar concerns such as transportation, availability of personal assistance services, or access to AT, it is important that those consumers be provided the opportunity to meet and form working groups to develop solutions. It is also important that the provider examine either how his or her role might be expanded to include needed services or how he or she can develop working agreements with other providers that offer those services. For the provider, such efforts necessitate a willingness to abandon territorial domain in favor of enhanced and more complete service provisions. On a more macro level, disabled people can form consumer advisory councils that help establish proactive guidelines and policies for individual service providers as well as for state and national disability agencies. For the providers and agencies, the challenge will be to develop such consumer advisory councils and to provide them with true authority and power. This will require that many individual providers and agencies examine how their behaviors, policies, and practices have served to exclude disabled people in favor of control by nondisabled professionals.

Fundamental to consumer-directed human services is a recognition that people with disabilities are the experts on their own lives. As the experts, people with disabilities hold more knowledge and understanding of their own needs and interests than do human services professionals. The individual with the disability is not a client, patient, or recipient of services (Tower, 1994) but is, instead, the director of which services are delivered. Redefining the relationship between human services professionals and individuals with disabilities serves to place consumers in control of and in direction of their services (Parent, Unger, Gibson, & Clements, 1994). Decisions regarding issues such as the nature and extent of inclusion, and where, how, and which services are to be provided must rest with disabled people themselves. Self-determination, or "the right to assume control in one's life; the right to define quality of life for oneself," is essential for empowerment (Brotherson et al., 1995, p. 4). Ward (as cited in Brotherson et al., 1995) has suggested that self-determination requires both the development of inner resources within people with disabilities and support from society. It "is a lifelong interplay between the individual and society, in which the individual accepts risk-taking as a fact of life and in which society, in turn, bases an individual's worth on ability," values, and fundamental human worth (Ward as cited in Brotherson et al., 1995, p. 12).

DUANE: EMPOWERMENT

In the previous case, Duane is at the point in his life at which he is beginning to understand empowerment. His friend has told him that he can find a job on his own, but now it is up to Duane to take the next step. The first employment application that Duane fills out will be a major expression of self-empowerment. He may learn that he does need support, perhaps even the support of a rehabilitation counselor and job coach, to be successful in changing employment. But he has learned that he does not have to continue in a job that he does not like without hope for change in the future. With adequate training, support, and AT to aid in his communication, Duane can change jobs or remain in his current job but change his ability to interact with his co-workers.

As with the terms *choice* and *self-determination*, empowerment can be a confusing concept and can have mixed implications for disabled people and human services professionals. Unfortunately, the philosophical appeal of the term *empowerment* has increased the potential for it to be interpreted as an intervention. Rehabilitation systems cannot give power or authority to disabled people. These systems can, however, stop trying to provide services in a manner that denies or takes away power, choice, and self-determination. If empowerment is thought of as a set of skills, such as time-management and training in public speaking or letter writing, that the professional will teach to the disabled person, then this is a continuation of the practices of paternalism and control. If, however, empowerment flows from the experiences of making choices and practicing self-determination, then it is likely to be an empowerment of emancipation and independent living.

Empowerment is an attitude as well as the practice of a set of skills and strategies. Fawcett et al. suggested that empowerment is a "process by which people gain some control over valued events, outcomes, and resources" (1994, p. 471). A sense of control over one's life is linked to having choices and options and to believing in self-determination, as well as to being able to influence consequences, the power to make decisions, and the knowledge of when and how to use power (Pomeroy, Demeter, & Tyler, 1995). As an ongoing process, empowerment is an individual as well as a group experience (Balcazar, Mathews, Francisco, Fawcett, & Seekins, 1994; Fawcett et al., 1994). In addition to considering individual and group processes, empowerment "may be exercised at different levels of change, including that of individual, family or kinship group, organization, neighborhood, city or town, or the broader society" (Fawcett et al., 1994, pp. 473–474). The empowerment that an individual or a group may experience in one context, such as within a particular agency or organization, may be different from the degree of control that may be experienced in another domain, such as a neighborhood or city (Fawcett et al., 1994). It may often be easier for disabled people to effect change within organizations such as rehabilitation services in which the number of disabled people seeking services is greater than in settings such as colleges or universities at which we often compose much smaller percentages of the work force or student body. For those of us who live with families or partners who have developed a progressive understanding and appreciation of disability, it is often common to be startled by negative comments that strangers may make and/or by discriminatory and oppressive policies and behaviors that restrict our access to and use of restaurants, movie theaters, and art museums.

Empowerment within the Disabled Community

Although it is important that disabled people attend to the individual dimensions of empowerment, such as the increased sense of control that an individual may feel as a result of effecting positive social change, this empowerment theory also can be used to blame "individuals for not having the skills or motivation to rise up out of powerlessness" (Ryan as cited in Wallerstein, 1993, p. 219). A focus on individual empowerment often seeks to improve self-esteem, job competencies, and literacy rather than seeking to change "the environmental conditions [that] contribute to not having power" (Wallerstein, 1993, p. 219). An expanded definition of empowerment also focuses on individuals participating with others, as a community, "to change their social and political realities" (Wallerstein, 1993, p. 219). Within this expanded definition, disabled people as a community are viewed as having the ability to identify their own problems and solutions, having the capacity to solve those problems, having the ability to provide a context within which community activities take place, and having the right to increased control and self-determination (Wallerstein, 1993).

Empowerment, then, is both a process and an outcome. As a social action process, empowerment is a strategy to combat a lack of control,

Through enhancing participation in community actions, reinforcing sense of community and social networks, promoting a belief in people that they can control their worlds and dealing to actual socio-environmental changes. Empowerment as an outcome contains dimensions that are both psychological (belief and motivation in one's ability to act collectively) and community (increases in local action and transformed conditions). (Wallerstein, 1993, p. 221)

Fisher (1994), using psychiatric disabilities as a frame of reference, developed a model of empowerment that is clearly applicable to other members of the disability community. The elements of this model emphasize consumer-survivor "defined goals, liberty, self-control of symptoms, peer support, elimination of discrimination, and provision of adequate material and social supports" (Fisher, 1994, p. 913). Although all of the elements are vital to full, self-determined self-empowerment of disabled people, five of these elements seem to be of particular importance. First, our achievement of self-defined goals assumes that we, as disabled people, must increasingly take control of and responsibility for our lives; others cannot and should not take control for us. Second, meaningful choices from a full range of possible types of social and health care options must be available, and our judgment should be valued. Third, "since no one else can speak for us, we need a voice in decisions that affect us in all aspects of our care" (Fisher, 1994, p. 914), including community living and vocational services. Fourth, elements essential to the well-being of all people are adequate housing, food, educational and work opportunities, financial support, and social supports. And, finally, we need to have the freedom to hold our own beliefs; to present our ideas and thoughts without fear of retaliation, retribution, being demeaned, or having our services and supports curtailed; and to decide with whom to associate, including primarily peer environments and consumer-run services.

As individuals with disabilities through and within our communities identify and analyze the barriers to our full and equal participation, strategies and solutions will be developed that reflect our culture and visions and that reinforce the principles of choice and self-determination, consumer-driven services, and supports. Advocacy, which is discussed next, is an essential element of the development of a framework for the realization of these principles.

SOPHIA: ADVOCACY

Sophia is in her 60s and has a medical condition that has affected her body to the point that she is unable to fulfill of any of her self-care needs. She needs 24-hour personal assistance services, which she receives in her own home. Sophia has battled the system for all of her life, from the time she was school-age and fought with her mother for her right to have a classroom alternative other than home-bound instruction. She was able to attend high school and college but was never able to obtain employment in the years preceeding Section 504 of the Rehabilitation Act of 1973 and the ADA. Sophia has acquired many political acquaintances over the years: congressmen, state legislators, governors, mayors, and city council representatives. She knows someone everywhere she goes. Although Sophia has given up her dream of being employed, she has turned all of her energies to being a self-appointed advocate for those who want to enter or remain in the work force. With her political connections, she has been successful in getting many people with disabilities "through the front door" to potential employers. There are many professionals within the vocational rehabilitation setting who are in awe of Sophia's advocacy abilities.

But what is advocacy, and how does one know if he or she is acting as an advocate? The independent living movement (of which Centers for Independent Living are examples), which supports the development of individual power and the achievement of self-determination, presents disabled people as capable of consumer initiative and control over adapted living and support services and as capable of political advocacy (Brooks, 1991).

Alper defined an advocate as "someone who acts on behalf of or for another person's cause" (as cited in Cunconan-Lahr & Brotherson, 1996, p. 352). Such advocacy, in terms of disabilities, commonly focuses on restructuring, improving, creating, and developing services and supports for people with disabilities and their families with an emphasis on community access, accommodation, and inclusion (Balcazar, Keys, Bertram, & Rizzo, 1996). Within this context, advocacy occurs by way of "actions" related to "issues." In their study of a Partners in Policymaking program, Balcazar et al. (1996) identified five categories of actions. These included making telephone calls; visiting offices and attending meetings; initiating media reports (e.g., writing letters, generating mass mailings); participating in radio interviews or writing newspaper articles; and other activities, as exemplified by giving presentations at schools, testimony at public hearings, participating in and conducting training sessions, and raising funds. Advocacy may also take the form of filing lawsuits, direct action demonstrations, and civil disobedience (Cagle, 1996; Gwin, 1996). As such, advocacy can be a formal (e.g., initiating legal actions or legislation) or informal (e.g., the advice that one individual may give to another) process or action (Cunconan-Lahr & Brotherson, 1996). In their study, Balcazar et al. define disability advocacy issues as including "any disability-related event or situation that requires action and that affects people with disabilities and/or family members" (1996, p. 344). Examples of such issues would be "unmet needs for information, services, or support [and] negative or positive changes in services and supports, budget allocations, or policies" (Balcazar et al., 1996, p. 344).

Considering all of the important roles, actions, and issues that advocates take on (as described in the preceding paragraph), our experiences of choice, self-determination, and empowerment will be adversely affected if we limit our definition of self-advocacy to someone who acts on our behalf. Consumer-driven advocacy is that which we must do for ourselves. It is clear that partners and allies are important elements of any full advocacy effort, but it is through *self-advocacy* that we often experience a more complete and positive image of who we are as disabled members of a disabled community. The impact and benefit of self-advocacy by disabled people should not be underestimated or minimized. In 1986, the Harris poll noted the following:

Only 40% of people with disabilities claimed to feel a strong sense of identity with other people with disabilities (with 20% saying they identified "somewhat strongly" with others with disabilities and 20% identifying "very strongly"). In the 1994 survey, for the first time, more than half of all Americans with disabilities said they identified strongly with others with disabilities (29% "somewhat strongly" and 25% "very strongly"). (N.O.D., 1994, p. 27)

When we witness the impact of being able to affect policy, to help develop and lobby for legislation, to remove people from nursing homes, and to expand community employment opportunities and options for ourselves, we become less dependent on professionals to do these actions for us. We are in greater control over our lives and our destinies, which serves to increase our personal power and belief in our capabilities. In this manner we are removed from the role of being a recipient. We recognize ourselves and then are recognized by others as the experts on our lives.

What Does Self-Advocacy Mean?

In addition to the independent living movement being an example of consumer initiative and advocacy, other examples include ADAPT (Tower, 1994), Leadership Education to Empower Disabled Students (Aune et al., 1996; Chelberg & Kroeger, 1995), People First (Williams & Shoultz, 1982), and the psychiatric survivor-consumer community (Byzek, 1996; Fisher, 1994). In a definition of self-advocacy as an activity, Cunconan-Lahr and Brotherson state that it is one form of advocacy, which "occurs any time people speak or act on their own behalf to improve their quality of life, effect personal change, or correct inequities" (1996, p. 352). In September 1991, the Second Annual People First Conference approved the following definition of *self-advocacy*:

> Self-advocacy is about independent groups of people with disabilities working together for justice by helping each other take charge of their lives and fight discrimination. It teaches us how to make decisions and choices that affect our lives so we can be more independent. It teaches us about our rights, but along with learning about our rights, we learn responsibilities. The way we learn about advocating for ourselves is supporting each other, and helping each other gain confidence in themselves to speak out for what they believe in. (as cited in Nelis, 1994, p. 1)

It is clear that self-advocacy is defined by more than the actions that we adopt and by the issues that we address. For people with disabilities, self-advocacy is an assertion of ourselves. We have firmly established our capability and our right to define and safeguard our rights. We reserve and assert the right to educate others, our brothers and sisters with disabilities, our families, allies, partners, and professionals regarding the issues that have an impact on our lives. Self-advocacy is about choosing and determining how we want to live, work, and recreate in our communities. It is also about feeling the power, as individuals and as a community, to act on our own behalf.

Role of Allies

This discussion would not be complete without considering the role and place of nondisabled people as allies in the pursuit of self-advocacy. As the term itself implies, self-advocacy is something that we do ourselves. But as many other minority groups have found, creating lasting change in the community requires the support and participation of people not as directly affected by the experience of discrimination, denial of rights, and estrangement (in this case, nondisabled people) (Wallace & Gilson, 1997). An ally is much more than, and different from, a partner. Although many allies are connected to disabled people in professional relationships, the alliance referred to by Wallace and Gilson (1997), and which is supported in this chapter, goes much beyond traditional consumer–professional work relationships. Although an advocate does not have to have a personal relationship with the disabled person with whom, or for whom, he or she advocates, an ally has a personal stake in another person's life. An ally is someone who has been touched in some way by a disabled person. Wallace and Gilson stated that

> All the allies that we know are either a family member, an extended family member, a friend of someone with a disability, or a person who has a non-visible disability which they have chosen not to disclose. We allies all have a story of how and when we were touched; something that has had a major significance in our life to the extent that it influences all of our thinking and action when working, living, learning or playing with individuals with disabilities. (1997)

Within this context, it is clear that there are a variety of roles for nondisabled people in supporting us as we advocate for disability-related issues. Whether that role is as an advocate/partner, as a human services professional, as a personal care provider, as a family member, or as an ally, true choice, self-determination, and empowerment require that we clearly articulate these roles and their functions. This discussion should not be misinterpreted as a call for exclusion of nondisabled people, but rather as a recognition of the impact and importance of self-advocacy for us as disabled people and for our brothers and sisters with disabilities.

DIMITRI: DEVELOPING A SENSE OF SELF

Fortunately for Dimitri, he was able to develop a sense of self despite the human services and health care professionals' failure to provide him with important information and support. Following a series of additional hospitalizations and moves to "new" communities, Dimitri decided that continued participation in a psychosocial program was not in his best interest. He did, however, take responsibility for self-control of his symptoms and began monitoring how his decisions regarding personal care—such as sleep, nutrition, and exercise—influenced his overall health status. This monitoring provided the basis for Dimitri to begin a series of self-initiated, therapeutic changes. He also chose to return to college to pursue an advanced degree. Following completion of his graduate degree, Dimitri was able to secure career-path employment in a field for which he had both aptitude and skills. Dimitri continued to periodically experience slight exacerbation of his symptoms, but by making meaningful choices and practicing his skills of self-determination, he realized more control over many dimensions of his life. Dimitri also made contact with the disability community, in which the evolving peer relationships provided him with a sense of value and support that he did not experience in the professionally run health care delivery system. Following time spent developing friendships with members of what he identified as his community, he began to gradually become involved in activities to fight discrimination, and he worked to protect the human rights and to improve the quality of services and supports for disabled people.

CONCLUSION

Services and supports provided to people with disabilities in a manner that supports the right to make choices, practices self-determination, and experiences the benefits of changing the social context through acts of empowerment and self-advocacy are not only more humane and progressive, but also are effective. People with disabilities continue to move toward more experiences of positive affirmation of themselves. A viable pan- or cross-disability community is developing along with an emerging cultural attitude that recognizes our history and future possibilities. As such, it will be important that professional human and health care services be adapted to support and enhance these changes. In addition to identifying the realities of our experiences, this chapter identified possibilities and probabilities for the future. It is within this spirit that professionals are encouraged to develop collaborative consumer-oriented relationships that promote a full realization of independent living for all disabled people.

REFERENCES

Americans with Disabilities Act (ADA) of 1990, PL 101-336, 42 U.S.C. §§ 12101 et seq.

Aune, B., Chelberg, G., Stockdill, S., Robertson, B., Agresta, S., & Lorsung, T. (1996). *Executive summary: LEEDS (Leadership Education to Empower Disabled Students) final report.* Minneapolis: University of Minnesota.

Balcazar, F.E., Keys, C.B., Bertram, J.F., & Rizzo, T. (1996). Advocate development in the field of developmental disabilities: A data-based conceptual model. *Mental Retardation, 34,* 341–351.

Balcazar, F.E., Mathews, R.M., Francisco, V.T., Fawcett, S.B., & Seekins, T. (1994). The empowerment process in four advocacy organizations of people with disabilities. *Rehabilitation Psychology, 39,* 189–203.

Brooke, V., Wehman, P., Inge, K., & Parent, W. (1995). Toward a customer-driven approach to supported employment. *Education and Training in Mental Retardation and Developmental Disabilities, 30,* 308–320.

Brooks, N.A. (1991). Self-empowerment among adults with severe physical disability: A case study. *Journal of Sociology and Social Welfare, 18*(1), 105–120.

Brotherson, M.J., Cook, C.C., Cunconan-Lahr, R., & Wehmeyer, M.L. (1995). Policy supporting self-determination in the environments of children with disabilities. *Education and Training in Mental Retardation and Developmental Disabilities, 30,* 3–14.

Bryan, W.V. (1996). *In search of freedom: How persons with disabilities have been disenfranchised from the mainstream of American society.* Springfield, IL: Charles C Thomas.

Byzek, J. (1996). Judi says: An interview with Judi Chamberlin. *Mouth: The Voice of Disability Rights, 7*(4), 10–13.

Byzek, J., & Ehman, J. (1996). NOT DEAD YET. *Mouth: the Voice of Disability Rights, 7*(2), 17–19.

Cagle, T. (1996). Power move: Get to an ADAPT action. *Mouth: The Voice of Disability Rights, 17*(2), 26–29.

Chelberg, G., & Kroeger, S. (1995). Tenets of disability discovery. *Disability Studies Quarterly, 15*(4), 19–21.

Chumbley, C., Collins, M., Elliot, J., Geake, L., Grant, M., Hague, J., Hock, T., Moore, J., & Tooth, T. (1992). Supported employment service issues. In V. Brooke, M. Barcus, & K. Inge (Eds.), *Consumer advocacy and supported employment: A vision for the future* (pp. 13–32). Richmond: Virginia Commonwealth University, Rehabilitation Research Training Center on Supported Employment.

Cunconan-Lahr, R., & Brotherson, M.J. (1996). Advocacy in disability policy: Parents and consumers as advocates. *Mental Retardation, 34,* 352–358.

Developmental Disabilities Assistance and Bill of Rights Act Amendments of 1976, PL 94-278, title XI, § 1107(d), 90 Stat.

Developmental Disabilities Assistance and Bill of Rights Act Amendments of 1987, PL 100-146, 42 U.S.C. §§ 6000 *et seq.*

Developmental Disabilities Assistance and Bill of Rights Act of 1990, PL 101-496, 42 U.S.C. §§ 6000 *et seq.*

Developmental Disabilities Assistance and Bill of Rights Act of 1994, PL 103-230, 42 U.S.C. §§ 6000 *et seq.*

Developmentally Disabled Assistance and Bill of Rights Act of 1975, PL 94-103, 42 U.S.C. §§ 6000 *et seq.*

Education for All Handicapped Children Act of 1975, PL 94-142, 20 U.S.C. §§ 1400 *et seq.*

Education of the Handicapped Act (EHA) of 1970, PL 91-230, 20 U.S.C. §§ 1400 *et seq.*

Education of the Handicapped Act Amendments of 1983, PL 98-199, 20 U.S.C. §§ 1400 et seq.

Education of the Handicapped Act Amendments of 1986, PL 99-457, 20 U.S.C. §§ 1400 et seq.

Fawcett, S.B., White, G.W., Balcazar, F.E., Suarez-Balcazar, Y., Mathews, R.M., Paine-Andrews, A., Seekins, T., & Smith, J.F. (1994). A contextual-behavioral model of empowerment: Case studies involving people with physical disabilities. American Journal of Community Psychology, 22, 471–496.

Fisher, D.B. (1994). Health care reform based on an empowerment model of recovery by people with psychiatric disabilities. Hospital and Community Psychiatry, 45(9), 913–915.

Freedberg, S. (1989). Self-determination: Historical perspectives and effects on current practice. Social Work, 34, 33–38.

Gilson, S.F., Tusler, A., & Gill, C. (1997). Ethnographic research in disability identity: Self-determination and community. Journal of Vocational Rehabilitation, 9(1), 7–17.

Grady, A.P. (1995). Building inclusive community: A challenge for occupational therapy. The American Journal of Occupational Therapy, 49, 300–310.

Grobe, J. (Ed.). (1995). Beyond bedlam: Contemporary women psychiatric survivors speak out. Chicago: Third Side Press.

Gwin, L. (Ed.). (1996). A collection of power moves. Mouth: The Voice of Disability Rights, 17(2), 12–16.

Heumann, J.E. (1993). Building our own boats: A personal perspective on disability policy. In L.O. Gostin & H.A. Beyer (Eds.), Implementing the Americans with Disabilities Act: Rights and responsibilities of all Americans (pp. 251–263). Baltimore: Paul H. Brookes Publishing Co.

Individuals with Disabilities Education Act (IDEA) of 1990, PL 101-476, 20 U.S.C. §§ 1400 et seq.

Individuals with Disabilities Education Act Amendments of 1997, PL 105-17, 20 U.S.C. §§ 1400 et seq.

Kregel, J. (1992). A consumer empowerment approach to the design of human service systems: Implementations for supported employment. In V. Brooke, M. Barcus, & K. Inge (Eds.), Consumer advocacy and supported employment: A vision for the future (pp. 33–48). Richmond: Virginia Commonwealth University, Rehabilitation Research Training Center on Supported Employment.

Mayerson, A. (1993). The history of the ADA: A movement perspective. In L.O. Gostin & H.A. Beyer (Eds.), Implementing the Americans with Disabilities Act: Rights and responsibilities of all Americans (pp. 17–24). Baltimore: Paul H. Brookes Publishing Co.

Mental Retardation Facilities and Community Mental Health Centers Construction Act of 1963, PL 88-164, 42 U.S.C. §§ 2670 et seq.

National Organization on Disability (N.O.D.). (1994). Closing the gap: Expanding the participation of Americans with disabilities. The N.O.D./Harris survey of Americans with disabilities—a summary. Washington, DC: Author.

Nelis, T. (1994). Self-advocacy: Realizing a dream. Impact, 7(1), 1, 15.

O'Shea, E., & Kennelly, B. (1996). The economics of independent living: Efficiency, equity and ethics. International Journal of Rehabilitation, 19, 13–26.

Parent, W., Unger, D., Gibson, K., & Clements, C. (1994). The role of the job coach: Orchestrating community and workplace supports. American Rehabilitation, 20(3), 2–11.

Percy, S.L. (1989). *Disability, civil rights, and public policy: The politics of implementation*. Tuscaloosa: The University of Alabama Press.

Pomeroy, E., Demeter, S., & Tyler, D. (1995). The help book: A case study in empowerment research. *Prevention in Human Services, 12*(1), 89–102.

President's Committee: Health Insurance Working Group. (1993, April 16). *Americans with Disabilities Act Employment Summit* (Issue paper). Washington, DC: Author.

Rehabilitation Act of 1973, PL 93-112, 29 U.S.C. §§ 701 *et seq.*

Scotch, R.K. (1984). *From good will to civil rights: Transforming federal disability policy*. Philadelphia: Temple University.

Scotch, R.K. (1989). Politics and policy in the history of the disability rights movement. *The Milbank Quarterly, 67*(Suppl. 2, Pt. 2), 380–400.

Shapiro, J.P. (1993). *No pity: People with disabilities forging a new Civil Rights movement*. New York: Times Books.

Shaw, B. (Ed.). (1994). *The ragged edge: The disability experience from the pages of the first fifteen years of* The Disability Rag. Louisville, KY: Avocado Press.

Smith-Hughes Vocational Education Act of 1917, ch. 114, 39 Stat. 929; U.S.C. 20 §§ 11 *et seq.*

Technology-Related Assistance for Individuals with Disabilities Act of 1988, PL 100-407, 29 U.S.C. §§ 2201 *et seq.*

Tower, K.D. (1994). Consumer-centered social work practice: Restoring client self-determination. *Social Work, 39*, 101–106.

Turner, E., Barrett, C., Cutshall, A., Lacy, B.K., Keiningham, J., & Webster, M.K. (1995). The user's perspective of assistive technology. In K.F. Flippo, K.J. Inge, & J.M. Barcus (Eds.), *Assistive technology: A resource for school, work, and community* (pp. 283–290). Baltimore: Paul H. Brookes Publishing Co.

Wallace, J.F., & Gilson, B.B. (1997). Disabled and non-disabled: Allied together to change the system. *Journal of Vocational Rehabilitation, 9*(1), 73–80.

Wallerstein, N. (1993). Empowerment and health: The theory and practice of community change. *Community Development Journal, 28*, 218–227.

Weber, M.C. (1994). Towards access, accountability, procedural regularity and participation: The Rehabilitation Act Amendments of 1992 and 1993. *Journal of Rehabilitation, 60*(3), 21–25.

Williams, P., & Shoultz, B. (1982). *We can speak for ourselves: Self-advocacy by mentally handicapped people*. Bloomington: Indiana University Press.

Zola, I.K. (1982). *Missing pieces*. Philadelphia: Temple University.

Zola, I.K. (1993). Self, identify and the naming question: Reflections on the language of disability. In M. Nagler (Ed.), *Perspectives on disability* (2nd ed., pp. 15–23). Palo Alto, CA: Health Markets Research.

CHAPTER

2

Self-Advocacy in the United States

Historical Overview and Future Vision

Alicia A. Cone

As noted in Chapter 1, throughout history, society has constructed varied definitions of disability. This construction has comprised myths, stereotypes, and misunderstandings about disability that generally have been accepted as true. People with disabilities have been viewed by society as deviants, menaces, angelic innocents, and poor unfortunates (Mason, Williams-Murphy, & Brennan, 1996). American society often operates under a flawed set of assessments of the needs and the place of people with disabilities (Gliedman & Roth, 1980).

The experience of disability is a culturally specific social construction that is tied to a particular point in time, with the key elements of that social construct varying according to the disability (Bogdan & Taylor, 1982; Brunk, 1991; Minow, 1990; Scheer & Groce, 1988). For example, in most American communities, people with developmental disabilities continue to be relegated to an inferior and segregated status. People without disabilities consider disability to be an integral and essential part of the social being of the individual with the disability; therefore, the person with a disability often is treated differently and is expected to behave differently from people without disabilities (Gliedman & Roth, 1980).

25

It is not surprising that individuals who face a debilitating condition often become alienated and isolated, given that American society places such a strong emphasis on achievement, perfection, and competition (Fine & Asch, 1988; Hahn, 1988; Scheer & Groce, 1988). Rhoades, Browning, and Thorin (1986) pointed out that when a difference is detected in an individual with a disability, that person often is identified as a deviant or as a failure. Therefore, those individuals who society has labeled as having disabilities are painfully aware of the stigma and prejudice associated with their socially devalued status, and they have a strong desire to be accepted as typical members of society (Bogdan & Taylor, 1976, 1982; Brunk, 1991; Edgerton, 1967; Mest, 1988; People First of Washington, n.d.-a, n.d.-b, 1990).

Bogdan and Taylor (1976, 1982) and Mest (1988) found that people with developmental disabilities do define themselves, to some degree, by the norms of society. But in large part, their sense of identity is based on their distinct, and often collective, life experiences. These studies also drew a distinction among being aware of being labeled, being aware of the negativity of the label, and actually accepting and internalizing the label. In reality, many people with developmental disabilities recognize and criticize the stigma associated with labeling (Bogdan & Taylor 1976, 1982; Mest, 1988). Furthermore, if the individual has support from friends, it is even easier to reject the label and stigma (Bogdan & Taylor, 1976; Mest, 1988). The rejection of the label is not a rejection of the disability but a rejection of the negativity that society erroneously attaches to having the disability.

A 1984 assessment of the California service system conducted by People First of California for the California State Council on Developmental Disabilities came to some very pointed conclusions:

> Many people are better off for not getting services from institutionalizing and devaluing parts of the system. . . . [W]hen all factors are the same, including the type and degree of biological impairment, the evidence seems strong that the ones who become able to lead the most normal lives are those who have been helped to the greatest extent outside of the traditional service system. . . . [T]he task force suggests a new phrase to be used to sum up the nature and effect of. . . the traditional system of services for the mentally retarded[:]. . . the retarding environment. . . . [The retarding environment] is found, tragically, in almost every type of program, and even more tragically, in the attitudes of so many of the keepers of the system. (People First of California, 1984, p. 10)

The common denominator among people with disabilities is having one's capabilities ignored and being underestimated as a skilled individual. People without disabilities often base their opinions solely on preconceived notions tied to the prevailing attitudes toward a specific disability. The self-advocacy movement, however, rejects the validity of those devaluing attitudes. Individuals with developmental disabilities have started to define themselves as full citizens with the same rights as everyone else (Driedger, 1989). Self-advocacy works to develop a system of supports that encourages interdependence as well as independence and a more useful public policy toward people with disabilities.

This chapter explores the self-advocacy movement because self-advocacy is critical to gaining employment and a career. Most people with developmental and other significant disabilities have not worked before and, therefore, do not advocate well for themselves in the workplace. This chapter begins with a definition of self-advocacy that includes clarification of the values, beliefs, and principles of self-advocacy. The chapter then discusses several influences on the self-advocacy movement including the parent advocacy movement, the civil rights movement, the disability rights movement, the emergence of consumerism and citizen participation, legislative initiatives, judicial factors, and the self-help group legacy. The relationship between self-help and self-advocacy is discussed further because self-help is an important part of a self-advocacy group. The discussion of self-help leads directly into a description of the self-advocacy movement of people with developmental disabilities in the United States.

SELF-ADVOCACY DEFINED

In the field of developmental disabilities, *self-advocacy* most often is defined as individuals with developmental disabilities advocating on their own behalf, but that definition only touches the surface. Williams and Shoultz (1982) described self-advocacy as people with developmental disabilities—individually and/or in groups—speaking and/or acting on behalf of themselves, on behalf of others, or on behalf of issues that affect individuals with developmental disabilities. For Williams and Shoultz, the keys to self-advocacy for people with developmental disabilities are pursuing their own interests, being aware of their rights, taking responsibility for dealing with infringements on those rights, and joining with others to pursue issues of the group and of individuals with developmental disabilities in general.

In 1991, a definition of self-advocacy was approved at the Second Annual People First Conference (September, 1991) and appeared in an article by Nelis:

> Self-advocacy is about independent groups of people with disabilities working together for justice by helping each other take charge of their lives and fight discrimination. It teaches us how to make decisions and choices that affect our lives so we can be more independent. It teaches us about our rights, but along with learning about our rights, we learn responsibilities.

The way we learn about advocating for ourselves is supporting each other, and helping each other gain confidence in themselves to speak out for what they believe in. (1994, p. 1)

The national self-advocacy organization Self Advocates Becoming Empowered stated the beliefs of the self-advocacy movement in a 1994 publication. To this group, self-advocates believe

That people with disabilities should be treated as equals. That means that people should be given the same decisions, choices, rights, responsibilities and chances to speak up to empower themselves as well as to make new friendships and renew old friendships just like everyone else. They should also be able to learn from their mistakes like everyone else. (1994, p. 2)

In addition, a publication by the International League of Societies for People with Mental Handicap (1994) further elaborated on the beliefs, values, and principles of self-advocates. A list of beliefs and values held by self-advocates includes the following: being seen and treated as a person first, having one's own identity, being able to make one's own choices, believing in one's value as a person, and having others believe in the self-advocate as a person. Equally as important are these five principles of self-advocacy that should be encouraged and followed as decision-making guidelines: empowerment, equal opportunity, learning and living together, avoidance of labels, and freedom from institutions. These principles deal with nonnegotiable rights such as the right to make one's own decisions, the right to take risks, the right to be treated the same as others, the right to have the same access and opportunities as others, the right to participation in the community, the right to be seen as a person, and the right to a life in the community with the necessary supports.

INFLUENCES ON THE DEVELOPMENT
OF THE SELF-ADVOCACY MOVEMENT

Several forerunners to the self-advocacy movement created fissures in the negative aspects of the social construct of disability (Brunk, 1991). Each of the following provided a necessary part of the groundwork for the development of the self-advocacy movement.

Parent Advocacy in Mental Retardation

According to Rhoades (1986), the self-advocacy movement rests on a solid foundation of parent advocacy that has existed in the field of mental retardation since the early 1950s. The creation of the National Association for Retarded Children (NARC) by parents of children with mental retardation in 1950 marked the beginning of organized advocacy. Members were united in two goals: 1) to obtain better opportunities and treatment for their children and 2) to work toward stimulating broad social and political change in the interest of citizens with mental retardation. This early advocacy movement did not involve, to any significant degree, self-advocates; however, it was a forerunner of advocacy movements of the 1960s and 1970s.

Civil Rights Movement

Rhoades et al. (1986) reported that during the 1960s and 1970s the United States experienced an unparalleled time of social unrest, largely precipitated by its underprivileged citizens. There was a climate of self-determination and self-direction, and citizens who believed that they were underprivileged began to assert their interests, rights, and citizenship. It was a time of *power to the people*. The consciousness of groups facing discrimination (e.g., women, racial minorities, individuals with physical disabilities) was significantly altered: "The social climate was also ripe for the collective action of handicapped persons to ensure their rights in a nonhandicapped world" (Rhoades et al., p. 71).

Scotch's (1984) classic book, *From Goodwill to Civil Rights*, pointed out that individuals with disabilities learned from the activists of the civil rights movement. People with disabilities learned to demand full integration into the mainstream of life, to insist on equal treatment, and to call for accommodation as necessary.

The civil rights movement had a significant impact on both professionals and people with disabilities:

> As a result of the civil rights movement, many professionals began to understand retardation as a social problem, one particularly tied to the persistence of poverty in America. At the same time, the civil rights movement was helping some people with mental retardation gain a new perspective on themselves. (Brunk, 1991, p. 17)

Disability Rights/Independent Living Movement

Rhoades (1986) described the history of the disability rights/independent living movement and its legacy to the self-advocacy movement. The disability rights movement is most often seen as an outgrowth of the civil rights movement of African Americans, which had begun in 1955. In the 1960s, many individuals with physical disabilities joined the African American civil rights movement to fight for their human, legal, and civil rights. Grassroots-level groups began to spring up across the United States. These groups fought for income, education, and medical benefits entitlements.

As part of this rights movement, in the mid-1960s students at the University of California at Berkeley formed the Physically Disabled

Students Program. In 1971, this group formed the first Center for Independent Living (CIL). Rhoades (1986) described this group as a self-advocacy group of people with physical disabilities. The Berkeley CIL served as the model for the country and offered services such as peer counseling, housing referral, and wheelchair repair. The CIL also served as an advocacy group, advocating in the areas of education, transportation, employment, and housing.

Individuals involved in the disability rights and independent living movements were involved with securing the passage of the Rehabilitation Act of 1973 (PL 93-112), which was, at that time, often referred to as the Civil Rights Act for people with physical disabilities. Individuals with physical disabilities had seen through the prevailing construct of disability and were taking it upon themselves to change their unequal status.

The Emergence of Consumer Advocacy

In the late 1950s and early 1960s, a separate, but related, movement began to emerge—the consumer movement. Rhoades summarized advocacy or the consumer movement as bringing "to light the extent to which consumers in the marketplace were morally and economically victimized by business and government" (1986, p. 71). American consumers demanded protection from fraud, deceptive practices, unsafe products, unfair methods of selling, and help in coping with the complexities in the marketplace.

In 1962, President Kennedy outlined the rights of consumers as follows: 1) the right to safety, 2) the right to be informed, 3) the right to choose, and 4) the right to be heard (Rhoades, 1986). For the first time, consumers of services had government-defined rights that were not to be violated, and providers of goods and services were given very specific obligations to meet. The mode for providing goods and services had begun to move away from *let the buyer beware* and more toward *the customer is always right.*

In line with this philosophy of consumer rights, Meenaghan and Mascari (1971) outlined a new model—predicated on competition among providers and on customer demand, choice, and control—for providing services to individuals with mental retardation and to families who had children with mental retardation. Meenaghan and Mascari called for freedom of choice among customers of services, recognizing that customers should do what is in their best interests and that services would improve if a state of competition existed among the various service providers.

It seems that this early call for consumer's rights among individuals with mental retardation did not go far. In the late 1990s, people with developmental disabilities are still devalued, still segregated, still not in control of their finances, and still have limited input into developing and getting the services that they want. In the developmental disability services system, control of the product (i.e., service or support) still does not rest in the hands of the buyer because a true supply-and-demand system has not been allowed to exist. Individuals with developmental disabilities still have to accept those services that are available.

Citizen/Client Participation

Citizen/client participation reflected a change in the role of social services. Meenaghan and Mascari (1971), Rhoades (1986), Segal (1972), and Sutherland (1971) described citizen/client participation as a new, radicalized perspective in the field of social welfare: "Marginalized groups of people were redefined as a political rather than [as] a behavioral problem" (Rhoades, 1986, p. 73). The theoretical focus shifted from changing the individual to challenging and changing the archaic systems (Segal, 1972). In theory, citizen participation referred to having groups of citizens serve as watchdogs over government programs, which would serve to redistribute power by rerouting government practices back to a more grassroots level (Rhoades, 1986; Segal, 1972).

Rhoades (1986) found that in some social welfare circles, social workers began to take the role of advocate for the people receiving services. Social services agencies began to assume a similar role for consumers of social services. Concurrently, recipients of these services pushed for the right to advocate for themselves in the planning of programs that had an impact on their lives. The intent of these concurrent actions was to focus the perspectives of service recipients on all welfare issues and to expose actions of the government and social welfare agencies that were antithetical to the perspectives of service recipients.

Citizen/client participation ideally meant citizen power and was seen by reformers and some people who were poor as a major force to change the conditions of poverty (Rhoades, 1986). In practice, unfortunately, it became nothing more than rhetoric and ritual, involving attitude surveys, neighborhood meetings, and public hearings. Public officials were able to prove that they had gone through the motions, when, in fact, they had not made any true reforms.

At the same time that people involved with social welfare were giving up on the idea of citizen/client participation, professionals in rehabilitation services were beginning to explore citizen participation: "Influenced by the radicalization of the social welfare field, a circle of professionals in rehabilitation were dedicated to promoting the success of client involvement in planning and directing rehabilitation programs" (Rhoades, 1986, p. 74). Professionals in the rehabilitation field were frustrated with the token involvement of people with disabilities in their own rehabilitation. Through citizen participation, efforts were made to involve customers of rehabilitation services in the decisions about service delivery.

Legislative Initiatives

Whereas the previous sections focus on the roles that social movements have played in bringing rights to people with disabilities, this section turns to many of the legislative initiatives that have helped to secure these rights. Many authors have examined the role of legislation in the social change that occurred from the 1950s to the 1970s (see Brunk, 1991; Chappell, 1991; Driedger, 1989; Litvin & Browning, 1978; Rhoades, 1986). In the 1950s, amendments to existing legislation (e.g., the Smith-Fess Act of 1920, PL 67-236; the Social Security Act Amendments of 1956, PL 84-880, which amended the Social Security Act of 1935, PL 74-271) provided for personnel training, for medical care for people who were poor, for aid to families with dependent children, for assistance to adults with permanent and total disabilities who were in economic need, for extension of diagnostic and counseling services for youth with mental retardation, and for innovation and expansion of vocational rehabilitation programs.

In the 1960s, civil rights and issues involving disability became a major concern of the federal government. Initiatives focused on ensuring basic civil rights for minorities (e.g., the Civil Rights Act of 1964, PL 88-352), on establishing special projects in maternity and infant care, on coordinating comprehensive mental retardation planning on an interagency basis, (e.g., the Maternal and Child Health and Mental Retardation Planning Amendments of 1963, PL 88-156), and on removing architectural barriers (e.g., the Architectural Barriers Act of 1968, PL 90-480).

In addition, there was a focus on meeting construction costs of research facilities in human development (e.g., the Mental Retardation Facilities and Community Mental Health Centers Construction Act, PL 88-164) as well as on training teachers and other specialists in special education. The Social Security Amendments of 1965 (PL 89-97) are noteworthy because they added the Medicare and Medicaid programs to the Social Security Act.

Attention also was devoted to preventive health services and early detection and treatment of disease among children (e.g., Title XIX of the Social Security Act Amendments of 1967, PL 90-248), to training and job placement of public assistance recipients to restore individuals to independence (e.g., the creation of the Work Incentives Program), and to extended evaluation of people with disabilities applying for vocational rehabilitation programs (e.g., the Vocational Rehabilitation Amendments of 1965, PL 89-333).

In the 1970s, there were several major legislative initiatives. The Developmental Disabilities Services and Facilities Construction Act (PL 91-517) introduced the concept of developmental disability (Wolfe, Kregel, & Wehman, 1996). In 1975, the Education for All Handicapped Children Act (PL 94-142) was passed, which guaranteed a free and appropriate public education to all children in the least restrictive environment.

Title XIX of the Social Security Act of 1971 (PL 92-223) required Intermediate Care Facilities for the Mentally Retarded (ICF/MR) to provide active treatment (Wolfe et al., 1996). In addition, the Social Security Act was amended to create Title XX (PL 94-103), which allowed for provision of services to a large group of people.

Supplemental Security Income (SSI) was created by PL 92-603. The SSI program addressed Medicaid benefits, contributed to deinstitutionalization, allowed for a trial work period, and contained provisions for a representative payee (Wolfe et al., 1996).

One of the most significant laws of the 1970s was the Rehabilitation Act of 1973 (PL 93-112), which had several provisions that pertained to self-advocacy in the rehabilitation services system. Rhoades (1986) outlined these provisions as follows. First, each state vocational rehabilitation agency was required to develop a plan showing how the views of consumers, as well as providers and other concerned people, were to be taken into account in policy making. Second, there was the mandate of the Individualized Written Rehabilitation Program, which was a requirement for consumers to participate directly in their rehabilitation. In its Title V, Sections 501–504, the Rehabilitation Act of 1973 mandated affirmative action programs for the employment of people with disabilities, banned discrimination on the basis of disability in any project receiving federal assistance, and created the Architectural and Transportation Compliance Board.

Rhoades (1986) noted that the legislation passed in the 1970s recognized the value of self-advocacy in service programs and required it in various ways—for example, by addressing the importance of seeking customer input at all program levels and of measuring customer satisfaction as a means of assessing quality, effectiveness, and appropriateness of services (Rhoades, 1986).

Judicial Factors

In addition to social movements and legislative actions, the courts also have had a major role in shaping the rights of people with disabilities.

Many authors have examined the impact of certain judicial rulings on the emerging disability rights movement (see Brunk, 1991; Kenefick, 1981; Scotch, 1984; Turnbull, 1990). In the 1950s, the most significant case in shaping disability issues was the 1954 Supreme Court decision in *Brown v. Board of Education*. In general, it set the principle of equal opportunity for education (Blake, Sale, & Erhart, 1996). The principles enunciated in *Brown* were an important basis for court decisions in the early 1970s that established the right to free and appropriate public education for children with disabilities and that culminated in the Congressional passage of PL 94-142 in 1975 (Turnbull, 1990).

Mills v. D.C. Board of Education (1972) and *Pennsylvania Association for Retarded Children (PARC) v. Commonwealth of Pennsylvania* (1972) dealt with the right to education for children with mental retardation and physical disabilities (Scotch, 1984). In *Mills*, the court ruled that no child could be denied a free public education because of mental health, behavioral concerns, emotional concerns, or physical disabilities (Hickson, Blackman, & Reis, 1995). The *PARC* class action suit resulted in a consent agreement stipulating that all children with mental retardation had a right to a free program of education and training, regardless of their degree of impairment (Hickson et al., 1995). Both cases also established the right to nondiscriminatory evaluation, the right to be educated with peers without disabilities, and the right to adequate consultation with parents (Blake et al., 1996).

In the 1970s, several decisions set important precedents. *Wyatt v. Stickney* (1972) addressed the right to a minimal level of institutional care, treatment, and habilitation. It was a clear statement of the specific requirements for institutional care for people with mental retardation. The court issued a statement of 49 minimal constitutional standards of care, treatment, and habilitation, in which the rights of individuals with mental retardation to habilitation and treatment were affirmed (Hickson et al., 1995). In addition, the case established the right to adequate instruction with proper goals (Blake et al., 1996).

Halderman v. Pennhurst State School and Hospital (1977) established a precedent for the closure of institutions. Judge Broderick ruled that all institutions violated the right to habilitation of people with mental retardation and must be expeditiously replaced by community programs (Hickson et al., 1995). It moved the litigation arena into the community "through a demand for closure of a state facility, extension of the class membership and a recognition that the court itself might not be the best source for promulgating standards of care for" individuals with mental retardation (Kenefick, 1981, p. 38).

Ricci v. Greenblatt (1972) provided for the provision of constitutional rights in the areas of health, safety, and suitable living environment for residents of Belchertown State School in Massachusetts. *New*

York State Association for Retarded Citizens, Inc., and Parisi v. Carey (1980), which addressed living conditions at Willowbrook Developmental Center in New York, set the protection from harm precedent. Federal Judge Judd ordered the reduction of the number of residents at Willowbrook from 5,400 to 250 and an emphasis on training individuals with disabilities in the community.

With *Wuori v. Zitnay* (1978), the precedent for a system of community services was set. This federal ruling attempted to detail every aspect of life at the institution and in the community that would be required to produce an acceptable quality of care.

These judicial decisions set precedents that secured better living conditions, an improved quality of life, integrated education, and provided community services for individuals with developmental disabilities. These rulings opened doors but did not fix every problem faced by people with developmental disabilities. Often the court decisions lacked a plan of action and someone to coordinate activities, and, occasionally, state legislatures refused to fund court mandates, which undermined the courts' intents (Kenefick, 1981).

SELF-ADVOCACY BY PEOPLE
WITH DEVELOPMENTAL DISABILITIES

Rhoades et al. (1986) noted that the social/civil rights movement of the 1960s and 1970s was led primarily by people who did not have mental retardation but who did have physical disabilities. Although this period of advocacy for people with disabilities brought about dramatic reforms, the birth of the self-advocacy movement for people with developmental disabilities went largely unnoticed by the general population. The self-advocacy movement, though, has grown since its inception, and, in the 1990s, consists of community-based groups that provide a forum for their members to learn, among other things, the rights and responsibilities of citizenship and to speak on their own behalf. The following section explores the history and origins of the self-advocacy movement in the United States.

Origins of American Self-Advocacy

The origins of self-advocacy by individuals with developmental disabilities in the United States can be traced back to the early 1970s. Shoultz (1990a) and Williams and Shoultz (1982) traced American self-advocacy from its roots in Swedish self-advocacy. In 1968, a Swedish parents' organization sponsored a conference for people with developmental disabilities; the participants listed the changes that they wanted in their programs and gave their list to the parents' organization (Shoultz, 1990a). It was a chance for ideas, concerns, and experiences to be shared. This is thought to have been the first national conference of individuals with developmental disabilities in the world; a second was organized in 1970 (Williams & Shoultz, 1982). Conferences followed in Great Britain in 1972 and in British Columbia, Canada, in 1973.

Several authors (Hayden & Shoultz, 1991; Shoultz, 1990a; Shoultz & Ward, 1996; Whittico & Ingram, 1994; Williams & Shoultz, 1982) carefully outlined the events that took place during that period in the United States. Five individuals from Oregon who were present at the 1973 conference returned to Oregon inspired with the idea of creating an organization that would organize conventions and be a voice for individuals with developmental disabilities. These five individuals made a commitment to one another that Oregon would hold a state conference, which occurred in October of 1974, and was entitled *We Have Something to Offer*.

From this conference was born the first self-advocacy state chapter in the United States, People First of Oregon. State conferences were held in California, Kansas, Nebraska, and Washington over the next 4 years, and self-advocacy organizations continued to grow from the grassroots level or local level to the state level (e.g., California, Colorado, Kansas, Nebraska, Pennsylvania, Tennessee, Virginia, Washington).

Many leaders within the self-advocacy movement began to view the next logical step as uniting the various grassroots level self-advocacy groups into a national organization. During the First North American People First Conference in 1990, a steering committee was formed to make recommendations about a national self-advocacy organization. The steering committee developed and used the following six questions to guide their recommendations about the development of a national group:

1. What are the issues the national organization wants to address?
2. What are the beliefs, purposes, and goals of the national organization?
3. What is the best way to structure the national organization?
4. What is the best way for a national organization to work with state and local self-advocacy organizations?
5. Who will be members of this national organization?
6. How can we get money to support the national organization? (Hayden & Shoultz, 1991, p. 1)

As a result of their deliberations, the steering committee recommended the following: 1) formation of a coalition of all state and local self-advocacy organizations, 2) creation of nine regional divisions of self-advocacy organizations, and 3) selection of two elected representatives from each region to serve on the National Steering Committee.

In all, the Committee developed 14 recommendations, which were voted on at the next national conference in September 1991. Passage of the recommendations is regarded "as the time when the national organization was born" (Whittico & Ingram, 1994, p. 2).

Through the early 1990s, the national organization grew and became more focused, and in 1992 it adopted the name Self Advocates Becoming Empowered and appointed national advisors; in 1995, the national organization was incorporated. In 1996, Self Advocates Becoming Empowered outlined its goals as follows:

1. Make self-advocacy available in every state including institutions, high schools, rural areas, people living with families, with local support and advisors to help.
2. Work with the criminal justice system and people with disabilities about their rights within the criminal justice system.
3. Close institutions for people with developmental disabilities labels nationwide and building community supports. (Shoultz & Ward, 1996, p. 233)

Self-Advocacy Group and Membership Profiles

Longhurst (1994) provided information on self-advocacy groups and their members in the United States, which has been summarized in Tables 1 and 2. Table 1 contains the self-advocacy group demographic information. Table 2 displays the demographic information of members of self-advocacy groups.

Self-Advocacy as a Social Movement

Bersani (1996), Driedger (1989), Rhoades (1986), Shakespeare (1993), and Shoultz (1996) discussed whether the self-organization and self-help of people with disabilities represent a social movement. Except for Bersani (1996) and Shoultz (1996), the main focus has been on individuals with physical disabilities; but clearly there is an argument to be made for self-advocacy as a social movement. Johnson, Larana, and Gusfield (1994) provided four indicators of a social movement: 1) Members go beyond their social roles, 2) a strong ideological change is represented, 3) a new dimension of identity emerges by drawing on a characteristic formerly seen as a weakness, and 4) the relationship between the individual and the movement is blurred.

As Bersani (1996) pointed out, self-advocacy groups have achieved each of these indicators. People with developmental disabilities have gone beyond social roles by organizing and taking control over their lives. Seeing individuals with developmental disabilities as leaders rather than as consumers represents a clear ideological change. What was once regarded as a weakness—having a disability—is seen as a strength in the late 1990s: Self-advocates are proud of who they

Table 1. Self-advocacy group demographics

Variable	Data
Group size	
Average	23 members
Range	1–150 members
1–10 members	23%
11–25 members	44%
26 or more members	33%
Group age	
Average	5 years
Range	Birth to 34 years
Meeting locations	
Human service settings	55%
Community locations	45%
State organization membership	
Yes	80%
No	20%
Average age	8 years
States with statewide self-advocacy organizations	Alabama, California, Colorado, Connecticut Illinois, Indiana, Michigan, Nebraska, New Jersey, New York, Oklahoma, Oregon, Tennessee, Texas, and Washington
Group activities	
Individual advocacy	How to be a good officer, rights, decision making, voting, advocating for individual rights
Group advocacy	Community education, closing institutions, contacting political leaders, developing self-advocacy curricula, developing employment opportunities, guardianship training, training for the criminal justice system, developing position statements, program evaluation, advocating for all people with disabilities, putting out newsletters
Self-help	Improving self-respect, labeling, assertiveness training, helping others, leadership training
Recreation	Social events, learning about relationships

From Longhurst, N. (1994). *The self-advocacy movement by people with developmental disabilities: A demographic study and directory of self-advocacy groups in the United States.* Washington, DC: American Association on Mental Retardation; reprinted by permission.

are, as is reflected in their writing and slogans (e.g., "Disabled and proud," "Don't think that we don't think"). An important final point is that self-advocates no longer advocate solely for themselves; they advocate for others and for the movement, and some are employed as paid professional advocates.

Table 2.   Self-advocacy membership demographics

Variable	%
Gender	
Female	51
Male	49
Marital status	
Single	95
Married	3
Divorced/widowed	2
Age	
13–20 years	4
21–35 years	44
36–50 years	38
51–65 years	11
65 years or older	2
Ethnic background	
European American	85
African American	11
Latino American	3
Asian American	<1
Other	<1
Living arrangement	
Institutions	10
Large group homes	6
Small group homes	27
Own home	24
Family	24
Foster	7
Other	2
Urban	71
Rural	29
Employment setting	
Segregated settings	57
Day programs	16
Sheltered workshops	41
Integrated settings	28
Supported employment	17
Competitive employment	11
School	4
Unemployed	6
Other	5
Disability label	
Mental retardation	80
Learning disability	11
Cerebral palsy	9
Physical disability	7

(continued)

Table 2. *(continued)*

Variable	%
Autism	1
Mental illness	4
Traumatic brain injury	<1
Other	2
Two or more disability labels	37
Length of involvement with self-advocacy	
Less than 2 years	50
2–4 years	28
5 or more years	22

From Longhurst, N. (1994). *The self-advocacy movement by people with developmental disabilities: A demographic study and directory of self-advocacy groups in the United States.* Washington, DC: American Association on Mental Retardation; reprinted by permission.

STANDARD FEATURES OF SELF-ADVOCACY GROUPS

As mentioned previously, self-advocacy groups can be considered part of a larger social movement. Self-advocacy groups also have certain shared characteristics. This section describes starting a self-advocacy group, supporting a self-advocacy group, setting goals for a self-advocacy group, and coping with difficulties faced by a self-advocacy group.

Starting a Self-Advocacy Group

Among self-advocacy groups, there is a common understanding of how to start a group. People First of Washington (n.d.-a) and People First of Nebraska (1993) identified and presented nine steps to starting a successful self-advocacy group: 1) Make sure that everyone understands what a self-advocacy group does and why people meet as a group; 2) decide on the responsibilities for getting the group going (e.g., place to meet, transportation, publicity); 3) find out how other groups work, and learn from them (e.g., invite another group to visit and talk); 4) decide on the rules for how the group will work together (e.g., officers, advisor, voting); 5) develop team spirit and a good working friendship with members; 6) decide on goals for the group (start small and build up); 7) decide on ways to reach the group goals, and formulate an action plan; 8) develop connections to the community; and 9) evaluate the group, and make changes.

Supporting a Self-Advocacy Group

Self-advocacy groups also share a common understanding of how to sustain the group. People First of Nebraska (1993) outlined many ways to support a self-advocacy group over time. It is the responsibility of the advisor or a committee of the self-advocacy group to ensure that people know the place and time of each meeting (e.g., call people, send letters or calendars, put up notices). The leaders of the self-advocacy group, particularly the president, should ensure that each advisor knows his or her job responsibilities, which is often accomplished through written contracts. Before group meetings, it is essential to have officers' meetings. These preparatory meetings are a time to practice, to get ready, and to discuss problems. The advisor usually assists with these preparatory meetings.

It is important to find ways to get everyone involved in the group (i.e., no member of the group should feel left out). Each member should have a job, a chance to talk, and something for which he or she is responsible. Materials and discussion should be presented in a way that is easy for everyone present to understand. The leadership, through group members' input, should monitor the group's goals to ensure that the goals meet the members' true needs. The advisor should help the group make a 3- to 6-month plan for the group, as well as help the group set annual goals. Meetings should be fun; therefore, most group meetings can be followed by a time to socialize and to enjoy refreshments. Last, any problems within or outside of the group should be addressed head on by the individuals involved. Part of self-advocacy is solving problems.

Setting Goals for a Self-Advocacy Group

Self-advocacy groups also have common areas in which they set group goals. People First of Nebraska (1993) suggested setting group goals in the broad categories of community integration, employment, education, getting along with others, personal and physical assistance services, home living/ownership, recreation and leisure time, medical and dental services, fundraising, financial management, and transportation.

These common procedures (i.e., how to start a group, how to support a group, how to set group goals) allow one self-advocacy group to help other self-advocacy groups form and grow. It saves members from having to reinvent the process each time a new group forms; one group is able to support another, and there is a continuity of experience.

Coping with Difficulties Faced by a Self-Advocacy Group

Self-advocacy groups and their members are often poor. Finding funding for self-advocacy groups can be very difficult. Searching for funding is an ongoing quest for grants, donations, stipends, salable products, and fund-raising ideas:

We have learned that it is very important to get funding from a number of different places. This is important so that you are not controlled by any one funder. Our funds come from county government, community organizations, private foundations, individual donors, and State and Federal funds. (Speaking for Ourselves, 1993, p. 16)

A second issue is group independence versus sponsorship (Shoultz, 1990b; Worrell, 1988):

There are basically two ways in which self-advocacy groups function across the country. Some, like several of the statewide organizations are independent, autonomous organizations that have their own boards of directors and make independent decisions about their own affairs. Others, both statewide and local organizations, are sponsored by larger organizations such as an advocacy organization, a parents' group, or a service provider. (Shoultz, 1990b, p. 7)

Shoultz (1990b) described the advantages and disadvantages of sponsored and independent groups. Sponsored groups have the following advantages: ease of finding a meeting place, having an advisor, having the means to mail notices to members, and possibly having more readily available knowledge and resources that will help the group to grow and learn about self-advocacy (Shoultz, 1990b). The disadvantages associated with being a sponsored group include less opportunity for the group to do the following: make its own decisions, develop the skills of self-advocacy, learn about the rights of people with disabilities, apply for funding in its own right, and put its own needs first (Shoultz, 1990b).

The advantages typically associated with independent groups include the following: the opportunity for greater control over its own affairs (e.g., making decisions, getting involved in controversies, applying for project funding), and for more ease participating in coalitions of groups that want the same thing (Shoultz, 1990b). The disadvantages of being an independent group typically include the following: more difficulty getting started, more likely to stop meeting if the advisor leaves, and less ease forming connections to the service system and to parent and advocacy organizations (Shoultz, 1990b).

CONCLUSION

It is important to understand the community and unity of the self-advocacy movement for people with disabilities. Self-advocacy is not self-involved or self-centered; it is a "statement by people with developmental disabilities that [they] want to be seen as people who have something to offer and skills to share, rather than [being] seen as people with handicaps or limitations" (People First of Washington, n.d.-b, p. 2). Self-advocacy is also a social/civil rights movement that is about building alliances and coalitions, working together to achieve personal and group goals, looking out for one another, learning, and fighting discrimination against great odds. It is an empowering experience that brings awareness of society and self (Miller & Keys, 1996).

REFERENCES

Architectural Barriers Act of 1968, PL 90-480, 42 U.S.C. §§ 4151 et seq.

Bersani, H., Jr. (1996). Leadership in developmental disabilities where we've been, where we are, and where we're going. In G. Dybwad & H. Bersani, Jr. (Eds.), New voices self-advocacy by people with disabilities (pp. 258–269). Cambridge, MA: Brookline Books.

Blake, K.A., Sale, P., & Erhart, L.M. (1996). Going to school. In P.J. McLaughlin & P. Wehman (Eds.), Mental retardation and developmental disabilities (pp. 49–68). Austin, TX: PRO-ED.

Bogdan, R., & Taylor, S. (1976). The judged not the judges: An insider's view of mental retardation. American Psychologist, 31(1), 47–52.

Bogdan, R., & Taylor, S. (1982). Inside out: The social meaning of mental retardation. Toronto, Ontario, Canada: University of Toronto Press.

Brown v. Board of Education, 347 U.S. 483 (1954).

Brunk, G. (1991). Supporting the growth of the self-advocacy movement: What we can learn from its history and activists. Lawrence, KS: Beach Center on Families and Disability.

Chappell, J. (1991). A movement toward independence: One perspective on the disability rights movement. In R.L. Akridge (Ed.), Peer support programs to promote independent living and career development of people with disabilities (pp. 19–32). Fayetteville, AR: Research and Training Center in Vocational Rehabilitation.

Civil Rights Act of 1964, PL 88-352, 42 U.S.C. §§ 1981 et seq.

Developmental Disabilities Assistance and Bill of Rights Act of 1975, PL 94-103, 42 U.S.C. §§ 6000 et seq.

Developmental Disabilities Services and Facilities Construction Act, PL 91-517, 42 U.S.C. §§ 6000 et seq.

Driedger, D. (1989). The last civil rights movement: Disabled people's international. New York: St. Martin's Press.

Edgerton, R. (1967). The cloak of competence: Stigma in the lives of the mentally retarded. Berkeley: University of California Press.

Education for All Handicapped Children Act of 1975, PL 94-142, 20 U.S.C. §§ 1400 et seq.

Fine, M., & Asch, A. (1988). Disability beyond stigma: Social interaction, discrimination, and activism. Journal of Social Issues, 44(1), 3–21.

Gliedman J., & Roth, W. (1980). The unexpected minority. New York: Harcourt Brace Jovanovich.

Hahn, H. (1988). The politics of human difference: Disability and discrimination. Journal of Social Issues, 44(1), 39–47.

Halderman v. Pennhurst State School & Hospital, 466 F. Supp. 1295 (E.D. Pa. 1977).

Hayden, M., & Shoultz, B. (1991). Self-advocacy by persons with disabilities ideas for a national organization. Minneapolis, MN: Research and Training Center on Community Living.

Hickson, L., Blackman, L.S., & Reis, E.M. (1995). *Mental retardation foundations of educational programming*. Needham Heights, MA: Allyn & Bacon.

International League of Societies for Persons with Mental Handicap (1994). *The beliefs, values, and principles of self-advocacy*. Unknown: Author.

Johnson, H., Larana, E., & Gusfield, J.R. (1994). *New social movements: From ideology to identity*. Philadelphia: Temple University Press.

Kenefick, B. (1981). Court decisions: The impact of litigation. In J. Wortis (Ed.), *Mental retardation and developmental disabilities* (Vol. XII, pp. 20–54). New York: Brunner/Mazel.

Litvin, M.E., & Browning, P.L. (1978). Public assistance in historical perspective. In J. Wortis (Ed.), *Mental retardation and developmental disabilities: An annual review* (Vol. X, pp. 196–213). New York: Brunner/Mazel.

Longhurst, N. (1994). *The self-advocacy movement by people with developmental disabilities: A demographic study and directory of self-advocacy groups in the United States*. Washington, DC: American Association on Mental Retardation.

Mason, J., Williams-Murphy, T., & Brennan, L. (1996). The need to reconfigure our hard drives. *Impact, 9*(3), 4.

Maternal and Child Health and Mental Retardation Planning Amendments of 1963, PL 88-156, 42 U.S.C. §§ 1305 *et seq.*

Meenaghan, T.M., & Mascari, M. (1971). Consumer choice, consumer control in service delivery. *Social Work, 16*(4), 50–57.

Mental Retardation Facilities and Community Mental Health Centers Construction Act of 1963, PL 88-164, 42 U.S.C. §§ 2670 *et seq.*

Mest, G.M. (1988). With a little help from their friends: Use of social support systems by persons with retardation. *Journal of Social Issues, 44*(1), 117–125.

Miller, A.B., & Keys, C.B. (1996). Awareness, action, and collaboration: How the self-advocacy movement is empowering for persons with developmental disabilities. *Mental Retardation, 34*(5), 312–319.

Mills v. D.C. Board of Education, 348 F. Supp. 866 (D.D.C. 1972).

Minow, M. (1990). *Making all the difference: Inclusion, exclusion and the American law*. Ithaca, NY: Cornell University Press.

Nelis, T. (1994). Self-advocacy: Realizing a dream. *Impact, 7*(1), 1.

New York State Association for Retarded Citizens, Inc. & Parisi v. Carey, Civ. No 80–7289, 72.85 (2nd Cir. June 4, 1980).

Pennsylvania Association for Retarded Children (PARC) v. Commonwealth of Pennsylvania, 343 F. Supp. 279 (E.D. Pa. 1972).

People First of California. (1984). *Surviving the system: Mental retardation and the retarding environment*. Sacramento, CA: State Council on Developmental Disabilities.

People First of Nebraska. (1993). *Speaking up for yourself and others: Some ideas for successful self-advocacy*. Lincoln, NE: Author.

People First of Washington. (n.d.-a). *A community where self-advocacy grows*. Clarkston, WA: Author.

People First of Washington. (n.d.-b). *Self advocacy is*. Tacoma, WA: Author.

People First of Washington. (1990). *The retarding or disabling environment*. Tacoma, WA: Author.

Rehabilitation Act Amendments of 1986, PL 99-506, 29 U.S.C. §§ 701 *et seq.*

Rehabilitation Act of 1973, PL 93-112, 29 U.S.C. §§ 701 *et seq.*

Rhoades, C.M. (1986). Self-advocacy. In J. Wortis (Ed.), *Mental retardation and developmental disabilities* (Vol. XIV, pp. 69–90). New York: Elsevier/North Holland.

Rhoades, C.M., Browning, P.L., & Thorin, E.J. (1986). Self-help advocacy movement: A promising peer-support system for people with mental disabilities. *Rehabilitation Literature*, 47(1–2), 2–7.

Ricci v. Greenblatt, Civ. No 72-469-T (D. Mass. 1972).

Scheer, J., & Groce, N. (1988). Impairment as a human constant: Cross-cultural and historical perspectives on variation. *Journal of Social Issues*, 44(1), 23–37.

Scotch, R.K. (1984). *From goodwill to civil rights*. Philadelphia: Temple University Press.

Segal, B. (1972). The politicalization of deviance. *Social Work, 18*, 40–46.

Self-Advocates Becoming Empowered. (1994). *Taking place*. Tulsa: People First of Oklahoma.

Shakespeare, T. (1993). Disabled people's self organization: A new social movement? *Disability, Handicap and Society, 8*(3).

Shoultz, B. (1990a). A short history of American self-advocacy. *Impact, 3*(4), 2.

Shoultz, B. (1990b). Independence or sponsorship: An issue for self-advocacy groups. *Impact, 3*(4), 7.

Shoultz, B. (1996). More thoughts on self-advocacy: The movement, the group, and the individual. *TASH Newsletter, 22*(10/11), 22–25.

Shoultz, B., & Ward, N. (1996). Self-advocates becoming empowered: The birth of a national organization in the U.S. In G. Dybwad & H. Bersani, Jr. (Eds.), *New voices self-advocacy by people with disabilities* (pp. 216–234). Cambridge, MA: Brookline Books.

Smith-Fess Act of 1920, PL 67-236, 29 U.S.C. §§ 31 *et seq.*

Social Security Act Amendments of 1956, PL 84-880, 42 U.S.C. §§ 101 *et seq.*

Social Security Act Amendments of 1965, PL 89-97, 42 U.S.C. §§ 101 *et seq.*

Social Security Act Amendments of 1967, PL 90-248, 42 U.S.C. §§ 1396d *et seq.*

Social Security Act of 1935, PL 74-271, 42 U.S.C. §§ 301 *et seq.*

Social Security Act of 1971, PL 92-223, 42 U.S.C. §§ 402 *et seq.*

Speaking for Ourselves. (1993). *Spreading the word*. Plymouth Meeting, PA: Author.

Supplemental Security Income (SSI) for Aged, Blind and Disabled, PL 92-603, 42 U.S.C. §§ 1381 *et seq.*

Sutherland, M. (1971). Consumer participation. *Journal of Rehabilitation, 37*(6), 18–21.

Turnbull, H.R., III. (1990). *Free appropriate education: The law and children with disabilities* (3rd ed.). Denver, CO: Love Publishing.

Vocational Rehabilitation Amendments of 1965, PL 89-333, 29 U.S.C. §§ 7000 *et seq.*

Whittico, P., & Ingram, T. (1994). The history and accomplishments of self-advocates becoming empowered. *Impact, 7*(1), 2–3.

Williams, P., & Shoultz, B. (1982). *We can speak for ourselves*. Bloomington: Indiana University Press.

Wolfe, P., Kregel, J., & Wehman, P. (1996). Service delivery. In P.J. McLaughlin & P. Wehman (Eds.), *Mental retardation and developmental disabilities* (pp. 3–27). Austin, TX: PRO-ED.

Worrell, B. (1988). *People first advice for advisors*. Downsview, Ontario, Canada: National People First Project.

Wuori v. Zitnay, No. 75-80-SD (D. Maine July 14, 1978).

Wyatt v. Stickney, 344 F. Supp. 387 (M.D. Ala. 1972).

The Promise of Self-Advocacy and Community Employment

Julie Ann Racino
with contributions from Perry Whittico

SAMUEL

Samuel Ellsworth[1] was one of the pioneers with the Lakes Region self-advocacy group in New Hampshire. He was elected the group's treasurer and was one of the co-chairpersons when the group started. According to the group's advisor, Samuel has gone through cycles in which self-advocacy was more or less important to him.

This chapter is based, in part, on two research studies with self-advocates (Racino, 1993b, 1995a) and coalition advocacy work; it is not intended to update national and international developments in self-advocacy.

The author wishes to thank those people who participated in the projects, including the following: Roberta and Jocelyn Gallant of New Hampshire; T.J. Monroe of People First of Tennessee; Alan Emerson and Bindy Bourgeois of Lakes Region Self Advocacy Group, New Hampshire; Beverly Evans of Sacramento, California; Thomas Acherson of Danbury, Connecticut; Joseph Wrinkle of Blue Springs, Missouri; Tammy Swartz of San Diego, California; Mary Faith D'Andrea of Watertown, Connecticut; Roland Johnson of Pennsylvania; and Lorelee Stewart, Judi Chamberlin, Pat Deegan, and Sherri Watson for cross-disability insights.

[1]A pseudonym.

Samuel lives in his own apartment downtown and has a job washing dishes at a local restaurant. His girlfriend, Susan, also belongs to the
self-advocacy group. Samuel loves music and takes it with him wher-
ever he goes, including when he rides his bike. He says that at work he
can "get people going," and the waiters and waitresses will dance and
so will the cook. He enjoys adding this excitement to other people's lives.
(Racino, 1993b)

As one of the major concerns of U.S. citizens and a national priority, the goal of full employment remains elusive for citizens with and
without disabilities. Employment, which is highlighted in the Americans with Disabilities Act (ADA) of 1990 (PL 101-336), has long been a
cause of self-advocates, disability activists, and psychiatric survivors[2]
and continues to be a priority in the independent living (including delivery of services through independent living centers [ILCs]), self-help,
and survivor movements (e.g., Chamberlin & Unzicher, 1991; Mems &
Bolton, 1992; People First of Washington, 1986; Weissman, Kennedy, &
Litvak, 1991).

This chapter briefly introduces the concept of employment as the
background for consumer-driven approaches for all citizens with and
without disabilities, presents the perspectives of self-advocates on 11
major issues concerning employment, and concludes with a hope for
change toward better quality lives.

EMPLOYMENT FOR CITIZENS WITH DISABILITIES

As reported by Lou Harris and Associates (1994) and the National
Council on Disability (1993), knowledge of the ADA has markedly increased since 1991. However, according to Lou Harris and Associates,
there have been no employment gains or "any significant increase in
earning power of working individuals with disabilities" since the mid-
1980s (1994, p. 93). Unemployment figures for people with severe or
significant disabilities continue to be inordinately high; for example,
unemployment was at 85% for people with severe psychiatric disabilities (Mancuso, 1990).

Reasonable Accommodations

With the passage of the ADA, businesses have made renewed efforts
nationwide to employ people with disabilities, including efforts to increase reasonable accommodations in typical worksites. Although conceptualized as applying to people with disabilities, many reasonable

---

[2]*Psychiatric survivors* is a term preferred by people who do not view themselves as
clients but as survivors of the service systems.

accommodations also hold promise for *all* workers. These reasonable accommodations include the following (Allen, 1994):

- Job restructuring (also, job sharing and enlargement)
- Modified work schedules[3] and reassignment
- Modified exams, training materials, and policies
- Modified equipment, readers, and interpreters
- Miscellaneous accommodations such as reserved parking spaces
- Personal assistants (as travel attendants) and temporary job coaches
- Use of paid and unpaid leave
- Assistive technologies

Barriers to Choice and Employment

Citizens with disabilities continue to face barriers in the workplace and employment sectors but also are hindered by barriers in disability systems, which affect all areas of life: recreation, employment, education, health, and home. As obstacles to choice and employment, these disability systems' barriers include the following (West, 1995):

- Policy conflict between vocational rehabilitation and disability policies
- Reimbursement mechanisms for day services (and insufficient case funds [Revell, Wehman, Kregel, West, & Rayfield, 1994])
- Financial disincentives to employment (including part-time employment without health benefits)
- Self-interest of sheltered workshops
- Limitations of federal programs for use on the job (e.g., Community Supported Living Arrangements, home and community-based Medicaid waivers [Racino, 1995a])

The barriers also include the continued separation of the disability systems of employment from the typical employment options and paths.

EMPLOYMENT FOR ALL CITIZENS
WITH AND WITHOUT DISABILITIES

Considered to be a part of full citizenship, the rights to employment, housing, recreation, and education have taken second place to the growth in the business economy and its effects on the work force and

---

[3]See, also, flextime and flexible work arrangements (e.g., Ronen, 1981; Swartz, 1978) as international innovations in business, industry, and the governmental sectors. The benefits of flextime include time for family, recreation, and control over personal life (e.g., medical, child care, shopping, adult education) (Ronen, 1981), and positive effects on public transportation and employee productivity.

on family and community life. From a political-economic perspective, the nature of the work force has shifted toward a service-informational economy, with changes in the following:

- Demographics (e.g., major increases in minority workers)
- Size and structure of organizations (e.g., reductions in middle management as part of downsizing)
- Division of labor (e.g., increased specialization, certification, and licensing)
- Factors that affect the lives of individual workers (e.g., growth in people working at home, expectations of career and job changes)

Often working conditions are ones in which loyalty and trust—part of employee–employer agreements of the past (and basic to new approaches to personal assistance and support)—also are shifting and affecting the very nature of labor management in the U.S. economy.

Compensation Packages and Employee Assistance Programs

The changing conditions in the marketplace may be viewed as leading to more flexible and comprehensive compensation packages with a greater emphasis on "flextime, day-care services, parental leave, unpaid leave, benefit options, and employee contributions to escalating health care costs" (Krannich & Krannich, 1994, p. 32). However, similar to employee assistance programs—"one of the most prevalent forms of accommodations" (Shaw, MacGillis, & Dvorchik, 1994, p. 117)—employers' compensation packages may evolve to be tools of management to reduce costs[4] and may represent the intrusion of new forms of social control (e.g., social requirements in areas of alcoholism) into the workplace (see Shaw et al., 1994).

Employment Concerns and Issues

As described from the disability sector, employment for all is based on several key principles: integration, income and benefits, choice (and introducing flexibility in the workplace), ongoing career advancement (and the marketability of workers), individualized and natural supports, equal access (versus diversity of access), and employment retention (Wehman & Kregel, 1995). These principles, however, are of general concern to all workers, with or without disabilities. The following are more specific concerns faced by American workers in the late 1990s:

- Fairness in employment, including hiring and terminations (at-will and contractual employment)
- A minimum wage, though raised by Congress in 1996, which remains particularly inadequate in urban areas

---

[4]See union concerns with flextime and potential negative effects on employees' economic position (Swartz, 1978).

- Discrimination on the basis of age, disability, gender, and ethnicity, and discrimination in part-time employment and in benefits packages
- Pensions and benefits, which are negatively affected by business reorganizations and bankruptcies and which are inadequately protected by law
- Employment law that can be biased against workers
- The declining strength of American unions
- Lack of health benefits, with concerns during times of financial and health crises
- Working conditions in unsafe industries and inability to choose socially conscious employment
- The need for youth employment and education, including technology access on a universal (i.e., global, multicultural) and community bases
- The need for two sources of income and how this affects working families, homes, and businesses (e.g., child care)
- The policies and politics of work and welfare reform, child support and employment, and income support remained as volatile issues affecting family and community life.

These developments in the United States have been occurring as such countries as Great Britain and the East European nations (e.g., the former Czechoslovakia) engaged in privatization plans, based in part on increasing competition as in a capitalistic society (see Racino, 1990). These contrast with approaches to foster social acceptance and cooperation.

CONSUMER-DRIVEN APPROACHES
TO EMPLOYMENT: DISABILITY AND EMPLOYMENT

Disability and employment have been publicly driven, in part, by perceived taxpayer concerns with the financial costs of disability and the economics of contribution (see Racino, 1995a). Based on the acceptance of theories of competition for scarce jobs and resources, cost savings from increased productivity, and lessened support services costs, this perspective contrasts with movements toward universal access and full employment (which may not result in cost savings but in richer lives and a richer society).

Employment efforts in disability have, in part, been targeted to change *societal stereotypes* (see also, Urban League of Onondaga Co., Inc., 1979), including stereotypes of perceived tokenism; to offer *benefits counseling* (Berkeley Independent Living Center, Racino, 1993b; Healy-Mills & Citrone, 1994) and *job placement and training to workers* (and co-workers); to incorporate *career planning* in vocational rehabilitation services (e.g., 100% of vocational rehabilitation agencies reported offering career planning [National Center for Youth with Disabilities, 1993]); and to begin with children (Chaikind, 1992) and youth in schools in the *transition to community life* (e.g., Bradford, Licata, & Lang, n.d.; Rusch, DeStefano, Chadsey-Rusch, Phelps, & Szymanski, 1992).

Most of these employment efforts target changes in the individual (e.g., applicant with a disability, human resources professional, supervisor), or in the workplace (e.g., business, human services employer), often with legal and social underpinnings. Some of these approaches, however, involve changes in the societal institutions that interact with youth (Jackson, Felner, Millstein, Pittman, & Selden, 1993; Stainback & Stainback, 1990), whereas others involve changes in the nature of free enterprise in the emerging global economy.

Individualized and Flexible Supports

The concept of individualized and flexible support services in community living (Knoll & Racino, 1988; Taylor, Racino, Knoll, & Lutfiyya, 1987) has been interpreted differently in the employment and rehabilitation fields. "Individualized" refers to each person's uniqueness, inclusive of support (some of which may be services) from diverse sources (e.g., an agency, a friend); "flexible" encompasses the nature of human beings and human life conditions and their capacities to change over time and the necessity for the community, agencies, families, or individuals to be able to respond. Consumer-directedness may or may not be used as part of the definition. (See Racino, 1995b, for separation of consumer-directedness from individualized and flexible support; and Racino & O'Connor, 1994, for research analysis of support.)

The ADA and Supports

The ADA assumes a different perspective than that of the movement in mental retardation toward natural supports or toward more employee- and family-responsive (i.e., "accepting") workplaces. The differences between the ADA and a supports perspective are primarily due to the reliance of the ADA on a minority (i.e., capability, autonomy) perspective, which is in contrast to supports that rely on societal acceptance and changes in the nature of society and its institutions for all citizens. Consumer involvement and consumer choice (e.g., from an array or a menu) are more common than efforts toward consumer-directedness (see Racino, 1995b, for innovative agencies' approaches to consumer choice and control).

Person-Centered Planning

People with mental retardation are often not involved in "important decisions in their lives, including choosing who they live with, where they work, and what medical services they receive. [This] lack of choice-making opportunities . . . is not the result of the presence of a cognitive disability" (Stancliffe & Wehmeyer, 1995, p. 319). Person-centered planning approaches (e.g., Mount & Zwernik, 1988; O'Brien, 1987; Steere, Gregory, Heiny, & Butterworth, 1995) provide individuals with a means to move away from professionally determined life outcomes—with the help of supportive people—toward planning for valued employment, recreation, education, housing, friendship, and family outcomes (see also Ludlum, Beeman, & Ducharme, 1991).

Consumer-Driven Services and Consumer-Informed Services

Consumer driven is a term that reflects business's efforts to market products and services in ways that are desired by potential markets or audiences (i.e., consumers or users of services or products). Marketing to *potential* users or buyers and to their "needs" and "wants" is viewed as more important for development than are the *views* of current consumers or users. This same concept can be applied to human services. In human services, the term *consumer directedness* often reflects decision making by the primary services consumer regarding the directions of his or her own life and reflects the ways in which services can support his or her hopes and dreams. The experience of a services user, however, may be one of being *consumed by* services, not as a user or director of the services (see Ebert, 1989).

Consumer-informed services or consumer involvement in services are more common in practice. Consumers may "inform" the design of services and products as part of ongoing services development. Consumers also may use total quality management techniques, which are often attributed to businesses that provide exemplar customer service (see Chapter 2); the consumers also should have access to information so that they can offer timely feedback. The involvement of the individuals in consumer-informed services delivery differs from their involvement in consumer-driven services, whereby people with disabilities make decisions regarding their careers and futures and actively "take control" of the employment process (often with the help of others) to realize those decisions. Such active direction may involve changes, such as new availability of transportation to employment and increased accessibility of workplaces (Harris & Associates, 1994).

Consumer-Driven Employment

Consumer-driven employment is based on the directions of the users of the products or services of businesses. It can be viewed from three different human services perspectives. The first perspective—the hiring of personal assistants by people with disabilities—highlights the rights of the employer (i.e., the person with a disability) in relationship to his or her employee (i.e., the personal assistant). This perspective maintains, largely, the institutional relationship as reflected in U.S. labor and contract law (see Racino, 1995a). The second perspective—the consumer as employee of an organization—reflects the push toward increased employee rights, such as the right to choose where one works and how accommodations will be made within the workplace. In the third perspective, employees may help to determine how the organization operates and creates products and services. The latter two approaches in human services, however, often are not considered within the realms of business outcomes and viability (and employee futures) or as part of a movement toward full community employment as determined in part by economic expansion and community growth and stability. Each of these approaches differs from the concepts of *natural supports* (employment with supports) and support across diverse environments, which may or may not involve consumer directedness as a primary organizing concept.

SELF-ADVOCACY, COMMUNITY, AND JOBS

"We do a lot of things that other people won't do" (Whittico, August, 1993, p. 2). Internationally, the self-advocacy movement of people with mental retardation has continued to expand, with "the number of identified self-advocacy groups increas[ing] from 55 to nearly 750 in the decade from 1985 to 1995" (Hayden, Lakin, Braddock, & Smith, 1995, p. 342). As Perry Whittico, a self-advocacy leader in New York, reports, the self-advocacy groups "that have survived over the years are the independent ones, because once you get state or federal money involved in advocacy, your funding can be taken from you or lost very easily in budget cuts" (1993, p. 1). (See also Shoultz, 1990/1991, for discussion on independence and sponsorship with self-advocacy groups.)

People think differently about what self-advocacy and empowerment mean. According to members and leaders of self-advocacy in New Hampshire, being part of a self-advocacy group also means having a place to meet other people, "to make new friends, and to unite old friends, and to be independent"; and to "be able to get what he (or she) wants, whether an apartment, a job or simply being heard" (Racino, 1993b, pp. 2, 4). The Minnesota Developmental Disabilities Council, in a 1992 national survey funded by the Administration on Developmental Disabilities, recommended that practices in self-advocacy and empowerment include career vision and supported employment, youth leadership (cooperative efforts of and friendships among youth with and without disabilities), and People First (a common name for self-advocacy groups and efforts).

ISSUES AND CONCERNS: SELF-ADVOCACY[5]

Major areas of concern and targets of work by self-advocacy groups include both common issues shared with the American people and concerns that may be specific to people's life experiences based on disability or human services involvement. These major areas of concern are highlighted in Table 1 and are discussed individually in this section.

Finding Good Jobs

At that time, it was hard to find jobs because there aren't many out there. . . . It was tough for me because I can't read or write very well so it was tough trying to find a job, you know, trying to find a job that you can do. (words of a self-advocate from the New Hampshire Lakes Region, Racino, 1993b, p. 5)

According to Harris and Associates, "two thirds of the adults with disabilities ages 16–65 want to work, yet are unable to find a job" (1994, p. 93). Finding jobs is compounded by problems with transportation (Rogan, 1992) and with potential loss of benefits (e.g., food stamps, a subsidized apartment, personal assistance, health care) and the need to absorb expenses such as providing transportation to and from the job. These expenses can make getting a job unaffordable, even for college graduates with physical disabilities (Racino, 1993b). Work disincentives make it very difficult to get out and join the work force (Racino, 1995a; see also Martin, Conley, & Noble, 1995), although Plans for Achieving Self Support, which offer other opportunities for covering work expenses, have had a positive impact for some people (Owen, 1992; Rheinheimer, Van Covern, Green, Revell, & Inge, 1993).

Receiving Good Pay and Benefits with
Control of Money and Cost of Living Increases

I don't like the fact that [every] time any of us get a job, welfare and social security always takes our benefits away from us, when we have a job that doesn't even pay us very well. . . . The paychecks that we get do not fit today's cost of living at all. (words of a self-advocate in Concord, New Hampshire, Racino, 1993b, p. 6)

---

[5]Unless otherwise noted, this section draws largely on interviews with self-advocates and psychiatric survivors on personal assistance services as part of the National Research and Training Center on Personal Assistance, Oakland, California (Racino, 1995a), and views of self-advocates and the independent living center in New Hampshire, as part of policy research of the Research and Training Center on Community Integration, Syracuse, New York (Racino, 1993b).

Table 1. Self-advocacy: Targets for employment change

Finding good jobs
Receiving good pay and benefits, with control of money and cost of living increases
Finding enjoyable work and making contributions
Moving money from sheltered workshops to community work
Providing reasonable accommodations
Closing institutions
Removing labels, stigma, and discrimination
Providing information and universal access to PAS
Obtaining fair treatment and promoting advocacy and freedom from abuse and coercion
Training by people with disabilities of people with disabilities
Receiving education and career planning and advancement

People First of Washington (1986) shared a report on the views of 100 self-advocates who attended the International People First Leadership Conference on employment. These perspectives included concerns about "not paying us enough money to live on. . . [to] pay rent, buy food, pay bills [and] by not giving us sick leave, vacations or medical benefits" and desires to be listened to, respected through a decent wage, and given "a chance to meet and know a variety of people" (Racino, 1995c, pp. 39–40; see also, Johnson & Racino, 1988; People First of New Zealand, 1993). Income should be adequate to pay for clothes and equipment (Racino, 1993a), and pay and benefits should not result in the loss of material support (e.g., homes, personal assistance) (see also, Center on Human Policy, 1989). People should have control of their own money, and money should not be used to control a person's actions or behaviors through case management or service coordination (Ebert, 1989).

Finding Enjoyable Work and Making Contributions

Betsy is one of the [New Hampshire] Lakes Region's [Self Advocacy group's] co-chairpersons, who [previously] worked . . . at a college [child] care center, which she really enjoyed. An advisor described Betsy, whose interests include art, reading, travel, letter writing, and rock and roll: "She'll help others (even) if she doesn't have the problems herself." (words of an advisor at Lakes Region New Hampshire Self Advocacy group, Racino, 1993b, p. 13)

Work is a form of contribution to society and to the lives of other people, in ways other than through taxes (the latter a common argument for people with disabilities working; see Racino, 1995a). Most people aspire to enjoy the time spent at work, whether through the work itself, the working conditions, or the people and benefits. In one of New Hampshire's researched case studies, people mentioned wanting to enjoy their work and their workday and contributing through what they do well, including how they get along with other people and how they advance toward successful futures (Racino [New Hampshire], 1993b). Enjoyable work includes both volunteer and paid positions; (paid) assistance should be available in both types of situations (Racino, 1995a).

Moving Money from Sheltered Workshops to Community Work

I'd rather have a coalition behind you rather than do it yourself because right now we are involved in the jobs issue for the sheltered workshops. . . . Right now we are asking to have the money recycled and reshuffled in other capacities. (Whittico, August, 1993, pp. 3, 7)

Self-advocates, together with parents, have also taken on controversial issues such as sheltered workshops (see Kennedy, 1988), which are often run by large, well-established community agencies. Sometimes, people have taken on the issues because they would prefer that the money be used for other employment options in the community (e.g., supported employment) (see Parents for Positive Futures in Taylor, Racino, & Walker, 1992). A state administrator shared a comment on the dilemma that is often discussed as part of advocacy strategy debates about whether to accentuate the positive or to take on the controversial position: "The sheltered workshops have a very large constituency, that if you polarize the constituency now, I am not convinced there is enough to win the battle" (Racino, 1993b, n.p. ; see also Center on Human Policy Advocacy Board, 1989, for discussion on segregated schools for children with emotional and behavioral needs).

Yet, some people with disabilities are concerned that personal assistance services (PAS) be made available in workshop settings (Racino, 1995a), which have often excluded people with physical and medical needs, resulting instead in other types of segregated day programs (e.g., day treatment programs). Other people are more concerned that these "habilitation" programs are based on an "old train-and-place model" of Medicaid active treatment (with different funding than sheltered workshops), which often preclude people from regular community employment (Racino, 1993b).

Providing Reasonable Accommodations

Reasonable accommodation is a modification to a job, the work environment, or the way things are done that enables a qualified individual with a disability to enjoy an equal employment opportunity. (Regulations to Implement the Equal Employment Provisions, 1991, 29 C.F.R. Part 1360.2)

Establishment of affordable, accessible, and consumer-controlled assistance services for people with disabilities ranked among the group's highest priorities (President's Committee on Employment of People with Disabilities, 1993).

Self-advocacy groups often are run by people with disabilities so that people will have an opportunity to learn how to speak for themselves and to work on different systemic and personal issues such as transportation accessibility, acquiring personal attendants, and establishing circles of friends (Racino, 1995a). From the perspective of complying with the ADA, issues involving transportation and personal attendants would be viewed in terms of providing reasonable accomodations (Racino, 1995a; Wehman, 1992); simple accommodations for people with some disabilities often cost less than $100 (Mancuso, 1990).

Personal assistance, including personal assistance at work, is highlighted in Table 2.[6] In the psychiatric, self-help movement, two key work accommodations are transportation and flexible work time (Racino, 1995a). In fact, flexible work time is considered a central accommodation for people with alcoholism as well (Shaw et al., 1994). As described previously, flexible work schedules are a work force concern, based on the concepts of individual differences and on the promotion of quality of life for all workers (Ronen, 1981). Another central issue for job applicants and employees is that "hidden disabilities" must be disclosed in order to qualify for accommodations under the ADA (MacDonald-Wilson & Whitman, 1995).

The major concerns with PAS (see Ratzka, 1991) in the context of the ADA and highlighted by psychiatric survivors include 1) who will define the assistance (i.e., the continuing implicit message that people do not know what is best for themselves) and 2) the role that service coordination and case management, which take personal control away from people's lives, will play in a person's life. In competitive jobs, people with disabilities may be concerned that the need or request for PAS can be perceived by the employer and co-workers as an incapacity to meet the requirements of the job (Racino, 1995a), especially when accommodations are not considered a regular part of the work culture and/or environment.

Closing Institutions

> You know I was in an institution for 11 years of my life and it was hell. (Self-advocate from Connecticut, Racino, 1995a, transcript)

---

[6]Particular thanks in this section to Judi Chamberlin, Pat Deegan, and Lorelee Stewart of the psychiatric survivor movement and Sherri Watson for her insights in brain injury.

Table 2. Types of personal assistance services (PAS)

Personal hygiene and care
- Getting dressed, moving out of chairs, getting ready for work, showering, getting in and out of bed, shaving legs or face, assisting with personal care and menstruation, brushing teeth

Therapies and exercises
- Obtaining therapies (e.g., physical and occupational therapy, respiratory therapy), and nursing
- Exercising (e.g., aerobics, jazz)
- Exercising memory

Interpretation[a] (as ongoing social, job, and personal need)
- Interpreting sign language
- Interpreting nonverbal communication
- Making telephone calls (e.g., prescription renewals, ordering)
- Interpreting speech

Financial management
- Budgeting money, going to the bank, writing checks, making payments to personal assistant(s), balancing checkbook, making change
- Keeping books on personal assistance payments, paychecks, and so forth

Home activities
- Cooking, baking, and putting together cookbooks
- Doing housekeeping, laundry
- Doing heavy cleaning and repairs
- Feeding/eating, drinking, sharing meals
- Writing letters
- Using washer and dryer and dishwasher
- Getting up in the morning; getting assistance at night
- Assisting with emergencies and providing backup assistance

Community activities
- Shopping (e.g., grocery, clothes); using coupons and reaching items in stores
- Going places locally (e.g., church, mall, walks, pool, fitness center, laundromat, coffee shop)
- Participating in social functions and sports
- Going on vacations and to events
- Participating in local entertainment (e.g., country and western dancing)
- Making telephone calls, stopping by to visit, keeping in touch
- Going to a beauty consultant, getting haircuts
- Going to the doctor and dentist
- Going to self-advocacy meetings

Jobs
- Making reasonable accommodations (e.g., flexible time, transportation)
- Working in office (e.g., administrative assistant)
- Making connections with work agencies (e.g., family connections)
- Traveling on business, including international consulting
- Making telephone calls
- Obtaining job coaching, on and off site
- Planning for career, finding jobs, and resumés
- Obtaining assistance with bathroom and eating (e.g., lunch)
- Working on computer, sorting papers, and assisting at the office
- Supporting people in workshops (and personal care at work)

(continued)

Table 2. *(continued)*

Adult education/volunteer work
- Attending adult education, (e.g., help with registration, classes, reading, writing, career changes)
- Volunteering at community sites
- Advocating for employment

Schools
- Providing information about options
- Participating in afterschool activities and "field trips"
- Assisting with personal care at school
- Providing one-to-one aides and student-to-student support
- Tutoring, helping with homework and notetaking

Families
- Raising a family with children
- Providing an alternative to residential foster care for youth

Relationships
- Dating and providing time with other youth
- Facilitating relationships with roommates, dates, and spouses

Transportation
- Driving cars, starting vehicles, washing cars and vans
- Traveling for business
- Assisting with traveling

Safety
- Teaching fire safety, installing lifelines; providing support in dealing with "con" people
- Assisting with getting out of bed in an emergency

Cognitive support and management
- Providing cognitive support (e.g., reading, writing, math)
- Sending cards and letters
- Assisting with calendars, schedules, and meetings
- Negotiating with personal assistant(s)
- Understanding words and how things went at meetings, particularly professional ones
- Reading materials, including prior to meetings, and writing things down
- Using the telephone
- Listening to nonverbal communication
- Assisting with organization and decision making
- Giving advice and helping people make up their minds
- Helping make medical decisions
- Setting up routines and helping with changes in everyday life
- Acting as facilitator, explaining things, helping people articulate things and converse

From Racino, J. (1995). *Moving toward universal access: Perspectives on personal assistance services: New models development.* Syracuse, NY, and Boston, MA: Community and Policy Studies; adapted by permission.

This table was made possible in part through the support of the National Institute on Disability and Rehabilitation Research (Grant #H13340005-95), Office of Special Education, Department of Education, awarded to Community and Policy Studies through the World Institute on Disability, California for a Research and Training Center on Personal Assistance Services.

[a] See also interpreters with people with "deaf-blindness" (Raistrick (1994–1995)).

The reason the work of our group started out a long time ago was just to . . . clos[e] SDC (a New York State institution in central New York); that was our original battle. When we succeeded and we were done, we just sort of decided we would do other things. (Whittico, 1993, p. 2)

Many of the interviews about PAS with self-advocates included discussions about institutional closure (Racino, 1995a). Personal accounts of institutional experiences, often in contrast to community experiences, emerged again in the late 1980s (see also Doherty, 1988). Community access was described in the interviews as shifting money to the community from the institution, having access to community places, closing the institution, and the community opening "their doors and giving people a chance" (Racino, 1995a, pp. 22–23). Community access, as supported by the ADA, was also described in terms of physical changes in the ways cities, towns, or communities approach areas such as public works and accessibility as more than simply physical changes (Racino, 1997).

Removing Labels, Stigma, and Discrimination

T.J. Monroe, a self-advocate originally from Connecticut, and now from Tennessee, said that people need to stop using the word mental retardation, which self-advocates have said is connected with being institutionalized, as not having potential, as being seen as "slow," and [as] not having opportunities to learn. (Racino, 1995a, p. 16)

Self-advocates are almost unanimous in their dislike of the term "mental retardation," with some self-advocates having a preference for no term, the term "learning disabilities," or the term "people with disabilities." Stereotypes, myths, and discrimination often have been connected with labeling (Muesser, 1996) and are major concerns of psychiatric survivors who believe that the label itself implies a lack of competency and capacity to make decisions about one's own life (Racino, 1995a).

People with diverse disabilities who have tried to use vocational rehabilitation services to enter or re-enter the marketplace have had longstanding concerns about stigmatization resulting from their disclosure of disability. Therefore, they face a major decision regarding whether to disclose their disabilities. (See Freedman & Fesko, 1996, for more information on "conscious choice" of disclosure; Urban League of Onondaga Co., Inc., 1979.) As Wehman and his colleagues have also reported, there is a tendency for both employers and employees (e.g., individuals with chronic mental illness or cerebral palsy) "to view the presence of an employment specialist at the job site as stigmatizing" (1991, p. 105).

If the job is a source of stress, people may be perceived as needing to overcome their own feelings of devaluation and worthlessness

(Racino, 1995a). Employers and human services professionals may be perceived as needing to have greater "disability awareness" (Racino, 1993a, 1993c, 1995a). For example, in seminars, employers were found to carry media stereotypes of people with disabilities (e.g., violent behavior, mental illness), of people with back injuries (e.g., reinjury costs), and of people with epilepsy (e.g., safety) (Green-McGowen & Racino, 1988; Urban League of Onondaga Co., 1979).

Providing Information and Universal Access to PAS

Everyone regardless of age or ability has the right to know about PAS. (Racino, 1995a, p. 14)

In the PAS interviews, *information access* was described as part "of a right to think freely"; *universal access* as one way of "trying to include everyone in society," including in jobs, in homes (e.g., affordable housing [People First of New Hampshire, 1994, p. 6]) and in classrooms; *decision making* as freedom from coercion; and personal assistance as offering hope of moving from controlling environments (Racino, 1995a). The right to universal access is described by Judy Heumann, international leader of the Independent Living Movement and Racino (1992):

While we acknowledge the desire and need of some people for support in decision making, in coordinating services and in other management roles, we believe that all disabled people, whether they have a guardian or not, should have access to information that affects or potentially could affect their lives. . . . Decisions about assistance with self direction should be a personal versus a professionally determined process. (assorted pp.)

Services users continue to report difficulty in obtaining information about "rights and responsibilities" in the vocational rehabilitation system (Freedman & Fesko, 1996). Children and youth need to have an opportunity to know that the programs or services exist, and consumers have a right to shop around for the programs that best satisfy their needs (Racino, 1995a). Children and adults with guardians also may not have access to controversial information (e.g., sexual education), which could be made available in places such as high schools and hospitals.

Obtaining Fair Treatment and Promoting
Advocacy and Freedom from Abuse and Coercion

Self-advocacy provides opportunities to act as a role model for others, and assist other people to "have a chance to be in the community, get them a regular job . . . trying to show them that they can be a person first." (words of a self-advocate in Tennessee, Racino, 1995a, transcript)

Mental health has absolute, enormous control, and when I talk with people from other disability groups, they are just amazed at the control. (words of a psychiatric survivor in Massachusetts, Racino, 1995a, transcript)

Fair treatment in self-advocacy often has been described as being treated as an adult (not as a child) and with respect (i.e., having equal worth as a human being), and with dignity. It also means freedom from abuse, both on the job and from assistants (Racino, 1995a). Themes in clubhouses[7] in the fields of psychiatric disabilities and brain injury also revolve around relationships of more equality and respect (see Propst, 1992).

Fair treatment can be reflected in working conditions, promotions, hiring and terminations, employee assistance and benefits, and in the day-to-day interactions on the job. It also means access to the community and to the same opportunities as other citizens and the right to refuse services (World Institute on Disability, 1991); and it means advocacy to prevent involuntary hospitalizations. Fair treatment with personal assistants also means paying decent wages with benefits and having access to the funds to do so (Racino, 1995a).

Training of People with Disabilities by People with Disabilities

[Training includes] undoing existing learnings that have been stigmatizing. (words of a psychiatric survivor, as cited in Racino, 1995a)

One of the repeated themes in the independent living (IL) and psychiatric survivor movements, which is also surfacing among individuals with mental retardation, is the need for "disability awareness," or "sensitivity training," which is an appreciation of the experiences of living with a disability and dealing with the systems. Another part of the training process is described as one of "unlearning" (e.g., behavior management) and getting past myths and stereotypes, for example, about the possibilities for the future and the capacities of people to make their own decisions about their lives (e.g., employment, community access, parenting). Because professional training sometimes gives the implicit message that the person with a disability does not know what is best for him- or herself, training can be provided directly by the person him- or herself and/or by other people with disabilities. Training also may include hiring one's own staff (Racino, Walker, O'Connor, & Taylor, 1993) and managing one's own money and assistance (Racino, 1995a, Whittico, 1994).

Obtaining Education, Career Planning, and Advancement

Children can "know that their career" will not be impeded by "small things unrelated to their skills," which employers can accommodate. (Chaikind, 1992, p. M8)

---

[7]Clubhouses are part of an international movement whereby people with psychiatric disabilities can come together and work with staff to operate the clubhouses. They are often described as having a transitional employment or work component, and they offer a variety of social events.

Parents and other caregivers should orient children toward career planning at an early age; opportunities to guide youth abound in the home, with playmates, at school, in libraries, in television, in restaurants, and in children's day-to-day lives (see Chaikind, 1992, on the ADA; Szymanski & Hanley-Maxwell, 1996, on choice and families' roles). Career planning includes opportunities to participate in extracurricular events in schools (Racino, 1995a) and may involve nontraditional options (e.g., entrenpreneurship for young women [Jones, 1995]). Career planning projects can be "designed to give the client the choice of deciding his or her own career plan" and to be "flexible according to what the client needs" to get a "job where [he or] she wants" (Racino, 1995a). The hope is that career planning can lead to diverse employment roles (Shafer, Banks, & Kregel, 1991) and lifelong pursuits.

Parents, like self-advocates, are concerned about their careers, and without support services, their children may be institutionalized and not given the opportunity to learn. And without support services, parents and self-advocates may be unable to work, to progress in careers, and to maintain balanced activities (Racino, O'Connor, Walker, & Taylor, 1991). To obtain good jobs, self-advocates typically want a good education, especially if previously denied that right. One self-advocate in New Hampshire explained the desire for quality education and the result of the denial of a good educational foundation as follows:

> Many of us who are undereducated, okay, we are made . . . to take jobs in cleaning, pushing broom handles all day long because of the fact vocational rehabilitation just doesn't want to increase our education. (words of a person with disabilities in New Hampshire Self Advocacy group, Racino, 1993b, p. 5)

The ADA offers hope for the future of children so that "they know they are several steps closer to equality" (Chaikind, 1992, p. M10) and that they can have the education and opportunities that lead to career-based employment.

CONCLUSION: THE PROMISE OF SELF-ADVOCACY

Self-advocates also may work to make changes such as closing institutions; obtaining transportation; acquiring real jobs and housing; securing rights for people with disabilities; using facilitated communication and real money; and controlling their own money, health, and choice. They may seek these changes through mailings, boards and committees, conferences, networking, luncheons, seminars, communication partners, and exchanges with other self-advocacy groups (Whittico, 1994). These efforts also might change the ways in which agencies operate (see Racino, 1994), may be collaborative or adversarial, and also may involve networking with other organizations. As Whittico explained, "people [are] set in their ways; parties never bridge the gulf between them to make decisions." Self-advocates can help "providers listen more to what consumers have to say" and begin to break "tunnel vision" (Whittico, 1994, n.p.) Personal accounts by self-advocates (see Worth, 1989, on leisure) and participatory action research also have been viewed as avenues for change (Pederson, Chaikin, Koehler, Campbell, & Arcand, 1993), together with citizen advocacy (Flynn & Ward, 1991).

Because everyone has been discriminated against in one way or another, self-advocacy holds promise in its political nature and also on the local grassroots level as a base for people (e.g., African Americans, Mexicans, Italians, Latinos) to seek strength in efforts to change the social, political, economic, and spiritual forces affecting lives in workplaces, industry, and businesses, and in schools and families. Self-advocacy, as part of a vision of communities of people coming together, remains an important avenue of hope for the future.

REFERENCES

Allen, J. (1994). *Successful job search strategies for the disabled: Understanding the ADA.* New York: John Wiley & Sons.

Americans with Disabilities Act (ADA) of 1990, PL 101-336, 42 U.S.C. §§ 12101 et seq.

Bradford, J., Licata, J., & Lang, C. (no date). *South Carolina Three Year State Plan, Fiscal Years 1995–1997.* Columbia, SC: Office of the Governor, Office of Executive Policy and Programs, Division of Health and Human Services; and the Developmental Disabilities Council.

Center on Human Policy. (1989). *A statement in support of adults living in the community.* Syracuse, NY: Syracuse University, Center on Human Policy, Research and Training Center on Community Integration.

Center on Human Policy Advocacy Board. (1989). *Board meeting on segregated schools for children with emotional and behavioral needs.* Syracuse, NY: Center on Human Policy.

Chaikind, S. (1992). Children and the ADA: The promise of tomorrow. *Exceptional Parent, 22*(2), M8–M10.

Chamberlin, J., & Unziker, R. (1991). Psychiatric survivors, expatients and users: An observation of organizations in Holland and England. *IDEAS Portfolio II,* 3–5.

Doherty, J. (1988, July 11). Groups seek closing of Syracuse center for retarded. *Syracuse Herald-Journal,* A1, A5.

Ebert, G. (1989). *Presentation on support: What are the meaning, characteristics and dimensions of support?* Syracuse, NY: Syracuse University, National Policy Institute on Support, Center on Human Policy, Research and Training Center on Community Integration.

Flynn, M., & Ward, L. (1991). "We can change the future"—Self and citizen advocacy. In S. Segal & V. Varma (Eds.), *The future for people with learning difficulties* (pp. 129–148). London: David-Fulton.

Freedman, R., & Fesko, S. (1996, July–September). The meaning of work in the lives of people with significant disabilities: Consumer and family perspectives. *Journal of Rehabilitation, 62*(3), 49–55.

Green-McGowen, K., & Racino, J. (1988). Consultation on people with complex medical needs living in institutions in the State of Maryland. Baltimore: KGM Associates and the Center on Human Policy, Syracuse University.

Harris, L., & Associates. (1994). N.O.D. Survey of Americans with Disabilities. Washington, DC: National Organization on Disability.

Hayden, M., Lakin, K.C., Braddock, D., & Smith, G. (1995, October). Growth in self advocacy organizations. *Mental Retardation, 33*(5), 342.

Healy-Mills, S., & Citrone, M. (1994). *Rhode Island Developmental Disabilities Council: Three year plan (1995–1997).* Cranston: Rhode Island Developmental Disabilities Council.

Heumann, J., & Racino, J. (1992). Whose life is it? The issue of control of personal assistance services. *Disability Studies Quarterly, 12*(3), 22–24.

Jackson, A., Felner, R., Millstein, S., Pittman, K., & Selden, R. (1993). Adolescent development and educational policy: Strengths and weaknesses of the knowledge base. *Journal of Adolescent Health, 14*, 172–189.

Johnson, R., & Racino, J. (1988). *Jobs and work: Workshop at the New York State Self Advocacy Conference.* Syracuse: New York State Self Advocacy Association with Speaking for Ourselves in Pennsylvania.

Jones, M. (1995). Smart cookies. *Working Woman, 91*, 50–52.

Kennedy, M. (1988). From sheltered workshops to supported employment. In R. Traustadottir (Ed.), *Supported employment: Issues and resources.* Syracuse, NY: Syracuse University, Center on Human Policy, Research and Training Center on Community Integration.

Knoll, J., & Racino, J. (1988). *Community supports for people labelled by both the mental health and mental retardation systems in the community.* Syracuse, NY: Syracuse University, Center on Human Policy. Community Integration Project.

Krannich, R., & Krannich, C. (1994). *Dynamite salary negotiations* (2nd ed.). Manassas Park, VA: Impact Publications.

Ludlum, C., Beeman, P., & Ducharme, G. (1991). *Dare to dream: An analysis of the conditions leading to personal change for people with disabilities.* Manchester, CT: Communitas Publications.

MacDonald-Wilson, K., & Whitman, A. (1995). Encouraging disclosure of psychiatric disability. *American Rehabilitation, 21*(1), 15–19.

Mancuso, L. (1990). Reasonable accommodations for workers with psychiatric disabilities. *Psychosocial Rehabilitation Journal, 14*(2), 3–19.

Martin, D., Conley, R., & Noble, J. (1995). The ADA and disability benefits policy. *Journal of Disability Policy Studies, 6*(2), 1–15.

Mems, B., & Bolton, B. (1992). A national survey of employment services and independent living. *Journal of Rehabilitation, 58*(4), 22–26.

Minnesota Developmental Disabilities Council. (1992). *Shifting patterns.* Minneapolis, MN: Author.

Mount, B., & Zwernik, K. (1988). *It's never too early; it's never too late: A booklet about personal futures planning.* St. Paul, MN: Metropolitan Council.

Muesser, K. (1996, July). A survey of preferred terms for users of mental health services. *Psychiatric Services, 47*, 760–763.

National Center for Youth with Disabilities. (1993, Winter). *Teenagers at-risk: A national perspective of state level services for adolescents with chronic illness and disability.* Minneapolis, MN: Author.

National Council on Disability. (1993). ADA Watch—Year One: A report to the President and Congress on progress in implementing the Americans with Disabilities Act. Washington, DC: Author.

O'Brien, J. (1987). A guide to life-style planning: Using the Activities Catalog to integrate services and natural supports. In B. Wilcox & G.T. Bellamy, A comprehensive guide to The Activities Catalog: An alternative curriculum for youth and adults with severe disabilities (pp. 175–190). Baltimore: Paul H. Brookes Publishing Co.

Owen, M.J. (1992). PASS: Plans for achieving self support. Exceptional Parent, 22(1), 24–26.

Pederson, E.L., Chaikin, M., Koehler, D., Campbell, A., & Arcand, M. (1993). Strategies that close the gap between research, planning and self advocacy. In E. Sutton, A.R. Factor, B.A. Hawkins, T. Heller, & G.B. Seltzer (Eds.), Older adults with developmental disabilities: Optimizing choice and change (pp. 277–326). Baltimore: Paul H. Brookes Publishing Co.

People First of New Hampshire. (1994, Winter). Self-advocate (Jocelyn Gallant) pursues options for affordable housing. People First of New Hampshire Newsletter, 7, 6.

People First of New Zealand. (1993, September). People First conference report. Rotura, New Zealand: Author.

People First of Washington. (1986). Introducing: What we want from employment programs. Tacoma, WA: Author.

President's Committee on Employment of People with Disabilities. (1993). In R. Douglas (1994), Operation People First: Toward a national disability policy. Journal of Disability Policy Studies, 5(2), 81–106.

Propst, R. (Ed.). (1992). The clubhouse [special issue]. Psychosocial Rehabilitation Journal, 16(2).

Racino, J.A. (1990, July). Consultation to Kings' Fund College, Great Britain [Consulting project]. Syracuse, NY: Syracuse University, Center on Human Policy.

Racino, J.A. (1993a). Center for Independent Living: Disabled people take the lead for full community lives. In J.A. Racino, P. Walker, S. O'Connor, & S.J. Taylor (Eds.), The Community Participation Series: Vol. 2. Housing, support, and community: Choices and strategies for adults with disabilities (pp. 333–354). Baltimore: Paul H. Brookes Publishing Co.

Racino, J.A. (1993b). Edited collection: Community integration and deinstitutionalization in New Hampshire. Syracuse, NY: Community and Policy Studies.

Racino, J.A. (1993c). Interview transcript, Y, Central New York: A study of the Ys in Central New York. Syracuse, NY: Syracuse University, Research and Training Center on Community Integration.

Racino, J.A. (1994). Creating change in states, agencies, and communities. In V.J. Bradley, J.W. Ashbaugh, & B.C. Blaney (Eds.), Creating individual supports for people with developmental disabilities: A mandate for change at many levels (pp. 171–196). Baltimore: Paul H. Brookes Publishing Co.

Racino, J.A. (1995a). Moving toward universal access to support: An edited collection on personal assistance services. Syracuse, NY: Community and Policy Studies (for the World Institute on Disability).

Racino, J.A. (1995b). Housing and support: Community living for adults with developmental disabilities. Journal of The Association of Persons with Severe Handicaps, 20(4), 300–310.

Racino, J.A. (1995c). PAS: Toward universal access to support: Annotated bibliography. Syracuse, NY: Community Policy Studies.

Racino, J.A. (1997). Youth and community life: Expanding options and choices. In S. Pueschel (Ed.), *Adolescents with Down syndrome: Toward a more fulfilling life* (pp. 359–380). Baltimore: Paul H. Brookes Publishing Co.

Racino, J.A., & O'Connor, S. (1994). "A home of our own": Homes, neighborhoods, and personal connections. In M.F. Hayden & B.H. Abery (Eds.), *Challenges for a service system in transition: Ensuring quality community experiences for persons with developmental disabilities* (pp. 381–403). Baltimore: Paul H. Brookes Publishing Co.

Racino, J.A., O'Connor, S., Walker, P., & Taylor, S. (1991). *An evaluation of innovative family support programs in Central New York.* Syracuse, NY: Syracuse University, Center for Human Policy.

Racino, J.A., Walker, P., O'Connor, S., & Taylor, S.J. (Eds.). (1993). *The Community Participation Series: Vol. 2. Housing, support, and community: Choices and strategies for adults with disabilities.* Baltimore: Paul H. Brookes Publishing Co.

Raistrick, K. (1994–95). Hiring interpreters for individuals who are deaf-blind. *American Rehabilitation, 20*(4), 19–22.

Ratzka, A. (1991). Personal assistance delivery models. *Independent Living: Disabled Peoples' International Newsletter, 1*(2), 2.

Regulations to Implement the Equal Employment Provisions of the Americans with Disabilities Act, 29 C.F.R. § 1360.2. (1991).

Revell, W.G., Wehman, P., Kregel, J., West, M., & Rayfield, R. (1994). Supported employment for persons with severe disabilities: Positive trends in wages, models, and funding. *Education and Training in Mental Retardation, 29,* 256–264.

Rheinheimer, G., Van Covern, D., Green, H., Revell, G., & Inge, K. (1993). *Finding the common denominator: A supported employment guide for long-term funding supports and services for people with severe disabilities.* Richmond: Virginia Commonwealth University Technical Assistance Center.

Rogan, P. (1992). Integrated employment for all. Syracuse, NY: Center on Human Policy, Syracuse University. In J. Racino (Ed.) (1993), *Community integration and deinstitutionalization in New Hampshire.* Syracuse, NY: Community and Policy Studies.

Ronen, S. (1981). *Flexible working hours: An innovation in the quality of worklife.* New York: McGraw-Hill.

Rusch, F.R., DeStefano, L., Chadsey-Rusch, J., Phelps, L.A., & Szymanski, E. (1992). *Transition from school to adult life for youth and adults with disabilities.* Sycamore, IL: Sycamore Press.

Shafer, S., Banks, P., & Kregel, J. (1991). Employment retention and career movement among individuals with mental retardation working in supported employment. *Mental Retardation, 29*(2), 103–110.

Shaw, L., MacGillis, P., & Dvorchik, K. (1994). Alcoholism and the Americans with Disabilities Act: Obligations and accommodations. *Rehabilitation Counseling Bulletin, 38*(2), 108–123.

Shoultz, B. (1990/91, Winter). Independence or sponsorship: An issue for self advocacy groups. *IMPACT: Feature issue on self-advocacy, 3*(4), 7.

Stainback, S., & Stainback, W. (1990). Facilitating support networks. In W. Stainback & S. Stainback (Eds.), *Support networks for inclusive schooling: Interdependent integrated education* (pp. 25–36). Baltimore: Paul H. Brookes Publishing Co.

Stancliffe, R., & Wehmeyer, M. (1995). Variability in the choice to adults with mental retardation. *Journal of Vocational Rehabilitation, 5,* 319–328.

Steere, D., Gregory, S., Heiny, R., & Butterworth, J. (1995). Lifestyle planning: Considerations for use with people with disabilities. *Rehabilitation Counseling Bulletin, 36*(3), 207–223.

Swartz, J.C. (1978). *A flexible approach to working hours.* New York: Amacom Books.

Szymanski, E., & Hanley-Maxwell, C. (1996, January–March). Career development of people with developmental disabilities: An ecological model. *Journal of Rehabilitation, 62*(1), 48–55.

Taylor, S., Racino, J., Knoll, J., & Lutfiyya, Z. (1987). *The nonrestrictive environment: On community integration for people with the most severe disabilities.* Syracuse, NY: Human Policy Press.

Urban League of Onondaga Co., Inc. (1979). *Project findings: Seminars on employment of handicapped for agencies and businesses.* Syracuse, NY: Author.

Wehman, P. (1992). The challenge of public transportation and mobility. In P. Wehman (Ed.), *The ADA mandate for social change* (pp. 135–153). Baltimore: Paul H. Brookes Publishing Co.

Wehman, P., & Kregel, J. (1995). At the crossroads: Supported employment a decade later. *Journal of The Association of Persons with Severe Handicaps, 20*(4), 286–299.

Wehman, P., Revell, G., Kregel, J., Kreutzer, J., Callahan, M., & Banks, D. (1991). Supported employment: An alternative model for vocational rehabilitation of persons with neurological, psychiatric, and physical disability. *Archives of Physical Medicine, 72,* 101–105.

Weissman, J., Kennedy, J., & Litvak, S. (1991). *Personal perspectives on personal assistance services.* Oakland, CA: World Institute on Disability.

West, M. (1995). Choice, self determination and VR services: Systemic barriers for consumers with severe disabilities. *Journal of Vocational Rehabilitation, 5*(4), 281–290.

Whittico, P. (1993, August). *Interview transcripts: Comments on New Hampshire self advocacy research report.* Syracuse, NY: Community and Policy Studies.

Whittico, P. (1994, May). *Interview transcripts: Comments on New Hampshire self advocacy research report.* Syracuse, NY: Community and Policy Studies.

Whittico, P., with Racino, J. (1994, May). *Advocacy and personal assistance services: Presentation at the Ohio statewide community living conference* (Ohio Department of Mental Retardation and Developmental Disabilities). Columbus, OH: Author.

World Institute on Disability. (1991). *International personal assistance symposium: Work group on PAS statement.* Oakland, CA: Author.

Worth, P. (1989). You've got a friend. In G. Allan Roeher Institute, *The pursuit of leisure: Enriching the lives of people who have a disability* (pp. 73–78). Downsview, Ontario, Canada: The G. Allan Roeher Institute.

CHAPTER 4

Developing a Career Path
Application of Person-Centered Planning

John Kregel

JILL

Jill is a 19-year-old young woman who is about to graduate from her local high school. While in school, Jill was labeled as having a significant cognitive disability as well as having cerebral palsy. Her employment preparation has consisted of work experience in a fast-food restaurant, developed as part of her school employment program, and part-time employment in a local grocery store. She has been fairly successful in each of these positions; and Jill, her family, and staff from the local supported employment agency are confident that she will be able to obtain employment after leaving school.

As part of her overall transition-planning process, staff from the school worked with Jill to initiate a series of person-centered planning activities with her family, adult services agency representatives, and school staff members. As a part of these meetings, Jill was asked whether she preferred working in a fast-food restaurant or in a grocery store; and at the meeting, the supported employment representative presented a plan for developing jobs in each of these industries. Later in the meeting, Jill and her mother were asked to describe her current recreational interests. Her mother indicated, among other things, that after lunch each day, Jill enjoyed walking to the end of her block to a child care center to watch the young children play. Her mother indicated that Jill had always enjoyed the presence of young children and had often spoken about visiting the child care center.

After hearing Jill's interest in this area, the person-centered planning meeting facilitator attempted to use Jill's recreational interest to focus her employment goals. Would she be interested in working in a child care center? When questioned, Jill was extremely excited to think that she could get a job that would allow her to work with children. A follow-up meeting was scheduled, and in the meantime, the facilitator began to scout for job opportunities involving working with children and arranged for Jill to visit the child care center with her mother.

PERSON-CENTERED PLANNING APPROACH

Person-centered planning is a term used to describe a group of approaches intended to organize and guide the efforts of an individual with a disability, his or her family members, friends, and service providers as they work collectively to assist the individual in pursuing his or her interests, desires, and goals. These approaches have evolved as an alternative to "traditional" multidisciplinary or interdisciplinary models, which are usually dominated by the expertise and perspectives of various professionals. In contrast, person-centered planning approaches are based on the belief that the individual should be the focus of the planning process and that the individual and those close to him or her are best able to plan for and meet future needs. In a person-centered plan, the individual is no longer viewed as a "client" but rather as the focus of the planning process and as the single greatest authority on his or her life.

Person-centered planning is referred to by various names, including individual service design (Yates, 1980), Lifestyle Planning (O'Brien, 1987), personal futures planning (Mount, 1989), Circle of Support (Perske & Perske, 1988), essential lifestyle planning (Smull & Harrison, 1992), Making Action Plans (MAPs) (Forest & Pearpoint, 1992), and Planning Alternative Tomorrows with Hope (PATH) (Pearpoint, O'Brien, & Forest, 1993). Each of these approaches emphasizes the development of program goals specific to the individual and the reflection of individual preferences, desires, and choices in the design and delivery of supports (O'Brien & Lovett, 1992).

Whereas person-centered planning approaches usually are applied to all aspects of an individual's life (Mount & Zwernik, 1988), Steere and his colleagues (Steere, Gregory, Heiny, & Butterworth, 1995) have illustrated how person-centered planning approaches can be used effectively to enable individuals to plan and direct their own careers. When applied to employment, key components of the person-centered planning process include the following: 1) focusing on individual preferences as opposed to impairments or limitations when exploring potential careers, 2) developing a vision of the type of job and work environment that will most contribute to the individual's self-chosen lifestyle, 3) developing short- and long-term goals that will allow the individual to obtain and maintain employment in a job that will contribute to his or her long-term career progression, and 4) coordinating a network of informal and formal supports that are as self-sustaining as possible and that assist the individual in all facets of the employment process.

The person-centered planning processes described in this chapter have significant implications for human services programs generally and for employment programs in particular. At one level, person-centered planning dramatically changes the way individuals with disabilities take control of their own careers. Decisions related to whether an individual should work, to the characteristics of different employment settings that are most highly valued by the individual, to the amount and type of support that will be required to help the individual succeed in an initial employment setting, and to who should provide that support will be significantly different when individuals with disabilities and their families are the primary source of decision making in the employment planning process. Similarly, a commitment to person-centered planning will undoubtedly change the values and practices of human services agencies.

Person-centered planning can occur in many different types of settings. The illustrations provided in this chapter are drawn primarily from community-based employment programs. Agencies providing supported employment and other types of community employment agencies are uniquely positioned to allow individuals with disabilities to select and direct their initial employment experience (Brooke, Wehman, Inge, & Parent, 1995). Public school transition programs are incorporating the concepts of Circle of Support and other approaches into the development of individualized transition plans. To ensure that individuals are able to enter the career of their choice on exiting from school, institutions of higher education can use person-centered planning techniques to develop career plans for college and university students with disabilities by coordinating academic programs with community-based employment experience (Getzel & Kregel, 1996). In the vocational rehabilitation system, the increased emphasis on self-determination and provider choice has set the stage for expanded use of person-centered approaches in the development of rehabilitation services plans (West & Parent, 1992).

Person-centered planning will challenge staff in employment agencies to do the following: 1) support job choices made by the individual, as opposed to supporting selections identified entirely by agency staff; 2) coordinate placement, training, and support efforts with family members, co-workers, and employers, instead of fulfilling all these functions with agency staff; and 3) accept and support naturally occurring changes in an individual's employment situation as the person learns from initial employment experiences and attempts to expand career opportunities. The next section describes the key components of several different approaches to person-centered planning.

APPROACHES TO PERSON-CENTERED PLANNING

Six specific types of person-centered planning approaches—individual service design, personal futures planning, essential lifestyle planning, Circle of Friends, MAPs, and PATH—are described in the following section. A comprehensive review of each of the strategies is not possible; instead, the information provided is intended to present a clear description of each of the approaches, identify similarities and differences across the various approaches, illustrate the evolution of the concept of person-centered planning since approximately 1980, and explain the relevance of each of the techniques to the process of planning one's career and obtaining employment.

Individual Service Design

One approach to person-centered planning, individual service design (Yates, 1980), evolved from efforts to implement the principles of normalization (Wolfensberger, 1972) with individuals who frequently challenge the services system. The individual service design process emphasizes the importance of understanding and appreciating the individual and his or her prior experiences. Typical opening questions are as follows: Who is this person? What experiences has he or she had? What would it be like to experience the events that this person has? This approach is designed to allow team members to empathize with the individual's prior history and to come to understand his or her motivation, hopes, fears, and desires. Based on this information, the team can more effectively identify a person's needs and identify the supports an individual might require to address those needs.

TIMOTHY

Timothy, an individual who had sustained an acquired brain injury (ABI) 36 months previously, continued to insist that he should be supported in his efforts to return to his prior job as a tire salesperson, even after staff members at the rehabilitation agency had clearly come to believe that memory and communication impairments resulting from the ABI made this alternative unfeasible. Through a series of planning sessions involving Timothy, his family, and his former employer, staff members came to realize how success and recognition in his former job had been a key part of Timothy's self-concept. They ultimately came to accept the fact that Timothy wanted to pursue his former position, understanding that he may not be successful in his former job, as a precondition to exploring other employment avenues.

Too often, local employment agencies working with individuals such as Timothy will be too quick to conclude that an individual's acquired disability is too extensive or too severe to allow him or her to return to a prior occupation. After conducting a series of evaluations, the agency may conclude that Timothy will be incapable of returning to prior employment and that efforts must be directed toward preparing him for an employment situation more consistent with his present level of functioning. Agencies that use individual service design, however, will be more likely to understand the depth of Timothy's desire to return to his previous job. Because they understand how important being a tire salesperson is to Timothy's self-image, staff may be more likely to take the steps necessary to allow Timothy to return to his prior situation or to more effectively cope with the fact that his previous job may not be a viable employment alternative at present. Staff may work with employers (past, present, and future) to identify areas in which reasonable accommodations may be needed. Timothy may contact rehabilitation engineers or assistive technology (AT) providers to identify technological aids that may help him with memory or communication impairments.

Personal Futures Planning

Another approach to person-centered planning is personal futures planning. A distinguishing feature of personal futures planning (Mount, 1989) is its attempt to apply principles from community development to life planning for individuals with disabilities as well as to the system designed to serve these individuals. When applied to an individual, personal futures planning uses the development of a "personal profile" to identify the person's capacities. These capacities, which form the basis of a vision of a desirable future for the individual, may evolve from a review of the person's life history, interpersonal relationships, and his or her ideas about the future. When applied to employment, this vision of the individual's future may focus not just on the person's next job but rather center on his or her long-term career goals. Consider, for example, a planning meeting held for Bob.

BOB

Bob is a college junior with a severe visual impairment. He is majoring in history. When asked about his career objectives, Bob indicated that he wanted to be curator of the Smithsonian Institution. Although few college students leave undergraduate programs and obtain major curator positions, the clarity and optimism of Bob's career vision made it easy for him to identify initial employment opportunities that would launch him on his way to his long-term goal.

Bob's vision was attained through the development and implementation of an action plan, which includes the following: 1) an image of the person's future, 2) the identification of potential obstacles and opportunities, 3) strategies for achieving the vision, and 4) the commitment on the part of all parties to implement the next steps of the action plan.

Personal futures planning tries to mobilize the strengths and abilities of the individual, his or her family and friends, and service providers to make small, positive changes in an individual's life. The group tries various solutions, reflects on their success, and then modifies the solution based on its results. It is important to note that personal futures planning also may apply to the services system itself. A key component of the model is its emphasis on assisting service provider agencies (and the individuals who work in these agencies) to change their activities and engage in meaningful system reform.

Essential Lifestyle Planning

A third strategy for implementing person-centered planning, essential lifestyle planning (Smull & Harrison, 1992), was originally developed as a strategy to assist individuals with significant disabilities to move from large, segregated institutions into integrated, community-based service alternatives. As such, the process devotes a great deal of effort to attempting to identify the individual's preferences and values through information provided by the individual, his or her family and friends, and institution staff members. The individual's "reputation" is discussed and analyzed to ensure that stereotyped notions of the individual and his or her potential do not taint long-range planning efforts.

The notion of prior negative stereotypes limiting the opportunities available to individuals with disabilities has particular relevance to employment agencies. Far too frequently, an individual is excluded from competitive employment programs either because 1) he or she has a "history" of displaying behaviors that staff members feel make it unlikely that the individual will succeed in a community-based setting, or

2) the individual is considered a "problem worker" or "troublemaker" in his or her present sheltered employment situation. It has been repeatedly demonstrated over a 20-year period (e.g., Kregel, Wehman, & Banks, 1989; Wehman, 1981) that individuals who have no prior work experience or who have previously displayed what staff members have termed "inappropriate behaviors" can succeed in competitive employment situations of their own choosing with proper supports.

BRIAN

Brian, an individual who had attended a sheltered workshop for 12 years, consistently engaged in stereotypic behaviors (e.g., rocking his body, touching his finger to his mouth) while he worked. His family and employment staff initially were worried that these behaviors would prevent him from succeeding in a community-based job. After starting a job as a courtesy clerk in a busy grocery store, the employment staff members were surprised that these behaviors were virtually eliminated, even without a specific behavior management program designed to target these inappropriate behaviors. Brian's parents believed that the increased stimulation of the community-based work setting and the increased expectations on the part of the grocery store manager were in large part responsible for the reduction in the inappropriate behaviors.

Essential lifestyle planning recognizes that some individuals with lengthy institutional histories may need some intensive, long-term supports. These supports are mobilized through a process that promotes competition among local service provider agencies. These agencies may respond to a challenge from the individual and the service system by entering into a contract with the service system that credibly addresses the individual's needs and safety while directly addressing the individual's desires, preferences, and values.

Circle of Friends

A Circle of Friends, also referred to as a Circle of Support, is a planning process that emphasizes the interdependent nature of relationships among individuals with disabilities, their families and friends, close acquaintances in the community, and paid professionals. The process focuses on the development of community connections that provide the supports an individual needs to live in a community, feel like a valued member of that community, and maintain lasting friendships.

The Circle of Friends planning process begins by gathering a group of individuals with disabilities (the process also can be applied to a single individual as well) to identify their own support networks and to plan changes based on the results of their reflection. The individual first draws four concentric circles on a piece of paper. He or she then places him- or herself in the middle of the circle and is guided through the process of completing the Circle of Friends.

The first circle is referred to as the *Circle of Intimacy*. The Circle of Intimacy comprises the individuals most intimate in the person's life— those who the person cannot imagine living without. Individuals generally list their family members, spouses, grandparents, or particular friends. The second circle—the *Circle of Friendship*—comprises individuals who are good friends but with whom the individual does not have an intimate relationship. People whom a person calls several times a week, people whom a person sees only once a year, or people whom a person has seen daily for 10 or more years all could be included in the Circle of Friendship, depending on the nature and depth of the relationship.

The third circle is the *Circle of Participation*. This circle consists of individuals who the person likes but who are not considered to be close friends. Members of organizations, members of networks to which the individual belong, and close acquaintances all may be included in the Circle of Participation. Individuals frequently list co-workers or classmates, choir directors or soccer coaches, members of a Sunday School class or a bowling team, or close neighbors as members of the third circle, the Circle of Participation.

The *Circle of Exchange* is the fourth, and final, circle. This circle usually comprises individuals who are paid to be in a person's life. A doctor, personal assistant, hair stylist, bus driver, physical therapist, service coordinator, dentist, job coach, rehabilitation counselor, or other paid professional all could be members of the Circle of Exchange.

Figure 1 is an example of a Circle of Friends completed by Mike, an 18-year-old adolescent with significant cognitive disabilities, as a part of his transition-planning process in a secondary special program. As noted in Figure 1, Mike indicates extensive support from his family in the Circle of Intimacy. He is also able to identify one aunt, a Sunday School teacher, and two friends in the Circle of Friendship, as well as a large number of paid service providers in the Circle of Exchange. Mike, however, has not identified anyone in his third circle, the Circle of Participation.

From one perspective, the only individuals in Mike's life appear to be his family, a couple of close friends, and a variety of paid service providers. Like many adolescents with significant disabilities, he may feel somewhat isolated and may desire additional social relationships. Expanding Mike's network of friendships and supports will require the commitment of a sizable number of the friends identified in the various circles. Current members of the Circle of Exchange could be involved in

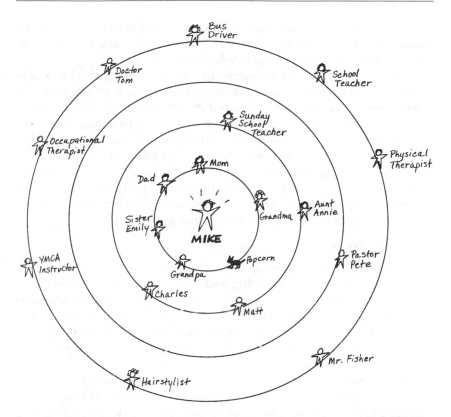

Figure 1. Circle of Friends completed by an adolescent with severe cognitive disabilities at Project Access (Rehabilitation Research and Training Center, Virginia Commonwealth University).

brainstorming ways that Mike could be more involved in social, recreational, and employment activities. These experiences may lead to the development of new relationships and friendships for Mike. In addition, Matt and Charles, current members of his Circle of Friendship, could make an extra effort to introduce Mike to others and increase his opportunities to develop friendships. Finally, those closest to Mike, members of his Circle of Intimacy, could commit themselves to providing Mike every opportunity to build close relationships with others and to participate in environments and activities that will provide him every opportunity to meet new people and to build lasting relationships.

Members in Mike's Circle of Friends also can be involved in helping him to achieve his employment goals. For example, the community members in Mike's Circle of Exchange could assist Mike in determining types of jobs that he might want to explore. Family members also can identify ways that they can promote job exploration experiences for Mike. Job shadowing opportunities or competitive work experiences could both increase social networks for Mike and contribute to the achievement of long-range employment goals.

The Circle of Friends is designed to allow an individual to assess his or her social situation and determine the extent to which he or she would like to increase friendships and expand social relationships. Implementing this planning process may be viewed as simple, but it requires sustained, intense effort by a variety of individuals to make the process work. A Circle of Friends should not be completed just once; rather, it is an ongoing process of identifying support needs and resources, combining the energies of a number of individuals to achieve a common goal, and regularly reassessing the individual's support network as his or her interests and needs change.

Making Action Plans

MAPs is one of several person-centered planning strategies developed by Marsha Forest, Jack Pearpoint, and their colleagues. Similar to the personal futures planning approach, the MAPs process is applicable to individuals, families, or organizations. A MAP is a tool that is used to collect information on individuals and/or families and to help them devise a plan of action that will allow them to achieve their ambitions and dreams.

A key feature of the MAPs approach is the reliance on a skilled facilitator. The facilitator should be an individual who is adept at listening to individuals who have rarely had the opportunity to plan and direct their own lives. Falvey, Forest, Pearpoint, and Rosenberg (1994) recommended the use of a trained facilitator who may not even know the individual and others involved in the planning process. A facilitator may have the advantage of entering the planning session without any preconceived ideas about what might be "best" for the individual and what is needed to help the individual achieve his or her potential goals.

A MAPs planning session begins with the person or group identifying and inviting those individuals whom they would like to participate in the process. As opposed to "traditional" planning approaches, which are often controlled entirely by paid service providers and are frequently held without the individual in question even being physically present, the individual is the focal point of all MAPs activities. Therefore, the individual decides who should attend. In addition, the individual becomes primarily responsible for identifying his or her dreams, nightmares, strengths, and plan of action.

Forest and Pearpoint (1992) identified eight key questions that form the basis of the MAPs planning process. These questions are summarized in Table 1. The session begins with each person introducing him- or herself and describing his or her relationship to the individual. The facilitator then leads the group in a discussion of the first question, "What is the purpose of the MAPs activity?" (see Table 1, Question 1). The group then tells the individual's or family's story (see Table 1, Question 2). By describing the individual's history, the key accomplishments and obstacles that have been overcome, and the major events in an individual's life, all of the participants begin to feel involved and connected to the process. The facilitator graphically summarizes input and asks the group to verify its accuracy, thereby maintaining the group's ownership of the activity.

The individual then is asked to identify his or her long-term dream (see Table 1, Question 3). Dreams need not be "feasible" or "realistic"; rather, dreams are used to identify an individual's real desire and motivation and to point the group's attention toward what the person really wants, as opposed to what might be attainable or "best" for him or her. What is important is that group members are accepting of the individual's dream and that they do not make value-based judgments.

An individual's "dream" may or may not relate to employment. Often, individuals will describe their dreams as related to independence, family, or relationships. For these individuals, employment may be viewed as a necessary short-term or long-term goal that will move them closer to their dreams. For other individuals, attaining a specific job or career may be closely aligned to their self-concept and become the focal point of the MAP.

The individual then is asked to identify his or her "nightmare" (see Table 1, Question 4). The nightmare represents the situation or outcome that the individual most wants to avoid. For some individuals, their nightmare may involve moving into a nursing home or institution. For others, it is an inability to financially support their families. Still others

Table 1. Questions addressed in a MAPs planning session

1. What is a MAP?
2. What is the person's history or story?
3. What are your dreams?
4. What are your nightmares?
5. Who is the person?
6. What are the person's strengths, gifts, and talents?
7. What does the person need?
8. What is the plan of action?

often describe nightmares related to health or to dying. A key feature of the MAPs process is that it requires the individual and group to acknowledge and face their "worst-case scenario" and actively plan to avoid that situation while striving to achieve the individual's dream.

The group then is asked to describe the individual (see Table 1, Question 5) and summarize his or her strengths and gifts (see Table 1, Question 6). These strengths form the basis for planning efforts to identify the opportunities, supports, and resources necessary to assist the individual in achieving his or her dream (see Table 1, Questions 7 and 8). Short-term goals are established that may create opportunities for the individual or secure needed support resources. These goals are then combined into a formal plan of action that specifies what will be done, who will do it, and when it will be completed.

Planning Alternative Tomorrows with Hope

The PATH process, an extension of the MAPs approach, includes the development of a more formalized, self-sustaining plan of action. Similar to the MAPs process, the PATH process involves the use of a facilitator and relies heavily on graphical representation of the results of the individual's and group's planning efforts. It differs somewhat from the MAPs process by adding specific checkpoints that can be charted to assess an individual's progress in moving toward his or her dream. A representation of the components of a PATH is provided in Figure 2.

The PATH process begins with the individual establishing his or her long-term goal or dream, which in the PATH process is referred to as the "North Star." The individual and group then pick a point in the intermediate future, generally from 6 months to 2 years, and "transport" themselves to that point in time. The group then visualizes the positive events that have occurred in the preceding time period to bring the individual to that future place. These events, which should be realistic for the identified time period, become the intermediate goals for the individual. At this point in the process, the facilitator turns the group's attention back to the present. The person, assisted by the group members, develops a snapshot of his or her present situation as it looks like at the present time, which is termed the *NOW*. Next, the PATH process focuses on the differences between the present (the NOW on the left of Figure 2) and the *GOAL*.

The PATH in Figure 2 was developed for Kevin, a 34-year-old man with spina bifida who had no prior employment experience. Kevin's dream focused on employment in a music store or in the field of music. He clearly indicated that he did not want "just any job." He wanted a job that had certain working conditions and that he was sure that he

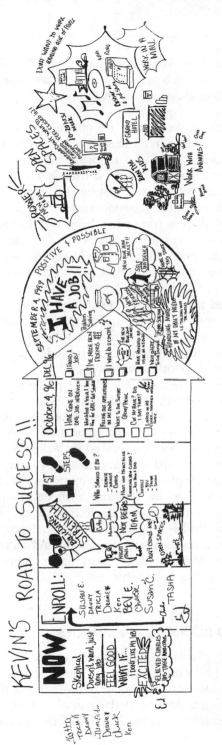

Figure 2. PATH developed at Project Access (Rehabilitation Research and Training Center, Virginia Commonwealth University) for an adult with spina bifida who wants to work in a music store.

would enjoy. He was, however, somewhat skeptical of the likelihood that he could obtain such a job because previous service providers had not been able to deliver the services and outcomes that they had described to him.

Kevin's goal focused specifically on obtaining a job. He felt that employment would help him in a number of ways, including increasing his self-confidence, adding to his disposable income, participating more in his community, and making new friends. For Kevin, employment was the focal point of his goal; but he also was interested in the economic, social, and recreation consequences of employment.

After the goal and time frame has been established, the group attempts to enlist the participation of others to help enable the individual to achieve his or her goal. Friends, family, service providers, agencies, and organizations can be "enrolled" to assist in the process. The group then devotes time addressing the realization that a great deal of effort will be required to achieve this goal. The individual, as well as the group members, must focus on acquiring and maintaining the personal strength necessary to succeed during the challenging time ahead. For Kevin, friends, service providers, and self-advocates were identified to assist in the job development process.

The remaining components of the PATH process establish intermediate time periods that will serve as milestones along the way toward the individual's goal. For each time period, the group identifies what must be done, who will do it, and when and where it will occur. Finally, the group develops what is termed the *FIRST STEP*. The facilitator guides the group toward identifying a specific action or set of actions that can be accomplished almost immediately. Returning to Kevin's case, Kevin focused on meeting with employment staff to begin arranging job-seeking activities, selecting an employment specialist, obtaining new clothes, and contacting some people who may help him. In all cases, emphasis is placed on the individual, his or her significant others, and team members working in combination to enable the individual's dream to be achieved.

COMMON THEMES ACROSS
PERSON-CENTERED PLANNING APPROACHES

The person-centered planning processes described in the previous sections have evolved over time. Subtle differences exist across the various approaches, yet there are a number of basic tenets that hold constant across the planning designs (Falvey et al., 1994). A number of these themes are identified in Table 2 and are briefly described in the next section.

Table 2. Common themes across person-centered planning approaches

1. Focus on the individual
2. Break down myths and barriers
3. Involve everyone
4. Dreams become realities
5. Art versus science
6. Importance of the facilitator
7. Importance of ongoing planning

Focus on the Individual

In a traditional approach to planning, the emphasis is often on professional information (e.g., test results, clinical impressions, behavioral samples). In a person-centered planning approach, however, the emphasis switches to the individual and to those significant people in his or her life who have direct knowledge of the person. This subtle shift dramatically changes who controls and directs the planning process.

Break Down Myths and Barriers

An individual with disabilities who has been served by human services programs, such as schools, vocational rehabilitation, or developmental disabilities agencies, has invariably developed a reputation. More often than not, this reputation is a combination of negative descriptors, such as "distractible," "noncompliant," "unstable," or "withdrawn." In most instances this reputation is extremely exaggerated and often quite destructive. In person-centered planning approaches, every effort is made to focus on the strengths and talents of the "real" individual and not on some inaccurate, stereotyped notion of who the individual may be.

Involve Everyone

Person-centered planning approaches are based on the recognition that human services agencies cannot and should not be responsible for identifying and meeting all of an individual's support needs. The individual, family members, friends, neighbors, classmates, and co-workers should be viewed as potential sources of support for the individual. Involvement of individuals from all segments of the community may enhance an individual's ability to establish and maintain long-term relationships.

Dreams Become Realities

The hopes and desires of individuals with disabilities are too frequently viewed by service providers as unattainable or "unrealistic."

Person-centered planning approaches, however, emphasize that an individual's "dream" may shed important light on that which the individual values most dearly. An individual's desire, which at first may seem far-fetched, often can be the springboard for the identification and attainment of realistic, satisfying goals.

GERONIMO

In a PATH meeting, Geronimo, a 25-year-old man who had sustained a brain injury, expressed a desire to be an aerobics instructor in a fitness center. Because his brain injury made it extremely difficult for Geronimo to ambulate and speak verbally, several members of the group expressed concern that employment as an aerobics instructor should be established as a 3-month goal for Geronimo. Other members of the group, however, responded favorably to Geronimo's dream and suggested that employment in a fitness center should be established as a 1-month goal, with movement into an aerobics instructor position identified as an intermediate, 3-month goal. With help from one of his neighbors, Geronimo found employment as a counter assistant in a fitness center, and he quickly came to be viewed as a valuable member of the staff. In only 4 months, Geronimo was assisting during several aerobics sessions each day. What an individual desires most often turns out to be a feasible goal, even if it is initially viewed with skepticism by others.

Art versus Science

Many of the person-centered planning approaches make considerable use of graphic representations throughout the planning process. Although some professionals have questioned the utility of these detailed "artistic" renderings, the MAPs and PATHs illustrated in the previous sections fulfill at least a two-fold purpose. First, they reinforce the belief that the planning process for the individual is more of an art than a science. Individuals' lives cannot be planned through simple formulas, and individuals' experiences do not follow linear progressions. The artistic representations of the planning process reflect the importance of incorporating innovative, spontaneous strategies into an individual's career path. Second, creating a permanent, artistic representation of the individual's plan is intended to increase the plan's value to the individual, as well as to all of the group members. Individuals are encouraged to take pride in and display their plans.

Importance of the Facilitator

Most person-centered planning approaches emphasize the importance of a skilled facilitator. The facilitator provides objectivity and is frequently able to center the group's attention on the concerns, desires, and preferences expressed by the individual. This is particularly important in situations in which the individual and his or her family may have little experience in making their needs known over the potential objections of paid staff members, or in instances in which service providers are just learning to move beyond their narrow professional focus into new, more supportive roles. People from many different personal and professional backgrounds can become effective planning facilitators. It is important that individuals acquire both the training and the guided experience necessary to fulfill this important role.

Importance of Ongoing Planning

Person-centered planning is not an activity that is completed once in isolation, never to be repeated again. On the contrary, person-centered planning activities should form the basis of a long-term, ongoing effort to enable the individual to establish new relationships and experience new opportunities, learn from those opportunities, and then revise his or her dreams and goals in light of his or her expanding base of experience and knowledge. The need for ongoing, long-term planning is particularly important in employment. For example, consider the following situation.

SUSAN

Susan is a 30-year-old woman with cerebral palsy. Overcoming considerable obstacles, Susan obtained a bachelor's degree in information systems from a local university. After obtaining her degree, Susan had a difficult time obtaining long-term employment. Finally, after 6 years without a full-time position, Susan obtained a computer programming job with the assistance and support of family members, a rehabilitation counselor, an employment specialist, a rehabilitation engineer, a supportive supervisor, colleagues, and friends. After holding this job for a number of years, however, Susan gradually came to the conclusion that the job did not meet her needs.

Susan had overcome multiple obstacles to obtain a well-paying job. She had received a promotion and recognition by her employer for the quality of her work, despite numerous professionals who had told her that she could never be successfully employed. By any standard, she would be viewed as successfully employed. Yet, the nature of her job duties left her looking for additional challenges. Susan reconvened those individuals who she had initially "enrolled" to help her obtain her first job. She asked these individuals to assist her again to move into a different job that would better meet her need for additional work challenges. She ultimately obtained a second job in which she earned less money but in which she was able to engage in more challenging types of programming activity.

Cautions in the Use of Person-Centered Planning Approaches

O'Brien and Lovett (1992) identified several issues to address when implementing person-centered planning approaches. Several of these issues have particular relevance for individuals seeking to develop a career path and for professionals interested in assisting the individuals.

First, some proponents of person-centered planning believe that the individual should have total control of his or her process and that the process should implement only those activities for which the individual has clearly communicated a preference. Other person-centered planning advocates will point out that some individuals with disabilities have extremely limited experience in work settings, due largely to limitations imposed by the services system, and, therefore, should be actively encouraged to investigate new possibilities.

This second point is particularly relevant to the process of developing a career path. Individuals who have not worked before may have a limited base from which to make lifelong career choices. It is unlikely that a person's first job will be his or her last. With this in mind, group members in person-centered planning processes will actively encourage individuals to explore a variety of jobs, including job shadowing or job tryout experiences, prior to selecting a job for long-term employment (Clark & Kolstoe, 1990; Kregel, 1989). At the same time, it is very clear that individuals are likely to be more satisfied with jobs that they have selected themselves and that they will stay in those jobs for a longer period of time (Kregel, Parent, & West, 1994; Parent, Kregel, & Johnson, 1996). For this reason, the individual should retain the right to make final decisions related to issues such as whether to work, the type of job he or she would like to acquire, and the amount and types of supports necessary for long-term employment success.

Second, most approaches to person-centered planning focus on all aspects of the individual's life. In these approaches, employment may be viewed as one avenue through which an individual is able to achieve a broader personal goal related to his or her independence, relationships with others, and self-esteem. Therefore, developing a career path cannot be done without considering how employment is related to all other aspects of an individual's life.

For other agencies implementing person-centered planning approaches, directly addressing employment is viewed as a catalyst that may subsequently lead to additional life changes and future planning activities. These agencies take a broad view of the value of work. For many individuals, employment has led to dramatic changes in all aspects of their lives.

For example, Parent and her colleagues (Parent, Kregel, & Johnson, 1996) conducted in-depth face-to-face interviews with more than 100 individuals who had obtained employment through a number of different supported employment programs. For a large percentage of these individuals, participating in employment had led to what they viewed as major life events or changes. Major life events included moving away from home for the first time and into one's own apartment, getting married or entering a long-term relationship, and moving to another city or purchasing a car. The experience of these individuals illustrates how success in employment can dramatically affect an individual's ability to direct and control his or her own life, relationships with others, and economic empowerment.

Third, proponents of person-centered planning and staff in employment agencies sometimes have differing views of the extent to which family members, friends, supervisors, and co-workers can and should be involved in the delivery of support services. Chapters 7 and 8 illustrate service delivery approaches that rely heavily on home, community, and workplace supports in the design and delivery of employment services. An emphasis on "natural" supports, however, does not eliminate or lessen the value of quality employment services provided by human services professionals in supported employment or other employment programs.

In instances in which sufficient supports cannot be identified from home, community, and employer services, human service professionals such as job coaches or job placement specialists should provide assistance as needed to implement each individual's plan. To do less would be to exclude individuals from employment opportunities based on factors over which they have no control. In addition, even when friends, neighbors, and/or co-workers are ready and willing to assist in the implementation of a plan, there is still frequently an important role to be played by employment specialists. For example, on the one hand, an individual's family or neighbors may be involved in locating a job for a specific individual; but the assistance of an employment specialist is necessary to identify and implement the accommodations necessary to enable the individual to perform the job. On the other hand, in situations in which the employer is willing to assist the individual to learn and perform the job, the employment specialist's involvement may be helpful in securing transportation to and from the jobsite or in arranging for needed types of AT and rehabilitation engineering.

CONCLUSION

Person-centered planning approaches are important tools that individuals with disabilities can use to gain control over and direct their own careers. When successfully implemented, these strategies can enable individuals to overcome the lowered expectations of professionals and others and establish career goals of their own choosing. Family members, friends, neighbors, community members, and paid professional staff members can combine to assist an individual to overcome the economic, attitudinal, and technological obstacles that sometimes stand in the way of meaningful and satisfying employment. Through ongoing participation, individuals will be able to use initial employment opportunities as starting points that will start them down the path of long-term careers.

REFERENCES

Brooke, V., Wehman, P., Inge, K., & Parent, W. (1995). Toward a customer-driven approach to supported employment. *Education and Training in Mental Retardation, 30*(4), 308–320.

Clark, G., & Kolstoe, P. (1990). *Career development and transition education for adolescents with disabilities.* Needham Heights, MA: Allyn & Bacon.

Falvey, M., Forest, M., Pearpoint, J., & Rosenberg, R. (1994). *All my life's a circle—Using the tools: Circles, MAPs, & PATH.* Toronto, Ontario, Canada: Inclusion Press.

Forest, M., & Pearpoint, J. (1992). Commonsense tools: MAPs and circles. In J. Pearpoint, M. Forest, & J. Snow (Eds.), *The inclusion papers: Strategies to make inclusion work* (pp. 52–57). Toronto, Ontario, Canada: Inclusion Press.

Getzel, E.E., & Kregel, J. (1996). Transitioning from the academic to the employment setting: The Employment Connection Program. *Journal of Vocational Rehabilitation, 6,* 273–287.

Kregel, J. (1989). Vocational and career education. In J. Wood (Ed.), *Mainstreaming: A practical approach for teachers* (pp. 352–391). Columbus, OH: Charles E. Merrill.

Kregel, J., Parent, W., & West, M. (1994). The impact of behavioral deficits on employment retention: An illustration from supported employment. *NeuroRehabilitation, 4*(1), 1–14.

Kregel, J., Wehman, P., & Banks, P.D. (1989). The effects of consumer characteristics and type of employment model on individual outcomes in supported employment. *Journal of Applied Behavior Analysis, 22*(4), 407–415.

Mount, B. (1989). *Making futures happen: A manual for facilitators of personal futures planning.* St. Paul, MN: Governor's Planning Council on Developmental Disabilities.

Mount, B., & Zwernik, K. (1988). *It's never too early, it's never too late: A booklet about personal futures planning.* St. Paul, MN: Metropolitan Council.

O'Brien, J. (1987). A guide to life-style planning: Using *The Activities Catalog* to integrate services and natural support systems. In B. Wilcox & G.T. Bellamy (Eds.), *A comprehensive guide to The Activities Catalog: An alternative curriculum for youth and adults with severe disabilities* (pp. 175–190). Baltimore: Paul H. Brookes Publishing Co.

O'Brien, J., & Lovett, H. (1992). *Finding a way toward everyday lives: The contribution of person centered planning.* Conference proceedings of the Pennsylvania Office of Mental Retardation. Harrisburg: Pennsylvania Office of Mental Retardation.

Parent, W., Kregel, J., & Johnson, A. (1996). Consumer satisfaction: A survey of individuals with severe disabilities who receive supported employment services. *Focus on Autism and Other Developmental Disabilities, 11*(4), 207–211.

Pearpoint, J., O'Brien, J., & Forest, M. (1993). *PATH: A workbook for planning positive possible futures.* Toronto, Ontario, Canada: Inclusion Press.

Perske, R. (1988). *Circles of friends: People with disabilities and their friends enrich the lives of one another.* Nashville, TN: Abingdon Press.

Smull, M., & Harrison, S.B. (1992). *Supporting people with severe reputations in the community.* Alexandria, VA: National Association of State Mental Retardation Program Directors.

Steere, D.E., Gregory, S.P., Heiny, R.W., & Butterworth, J. (1995). Lifestyle planning: Considerations for use with people with disabilities. *Rehabilitation Counseling Bulletin, 38*(3), 207–223.

Wehman, P. (1981). *Competitive employment: New horizons for severely disabled individuals.* Baltimore: Paul H. Brookes Publishing Co.

West, M.D., & Parent, W.S. (1992). Consumer choice and empowerment in supported employment services: Issues and strategies. *Journal of The Association for Persons with Severe Handicaps, 17,* 47–52.

Wolfensberger, W. (1972). *The principle of normalization in human services.* Toronto, Ontario, Canada: National Institute on Mental Retardation.

Yates, J. (1980). *Program design sessions.* Stoughton, MA: Author.

Strategies

As discussed in Section I, a philosophical foundation of self-determination and a person-centered orientation is crucial for one's long-term employment and career satisfaction. Without the appropriate strategies for implementation, however, individuals with disabilities and the programs that work with them, as well as with their families, will be unable to attain their visions. Section II, therefore, presents strategies for securing satisfying employment. The authors explore vocational evaluation, training techniques, the importance of supported employment, and assistive technology (AT).

Vocational evaluation, historically, has not always been "friendly" to individuals with significant physical or intellectual disabilities. In the chapter presented by Ms. Sherron Targett and her associates, there is an emphasis on involving the consumer in the evaluation process. The chapter focuses on ways to personalize vocational evaluation and the roles that situational assessments play in the information gathering process. Understanding a person's abilities and strengths and how they fit the individual's desired career path are the first steps toward designing a vision of fulfilling employment.

Because many individuals with disabilities enter the workplace needing substantial training, it should not be surprising that they *initially* cannot complete their assigned workplace tasks. This, however, should not be considered an ending point but instead should be considered a beginning point for implementing training. A key component of establishing satisfying careers is to tailor each person's training to his or her particular needs. Whereas in the past training was not tailored to particular jobs and job needs, training that is geared toward gaining specific, useful competencies can break down barriers to full employment and help to establish competitive and fulfilling career paths for people with disabilities. In the chapter by Dr. Grossi and her colleagues, the focus is on consumer-driven training techniques. This approach uses consumer input to devise behavioral instruction techniques based on consumer needs. Grossi's chapter leads the way nicely into the next two chapters, which explore supported employment and maximizing the use of community and workplace supports. Dr. Parent and Ms. Unger and colleagues discuss issues related to self-advocacy, the role of the employment specialist, and the types of supports available in the workplace. The strategies presented in these chapters represent the major techniques that consumers, families, and helpers such as rehabilitation counselors and employment specialists have at their disposal for implementing the career vision of the person with disabilities.

The section concludes with a user's perspective on making accommodations in the workplace through AT. Ms. Armstrong and Ms. Wilkerson present ways to acquire and use assistive technology as well as methods for evaluating its efficacy in different types of job situations. Assistive technology does not have to be expensive or complicated, but it is a resource that too many individuals with disabilities and employers and employment specialists do not utilize sufficiently. Readers will find a significant breadth of information to complement supported employment, training techniques, and vocational evaluation strategies.

CHAPTER

Consumer Involvement in Vocational Evaluation

Pamela Sherron Targett,
Shirley S. Ferguson, and Jay McLaughlin

JIM

Jim, who was born with cerebral palsy and who uses a walker and a scooter, had been through the vocational rehabilitation system in the past, including participation in a vocational evaluation. The evaluation recommended employment at a sheltered workshop rather than in competitive employment. Frustrated with this outcome, Jim chose to stay at home and collect disability income. Two years later, a friend encouraged Jim to reapply for vocational rehabilitation services. During the initial interview with his new rehabilitation counselor, Jim explained how the past evaluations had lowered his motivation and self-esteem. He also expressed the feeling that several past testing procedures (a vocational evaluation and a psychological evaluation) were unfair and that the instruments were inappropriate for evaluating his potential. The vocational evaluation included several pen-and-paper tests, which were difficult for Jim because of his limited dexterity and, therefore, indicated that he had limited vocational potential. The recommendation for Jim was participation in a work adjustment program at the local sheltered workshop to further evaluate his potential. Jim described this experience as humiliating and nonproductive. He disagreed with the evaluator's diagnosis of mental retardation and believed that the evaluation procedures were not designed to meet his needs.

Jim's new vocational counselor used a consumer-driven approach to career counseling. Together, they explored career interests that Jim identified. Jim became active in the process by conducting informational interviews with prospective employers. Rather than participating in work adjustment at the local workshop, Jim volunteered at a local company that he had researched. Jim performed well enough in the volunteer experience that he was offered a permanent position with the company. Within a year, Jim had his own office and job security. Jim's overall quality of life as well as his self-esteem had improved.

Consensus has emerged in the rehabilitation field that traditional vocational assessment measures relying on standardized conditions, administration, and normed scoring that take place in a facility or in an evaluation room do not supply an adequate amount of information about an individual's true capability to function in a real-world environment. Traditional vocational assessment measures also make incorrect predictions about the eventual employment status of people with disabilities (Anthony, Cohen, & Farkas, 1990; Bullis, Kosko, Waintrup, Kelley, & Isaacson, 1994; Mcloughlin, Garner, & Callahan, 1987; Peters, Koller, & Holliday, 1995).

People with disabilities often fall victim to a system that allows human services providers to direct their lives. Some vocational evaluators may believe that the consumer is not able to make realistic career choices or to obtain employment without the assistance of the "professional." The vocational evaluator may enter the consumer–evaluator relationship believing that he or she knows what is best for the consumer. In essence, the evaluator truly believes that his or her knowledge about the consumer is more accurate than the knowledge of the consumer him- or herself. After all, this individual would not be seeking assistance if he or she could obtain employment on his or her own. This view reinforces the dependency of the consumer on vocational rehabilitation service providers.

Oftentimes, evaluation results are used to set goals for individuals who remain passive in the process. This may result in consumers accepting dead-end jobs with no satisfaction, jobs that they did not choose, and/or jobs that they did not work hard to obtain. Obviously, this lack of ownership leads to a lack of interest and commitment, which may ultimately lead to job separation. Consumers must learn how to get involved in the rehabilitation efforts, including the vocational evaluation.

Through the years, rehabilitation programs have sought innovative evaluation methods that provide meaningful information related to needs, skills, preferences, and experiences. This chapter describes an assessment paradigm that does not rely on standardized procedures. This approach promotes individualization, provides functional information, and encourages the consumer to be actively involved in all phases of the vocational evaluation process.

A vocational evaluation can be an integral part of career planning for people who enter the vocational rehabilitation system. Vocational evaluation is useful for a consumer who does not know what he or she wants to do or which job fits his or her skills and abilities. This chapter, which focuses on identifying consumer wants, skills, and abilities, first discusses two approaches to vocational evaluation that are used whenever a person plans to return to an preexisting place of employment or possesses a special skill or knowledge base that, if intact, may guide the job search.

RETURN-TO-WORK ASSESSMENT

The first approach, a return-to-work assessment, can be useful when a consumer plans to return to existing employment. Table 1 presents some general guidelines on how one program has approached this type of assessment. In each of the following scenarios, an on-the-jobsite assessment may provide insight into the person's ability to perform essential functions with and without reasonable accommodations:

1. *The rehabilitation team (prior to medical release) is seeking information on the person's ability to perform the essential functions of the job with or without accommodation and on whether this person can perform the job without posing a direct threat to the health or safety of him- or herself or to others.* For instance, prior to injury, Jack was part of a team that operated a machine that manufactured tea bags. Jack's employer and co-workers are looking forward to his return to work. Jack's physician is in the process of determining his medical restrictions related to his return to work.

2. *The worker may need to request reasonable accommodation but needs technical assistance to determine the type(s).* For example, Jane is an 18-year-old female who sustained a spinal cord injury as a result of a skiing accident. Prior to injury, she worked in the inventory control department of a machine parts packaging distribution center. Although her employer is holding her position open, Jane is skeptical about her ability to return to work. An on-the-job or jobsite assessment can be used to identify the potential need for accommodations and supports (e.g., accessibility to the workplace, rearrangement of employee's workstation, restructured job duties).

Table 1.   Return-to-work assessment

Meet with customer to determine interest and willingness to participate in return-to-work assessment.

Obtain permission to contact employer and agreement to participate in the assessment.

Contact employer.

Review relevant information from referring agency.

Obtain assessment data (e.g., physical restrictions, cognitive and communication skills) from rehabilitation team (if applicable).

Perform job analysis.
- Interview customer.
- Interview supervisor and workers.
- Obtain existing job description and performance evaluation.
- Observe personnel on the job.

Review job analysis with employer and make revisions.

Review job analysis with rehabilitation team (if applicable).

Design assessment process.

Review assessment process and coordinate scheduling with employer.

Revise assessment tools.

Perform assessment.
- Verbal (if applicable)
- Observational

Write report.

Review outcome with customer and rehabilitation team.

Determine next course of action.

Note: To be conducted at the consumer's place of employment.

3. *The employer (postmedical release) has requested that the doctor conduct a medical evaluation or inquiry to advise the employer on the individual's functional abilities and limitations in relation to the job functions and about whether the individual meets the employer's health and safety requirements.* For example, Roberto's job requires lifting items weighing 50 pounds or more on a continual basis. He also operates a forklift in a heavily populated environment. The employer has concerns about Roberto's as well as the other workers' safety.

4. *The worker returned to work without support and is having difficulty performing his or her job effectively.* An assessment may be used to assist with a determination of whether he or she can perform essential job functions with or without reasonable accommodations. For example, Tom sustained a brain injury as the result of an assault in the parking lot of a fast-food restaurant at which he was employed as a manager. He returned to work without support. Three months later, during a medical follow-up visit, he reported to his physician

that he was experiencing difficulties at work. His troubles centered around completing routine paperwork such as scheduling, inventory, and shipping supply requests.

RESIDUAL SKILLS AND ABILITY ASSESSMENT

Although some individuals may have jobs to which to return, other people may enter the vocational evaluation process without jobs but may have a keen interest in pursuing employment opportunities that require the use of specialized skills or educational backgrounds. So that a consumer can make an informed decision about whether to seek employment that requires a particular ability, a residual skills and ability assessment can be performed to determine his or her current knowledge or skill level. A residual skills and ability assessment typically focuses on surveying previously acquired skills to measure the potential to use such abilities in a proficient manner. A basic outline of the procedures used by one program is presented in Table 2. The following two case studies provide examples of situations in which residual skills and ability assessments might be warranted.

JOHN

John had worked as a shoe repairman for 25 years prior to his stroke 7 years ago. He indicates an interest in obtaining employment but is unsure of what he wants to do. He reports having enjoyed the shoe repair business but does not know if he still has the ability to do a good job.

John's vocational rehabilitation counselor helped him locate a local repair shop in which a situational assessment could be set up.

Table 2. Residual skills and ability assessment

Meet with the customer and referral source to determine area of vocational interest.

Obtain previous work history and job descriptions if possible.

Obtain medical release, if needed.

Develop an assessment site(s).

Hire an expert consultant, if needed.

Design assessment tools.

Perform the assessment.

Obtain feedback from expert (written report).

Write report.

Review outcome with customer and referral source.

Determine next course of action.

During this 1-week assessment, John became reacquainted with current shoe repair techniques and had an opportunity to demonstrate his abilities. The owner of the shop was so impressed with John's talents that he offered him a job.

MISSEY

Missey had been self-employed as a hair stylist for 10 years prior to an accident that adversely affected the use of her arms and hands. She would like to continue her career as a stylist but does not think this will be possible because of her physical limitations.

Use of a Consultant

Depending on the complexity of the job, a consultant may be hired to assist with designing and implementing the assessment. For example, Linda sustained a traumatic brain injury 4 years ago. Prior to the accident, she programmed machines to produce parts for sewing machines. She moved to a smaller urban area a year ago and would like assistance in finding out if she can utilize her programming talent in the job market. The consultant should be someone who could be considered an expert in the field or area that is to be assessed. In general, the vocational evaluator takes responsibility for contacting a consultant, coordinating the effort, and designing the assessment tool. The evaluator also actively participates in the assessment by observing and collecting data. An array of observable variables, such as consistency in performance, ability to remain on task, use of compensatory strategies, and control of quality can be documented by the examiner.

Individualization Is Essential

Both the return-to-work assessment and the residual skills and ability assessment are highly individualized and may take significantly more time to set up and perform than standardized evaluation procedures. Nevertheless, if a vocational evaluation program is going to be responsive to consumer needs, it should offer these types of evaluations.

PERSONALIZED VOCATIONAL EVALUATION

A great number of people who enter the vocational evaluation process will possess limited or no previous work experience. These individuals may benefit from a chance to explore vocational alternatives in an effort to gain a better self-understanding related to work. This knowledge then can be used to assist the person with establishing a description of a desirable career path and with finding a job. This type of assessment is referred to as a personalized vocational evaluation. Suggested steps for the personalized vocational evaluation include the following: 1) orientation, 2) intake interview, 3) assessment, and 4) report on outcomes. The remainder of the chapter provides recommendations for the completion of each of these steps, with an emphasis on how the examiner might promote consumer involvement.

Step 1: Orientation

The first activity in a personalized vocational evaluation involves familiarizing the consumer with the vocational evaluation process. The goal is to provide information so that the consumer can determine if an evaluation would be helpful and, if so, begin to acquaint the person with the process. It is also the first step toward facilitating the consumer's active participation in the decision-making process. During orientation, the designated personnel will be educating the potential participant about the process. This in-service might include the following topics: a review of program values and philosophy; an overview the vocational evaluation process, with an emphasis on consumer involvement; an explanation of the timeliness of referral; and an explanation of consumer rights and responsibilities. Effective communication at all levels is imperative for a successful orientation.

Review of Program Values and Philosophy Vocational evaluation programs should establish a clear set of values and philosophies to direct service delivery and to provide consumers with a rationale for services. This will help evaluators focus efforts on methods that promote opportunities for people with disabilities to fulfill their vocational dreams. This valuable information also should be shared with the consumer, who as a potential customer, is trying to decide whether to use a particular program's services. When developing a set of guiding philosophies, it may be useful to review the following principles:

- Everyone can be trained to work on the job; a person does not have to be "work ready" to work.
- The vocational evaluation process should place an emphasis on consumer wants and should provide insight into the supports needed to explore and/or reach goals.
- There should be no prerequisites for participation, except that the person should express a desire to work.
- Testing should be used only when absolutely needed because measures of existing aptitudes, interests, and traits cannot be used to predict subsequent learning, performance, and adjustment on the job.
- Evaluation should occur in real, not artificial or simulated, environments. The best way to determine skills is actual training on the task.

- Individuals do not have to have marketable skills. Emphasis should be placed not only on what the person can do now, but also on what supports will enhance success at work.

Overview of the **Vocational Evaluation Process**   When providing an overview of the vocational evaluation process, some individuals may benefit from examples of the reasons why other people have decided to participate in vocational evaluation. In addition, the vocational evaluator can provide a general description of the different approaches used during the process. Reasons why a person might chose to participate in a vocational evaluation include the following:

- To explore career interest
- To gain information on functional abilities and on how to maximize personal assets in the work force (through vocational choice)
- To identify the training or education that is needed to go into a desired field
- To identify work that takes advantage of training or education the consumer has or plans to get
- To identify ways that the person can participate in the job search
- To identify accommodations that may be needed to perform specific job tasks
- To learn how new information best should be presented to increase speed of learning
- To learn which types of environmental work conditions may promote successful performance
- To learn about different service support options

Explanation of the **Timeliness of Referral**   Although considerations related to the timeliness of referral should have taken place prior to referral, it may be wise to revisit this issue during the orientation. Factors to consider regarding the timing of the evaluation include recent changes in medications or dosages; medical stability; and, if a traumatic injury has occurred, the passage of time since the injury occurred. Any one or a combination of these factors could affect the results of the evaluation.

Explanation of **Consumer Rights And Responsibilities**   The consumer's rights and responsibilities should be reviewed and explained. Among the consumer's rights are the following:

- To attain the best services available within the mission and capabilities of the program
- To be treated with courtesy and respect
- To give or refuse permission for services
- To plan and participate in the evaluation
- To expect privacy when collecting personal information and discussing outcomes

- To have communications and records treated confidentially
- To make decisions or appoint someone to make decisions on his or her behalf
- To know how complaints will be handled (e.g., with an interpreter or assistive device when he or she has a communication impairment or does not speak or understand the staff's language)
- To stop and withdraw from the process at any time

The consumer's responsibilities are as follows:

- To provide information on vocational desires
- To follow the agreed-on evaluation plan
- To make known his or her understanding of the vocational evaluation plan
- To express complaints or problems with services
- To be respectful of staff

One way to develop a set of rights and responsibilities is to hold consumer forums that bring together a group of people and ask them to provide insight into what the rights and responsibilities of the consumer should be. The participants develop a set of standards after reviewing and revising the original ideas.

Effective Communication   When planning an orientation, it is important that the presenter give thought to the most effective way to impart his or her knowledge clearly and concisely. The presentation will vary depending on the potential consumer's communication skills and ability to comprehend. Some techniques to ensure that the consumer understands are to avoid using jargon, to adjust word choice, and to use visual representation (e.g., photographs, videotaped footage).

In cases in which these techniques are ineffective, the vocational evaluator can use alternative and creative strategies for facilitating the participation. In some cases, a person may not be able to actively participate in deciding whether to participate in an evaluation. Instead, his or her opportunity for decision making will take place during the course of the evaluation. As the person participates in various assessment approaches, the evaluator will seek the person's approval or disapproval for an activity by observing his or her behavior. To make this interpretation, the evaluator must be attuned to how the individual expresses satisfaction and dissatisfaction. Communicating in advance with the people who play a significant role in the person's daily life may be the most useful way to determine these signals. At the close of the orientation, the orienteer should solicit some feedback—either formally or informally—as to the effectiveness of the presentation from those who participated.

When the orientation is finished, the consumer then decides whether he or she will take part in a vocational evaluation. If the person chooses to continue, the next step will be to introduce the evaluator, or examiner, if this has not already taken place. To discern the consumer's expectations for the process, the evaluator can conduct an intake interview.

Step 2: Intake Interview

The goal of the intake interview is to obtain information for planning purposes, which involves determining which questions should be addressed during the course of the evaluation. At this time, the vocational evaluator also will begin to establish rapport with the consumer. At the first meeting between the vocational evaluator and the consumer, a special set of dynamics will be operating, as there are fears and hopes, expectations, reservations, awareness, and lack of awareness (i.e., known and unknown information about skills and talents). During the intake interview, the evaluator begins to generate facts for effective planning and to identify strengths and possible career paths. Effective planning requires that the vocational evaluator achieve an accurate understanding of the person's world and communicate that understanding back to the person. To do this, the evaluator must put aside his or her agenda and preconceived notions and allow the consumer's world to enter his or her awareness.

Planning may begin by establishing a direction for the evaluation, which may be achieved by gaining insight into the areas discussed in Table 3. The interview should be ended by pointing out strengths so that the person leaves feeling positive. Aside from developing rapport, a major outcome of the intake interview is to develop a recommendation for a customized approach to the personalized vocational evaluation.

Throughout the work evaluation process, the vocational evaluator creates a dialogue with the consumer that promotes choice and involvement. This is particularly important during intake, as the initial conversations between consumer and evaluator can have a positive or negative impact on the relationship and evaluation results. During the intake interview, the evaluator can enhance the dialogue with the person by reducing the individual's anxiety and by listening carefully. Table 4 offers suggestions on how to increase the individual's comfort level. Remember, when the person is at ease, he or she will feel free to talk.

Encouraging Consumer Ownership The evaluator can encourage the consumer to take ownership and to be an active participant in the planning process. Service providers can achieve this by refraining from talking and by listening to the needs of the consumer. A critical aspect of listening carefully involves communicating an understanding

Table 3. Establishing a direction for the evaluation

Motivation
- What brings you here today?
- What would you like to learn from participation in evaluation?

Personal history
- Tell me about yourself; Who are you?

Strengths and interests
- What do you do well?
- What do you like about yourself?
- What would you like to do better?
- What do you enjoy doing?
- Describe your ideal job.

Volunteer or work history
- What types of work have you performed in the past, and for how long were you employed?
- What are the reasons that you remained at or left these jobs?
- What are the most difficult problems you faced at work? How were they handled?

Self-perception
- How does your disability limit you from doing what you want to do?
- How does your disability limit you from gaining employment?
- What have you tried to do to alleviate these issues?

Support systems
- How does your family feel about your going to work?

of what has been said back to the consumer. This can be done by paraphrasing the consumer's words.

Results of a 1995 ongoing consumer satisfaction survey completed by consumers of the Virginia Department of Rehabilitative Services revealed consumers' dissatisfaction with counselors' abilities to hear consumers' needs. One recommendation was to provide more training in listening skills for counselors (Magill, 1995). (See Table 4 for a list of basic listening skills.)

Step 3: Assessment

If people with disabilities are not going to have vocational goals dictated to them, they must learn to make choices, even when this means taking a risk. The responsibility of learning to make choices lies not only with the consumer who must choose to become more active in the vocational process, but also with vocational evaluators who can promote an atmosphere that encourages participation, self-exploration, and choice.

Some evaluators may feel that consumers' vocational goals are unrealistic. The evaluators' reactions to this perception may be to redirect

Table 4. Reducing anxiety, encouraging customer participation, and listening for information

Environment
- Move away from the desk.
- Tell the person in advance if notes are being taken and how the notes will be used.
- Meet in privacy and reassure the person that the meeting is confidential.
- Get out of the office environment, for instance, talk with the person over coffee at a café or while taking a walk.
- Get rid of environmental distractions, and create a quiet atmosphere.

Body language
- Eye contact should be normal.
- Keep eye contact constant without staring.
- Avoid looking away, which is inattentive.
- Relax your body.
- Speak in a normal tone of voice.
- Promote the person's self-confidence by giving pats on the back.
- Demonstrate interest and promote broader responses by nodding, frowning, or smiling, and by using brief comments that encourage the speaker to share.

Spoken language
- Offer some personal information about yourself first (e.g., what you like to do).
- Invite the person to address you on a first-name basis.
- Gain permission on how to address the person.
- Call attention to the person's assets and successes.
- Encourage the person to expand on thoughts.
- Show interest by restating your understanding of how the person feels.
- Adjust your choice of words to a level that will promote understanding; do not use jargon.
- Reduce the unknown by describing the process.
- Give the person an opportunity to ask questions and check out his or her expectations.
- Provide an invitation that encourages the person to speak but does not specify what should be said.
- Be sure you understand a speaker's idea by asking questions and by paraphrasing what is stated.
- Give the speaker feedback by asking questions and by making comments that show that you are listening.

consumer goals. Instead, the evaluators should take the time to help the consumer understand the concept of a career path. Consumers can be assisted in identifying short-term goals that lead to the achievement of long-range goals. For example, consider a consumer who comes to the evaluation process with little or no work experience but with a goal of becoming an owner of a store. First, he or she might be counseled on how owning a shop is a long-range goal and how learning how to stock inventory in a retail establishment would be a short-term goal but perhaps a necessary step to understanding the retail business and achieving the long-range goal of store ownership.

Another consumer may have the goal of becoming a doctor. Rather than stating that the consumer does not have the intelligence to accomplish this goal, the evaluator can work with the consumer to explore the requirements necessary to achieve this goal. By providing information to the consumer regarding the university acceptance requirements, the number of years of college education required, and the skills needed for this profession, consumers often will come to the self-realization that the goal needs adjustment. A consumer may go as far as taking a course to see how well he or she performs. Sometimes, only an unsuccessful attempt to fulfill a goal will allow the consumer to see that his or her direction requires some adjustment. Whenever a person exits the vocational evaluation process with a better understanding of him- or herself, it is a victory.

In many cases, consumer goals may be indeed unrealistic; but we all have dreams. These dreams are the very things that keep us going and that keep us achieving. Also, because no one has foresight into what the future holds, at times we are sure to be amazed when someone reaches a goal that was thought by others to be impossible to reach.

The vocational evaluator can recommend activities that will help define the participant's vocational expectations. In addition, the results of the activities provide beneficial information for the job search process. A description of some possible approaches to evaluation follow, including situational assessment, person-centered career planning, community assessment, home visit, self-assessment inventory, self-assessment interview, career exploratory interview, career search exercises, review of records, and tours with local businesses. The reader should keep in mind that this list is not intended to be all inclusive. Instead, it is hoped that it will stimulate ideas on the creative ways to approach the vocational evaluation process for consumers with severe disabilities and to promote consumer participation.

Situational Assessment   Enabling a consumer to identify and plan vocational goals requires background knowledge of his or her preferences, abilities, and support needs. Situational assessments allow consumers to explore interests in job duties and environments and permit the examiner to observe the consumer in a variety of settings to determine his or her strengths, response to training strategies, and support needs. The actual worksites used in this type of assessment offer characteristics typical to most environments, such as varying levels of supervision, interruptions to routine, and distractions.

Site Selection   Sites are selected with the objective of procuring diverse environments and job duties for comprehensive assessments. For example, one site may allow the examiner to observe a consumer's physical abilities (e.g., standing, lifting), whereas another may emphasize the motor skills used in a job that is sedentary in nature. The worksites developed also should be selected to offer the consumer a range of experiences and diverse information, such as outdoor/indoor settings, physical/sedentary work, high/low levels of supervision, and opportunities for frequent/infrequent communication.

- *Outdoor/indoor settings*   Primary observations at outdoor worksites focus on such physical abilities as standing, walking, stooping, bending, and lifting. Environmental conditions may also be a critical factor. Although physical restrictions and medications already should have been discussed with the consumer and his or her primary physician, new information, such as the effect of temperature changes on seizure activity and whether medications are sensitive to sunlight and heat, may be observed. Indoor settings, however, often eliminate many of the uncontrollable weather variables associated with outdoor work. There are also a variety of aesthetic options to be explored, such as lighting systems, dress codes, and noise levels.

- *Physical/sedentary work*   Worksites developed to assess individual levels of physical ability explore a range of physical demands and endurance levels, such as the ability to stand and maneuver. Sedentary work, such as data entry, focuses on a worker's ability to meet production standards while maintaining quality control checks. In this case, a worksite providing the opportunity to explore activities such as hand and finger manipulation is used.

- *High/low levels of supervision*   Determining an individual's desired and optimal level of supervision for performance is often a crucial variable in employment maintenance. The examiner also may have the opportunity to collect information regarding instructional preferences and effectiveness of strategies.

- *Frequent/infrequent levels of communication*   Varied worksites afford the examiner and consumer with opportunities to learn about receptive and expressive communication skills. The examiner also is provided the opportunity to determine the effects that different communication styles may have on learning.

Other Factors in Site Selection   To individualize the process and maximize consumer involvement, the examiner can encourage the consumer to select sites and to choose which information he or she desires to gain as a result of participation. Finalizing the site selection should be based on the consumer's preference. Ideally, a worksite would be available for any vocational goal; although this is unrealistic, choosing sites that offer diversity is achievable. Often, the person may not have a vocational goal and uses assessment to gain knowledge related to interests.

Another way to select sites would be to have the consumer decide what skills to assess, then the examiner will be better able to recommend which jobsites may be best suited to evaluate these skills. A vocational skills checklist can be developed for each site. The list should include the various types of skills and interests that could be explored at each site.

Site Development Site development involves activities, selection of employment sites that offer a variety of entry-level jobs that are well represented in the labor market, and the development of data collection tools in order to quantify task performance. Table 5 outlines the basic steps for developing situational assessment sites.

Although a variety of worksites may meet most vocational assessment objectives (evaluating generalizable skills), in some cases new specific evaluation sites may be needed to meet the consumer's desires.

Table 5. Developing situational assessment sites

1. Identify businesses that permit broad-based comprehensive assessment. Hospitals and universities are excellent assessment sites because they possess a variety of positions.
2. Contact the personnel director by letter, and follow up to schedule an appointment to visit the company. During the visit, describe the purpose of situational assessment and responsibilities of the employer, evaluator, and customer during an assessment. When the company approves participation, schedule an appointment to meet with department supervisors.
3. Meet with supervisors, and identify positions for situational assessment.
4. Arrange to observe workers performing the targeted jobs, and perform a job analysis.
5. Develop a position description, including a checklist that identifies the variables to be assessed.
6. Determine standards, and develop tools for measuring skill acquisition and production levels.
7. Determine types of adaptive equipment or compensating strategies that could be used.
8. Take pictures or get videotape footage of sites to share with consumers.
9. Determine protocol to follow for setting up an assessment, such as what times of day or days that he or she is available, contact person, and length of advance notice needed.

Brief descriptions of six assessment sites developed by one program follow:

- *Library* The card-checking position at the university library requires an individual to use a computer terminal to enter library card data for verification of location and call number information. The individual will enter the appropriate code, taken from the library card, to the library collections records program to initiate a search. For each record assessed, discrepancies in location codes and/or call numbers are to be noted by writing the program data on the card. This worksite may be used for a part-time or full-time assessment.
- *Central supply* The supply room order filler position at the university hospital requires an individual to stock hospital floor carts with medical-related items. The order filler uses a computer printout, which indicates item name, identification number, and quantity needed. The employee locates the item needed and pulls the correct quantity required, then he or she writes the order's status (e.g., completed) on the printout.
- *Print shop* A materials handler at the print shop is required to maintain and program a photocopier, to photocopy materials, and to check all work to ensure quality. The individual also provides customer service.
- *Finance department* The duties of a clerical aide in the university accounting department requires an individual to sort incoming mail into categories (e.g., invoices, statements, checks, personal mail) and to meter outgoing mail; to copy, collate, and staple documents; and to file documents alphabetically.
- *Grounds and landscaping division* The landscapers working throughout the grounds of the university hospital are responsible for maintaining the property. Activities are seasonal (e.g., weeding flowerbeds, sweeping sidewalks, removing trash, raking or blowing fallen leaves).
- *Gymnasium* The janitorial position at the university gymnasium requires an individual to maintain the general-use areas. He or she sweeps and mops floors, dusts stair rails, cleans the full-length mirrors, and stacks gymnastic mats after aerobic exercise classes.

Rating Performance A consumer's performance of job duties at the assessment site is evaluated on the basis of new learner data that the examiner collected during site setup activities. One program randomly selected 10 volunteers to perform the tasks at a given worksite and collected data related to learning how to do the job and to productivity. A consumer's performance then is evaluated relative to the average figures generated by the norm group.

Situational assessment can give the consumer an opportunity to work in actual employment settings. The consumer explores interests, different types of work environments, preferences for instructional/ training strategies and potential jobsite support needs. The consumer can be heavily involved in the process. For instance, the person could select the community-based assessment site, the type of position to experience, the length of assessment period, and the schedule. The consumer also might identify different skills, abilities, and worker traits that he or she would like to have assessed during the situational assessment.

Person-Centered Career Planning An alternative to assessing needs through testing and labeling is conducting "person-centered planning." This process focuses on abilities rather than impairments. It is planning the best quality future for a person based on strengths, preferences, and dreams for a lifestyle. During this process, a team works with the person to decide on a schedule of events and supports that will organize available resources to move toward the future (Pearpoint, O'Brien, & Forest, 1993).

This type of team approach that involves those people who play a significant role in the person's life may be an effective way to assist some people with learning more about strengths and abilities. A primary goal of this technique is to assist the future worker with becoming more familiar with interests and personal strengths. This is the very essence of effective vocational evaluation (see Chapter 4 for a detailed discussion of person-centered career planning).

Using the PATH strictly for a career exploration is demonstrated by a federal demonstration project, Project Access (Inge, 1996). A quick overview of the PATH process follows. First, the customer, who is referred to as the "focus person," is asked to develop a relationship MAP. This involves having the focus person brainstorm the names of individuals involved in his or her life, such as family members, friends, and members of social organizations. Next, the person reviews the relationship MAP and selects people to invite to a meeting to discuss his or her vocational dreams. The outcome of this session will be a PATH, and those who choose to attend are referred to as the "Path Finders."

During the PATH, a mediator assists the "focus person" with leading a career exploration process, as summarized in the following: Participants first describe the person's ultimate vocational outcome and describe the accomplishments that would lead to such an outcome. The group develops a "picture" of the focus person's future, then identifies supports needed for reaching the vocational goal; group members then commit to assisting the focus person in reaching this goal. The group develops a list of objectives to be accomplished within 30 days. The PATH is given a title, and a direction for job development activities is generated. At scheduled intervals, the PATH is reviewed to document progress to date and develop new goals.

Community Assessment One useful technique for determining preferences and functional ability is to conduct a community assessment within the individual's neighborhood. Going into the community provides individuals with the chance to show the evaluator their skills and preferences.

Home Visit During a home visit, program staff have an invaluable opportunity to learn about the individual's residential environment, observe family interactions, discuss any concerns of family members in pursuing a vocational direction, and collect information on hobbies or chores that the individual performs at home. Although the evaluator may find it useful to conduct a structured interview during a home visit, a wealth of information can be gathered simply by spending a couple of hours chatting informally in the consumer's home.

Self-Assessment Inventory In the book *Job Strategies for People with Disabilities*, Melanie Witt (1992) outlined a method for self-assessment. The mission of the process is to have the individual focus objectively on current work values, personal values, interests, and personality traits and skills. On completion of the exercises, the consumer should have a clearer understanding of what makes him or her unique in the workforce. People who participate in this process should be better able to answer these questions:

• What do I want the most from work?
• What is important to me?
• What do I like to do best?
• What are my personality traits?
• What are my skills and aptitudes?
• What is my true ability?
• What am I willing to trade for what I want to get?

Programs also can dispense self-assessment tools, such as the one shown in Figure 1, that let the person evaluate skills related to activities of daily living.

Self-Assessment Interview Self-assessment also can be performed using an interview method. The vocational evaluator guides the person to focus as objectively as possible on him- or herself and to explore current work interests, skills, and values. Sample questions might include the following:

• Can you describe a typical day?
• What is your favorite thing to do?

Life Activities Interest Survey

Name: _____

Check off activities that you do, circle the ones that you enjoy doing, and cross out the ones that you dislike.

AT HOME
Makes beds
Changes linens
Dusts furniture
Sweeps floor
Vacuums carpet
Cooks on stovetop
Cooks in oven
Cooks in microwave
Cooks out on grill
Follows recipes
Sets table for dining
Washes dishes
Loads dishwasher
Operates dishwasher
Takes out trash
Scrubs bathroom
Waters plants
Feeds pets
Babysits
Supervises others
Mows lawn
Rakes leaves
Maintains shrubbery
Plants flowers
Plants vegetables
Maintains a garden
Cans/freezes vegetables
Performs household
  repairs
Washes clothes
Dries clothes on line
Operates washer/dryer
Uses computers

Sets thermostat
Makes shopping list
Stores groceries
Unloads groceries
Answers telephone
Takes messages
Makes calls to order
  food/service
Schedules appointments
Bathes others
Assists others with
  dressing
Operates answering
  machine
Changes car oil
Washes car
Operates television
Operates remote
Operates VCR
Operates stereo
Other: _____

RECREATIONAL
Reads
Makes things (hobbies)
Bikes
Walks/Jogs
Exercises
Bowls
Fishes/Hunts/Camps
Boats
Sews
Swims
Other: _____

COMMUNITY
ACTIVITIES
Drives car
Attends health club
Rides bus
Shops
Attends club meetings
Goes to movies
Goes to restaurants
Rides public
  transportation
Volunteers
Runs errands
Attends religious
  activities
Rents videos
Other: _____

FINANCES
Pays bills on time
Maintains checkbook
Makes change
Other: _____

SELF-CARE
Monitors/administers
  medication
Sets alarm clock
Brushes teeth
Bathes
Dresses
Clips nails
Shaves
Other: _____

Figure 1. Life activities interest survey, a self-assessment tool used to evaluate skills related to activities of daily living.

- What do you dislike doing?
- How do you spend your leisure time?
- What other types of things would you like to do during your leisure time?
- Can you describe your past accomplishments?
- What things have you done that made you or someone close to you proud?
- What are your current abilities?
- What do you do well?
- What do you do best?
- What do you do better than others?

In some cases, it may be beneficial to include other people in the self-assessment process. Those asked to participate might include anyone who spends time with the person—specifically, those who know the person best. The consumer may choose to provide names of people to contact who might have useful information related to their skills and abilities. The interviews may be one-to-one, group, informal, or structured. Potential interviewees might include teachers, previous employers, physicians, friends, rehabilitation professionals, and significant others. The consumer should be encouraged to attend and lead the interview process. The following are questions that can be asked of the interviewees:

- What skills does X possess?
- What skills have you seen X learn?
- What has X learned and accomplished in school?
- What has X learned and accomplished at home?

Career Exploratory Interview Exploratory career interviews offer the consumer an opportunity to learn about someone else's experiences. By asking workers about their jobs, the individual can learn about career development. As indicated, the examiner should assist the consumer with determining who to interview and with formulating the questions to be asked, performing the interview, and following up afterward. Please refer to Table 6, which outlines the exploratory career interview process. Exploratory interviews can help the consumer obtain information about the abilities required to do a job, skills training needed, and how this career choice might influence the way he or she lives.

Career Search Exercises Numerous tools, such as standardized career interest inventories and computerized vocational assessment instruments, are available to programs. Many of these tools are not specifically developed for people with physical and cognitive disabilities, and this must be taken into account when interpreting results.

Table 6.   Exploratory career interview steps

Step One: Choose who to interview, and schedule a time to meet.
- Think about who you know.
- Do you know someone who you would enjoy interviewing?
- Does someone you know know someone who you would enjoy interviewing?

Step Two: Prepare a list of questions.
- Tell me about the jobs that you have held.
    How did you choose those jobs?
    What did you do in each job?
    What did you like or dislike about each job?
- How did you get this job?
    How do you spend a typical day?
    What do you like best about this job?
    What do you dislike about this job?
- Did work influence your free time or family life?
- What do you hope to be doing 10 years from now?
- Describe your dream job. Why do you want to do that?
- What advice would you have for someone entering the workforce?
- Who else could I contact to learn more about this type of work?

Step Three: Conduct the interview.

Step Four: Write a thank you letter.

Step Five: Discuss the results of the interview and how it influences career direction.

Nonetheless, the experience of actually working through a career search exercise with a consumer can yield valuable assessment information in addition to helping the individual identify potential jobs.

Review of Records   If records are reviewed, they must be current. In addition, records should not be taken at face value and lead to forming preconceived notions. Evaluators should take the time to determine the records' usefulness relative to the person's vocational goals.

Tours with Local Businesses   The evaluator can set up tours of local businesses so that the consumer can gather information and ask questions. This approach provides a valuable means for learning more about consumers' interests and abilities, as well as about a potential occupation, industry, or employer. Observing the consumer asking questions and collecting information may yield valuable data on a number of variables related to social and communication skills.

Step 4: Evaluation Results

Many people who have never before gone into the job market perhaps have not spent much time assessing work interests and skills. Personalized vocational evaluation provides an opportunity to do this assessment and can serve as the first step toward developing a career path.

After the evaluation, a report can be generated; this report should be presented in a way that others can use. One way to arrange the information is to develop a consumer profile. The profile might include the following: consumer assets (skills and interest), consumer personal experiences (in terms of daily life, education, work, and other activities), consumer work values or rewards expected, consumer support preferences and needs, and a determination of how each of these factors relates to career choice.

CONCLUSION

The focus of a personalized vocational evaluation should be on a consumer's abilities and strengths rather than on disabilities and limitations. The evaluation provides the consumer and rehabilitation professionals with a direction for career development as well as with insight into the skills that the person has to offer to business immediately. It is important that the consumer be encouraged to become actively involved in the vocational evaluation process by deciding if assessment would be helpful, choosing factors to have assessed, selecting approaches for obtaining information, and providing feedback on the effectiveness of the evaluation process.

Everyone has limitations as well as something to contribute to society. The challenge we face is to overcome these limitations rather than allowing them to incapacitate us. Also, we all should be encouraged to reach for our dreams even if it means taking the risk of not succeeding at anything. As Helen Keller once said, "Life is either a daring adventure or nothing" (1957, p. 17).

REFERENCES

Anthony, W.A., Cohen, M.R., & Farkas, M.D. (1990). *Psychiatric rehabilitation*. Boston: Boston University, Center for Psychiatric Rehabilitation.

Bullis, M., Kosko, J., Waintrup, M., Kelley, P., & Isaacson, A. (1994). Functional assessment services for transition, education, and rehabilitation: Project FASTER. *American Rehabilitation, 20*(2), 9–19.

Inge, K. (1996). *Project Access*. Washington, DC: U.S. Department of Education (Federal Grant No. H128T50065).

Keller, H. (1957). *The open door* [poster]. Garden City, NY: Doubleday.

Magill, K. (1995). State Department of Rehabilitative Service Consumer Satisfaction Survey; Unpublished raw data.

Mcloughlin, C.S., Garner, J.B., & Callahan, M.J. (Eds.). (1987). *Getting employed, staying employed: Job development and training for persons with severe handicaps*. Baltimore: Paul H. Brookes Publishing Co.

Pearpoint, J., O'Brien, J., & Forest, M. (1993). *PATH: Planning alternative tomorrows with hope, a workbook for planning positive possible futures*. Toronto, Ontario, Canada: Inclusion Press.

Peters, R.H., Koller, J.R., & Holliday, G.A. (1995). A functional assessment approach to strategy development and implementation for a person with a specific learning disability: A case study. *Journal of Applied Rehabilitation Counseling, 26*(3), 30–35.

Wehman, P., & Sherron, P. (1995). *Off to work: A vocational curriculum for individuals with neurological impairment.* Verona, WI: Attainment Company, Inc.

Witt, M. (1992). *Job strategies for people with disabilities; Peterson's guides.* New York: Longman.

CHAPTER

6

Consumer-Driven Training Techniques

Teresa A. Grossi,
Jennifer Regan, and Beth Regan

JENNY

Jenny is an 18-year-old high school senior who lives at home with her parents and younger brother and sisters. Since she was in preschool, she has received special education services for students with developmental disabilities. Jenny loves to be around people and take vacations with her family, and she participates in all aspects of the family life. With four siblings, Jenny has always been expected to fulfill her part of the household chores and responsibilities. Jenny is responsible for making her bed, picking up her clothes, weekly vacuuming, and cleaning the bathroom. Like most other teenagers, Jenny needs occasional assistance and monitoring. Each sibling is responsible for specific jobs in the kitchen, which are rotated monthly: washing dishes, setting the table, clearing and wiping the table and counters, and sweeping the floor. Once a month, each child is expected to assist with washing and drying the clothes.

Regardless of whether adaptations or modifications are needed for certain activities, Jenny is always expected to participate. For example, when the family visits the local library, Jenny has always been expected to check out books of her interest. If she is unable to read the book alone, Jenny is read to or assisted by her parents or siblings. Jenny's equal participation in household chores and family activities has not only taught her daily living skills for future use but has heightened her family's expectations of her abilities.

Since she was 14 years old, Jenny has participated in some form of work experience. Her first work experience was helping with a variety of tasks in a local church twice a week after school. During her junior high school years, Jenny worked at a center for older adults, assisting during the lunch hour. Besides her nonpaid work experiences, Jenny has served as the high school girls' basketball manager for 2 years and participates in a number of in-school clubs such as the yearbook, Interact, and Youth-to-Youth. Each of these nonpaid work experiences and social activities has complemented her home activities to help Jenny begin developing a work ethic and social connections to her community.

For the past 1½ years Jenny has been employed part time at a family-style restaurant. With the assistance of two different employment specialists, Bob and then Sharon, Jenny started out washing dishes. Since then, Jenny has learned how to clean tables, sweep floors, stack silverware, serve on the food line, make sandwiches, and help pack food for the drive-through window. Throughout the remainder of this chapter, examples illustrate how Jenny and her parents have been active participants throughout the training process.

Competitiveness among the business community has forced companies to change their approaches to management. To lower costs, to increase effectiveness and efficiency, and to meet the customers' demands, companies have begun to focus their efforts on quality. Key phrases such as *total quality management (TQM)* or *continuous quality improvement* have been used to describe an approach to enhance the quality of products or services in a variety of businesses. To initiate change toward a quality orientation, organizations begin by defining the customer to determine the quality characteristics that their product or service requires to satisfy the customer. It is the customer who will ultimately define quality.

Albin (1992) brought TQM to the employment field for people with severe disabilities. Throughout her book, Albin emphasized the importance of all members of an organization using a quality improvement process and becoming obsessed with quality. If quality outcomes are expected for individuals with severe disabilities, then the people providing the direct line services must have the knowledge and skills to enhance consumer satisfaction.

Providing quality supported employment services begins by having an organization define who receives their services. People with disabilities typically serve as the primary consumer of supported employment services. Consideration must be given to other stakeholders such as employers, family members, and funding agencies. In a consumer-driven approach, the shift of control is from the service providers to the person with a disability. Consumers are empowered in the supported employment process when they can express preferences and desires; choose types of employment, service providers, and types and levels of services and supports to facilitate employment; control their careers; and choose without excessive external influences. Consumer satisfaction with supported employment services and outcomes helps keep an organization oriented to improving quality.

Family participation in the supported employment process is critical to successful employment for people with disabilities. In the 1990s, there are two generations of families: one whose children have grown up in segregated settings with limited options for services and little opportunities for choices; and another whose children are growing up in integrated settings with a greater movement toward community inclusion—school, home, work, and recreation. Each families' experiences with services and service providers will influence their attitudes and involvement in the supported employment process. It is understandable that family members' opinions have more influence on the person with a disability than the opinions of a professional who comes and goes in a person's life. Professionals must be sensitive to the choice and to the value system of consumers and their families. Families' concerns, such as ensuring safety and protection and the need for meaningful activities throughout the day, must be validated and addressed. For example, if a consumer with a severe cognitive disability is working 25 hours per week, the family may need other supported activities and supervision during the time the individual is not working. When given opportunities to choose and participate, families can be valuable assets to professionals during the training process. Families are the experts for their children and can provide valuable information about interests, preferences, skills, abilities, activities that the individuals engage in around the house and neighborhood, and effective teaching methods that can be used during the training process.

Employers' satisfaction with quality supported employment services is critical for ongoing support, integration, and future placements. Job developers must be knowledgeable and skillful in balancing the needs of employers and consumers with disabilities. Employers who experience quality supported employment services may serve as advocates and communicate the benefits to other potential employers. Employers can provide recommendations to other employers through letters, telephone calls, testimonials, personal meetings, or other informal channels such as lunches or social gatherings. Employer expectations may differ from those of consumers and family members; therefore, supported employment service providers must have a clear understanding of the different expectations and quality outcomes from the various stakeholders.

QUALITY PEOPLE, QUALITY SERVICES

The foremost indicator of a quality supported employment program is the quality of services provided by the community employment personnel. To be effective, direct line service providers should view their work as a continuous process of improvement. In community after community, the authors have found employment specialists who were paid low wages with little or no training and who were frequently viewed as nonprofessionals, yet they were expected to provide quality services.

The need for well-prepared employment specialists has been identified and discussed for a number of years (Agosta, Brown, & Melda, 1996; Everson, 1991; Hanley-Maxwell, Bordieri, & Everson, 1990; Renzaglia & Everson, 1990; Wheeler, 1990). A survey of employment specialists (job coaches) conducted by John Agosta and colleagues found that employment specialists earned low wages and that more than half received 8 hours or less of training. Agosta and colleagues also noted the need for employment specialist training in various areas including strategies for enhancing natural supports within the jobsite. If employment specialists are going to remain as the primary support provider, the gap should be closed between their responsibilities and expectations and the amount that systems are willing to increase the overall investment of training, support, and compensation given to enhance their performance (Agosta et al., 1996).

Certifying professionals who provide supported employment services has been actively discussed and debated by a number of supported employment advocates (Condon, Carson, Freeman, & Pellegrino, 1993; Dileo & Flippo, 1996; Killam, Flippo, Drouet, & Keul, 1996; "Thoughts on Certification," 1995). The premise of certification is to ensure basic quality services by competent providers. The complex issue of certification will not be resolved overnight; however, the aforementioned authors agree on the need for well-trained, competent providers to meet the expectations of people with disabilities, family members, employers, and funding agencies.

Selecting an Employment Specialist

At one time or another, each of us has been a seeker or recipient of a service (e.g., medical doctor, carpenter, plumber) or product (e.g., vacuum cleaner, automobile, coffee maker). Selecting an employment specialist to provide supported employment services can be analogous to selecting a doctor. Whether one is relocating to a new town, has a specific illness, or is dissatisfied with his or her current physician, choosing the right doctor is not easy. In any of these situations, it can be time-consuming to find a good doctor. Most searches for doctors are started by asking for recommendations from family members, friends, neighbors, or co-workers. Of course, there are other sources that may help one find a doctor: doctor referral services, newspaper advertisements, company personnel office health care lists, or telephone directories. Inlander (1993) provided recommendations for people to become savvy consumers. A few of Inlander's recommendations on how to negotiate the maze of the American health care system and how to choose the right doctor are listed here: 1) Check board certification; 2) ask for a get-acquainted visit; 3) make it clear that all tests and consultations to other physicians must be specifically approved by you prior to ordering; and 4) discuss all options before agreeing to tests.

Similar recommendations can be given to consumers when selecting an employment specialist and can be implemented throughout the training process. As discussed previously, the debate over certification continues; however, well-trained, competent service providers are expected, and competency often is assumed by consumers and family members. In many communities in which multiple supported employment service providers are available, funding agencies can give consumers and their families opportunities to choose a particular provider.

Brooke, Wehman, Inge, and Parent (1995) presented a series of questions to use when interviewing supported employment service providers. These questions help guide consumers in selecting the agency or service provider. Several questions focus specifically on the employment specialist (e.g., number of employment specialists employed by the service provider, average length of employment for employment specialists, opportunity of choice of employment specialists, opportunities to assess satisfaction). Once a supported employment provider or agency is selected, the next step is for a consumer to choose the right employment specialist. A common practice for supported employment services providers is for program managers to assign an employment specialist to a consumer based on availability and caseload; other factors such as type of work, gender, and personality also may be taken into consideration. Another common practice is that the roles of the job developer and employment specialist (job coach/trainer) are assumed by different people. Communication between the job developer and employment specialist is critical to ensure that the consumer's preferences and needs are met. Table 1 presents a series of questions for consumers to consider when interviewing employment specialists.

For parents and family members, getting to know the employment specialist is essential to building trust and feeling assured of their child's safety and security. Parents and family members who are ac-

Table 1. Questions for selecting an employment specialist

What is your philosophy in teaching individuals with disabilities on job sites?

What types of disabilities have you had experience in working with?

What type of training have you had to teach individuals with disabilities?

What makes you qualified to work with me?

How will you get to know me and my likes, dislikes, and needs?

What type of job information do you have from the job developer before working with me on the job (if different person assumed job developer role)?

How will you represent my interests with me on the job?

What is your job at my worksite?

Would you provide me with references from people with disabilities, family members, and employers whom you have worked with in the past?

What are your communication procedures with me, my family, and my employer?

Can you tell me how you will include my preferences when selecting teaching methods to help me learn my job?

How do you know if I am satisfied with your services?

---

tively involved in the supported employment services play a vital role in supporting the new employee throughout the employment process. Community job placements often are associated with the frequent changing of co-workers, supervisors, and professionals; but parents and family members can be constant sources of support. Professionals who have built a positive working relationship with parents and family members are those identified as understanding family systems, family lifecycles, and family stress and coping styles (Singer & Irvin, 1991). For example, most parents do not allow their child to go off with a stranger, yet supported employment service providers are asking parents of young adults or adults with the most severe disabilities— including cognitive disabilities—to take a risk and feel comfortable about their child being with a stranger in the community. The rationale is that these strangers are professionals! The same questions presented in Table 1 can be used or modified by parents, family members, friends, or advocates to assist the individual with a disability in selecting an employment specialist.

IF WE ONLY KNEW!

Jenny and her mother, Beth, received a call from Jenny's vocational rehabilitation counselor regarding a job opening. Jenny and Beth met the employment specialist for the first time when arriving at the family-style restaurant for the interview. Beth's obvious concerns centered around the fact that she knew nothing about this person who would be responsible for her daughter on her first paid job. More important, this person knew nothing about Jenny, her strengths, her needs, and what her family expected from the work experience for Jenny. The unfamiliarity with Jenny became evident when Bob, the first employment specialist, assumed she was capable only of washing dishes. Jenny and her parents did not know the employment specialist prior to beginning the job. A great deal of unnecessary worry, miscommunication, and lack of role identification on all parties could have been avoided if the same questions presented in Table 1 were used by the family prior to arriving at the jobsite. Beth and her husband both believe that having this information prior to Jenny working with a new employment specialist would have helped them feel more comfortable about taking the risk of community employment, would have clarified their role in supporting Jenny in her work experience, and would have allowed them to establish expectations of themselves and of the employment specialist.

Meeting the Expectations

People purchasing a product or a service have certain expectations. When eating in a restaurant, diners expect pleasant, comfortable, welcoming surroundings, and attractive food delivered in a timely manner. High quality often is evaluated by tasteful food, efficient service, friendly personnel, and cleanliness, with the ultimate goal of satisfying the customer.

Consumers, family members, and employers have certain expectations of the various rehabilitation systems and individuals providing supported employment services. Although consumers' expectations of services providers may vary, the following are a few reasonable expectations consumers have for professionals.

The Professional Is Committed to the Consumer The foremost assumption by consumers and/or family members is that the direct service provider believes in the individuals for whom he or she works: people with disabilities. A second assumption is that the quality of services will be high. With a renewed emphasis on corporate quality, consumers have come to expect quality services. A quote from a large corporation's training newsletter helps focus the consumer-driven approach: "Customers are not an interruption of your work; they are the reason for your work" (Boston Beacon, 1996). Likewise, in a consumer-driven approach to supported employment, committed professionals should remember that the ultimate reason for their work is to assist people with disabilities in designing and participating in meaningful careers. Satisfactory employment outcomes can result from committed professionals who believe in the supported employment philosophy and methodology and who have adequate training to implement their knowledge and skills.

The Professional Understands the Cultural and Value Systems
Schoor asserted that "successful programs [interactions] see the child in the context of family and the family in the context of its surroundings" (1988, p. 257) [brackets added]. Time spent with the consumer and family members increases the awareness of families' cultural and belief systems. An individual's family life, neighborhoods, religious affiliations, and community organization memberships may provide insight into the family's cultural system. For example, knowing that Jenny actively participates in family gatherings and outings tells the employment specialist of the high level of family support, the importance of family membership, and the need to regularly communicate with Jenny and her parents on her progress.

The Professional Will Communicate Regularly Ongoing communication among all individuals throughout the training process is vital for continuous quality improvement. Communication helps enhance the support from employers and family members to the consumer. Each consumer and/or family member will have different expectations of communication patterns. Communication expectations can be met by asking the consumers, family members, and employers their preferred frequency of communication regarding progress. If concerns arise, communication should occur immediately. For example, during the first weeks of employment, family members may prefer daily communication with the employment specialist while gradually reducing the frequency later in the employment process. Using effective communication skills will obviously avoid misunderstandings (see Friend & Cook, 1992). No matter how effective the communication skills, consumers, family members, and employers prefer to communicate with employment specialists without the professional jargon and technical terms. When professional jargon and terms are necessary, employment specialists should remember to describe terms explicitly and check for understanding and clarification.

The Professional Explores the Families' Knowledge Bases Many families are unfamiliar with the supported employment process, the rehabilitation systems, and community resources available. Consumers and family members expect service providers to inform them of the available resources and options; therefore, employment specialists should continually familiarize themselves with the various available community resources. Ongoing needs assessments will help each family member to identify concerns and to address issues at his or her comfort level.

The Professional Will Act as an Advocate The role of an advocate is to "seek change by supporting, speaking out, or acting on behalf of" the consumer (Moon, Inge, Wehman, Brooke, & Barcus, 1990, p. 418).

An employment specialist cannot act on behalf of a consumer if he or she does not know the consumer or his or her family. In some cases, a consumer will be able to communicate his or her preferences and desires and act as his or her own advocate; in other cases, observing the individual's behavior and soliciting information from family and friends will help ensure accurate communication on behalf of the consumer.

The Professional Will Use Consumer or Parent Mentors Connecting consumers and family members to other consumers and families who have gone through the supported employment process may aid those individuals feeling some hesitation, uncertainty, and confusion about community employment. Consumer mentors help other consumers with employment decisions, assist in maneuvering the rehabilitation systems, and provide support during the employment process by acting as role models. Parent mentor programs assist families of school- and adult-age children during the individualized education program process, transition process, or to maneuver through adult agencies. Issues such as guardianship, estate planning, wills, work incentives, supplemental security income or social security disability insurance (SSI/SSDI), and trust funds also are addressed. Family members frequently rely on parent mentors or other parents because of their mutual understanding of having a child with a disability, their experiences of working with the various education and rehabilitation systems, and their connections in the community.

Getting Acquainted

The first step in laying the foundation of a solid working relationship is the getting acquainted period. Developing a consumer or vocational profile (Mcloughlin, Garner, & Callahan, 1987) provides a picture or "snapshot" of the consumer, which includes his or her strengths, desires, needs, and expected employment outcomes. The consumer profile information is gathered by spending time with the consumer and his or her family members as well as by a number of different other sources such as teachers, relatives, residential providers, past employers, and previous records. The consumer profile includes establishing a vision with the consumer and his or her family members, identifying possible community and business supports, conducting situational assessments, identifying support needs, interpreting formal records, and directing job development activities. When different people assume the role of job developer and job trainer, the employment specialist responsible for jobsite facilitation and training does not always have the opportunity to go through the consumer profile process and "get to know" the consumer and family as desired. The authors highly recommend that every person responsible for providing direct services (job developer, jobsite facilitator, and follow-along person, if a different person) should be involved in the consumer profile process. Reading a consumer profile is not an adequate substitute for establishing a relationship with the consumer. Table 2 shows some basic "getting to know" questions that an employment specialist can ask consumers and his or her family members. The questions are not to take the place of a consumer profile but to supplement it and to be used prior to working with a consumer on a jobsite. This information also can be useful in helping to make social connections with co-workers.

The questions in Table 2 provide basic information about likes and dislikes, participation in community experiences, and effective teaching methods. The information is gathered by spending time with the consumer in a variety of community locations such as restaurants, shopping malls, or museums. Each question requires elaboration based on the consumer's response. If this information were obtained prior to Jenny starting one of her nonpaid work experiences, a number of issues or incidents might have possibly been avoided or enhanced. For example, Jenny had difficulty at a center for older adults because she avoided a certain area; therefore, she did not perform all of her job tasks. After a great deal of time and discussion, the transition coordi-

Table 2. Getting to know the consumer

Have you worked before? If so, where?

What makes you excited about working?

What kinds of things do you like to do? (For individuals who have more communication difficulties, give specific examples (e.g., Do you like being around people or to work with animals? Do you like office work such as filing, stapling?).)

What kinds of things do you like to do at home?

What kinds of jobs or chores do you do around the house?

What do you like to do in your free time?

How do you learn best? Do you like someone to show you how to do a task then let you perform it? Do you like people to just tell you and let you do it?

Are there any teaching methods that should be avoided or that are ineffective? Explain.

What are things that you do not like?

Who do you spend time with? What are some things you do with your family or friends?

Are there any areas that you are working on now to learn better (e.g., cooking, eye-contact, banking)?

If you could be anything, what would it be?

Note: Information from the above questions should be gathered while spending time with the consumer in a variety of community locations.

nator determined that Jenny avoided the area because one of the nurses brought her puppy to work for the residents to enjoy. No one at the center knew that Jenny was afraid of animals. Another example in which prior information would be valuable would be for Jenny's current job. Bob, the employment specialist, would have known of the various chores Jenny performed at home and could have presented her with opportunities to try more challenging tasks.

ROLE OF THE EMPLOYMENT
SPECIALIST DURING THE TRAINING PROCESS

During the training process, the primary job function of the employment specialist is the facilitation of jobsite training and supports. Brooke et al. (1995) described two primary roles of the employment specialist in a consumer-driven approach during training: consultant and technician.

Consultant's Role

Numerous definitions of consultation have been offered from both the business and education or human services fields (see Friend & Cook, 1992; Heron & Harris, 1993). The role of a consultant in schools and human services agencies has been described historically as a triadic process in which the consultant (a specialized professional or expert who imparts knowledge) works with a consultee (an individual or a group of agency personnel) in a voluntary and reciprocal relationship with work-related concerns (typically a student or consumer). Consultation is often indirect in cases in which the student or consumer do not directly participate in the interaction but benefit from the process (Friend & Cook, 1992). During the 1990s, the term *collaborative consultation* has evolved in the literature. Heron and Harris described collaborative consultation as "each party bringing different kinds of knowledge to each stage of the process. Further, collaborative consultation implies that each party in the consultation plays an active role in the design, implementation and evaluation of the program" (1993, p. 5).

The fundamental assumption of a collaborative consultation approach supports the premise of a consumer-driven approach to training. An employment specialist enters into a consultant relationship with all the stakeholders of supported employment services—consumer, family members, and supervisor or co-workers. The consumer and/or family members provide information based on past experiences; share preferences to solutions and accommodations; and provide input into the design, implementation, and evaluation of the training program and services. To assist the consumer in maintaining employment, the employment specialist provides information and recommendations based on knowledge of technical skills, community resources, or other potential support. Co-workers provide information and recommendations based on the knowledge of the specific job duties or tasks and of the work culture. The following case study explores ways in which an employment specialist can capitalize on stakeholders' knowledge and experiences.

THE EMPLOYMENT SPECIALIST AS A CONSULTANT

Consumer

Sam (the consumer) had just been hired to work in the mail room of a large hospital. As a new employee, Sam was given a choice of having his check directly deposited into his bank account or receiving it in person on payday. Carl, the employment specialist, provided Sam with the advantages and disadvantages of both options before he chose. Sam chose the direct deposit because he liked Carl's recommendation of eliminating the possibility of losing the check.

Employer/Co-workers

Kathy is an employee who is assigned to teach Sam his new job duties in a hospital mail room. Carl, the employment specialist, observed Kathy and Sam throughout the morning. Toward the end of the lunch break, Carl met with Kathy and Sam for a few minutes to see how things were going. Sam and Kathy felt things were going well, but Kathy identified a few concerns. For example, she does not think Sam is really listening when she gives him directions. When Carl reviewed his morning notes, he agreed and suggested to Kathy, "You may want to try to simplify your explanations by only giving one or two directions at a time, and keep them short and direct. Too many words and directions sometimes confuses Sam. For example, this morning you told Sam when he finished sorting the mail by room numbers, to stack them on the cart by floors, take the cart near the window, then go check for additional mail in each of the baskets, and begin sorting the mail again by room numbers. Until he learns his job, you may want to give him only one direction at a time."

Family Members

Sam's mother complained to Carl that she has to constantly remind Sam to remember his name tag and lunch for work. Carl suggested to Sam and his mother that while laying his clothes out for work the night before, he may want to put his name tag on his shirt so that he would already be wearing it in the morning. Carl also suggested putting a picture of a lunch bag where Sam will be sure to see it before leaving for work, such as on the door. Both Sam and his mother were willing to give Carl's suggestions a try.

Technician Role

The technician role requires the employment specialist to be competent in a variety of technical skills. Employment specialists should possess the following knowledge and skills:

- Understand the latest technologies that would assist an individual with disabilities to enter and maintain employment or a career.
- Implement instructional strategies to provide training, as needed.
- Identify and implement appropriate instructional strategies to teach new skills, to use systematic instructional techniques, compensatory strategies, natural cues, and reinforcement strategies.
- Become skillful in systematically fading instructional cues and physically removing themselves from the jobsite to ensure acquisition and maintenance of a skill.

The level of social and physical integration for an employee with a disability in the employment setting is also dependent on the role of the employment specialist. Employment specialists should facilitate interactions with co-workers as much as needed while taking caution not to block naturally developing relationships. For example, after answering the "getting to know" questions (see Table 2), the employment specialist can use a number of social topics to facilitate interactions with co-workers. When one of Jenny's co-workers was discussing his vacation plans, Sharon, the employment specialist, mentioned how Jenny and her family had just returned from a trip to Colorado. The co-worker began to ask Jenny a number of questions about her trip as Sharon removed herself from the conversation and from physical proximity.

The following case study explores how the employment specialist as a technician can incorporate the knowledge and skills of various stakeholders.

THE EMPLOYMENT SPECIALIST AS A TECHNICIAN

Consumer

Jenny is responsible for sweeping and mopping a large room with several tables and chairs at the restaurant. Her co-worker informed Sharon, the employment specialist, that Jenny is missing many parts of the room, and although she is willing to support her, Jenny needs much more time to learn the job then she can give her. Sharon immediately works with Jenny on deciding how best to teach her the tasks, while including the co-workers in the training as much as possible. Sharon divides the room into sections using the rugs on the floors as natural cues and directly teaches Jenny the tasks. Jenny then learned to self-monitor her job duties by using a picture checklist to ensure all tasks are completed.

Employer/Co-workers

Kelly, Jenny's supervisor, felt overwhelmed while teaching Jenny her new tasks. Kelly told Sharon, the employment specialist, that Jenny was having difficulty staying on task throughout her work shift and believed that many of the tasks were too difficult for Jenny. After observing, Sharon sat down with Jenny and Kelly to problem-solve together. Sharon had Kelly list all of Jenny's job tasks, then Sharon suggested prioritizing the tasks that needed to be completed during the shift. Kelly identified a task to be completed at the beginning and end of each shift, which would require Jenny to be independent. Sharon suggested a number of tasks that—until Jenny became independent—she could complete with support from co-workers. Specific task problems such as using a ladle to pour hot liquids into a container, sorting silverware into specific containers, and wiping tables required Sharon to teach Jenny directly by modeling and physical guidance.

Family Members

One of Jenny's tasks at the restaurant is to make sandwiches. Sharon, the employment specialist, mentioned to Beth, Jenny's mother, that Jenny was having difficulty using a knife to cut the sandwich. It seemed that most sandwiches were ripping. Sharon showed Beth how she was teaching Jenny at work to make and cut sandwiches correctly. Beth then practiced cutting sandwiches with Jenny at home.

THE CONSUMER–PROFESSIONAL PARTNERSHIP

For consumers to obtain the quality outcomes expected during the supported employment process, consumers, family members, professionals, and employers must join efforts and work as equal partners. The basic tenet of a collaborative partnership is that each person comes together as an equal and brings a potential source of expertise to support one another to obtain the highest quality of outcomes. How consumers provide input will vary according to each person's abilities. For example, consumers with more cognitive and communication abilities may be able to easily express their wants, likes, and dislikes, whereas consumers with more severe cognitive and communication impairments may require an employment specialist to make observations;

present alternatives; and seek information from family members, friends, and others who have knowledge of previous experiences with the consumers.

When soliciting consumer involvement, three major points should be considered: 1) All consumers, regardless of the severity of their communication skills, should be encouraged to express their choices and opinions (using augmentative and alternative communication devices as much as possible); 2) some consumers may have good speech articulation but may not be able to accurately communicate likes or dislikes; observations and input from family members may be helpful; and 3) caution should be taken for individuals whose choice may be potentially harmful to them (e.g., if an employee with a dual diagnosis of severe mental illness and mental retardation chooses not to take a prescribed medication, then the employment specialist may need to develop strategies to ensure that the medication is taken [Wehman, Sale, & Parent, 1992]).

Marketing the Training Process

When the roles of the job developer and the employment specialist are assumed by different people, it is critical that the job developer communicate the role and responsibilities of the employment specialist to the employer to meet employer's expectations and for integration of the employees with disabilities. Mank, Cioffi, and Yovanoff (1996) conducted a study on the use of natural supports in employment settings, termed "typical employment features" by the authors. The results showed that the more typical or similar the features of employment—job acquisition and hiring, compensation package, similarity in work roles, and orientation and initial training—the higher level of integration and interaction, hourly wages, and compensation. Consumers with mild disabilities tended to be better integrated and earn more than those with severe disabilities; however, for all levels of disabilities, those with more typical employment status achieved better employment outcomes and better integration.

When negotiating jobs, job developers must be aware of how each feature of the employment setting is critical to quality outcomes. Situations will occur when certain features are compromised. For example, if an application process includes an interview, the employee with a disability who uses an augmentative communication device will require support as will the interviewee. Job developers must communicate the specific jobsite negotiations to the employment specialist to ensure quality outcomes. During job negotiations, the job developer must determine 1) the orientation process, 2) who is responsible for training, and 3) the training procedures and process.

Determine the Orientation Process   Most companies have an orientation program for new employees. The size and type of the company often determine the extent of the orientation and training process. Larger companies tend to have a more structured program lasting from 1 day to 6 weeks or longer, whereas smaller companies may have more informal orientation procedures. The consumer and the employment specialist together should determine the orientation process that best meets the consumer's needs and the employment requirements. The following information should be determined:

1.   What is the typical orientation process for new employees?
2.   How are other employees in similar positions trained?
3.   Who is responsible for conducting the training?
4.   How long does it take typical employees to learn the job?
5.   Do new employees have a mentor or someone they can go to for assistance or questions?

JENNY BEGINS HER NEW JOB!

When beginning her job at the family-style restaurant, Jenny, her employment specialist, and supervisor, Kelly, worked collaboratively on how to adapt the typical orientation process to best meet Jenny's needs. The typical orientation process for all new employees is to complete required employment papers, tour the restaurant, answer questions after viewing a videotape, read the training manual and answer questions, and learn the specific job duties. The managers are responsible for training because new employees are taught to learn a number of different job stations.

All questions and suggestions were directed to Jenny, giving her the opportunity to participate in deciding the type of modifications for the orientation process. Although the employment specialist offered to accompany Jenny on the restaurant tour, Jenny chose to go alone with the manager. When viewing the videotape of the basic work requirements, safety and health issues, and issues related to specific cooking procedures, Kelly suggested that Jenny view the first two sections of the videotape that were pertinent to her job. Jenny had a choice of either responding to the questions alone or having the employment specialist assist with reading the questions. Jenny chose the assistance of the employment specialist. The employment specialist suggested that the manager highlight sections of the training manual pertinent to Jenny. Jenny read the manual with the assistance of the employment specialist and again at home with her parents.

Determine Who Will Conduct Training   Training procedures for new employees vary according to the size and type of company and specific job positions (e.g., computer data entry versus receptionist). Many large corporations have a training department, whereas small companies may assign an employee to teach the new employee his or her job duties. For employees with disabilities, a number of scenarios could occur in a given employment setting. No matter which training approach is chosen, the consumer must be actively involved in the decision-making process.

Employer Assumes Training Responsibility Some employers prefer teaching a new employee with a disability without an employment specialist present; however, employers should be well informed of the availability to call on an employment specialist if assistance is needed. This scenario occurs more frequently if employers have had past experiences working with employees with disabilities and more typically with individuals with mild disabilities. Some consumers, especially those with mental illness, may prefer the employment specialist not to be present due to stigmatization.

The employment specialist is available for consultation on a daily basis or on a schedule preferred by the consumer and employer. It is quite acceptable for an employer to call the employment specialist to assist more directly when the employer recognizes that the training is more time consuming than anticipated or recognizes the need for consultation on various issues.

Employer Requests that an Employment Specialist Be Present, Just in Case. . . Many employers prefer to use co-workers to train and to support new employees with disabilities. The presence of the employment specialist may be requested by the employer to increase the comfort level, to answer questions, and to provide support to the co-workers and to the consumer. The employment specialist may model methods to co-workers to teach the new employee or provide information to co-workers about how to better work with the new employee such as communication skills, health-related issues, or social skills. The employer directs the activities of the employment specialist based on the needs of the consumer and co-workers.

Employer Requests an Employment Specialist Many employers request and/or prefer that an employment specialist be present during the training process. Several of these employers prefer an employment specialist to assist with training because of the following: 1) a lack of available co-workers to teach the new employee for the length of time required, 2) the severity of the disability may require more support for both co-workers and the new employee, 3) the type of job (e.g., little supervision), 4) the lack of experience working with people with severe disabilities, and 5) past experiences (e.g., "I've always had a job coach who does the training").

FACILITATING JOBSITE TRAINING AND SUPPORT

The first two options described in the previous section—the employer provides the training or the employer uses the employment specialist as a backup—offer more natural and less intrusive approaches for facilitating employment by limiting the involvement of an external agent in the training process. Through active discussion with the consumer and the employer, the employment specialist can determine and implement their preferences for training and support needs. The following sections discuss the role of supports in training and the subsequent fading of supports.

Initial Training and Skill Acquisition Phase

Recommended practices for teaching individuals with severe disabilities in supported employment settings have been well documented. (For detailed jobsite training procedures and strategies, see Buckley, Albin, & Mank, 1988; Inge, Barcus, Brooke, & Everson, 1991; Mcloughlin et al., 1987; Moon, Goodall, Barcus, & Brooke, 1986; Moon et al., 1990; Rusch, 1990; Wehman et al., 1992.)

Components of the initial training and skill acquisition phase include 1) establishing a training schedule; 2) providing task analysis of job duties to be instructed; 3) establishing an instructional program to include reinforcement procedures, job duty analysis, training/instructional procedures, and data collection procedures; and 4) developing a contingency plan, if appropriate.

Establishing a Training Schedule Conducting a jobsite analysis requires an employment specialist to observe and, at times, to participate in the workplace activities. Certain job duties and the preferences of the employer will dictate when specific job tasks need to be completed during the work shift. In other situations, an employee may have a list of job duties that can be completed with flexibility during the work shift. Variations within the day or across days must be noted on the job analysis form. When job duty requirements allow for flexibility, the consumer works closely with the co-worker(s) and employment specialist to develop a training schedule.

The employment specialist also should pay special attention to the social milieu of the company and to the environmental events or characteristics. Analysis of co-workers' and supervisors' interactions, topics of conversations, rituals, teasing patterns, and taboos will aid in facilitating social integration in the workplace. Environmental characteristics such as work space, number of people in the area, noise level, or other working conditions can be associated with certain social or behavior problems.

DEVELOPING A TRAINING SCHEDULE FOR JENNY

Jenny's job duties at the family-style restaurant included washing dishes, sweeping and mopping the floor, filling gravy bowls, and filling the silverware trays throughout the restaurant. Other duties included assisting on the line to serve food and wiping tables. The employer required Jenny to start her shift by filling the gravy bowls and to end her shift with checking and filling silverware trays. Together, Jenny, her supervisor, and the employment specialist established the remainder of the work schedule. A picture list was developed from which Jenny could choose tasks to be completed.

Unless the supervisor requested Jenny to perform a specific task, she was required to make a decision on the task to be completed. For example, if the dishes are stacked up on the counter, then she should begin washing dishes; if customers are lining up to receive their food, she should assist on the serving line. This procedure was developed to give Jenny more control of her job while also working on her decision-making skills.

The supervisor took the overall responsibility for training but requested the employment specialist to be available as needed. The employment specialist and supervisor worked as partners to teach Jenny her new job tasks. When the supervisor directly taught Jenny a task, the employment specialist stood at a distance, inconspicuous but in Jenny's view. Several occasions arose when the supervisor needed to attend to other duties or believed that certain tasks were more difficult and would require longer training; during this time the employment specialist provided direct instruction to Jenny.

Providing Task Analysis of Job Duties to Be Instructed From the list of job duties, the consumer and employment specialist determine which job tasks will have a greater likelihood of needing extensive training. A task analysis, which breaks tasks into smaller steps to facilitate efficient and effective training, is developed for each identified task. The component steps may need to be more detailed for consumers with severe cognitive disabilities and much less detailed for consumers with psychiatric disabilities. When developing task analyses, the target work behavior should be listed, and the component steps should be stated in terms of observable behavior. For example, instead of "find the ladle," a more explicit wording would be "pick up the ladle," because the act of picking up the ladle is an observable behavior. Involving supervisors and co-workers in developing the task analyses can provide valuable information to ensure correct procedures for completing a task.

Baseline data are collected on the consumer's current performance level to determine which steps of the task the consumer can perform without assistance and which steps he or she needs assistance to complete. Assessment information should also include non–task related duties (e.g., clocking in and out, uniform requirements) and social behaviors (e.g., greetings, appropriate social interactions). The assessment information can be used not only to develop the instructional program but also to determine training responsibilities between the co-worker and the employment specialist. For example, when the assessment data indicate that certain steps of the task will likely take numerous trials to learn, the employment specialist may take a greater responsibility for training the identified steps, and the co-workers can assume responsibility for the other steps.

Establishing an Instructional Program The core of the acquisition phase of training is the instructional program. The importance of knowing the consumer and how the consumer learns best is essential during this phase. The information from the consumer profile or the "getting to know" questions (see Table 2) can help when developing the instructional program, especially in developing reinforcement procedures. Consumer involvement can occur by soliciting ideas for preferred training methods or by determining which methods have proved effective in past experiences.

Reinforcement Procedures The most powerful teaching tool available is reinforcement. The first two steps in using reinforcement for jobsite training is identifying naturally occurring reinforcers and identifying what is reinforcing for an individual at a given time.

Naturally occurring reinforcers on jobsites include praise from supervisors, co-workers, or customers; social reinforcers such as time spent with co-workers; and paychecks. Some individuals require additional reinforcers such as tokens (e.g., checkmarks exchanged at a later time for a preferred object or activity). Care should be taken when selecting a reinforcer and a delivery mechanism to avoid demeaning the consumer. Using age-inappropriate reinforcers such as Barney stickers or presenting the reinforcer in a manner that causes embarrassing attention to the consumer should be avoided at all times.

Identifying what is reinforcing for a given individual requires consumer input. Reinforcement information also can be obtained by asking the consumer, by observing the consumer, and by getting input from family members or others who have worked with the consumer in the past. The "getting to know" questions (see Table 2) may assist employment specialists to identify likes and dislikes and preferred activities. Knowing what is reinforcing to an individual also can be used to teach choice-making and provide access to additional reinforcers. For example, income from a paycheck can be used to make purchases or to participate in community activities such as sporting events.

USING REINFORCEMENT WITH JENNY

Identifying reinforcers for Jenny on the jobsite was rather easy for her supervisor, Kelly. After talking to and watching Jenny for a few days, along with speaking to her mother and the employment specialist, Kelly knew Jenny responded well to praise and enjoyed interacting with the other co-workers. When low motivation and avoidance of specific tasks occurred, Kelly used reinforcement to help Jenny improve her performance.

The first situation occurred when Kelly noticed Jenny moving rather slowly to complete her tasks. After the employment specialist discussed with Kelly how and when to provide Jenny with praise, Kelly began telling Jenny what a great job she was doing when working on her task. She also provided encouraging words such as "C'mon Jen, we have to work faster, I'm going to need those dishes real soon," or "Thanks Jen for helping to get all of the bowls filled with gravy, you're such a big help!" Kelly soon observed Jenny moving much quicker.

The second situation occurred when Kelly noticed Jenny was not completing her tasks of sweeping and mopping. She seemed to have difficulty staying on task. Through brainstorming with Jenny, her mother, and the employment specialist, a few possible problems were identified and solutions were developed. Beth, Jenny's mother, felt it was not the actual task but the fact that Jenny performed the task alone. Jenny said she preferred to help the drive-through attendants. Kelly mentioned it was very feasible to allow Jenny to assist the drive-through attendants but only after she finishes her sweeping and mopping. Providing Jenny with a preferred job task after completing a less favored job task increased Jenny's attention to the less desirable tasks.

Instructional Procedure An employment specialist must be competent to effectively design and implement a program of instructional procedures—specifically systematic instruction—to meet the needs of the consumer (Test & Wood, 1997). Instructional procedures should be written with enough detail to enable a person unfamiliar with the training setting and tasks to understand the procedures. Writing a detailed program is especially important when a substitute employment specialist may have to cover for the primary employment specialist and to maintain prompting consistency among trainers.

Based on the assessment data using the task analysis, an employment specialist can determine what steps of the task need instruction and the level of assistance required. The type of assistance or level of prompting strategies used during the acquisition stage generally move from less intrusive to more intrusive (e.g., verbal prompting to physical guidance). Together, the employment specialist and consumer design a program to meet the specific needs of the consumer. Information from the consumer or family members and other significant people who have worked with the consumer in the past can help determine how the consumer learns best. For example, some individuals learn a task by watching and listening to a co-worker demonstrate the task three or four times, whereas other individuals, especially those with the more severe disabilities, may have a greater need for intensive instruction over longer periods of time. Knowing a specific consumer is tactile defensive would suggest to the employment specialist to avoid physical guidance or hand-over-hand assistance. This information prior to training can save time and avoid frustration on the part of the consumer, co-workers, and employment specialist.

The employment specialist can determine which training techniques are acceptable for the specific worksite. Only instructional strategies that are typical, nonintrusive, and acceptable for the given worksite should be used. For example, an employment specialist should avoid using physical guidance in a crowded area. The respect and dignity of the consumer must be considered at all times as well as the image portrayed to the co-workers and to the general public. Employment specialists must remember that they are serving as role models for co-workers to teach and interact with consumers.

Consumer's choice-making skills can be utilized and/or improved while receiving instruction on specific job tasks. Deciding whether to first wash the dishes or the pots and pans or to begin sweeping on the right side or the left side are examples of giving consumers more control while learning a new task. The shift of control also can be accomplished by ensuring that all work-related interactions and directions from the employer are directed to the consumer. For example, if a supervisor needs the consumer to work faster or wants to determine whether the consumer likes his or her work, then the supervisor must communicate directly to the consumer rather than indirectly through the employment specialist. Finally, teaching consumers to respond to naturally occurring cues can increase task independence and decision-making skills; for example, seeing customers waiting in line could cue a consumer to stop what he or she is doing and serve the customer. Responding to natural cues enhances good choice-making skills and ultimately supervisor satisfaction.

Data Collection   Data-based decisions lead to successful and effective supported employment implementation. The purpose of data collection is to analyze information to increase the likelihood of employment success (Wehman et al., 1992). Two significant errors in judgment can result from not taking direct and frequent measures of a consumer's behavior: 1) Effective instructional programs are discontinued, and 2) ineffective instructional programs are continued (Heward, Barbetta, Cavanaugh, & Grossi, 1996).

Data collection during the acquisition phase of the training process is used to evaluate the effectiveness of a specific instructional strategy, to make program changes such as adding external cues or modifying tasks, and to document continued funding for placement. Collecting production data may indicate the need for a specific intervention to help an employee work faster or be used for saving a placement when a supervisor questions an employee's performance. Data also may be collected on social behaviors such as the number of times an employees sits down on the job. One of the major challenges faced by employment specialists is to make data collection as unobtrusive and simple as possible. The reader is referred to Moon et al. (1986, 1990) for specific data collection techniques.

Consumer involvement in data collection and the data-based decision-making process can be accomplished in several ways. First, data collected during the training and follow-along phase should be shared with consumers to provide feedback on a specific task performance. Graphing data provides the consumer with visual feedback of skill acquisition or production performance. Second, the consumer can be taught to self-monitor his or her own work productivity or social behavior. Self-monitoring has been shown to increase work productivity and social behaviors in community work settings for employees with disabilities (Grossi & Heward, in press; Mank & Horner, 1989; Wheeler, Bates, Marshall, & Miller, 1988). Third, consumers can use data to recruit reinforcement from supervisors and co-workers (Mank & Horner, 1987). Although the employees were not taught to recruit feedback and attention from others in the Grossi and Heward (in press) study, the study noted that on occasions when the employee told the chef that because he was doing such a great job scrubbing pots and keeping up with the dishes based on his self-monitoring chart, he deserved a special dessert. The chef agreed and gave the employee a dessert at the end of his shift.

Developing a Contingency Plan   Developing a contingency plan is a proactive approach to anticipate unforeseen situations that may occur on a jobsite. Knowing the consumer and having consumer input, however, will help avoid or anticipate some of the potential problems that may arise. Contingency plans are designed to prepare for non–task related concerns such as medical or behavior issues (e.g., preparing a plan with a consumer for the possibility of his or her electronic communication device not working when the job requires greeting customers or for specific consumers with a history of behavioral concerns). The plan clearly states the expectations, how to respond for certain behaviors, and consequences.

Developing Fading Plans

Fading occurs when external supports such as artificial cues and the employment specialist on the jobsite are systematically and gradually withdrawn. Technically, the employment specialist should start fading from the jobsite on the first day. If the role of the employment specialist has been communicated appropriately, then the consumer and the employer will be prepared for the fading process.

The employment specialist, consumer, and employer should develop a written, systematic fading plan, and eventually a support plan. Before deciding to fade, task acquisition, training, work quality, and production rate data should be reviewed. The data will indicate when to begin fading prompting strategies, thinning reinforcement schedules, and increasing the physical distance of the employment specialist from the consumer and supervisor and/or co-workers. Complete fading may require transferring prompts and delivery of reinforcement to supervisors and co-workers. Consumer's and supervisor's and/or co-worker's preferences when developing the fading schedule should be given high priority. For example, if an employer suggests working with the consumer alone for a few days without the employment specialist present on the jobsite, then the employment specialist must comply with the request.

A consumer's social participation at the jobsite should be considered when developing a fading and support plan. Employment specialists may have to advocate on behalf of the consumer while continuing to identify co-worker advocates and supports. Specific types of supports needed for the consumer should be decided while fading from the jobsite. For example, Lori, a woman with cerebral palsy, has difficulty straightening her pants and belt buckle after using the restroom. Identifying one or more co-workers to help Lori, if necessary, after she uses the restroom should be part of the support plan. The support plan can be used by supervisors and co-workers to remember the type of supports needed and to teach new co-workers how to support the consumer.

Again, involving consumers and family members when developing the fading and support plan is critical for employment success. Issues that occur outside the job setting but that have an impact on work should be included in the support plan. If a specific consumer who relies on public transportation gets anxious when the bus is late, then documentation in the support plan can help co-workers better understand the consumer's behavior and how to provide reassuring comments and support. Other examples to help co-workers support a new employee include the names of the consumer's parents and siblings, what to do when the electric wheelchair malfunctions, and reminders of how to handle specific instances such as seizures or when a consumer displays inappropriate social behaviors.

Finally, consumers should be taught self-management strategies such as antecedent cue regulation, self-evaluation, self-monitoring, or self-instruction. Self-management strategies place a consumer in a position of control over his or her environment and promote independence by reducing control from an external agent. Self-management strategies have been shown to facilitate the generalization and maintenance of skills (Wacker & Berg, 1986).

CO-WORKER SUPPORT FOR JENNY

Kelly, the supervisor, and many of the co-workers have taken an active role in supporting Jenny to meet her needs. The support plan includes descriptions of how Jenny learns best, procedures for teaching Jenny a new task, suggestions on how to respond to Jenny when she gets frustrated, and reminders for Jenny to look at people when speaking. When Jenny is interacting with unfamiliar people she tends to look at the ground. Co-workers practice with Jenny by interacting with her during breaktime; then they have her practice eye contact while serving customers on the food line. Frequent remarks are heard on the serving line such as "That's right Jenny, we need more potatoes," or a whispering reminder, "Don't forget to look at the next customer."

Jenny continues to learn new tasks without the need of an employment specialist. The employment specialist has given the supervisor and co-workers "the tools" to continue to teach and support Jenny. The employment specialist is now consulted only on an as-needed basis.

EVALUATING THE TRAINING PROCESS

To enable a continuous quality improvement process, supported employment programs must frequently solicit feedback from consumers, family members, and employers to adjust support services accordingly. Employment specialists must evaluate their own behavior to ensure a consumer-driven approach throughout the training process. Figure 1 presents self-evaluation questions for the employment specialist to ask him- or herself so that he or she can ensure a consumer-driven approach to training.

The purpose of consumer satisfaction surveys is to assess which components of the training process the consumer considers important and to evaluate the performance in each of these areas. Figures 2 and 3 present questions to assess the consumer's and employer's satisfaction with the training process. The results of the consumer's and employer's surveys should be used to direct actions for continuous quality improvement.

Employment Specialist Self-Assessment Guide for the Training Process

1. Did I get to know _consumer's name_ /family members prior to and during the first week of work?

   Not at all | Somewhat | Fairly well | Very well

   Comments:

2. Did I establish a preferred communication schedule with _consumer's name_/ family members and communicate as requested regarding training progress?

   Not at all | Somewhat | Fairly well | Very well

   Comments:

3. Did I include _consumer's name_ and consider his or her preferences in the decision-making during the orientation, training, and fading process?

   Never | Sometimes | Most of the time | Always

   Comments:

4. Did I solicit information from the consumer, family members, and other sources on effective training methods for _consumer's name_?

   Never | Sometimes | Most of the time | Always

   Comments:

5. Did I give _consumer's name_ choices throughout training?

   Never | Sometimes | Most of the time | Always

   Comments:

6. Did I advocate as best as I could on _consumer's name_ behalf?

   Not at all | Somewhat | Fairly well | Very well

   Comments:

7. Did I facilitate social interactions between _consumer's name_ and co-workers by getting to know the work culture?

   Not at all | Somewhat | Fairly well | Very well

   Comments:

8. Did I communicate with the employer regarding training progress?

   Never | Sometimes | Most of the time | Always

   Comments:

9. Overall, did I implement a consumer-driven approach by viewing _consumer's name_ as a partner throughout the training process?

   Never | Sometimes | Most of the time | Always

   Comments:

10. Did I use the employer and/or co-workers as partners throughout the training process by soliciting their preferences, ideas, and typical procedures?

    Never | Sometimes | Most of the time | Always

    Comments:

Figure 1. Self-assessment guide to be used by employment specialist after the training process.

1. Did the employment specialist get to know you before and during the first week of work, including your strengths, likes, dislikes, and needs?

    Not at all   Somewhat   Fairly well   Very well

    Comments:

2. Did the employment specialist include you in the decision-making during the orientation, training, and fading process?

    Never   Sometimes   Most of the time   Always

    Comments:

3. Did the employment specialist ask how you learn best and what teaching methods work better for you?

    Never   Sometimes   Most of the time   Always

    Comments:

4. Did the employment specialist give you choices throughout the training process?

    Never   Sometimes   Most of the time   Always

    Comments:

5. Did the employment specialist represent your interests as best as he or she could on the job?

    Not at all   Somewhat   Fairly well   Very well

    Comments:

6. Did the employment specialist help you get to know your co-workers?

    Not at all   Somewhat   Fairly well   Very well

    Comments:

7. Was the employment specialist there when you expected him or her to be there?

    Never   Sometimes   Most of the time   Always

    Comments:

8. Did the employment specialist communicate with you as requested through-out the training process regarding your progress or related information?

    Not at all   Somewhat   Fairly well   Very well

    Comments:

9. Overall, how satisfied are you with the training services?

    Not at all   Somewhat   Fairly well   Very well

    Comments:

Figure 2.   Form to evaluate consumer satisfaction of the employment specialist's services to be completed following the training.

Employer Satisfaction Form

1. Did the employment specialist help you better teach and work with _consumer's name_ (e.g., show you specific strategies, give you suggestions)?

   Not at all   Somewhat   Fairly well   Very well

   Comments:

2. Did the employment specialist include you and/or the co-workers throughout the training process, (e.g., seek information from supervisor/co-workers, provide you with the support needed or requested)?

   Not at all   Somewhat   Fairly well   Very well

   Comments:

3. Was the employment specialist present when you expected him or her to be here?

   Never   Sometimes   Most of the time   Always

   Comments:

4. Did the employment specialist communicate with you as desired throughout the training process regarding progress or related information?

   Not at all   Somewhat   Fairly well   Very well

   Comments:

5. Overall, how satisfied are you with the training services?

   None at all   Somewhat   Fairly well   Very well

   Comments:

Figure 3. Employer satisfaction of the employment specialist's services to be completed following the training.

CONCLUSION

A consumer-driven approach to training requires the consumer and/or family members, the employment specialist, and employer to work together as equal partners. A collaborative relationship requires each partner to play an active role in the design, implementation, and evaluation of the supported employment training process. To actively involve the consumer in the training process and advocate on his or her behalf, an employment specialist must have a clear understanding of the consumer's preferences, strengths, desires, and needs. This understanding can be accomplished only by spending time getting to know and building a relationship with the consumer.

To ensure quality outcomes demanded by consumers, employment specialists must be well prepared and competent to serve both as a consultant and as a technician during the training process. Because consumers, family members, and employers are the recipients of supported employment services, assessing quality outcomes and satisfaction is essential for supported employment programs to practice the principles of continuous quality improvement.

REFERENCES

Agosta, J., Brown, L., & Melda, K. (1996). Who is doing job coaching and what do they think about supported employment? *Facing the future: Best practices in supported employment*. St. Augustine, FL: Training Resource Network, Inc.

Albin, J.M. (1992). *Quality improvement in employment and other human services: Managing for quality through change*. Baltimore: Paul H. Brookes Publishing Co.

Boston Beacon. (1996). Boston Chicken, Inc.

Brooke, V., Wehman, P., Inge, K., & Parent, W. (1995). Toward a customer-driven approach of support employment. *Education and Training in Mental Retardation and Developmental Disabilities, 4*, 308–320.

Buckley, J., Albin, J.M., & Mank, D.M. (1988). Competency-based staff training for supported employment. In G.T. Bellamy, L.E. Rhodes, D.M. Mank, & J.M. Albin (Eds.), *Supported employment: A community implementation guide* (pp. 229–245). Baltimore: Paul H. Brookes Publishing Co.

Condon, E., Carson, B., Freeman, T., & Pellegrino, C. (1993). Employment specialist, job coach, job trainer, job coordinator, trainer, advocate: What is the professional identity of supported employment direct service personnel? *The Advance, 4*(2), 1–2.

Dileo, D., & Flippo, K. (1996). The road to certification in supported employment: Ensure professionality or reduce innovation? *Facing the future: Best practices in supported employment*. St. Augustine, FL: Training Resource Network, Inc.

Everson, J.M. (1991). Supported employment personnel: An assessment of their self-reported training needs, educational backgrounds, and previous work experiences. *Journal of the Association for Persons in Supported Employment, 16*, 140–145.

Friend, M., & Cook, L. (1992). *Interactions: Collaboration skills for school professionals*. White Plains, NY: Longman.

Grossi, T.A., & Heward, W.L. (in press). Using self-evaluation to improve the work productivity of trainees in a community-based restaurant training program. Education and Training in Mental Retardation and Developmental Disabilities.

Hanley-Maxwell, C., Bordieri, J., & Everson, J. (1990). Issues related to the preparation of administrative personnel for supported employment roles. *Rehabilitation Education, 4*, 277–286.

Heron, T.E., & Harris, K.C. (1993). *The educational consultant: Helping professionals, parents, and mainstreamed students* (3rd ed.). Austin, TX: PRO-ED.

Heward, W.L., Barbetta, P.M., Cavanaugh, R., & Grossi, T.A. (1996). *A dozen common teaching mistakes and what to do instead*. Manuscript in preparation.

Inge, K., Barcus, J.M., Brooke, V., & Everson, J. (1991). *Supported employment: Staff training manual*. Richmond: Virginia Commonwealth University, Rehabilitation Research and Training Center.

Inlander, C.B. (1993). *One hundred and fifty ways to be a savvy medical consumer*. Avenel, NJ: Random House.

Killam, S.G., Flippo, K., Drouet, R., & Keul, P. (1996). APSE's certification committee recommendations on the certification of supported employment personnel. *The Advance, 6*(4), 1–5.

Mank, D.M., Cioffi, A., & Yovanoff, J. (1996, July). *Oregon natural supports project.* Paper presented at the annual Association for Persons in Supported Employment Conference, New Orleans, LA.

Mank, D.M., & Horner, R.H. (1987). Self-recruited feedback: A cost effective procedure for maintaining behavior. *Research in Developmental Disabilities, 8,* 91–112.

Mcloughlin, C.S., Garner, J.B., & Callahan, M. (1987). *Getting employed, staying employed: Job development and training for persons with severe handicaps.* Baltimore: Paul H. Brookes Publishing Co.

Moon, M.S., Goodall, P., Barcus, M., & Brooke, V. (1986). *The supported work model of competitive employment for citizens with severe handicaps: A guide for job trainers.* Richmond: Virginia Commonwealth University, Rehabilitation Research and Training Center.

Moon, M.S., Inge, K.J., Wehman, P., Brooke, V., & Barcus, J.M. (1990). *Helping persons with severe mental retardation get and keep employment: Supported employment issues and strategies.* Baltimore: Paul H. Brookes Publishing Co.

Renzaglia, A., & Everson, J. (1990). Preparing personnel to meet the challenges of contemporary employment service alternatives. In F.R. Rusch (Ed.), *Supported employment: Policies, practices, and issues* (pp. 395–408). Sycamore, IL: Sycamore Publishing.

Rusch, F.R. (Ed.). (1990). *Supported employment: Policies, practices, and issues.* Sycamore, IL: Sycamore Publishing.

Schoor, L.B. (1988). *Within our reach: Breaking the cycle of the disadvantaged.* New York: Anchor Books.

Singer, G.H.S., & Irvin, L.K. (1991). Supporting families of persons with severe disabilities: Emerging findings, practices, and questions. In L.H. Meyer, C.A. Peck, & L. Brown (Eds.), *Critical issues in the lives of people with severe disabilities* (pp. 271–312). Baltimore: Paul H. Brookes Publishing Co.

Test, D.W., & Wood, W.M. (1997). Rocket Science 101: What supported employment specialists need to know about systematic instruction. *Journal of Vocational Rehabilitation, 9*(2), pp. 109–120.

Thoughts on certification: Results of APSE's member survey on certification of employment specialists, job coaches, and consultants. (1995, January). *The Advance, 6*(1), 4.

Wacker, D.P., & Berg, W.K. (1986). Generalizing and maintaining work behavior. In F.R. Rusch (Ed.), *Competitive employment issues and strategies* (pp. 129–140). Baltimore: Paul H. Brookes Publishing Co.

Wehman, P., Sale, P., & Parent, W. (1992). *Supported employment: Strategies for integration of workers with disabilities.* Stoneham, MA: Butterworth-Heinemann.

Wheeler, J.D. (1990). The effects of educational backgrounds and population served on the perceived training needs of employment training specialists in supported employment. *Rehabilitation Education, 4,* 347–358.

Wheeler, J.J., Bates, P., Marshall, K.J., & Miller, S.R. (1988). Teaching appropriate social behaviors to a young man with moderate mental retardation in a supported competitive employment setting. *Education and Training in Mental Retardation, 23,* 105–116.

CHAPTER

7

Supported Employment

Consumers Leading the Way

Wendy S. Parent, Alicia A. Cone,
Ed Turner, and Paul Wehman

I want to work! What do I do?
Who can help me get a job?
Where do I go to get the services I need?
What happens to my supplemental security income (SSI) if I go to work?
I don't have any transportation. How can I get to and from work?
I talked with the people at one agency, and they said they couldn't
    help me. Now where do I go?
I told the professionals what kind of job I wanted, and they said that the
    job isn't appropriate. How do I get people to listen to me?
I don't know where I want to work. How can I find out what I want to do?
The professionals asked me if I wanted to work here or there, but I don't
    want either one. How do I get them to look at other employment
    options?
I was told that I needed more time to get ready to go to work, but I
    don't want to wait. What do I have to do to get a job now?
A professional offered me a job working 20 hours a week at minimum
    wage, but that is not enough for me to live on. They said better jobs
    are hard to find. Now what do I do? If I take the job, I can't live; and

The authors thank Kathy Boes and Joan Kisicki for their assistance with writing this
chapter and for their tremendous contributions.

if I turn it down, I will be considered unmotivated and may never get another offer.

I called the agency to tell them that I found a job and needed support to learn how to do it. They told me I had to wait my turn after the many people ahead of me on the list of services. Does that mean I have to turn the job down?

I keep asking for more support on the job, but the professionals say they do not have enough funding to give me what I need. How can I get the type and amount of support that will help me be able to do my job?

I have a job, but I don't like it, and the professionals say they can't help me find another as long as I am employed. What can I do to find the job that I want?

My present job is boring and doesn't pay enough. I would like a job with more responsibility, more hours, and more money. Where can I go for help to advance my career?

All too often, individuals with severe disabilities can be heard voicing issues like these and expressing similar frustrations with their employment situations and personal experiences with the service delivery systems. Systems often are not designed to achieve their fundamental purpose: to provide individuals with assistance in achieving specific, requested goals. For example, some people want first jobs, others want to change jobs, still others want to change some aspect of their jobs, whereas others want to pursue career advancement opportunities similar to the rest of the labor force (Parent, 1996). But unlike the general population, people with disabilities face substantial obstacles and red tape that makes seemingly natural life progressions difficult to accomplish. Agency regulations, staff shortages, funding criteria, professional attitudes, and lack of knowledge contribute to the challenges associated with obtaining employment for individuals with disabilities and contribute to the challenges associated with receiving the critical supports that would allow these individuals to be successful on the job. As a result, more than two thirds of individuals with disabilities are unemployed, and many more are underemployed in low-paying, entry-level positions despite their desires for more advanced and varied career opportunities (Harris & Associates, 1994; Parent, 1996). The difference between these unfulfilling outcomes for some people with disabilities and achieving independent living and/or successful careers for others is often the degree of self-determination and level of self-advocacy skills exhibited by the two groups (Turner, 1995, West, Barcus, Brooke, & Rayfield, 1995). This chapter focuses on providing individuals with information and resources aimed at promoting the development and use of their own self-advocacy skills to achieve career fulfillment.

WHAT IS SELF-ADVOCACY, AND WHY IS IT IMPORTANT?

To many people, self-advocacy is defined as advocating on one's own behalf, but that definition only touches the surface. Williams and Shoultz (1982) described self-advocacy as people individually and/or in groups speaking and/or acting on behalf of themselves, on behalf of others, or on behalf of issues that affect individuals with developmental disabilities. For Williams and Shoultz, the keys to self-advocacy are people pursuing their own interests, being aware of their rights, and joining with others to pursue issues of the group and of individuals with developmental disabilities in general. In September 1991, a definition of self-advocacy was approved at the Second Annual People First Conference and appeared in an article by Nelis (1994) (see Chapter 1). This definition emphasizes the importance of people with disabilities working together to learn their rights, responsibilities, and decision-making skills so that they can speak for themselves about their wants and beliefs. Another group, Self-Advocates Becoming Empowered, offers a similar definition:

> [Self-advocates] believe that people with disabilities should be treated as equals. That means that people should be given the same decisions, choices, rights, responsibilities and chances to speak up to empower themselves as well as to make new friendships and renew old friendships just like everyone else. They should also be able to learn from their mistakes like everyone else. (1994, p. 2)

It is important to understand the sense of community and unity of the self-advocacy movement. Self-advocacy is not self-involved or self-centered. It is a statement by people with disabilities that they want to be seen as people who have something to offer and skills to share, rather than to be seen as people with "handicaps" or "limitations" (People First of Washington, n.d.-a; n.d.-b). Self-advocacy is a social rights movement that is about building alliances and coalitions and about working together to achieve personal and group goals. Self-advocates look out for one another, learn from each other, and fight discrimination against great odds and often at a high personal cost.

Why should people with disabilities *self*-advocate? Are there not kind and caring advocates who could speak for individuals with disabilities? Hoffman (1992) offered perhaps the best reason of all: Individuals with disabilities are the experts about their disabilities. Every day they learn things, teach things, and see things from the point of view of people with disabilities.

People with disabilities cannot rely on others to enhance their life opportunities, to promote progressive public policies and research, and to advance services that address individual choices and human rights. To accomplish these goals, it is imperative that individuals with disabilities self-advocate so that policy makers, educators, service providers, and any other person who supports them, hears and understands the point of view of people with disabilities. Decisions that affect and that have an impact on the future of people with disabilities must reflect their input and guidance.

Experienced self-advocates have identified three major reasons for advocating for competitive community employment: 1) People with disabilities have a right to real wages for real jobs; 2) sheltered work is really exploitation; and 3) anyone can be trained and or supported to do a real job in the community (Johnson, 1996; T. Nelis, personal communication, May 30, 1996).

As of 1996, there were more than 125,000 individuals participating in supported employment nationwide (Virginia Commonwealth University, Rehabilitation Research and Training Center, 1996). There are still, however, countless others who are unemployed or underemployed (e.g., in sheltered workshops) who should be competitively employed.

In general, self-advocating is important in the area of employment because if an individual is not working, self-advocacy will help him or her find a job; and if an individual's current employment is not meeting his or her needs, self-advocacy will help him or her locate better opportunities. Specifically, people who self-advocate during an employment search will be able to identify the job they want, specify the working conditions, determine the wage level, select the job location, and decide the hours that will be worked (Wehman, 1992). When self-advocating leads to obtaining competitive employment, an individual—often for the first time—has a choice in the labor force, earns a decent wage, develops a real work history, and realizes community inclusiveness (Wehman, 1992).

The bottom line is that if an individual with a disability is going to benefit from employment, that person must be supportive of, involved with, and have input into every phase of the employment process. Learning the skills necessary to be an effective self-advocate is one sound strategy for ensuring that a person's interests, choices, preferences, and decisions are heard and followed. Therefore, the focus of the rest of this chapter is on practical strategies for enhancing self-advocacy skills, with an emphasis on supported employment. Specifically, the chapter describes the concept of supported employment, discusses the role of key people and agencies, presents tips on making choices and ensuring that one's voice is heard, and highlights strategies for developing self-advocacy skills.

WHAT CONSUMERS AND ADVOCATES NEED TO KNOW

The primary resource to help people get the jobs and supports that they would like is for them to know what jobs and support options are available and if the resources are lacking, to know what potentially could be available to assist them with becoming employed. It is impossible for an individual to make informed decisions or to adequately pursue something that is very important with incomplete or inaccurate information. A major criticism reported by people with disabilities is that professionals do not provide them with complete information to allow them to make fully informed choices (Brooke, Barcus, & Inge, 1992; West & Parent, 1992). Rather, professionals often share only what they know, which may be limited in scope or based on personal judgment; they pre-screen and selectively choose information without the consumer's input; or they phrase questions in an "either/or" format that greatly restricts the consumer's options. The only way to truly make choices is to know what is available, to know what potential exists, to know what is needed to obtain it, and to have the critical skills to make it happen. Knowledge is power, and individuals with disabilities need to "know" if they are going to be able to accomplish their career and life goals.

WHAT IS SUPPORTED EMPLOYMENT?

Supported employment is a vocational option that provides people with disabilities with individualized supports that will assist them with achieving their employment goals (Wehman & Kregel, 1985; Wehman, Sale, & Parent, 1992). Supported employment allows an individual with disabilities to obtain competitive work in typical businesses in the community doing the same kinds of jobs as people without disabilities. Individuals earn comparable wages, work regular hours, perform their jobs among co-workers without disabilities, and have access to opportunities for climbing the career ladder.

Supported employment was developed for those individuals with severe disabilities who need intensive support to find a job, to learn how to do a job, to keep a job, and/or to deal with the multitude of work-related issues that can affect one's employment. Supported employment focuses on work, not on getting ready for work, not on having all of the skills before going to work, and not on meeting human services criteria before entering the competitive job market. An individual must simply want to work and meet the requirements specified in the Rehabilitation Act Amendments of 1992 (PL 102-569). This law defined support employment as follows:

The term "supported employment" means competitive work in integrated work settings for individuals with the most severe disabilities for whom competitive employment has not traditionally occurred; or for whom competitive employment has been interrupted or intermittent as a result of a severe disability; and who, because of the nature and severity of their disability, need intensive supported employment services . . . and extended services . . . to perform such work. (§706[18][A])

A person who is provided with supported employment should be served at his or her current skill level, and the supports should bridge the gap between the individual's skills and the requirements of the job. Supported employment is targeted to those individuals who have traditionally been unemployed or underemployed, to those who are idle at home, to those who are participating in sheltered workshops, or to those who are enrolled in ongoing training or readiness programs. In fact, if someone has been told that he or she must get ready to go to work, that he or she is unemployable because of a disability that is too severe, or that a workshop situation would be the most appropriate placement, then it is likely that the person would be a good candidate for supported employment. A job coach or employment specialist can be a key participant in the process of securing a job with accepting overall responsibility for ensuring that any issue that can affect an individual's employment is addressed.

WHAT IS THE ROLE OF THE JOB COACH?

Supported employment services are provided by a job coach or employment specialist who is responsible for conducting individualized consumer assessments, contacting employers and locating jobs, making job placement arrangements, providing jobsite training, assisting with work-related issues, and providing ongoing support (Brooke, Inge, Armstrong, & Wehman, 1997). Each of these roles is explored in more detail in the next section. In general, however, the role of the job coach is multifaceted and includes anything related to the individual's employment situation. Individuals can choose the extent and intensity with which they would like the job coach to be involved: The job coach may assist at every level, assist just for particular activities, or act only "behind the scenes." No matter the degree of job coach assistance an individual would prefer, it is important to be aware that the role of the job coach is to provide direct services, to coordinate or facilitate a variety of supports, or to assist the individual with gaining access to whatever services or assistance that is desired (Brooke, Wehman, Inge, & Parent, 1995; Wehman & Melia, 1985).

In many cases, a single fear or a general fear of the unknown (e.g., concern about losing SSI benefits, making new friends, finding transportation) can interfere with an individual's decision to go to work. Just by knowing what the job coach can do, by knowing the resources that he or she can share, and by having him or her available to answer questions as they arise can alleviate many concerns and are often the catalysts that can have a positive impact on an individual's employment outcome.

Conducting Individualized Consumer Assessments

The major focus of assessment is getting to know the individual. The job coach should spend time with the person and his or her family or advocate to share information about supported employment, to find out their interests and lifestyles, and to respond to any questions or ideas that anyone may have. It is paramount that the job coach schedule a time that is convenient to the individual in a comfortable location, such as at his or her home or at a restaurant over lunch, and that the visits be repeated several times. Without informal time together it is unlikely that each will begin to build rapport and get to know one another; it is also unlikely that the person's desires, dreams, and preferences will ever truly be made known.

In addition, other sources of assessment information through records, observation, or interviews can be identified such as educational background, previous employment or work experience, community-based training or volunteer activities, significant people or services providers, and so on. Community and situational assessments are other ways that the job coach and individual can spend time together exploring his or her skills and interests. At the same time, these assessments enhance opportunities for making choices about the job and employment situation (e.g., type of business, location, environment, coworkers, supervision) (Moon, Inge, Wehman, Brooke, & Barcus, 1990; Parent, Unger, Gibson, & Clements, 1994).

Contacting Employers and Locating Jobs

The primary emphasis of job development is to find a job that best matches the preferences and chosen job attributes expressed by the individual. The job coach uses knowledge gained about the business community through labor market screening activities (Nietupski, Verstegen, & Petty, 1995) and the information shared by the individual during assessment activities to identify and explore potential jobs that might be of interest. In essence, the job coach functions as the eyes of the person by assessing the job on the critical elements important to the individual, which is similar to anyone who approaches an employer for possible employment.

Through employer contacts, discussions with key personnel, and observations of a given business, the job coach can determine the employer's expectations, the specific job requirements, and the supports already available in the work setting. Frequent and ongoing communication between the individual and job coach can ensure that job development is moving in the direction that the consumer would like. In addition, the sharing of information discovered from employers, job openings that have been explored, and particular aspects of different kinds of positions can help the individual make choices based on actual availability.

Making Job Placement Arrangements

Once a job is found, the job coach assists the individual with the many activities to be completed to secure and start the job. Accompanying the consumer on an interview with the employer, negotiating work schedules and job accommodations, advocating on behalf of the new employee, "breaking the ice" to help everyone get to know one another, and sizing up the availability of worksite supports and their accessibility are a few of the many responsibilities completed before the first day of work. In addition, the job coach is available to ensure completion of necessary employment forms, Social Security reporting and documentation, transportation arrangements and training, and any other activities related to commencement of the individual's work.

Providing Jobsite Training and Assisting with Work-Related Issues

A unique feature of supported employment is that an individual does not need to know how to do the job or to be at a certain level before he or she can begin working. Instead, the job coach accompanies the individual to work beginning the very first day of employment and provides training directly at the jobsite while the actual work is being performed. The worker is paid minimum wage or more during this training period. The job coach teaches the job duties in the context in which they occur while ensuring that the work is completed as expected. In addition, the job coach can facilitate social relationships by supporting and modeling for the individual and co-workers. It is important to note that it is within the role of the job coach to act as an employee of the company during the training period, wearing similar clothing and following the same rules and schedules as everyone else. Acting as an employee is essential for the job coach to learn the true social culture of the workplace so to better facilitate "fitting in" for the new employee and "tapping into" the natural supports on the job.

Bridging the Gap   The job coach offers a variety of support resources and options aimed at bridging the gap between what the individual can do and what is expected by the employer. These can include behavioral training techniques, compensatory strategies, rehabilitation engineering, assistive technology, community and workplace supports, job modifications, job carving, and job sharing (Brooke et al., 1997; Unger, Parent, Gibson, & Kane, 1997). The job coach should be knowledgeable about different support alternatives and should be resourceful at making them available to the individual. The job coach also should provide whatever degree of assistance is necessary to allow the worker to choose the support that best matches his or her personal preferences, learning style, training needs, and the worksite environment. Regular communication among the job coach, the individual, the individual's family or advocates, and employer is critical to proactively address any problems or issues, monitor satisfaction of all parties, and keep all stakeholders informed of events affecting the employment situation.

Provide Ongoing Support

Once the individual has mastered the job and is satisfied with his or her current work status, the job coach gradually reduces time with him or her, both on and off the jobsite. Another unique aspect of supported employment, however, is the availability of the job coach to assist, on an ongoing basis, with issues and support needs as they arise. These issues can be job related, such as a change in supervision, new work responsibilities, or desire for career advancement or to change jobs; or they can be personal, such as a change in living arrangements or conflict with a co-worker. Ongoing support can take the form of making telephone calls, visiting on the job or at home, observing work performance, completing supervisor evaluations, conducting personal satisfaction measures, and using other data collection procedures on a regular basis. It is important to note that the provision of long-term supports is continuous and ongoing for the duration of the individual's employment and is not only on an as-needed or on a time-limited basis.

WHICH AGENCIES CAN ASSIST WITH OBTAINING SUPPORTED EMPLOYMENT SERVICES?

The criteria for determining who is responsible for supported employment services delivery often is based on funding structures and disability labels, which vary from state to state. The primary agencies that play a critical role are the school systems, vocational rehabilitation agencies, mental health/mental retardation or developmental disability agencies, and supported employment providers. Typically, an individual will be referred to a vocational rehabilitation agency for initial employment activities. On determining eligibility for services and benefits from supported employment, the vocational rehabilitation agency will contract with a supported employment provider for assistance from a job coach. This time-limited phase, beginning at the start of employment and continuing through jobsite training, is typically funded by the vocational rehabilitation agency and can last up to 18 months. Individuals who are in school can receive supported employment services directly from their school or can be referred to a provider, who is paid for by the individuals' education programs. It is extremely important that linkage and involvement with vocational rehabilitation be made regardless of whether funding is provided. The vocational rehabilitation system is the service system for adults, which is similar to the school system for youth and young adults; however, it is important to note that rehabilitation is an eligibility—not an entitlement—program, and application must be made to utilize any or all of an agency's services.

The extended services, or follow-along, phase is initiated at the end of the time-limited phase. The extended services phases begins at the point of stabilization and lasts for as long as the individual is employed. Definitions and criteria for determining stabilization can vary across states but generally indicate a time when individuals require less intensive support to maintain their jobs. For example, in Virginia, stabilization occurs when job coach intervention time is reduced to 20% or less for 4 consecutive weeks (Virginia Department of Rehabilitative Services, 1994). In many cases, this interagency transfer involves a shift in funding only, with no disruption in services; in other cases, changes occur with both the funding source and the provider. For example, sometimes the funding system will shift from vocational rehabilitation to the mental health/mental retardation agency, but the job coach who provides services will remain the same. Similarly, other situations will involve a change in job coaches from one provider to another provider or agency in addition to a change in funding sources.

A variety of agencies can be responsible for extended services; the mental health/mental retardation or developmental disability agencies, however, are the most frequent. Examples of other funding sources include Medicaid Waiver or through the Job Training Partnership Act of 1982 (PL 97-300); other state agencies, such as the Department of Labor; and Social Security Work Incentives, such as Plans for Achieving Self Support or Impairment Related Work Expense. A critical factor limiting the number of participants in supported employment is the lack of extended services funding sources or providers. Without a commitment of extended services, the initial time-limited services through vocational rehabilitation cannot be initiated. For those individuals who do not qualify for services from the designated agencies, for those who do not have service providers in their localities, or for those who face tremendously long waiting lists for extended services, creative and innovative approaches in the provision of on-going supports can be developed and implemented (Parent et al., 1994).

Determining which agency is responsible for certain activities is critical for gaining access to desired services and supports. Table 1 highlights the roles of key people who represent the major agencies involved with supported employment. Armed with reasonable expectations for the services provided by different agencies, a consumer is in a better position to advocate for high-quality assistance. More specific information about a particular agency can be acquired through a telephone call, or better yet, through a personal meeting. It may take several calls to find the right agency and to identify the appropriate person within the organization; but once an appropriate person or agency is identified, it is useful to gather as much information as possible, which will facilitate present and future planning for services.

WHAT ARE THE CONSUMER'S AND FAMILY MEMBERS' ROLES?

In any endeavor, the first step to getting what one wants is determining what it is that is desired. It is important to think about an individual's dreams and goals and the pathways to making them realities without being limited by other people's past expectations for the individual. The Individual Supports Assessment Form located in Appendix A can be a useful tool for exploring job characteristics and creative support options that might be of interest to an individual. Other strategies to assist with the discovery of available resources include visiting businesses in the community, talking to people who are employed, meeting with employers, attending job fairs, and looking at the newspaper. Through simple awareness, stakeholders can help generate potential job opportunities for the individual. For example, when shopping at the grocery store, a family member could glance around to see what different employees are doing or could approach the manager about potential openings.

On a similar scale, it is critical to try out new experiences and get involved with activities in the local community. The best job leads and employment information often come from personal acquaintances during informal conversations and participation in mutual events. For example, joining a civic organization, taking a personal development course, pursuing a hobby, or forming an interest group can provide a forum for communication. Not only does this open up doors to new opportunities, but also these additional experiences contribute important information for building an impressive resumé. A worksheet and an example of a functional resumé that can help in the employment search is located in Appendix B.

Table 1. Roles of key people involved in supported employment services delivery

Teacher	Rehabilitation counselor	Service coordinator
• Provide community-based work experiences.	• Meet with the individual and his or her family or advocate.	• Determine the individual's needs and preferences.
• Teach self-advocacy skills.	• Explore the individual's career interests.	• Learn what school and other adult service agencies have to offer.
• Learn what adult and community agencies have to offer.	• Find out individual preferences for jobs, services, and supports.	• Share information about available services and supports.
• Visit businesses and find out their expectations/requirements.	• Learn what school and other adult service agencies have to offer.	• Arrange desired services and supports (e.g., health, employment, housing, recreation, financial, education).
• Communicate with the student and family.	• Share information about all available service and support options.	• Coordinate on-going services and supports.
• Help with exploring career goals.	• Participate in transition planning meetings.	• Communicate regularly with key people.
• Assist with determining learning styles, support needs, and support preferences.	• Assist with identifying individual choices.	• Advocate on behalf of the consumer.
• Participate in transition planning meeting.	• Develop a plan for achieving the individual's career goals (e.g., objectives, people responsible, timelines).	
• Develop an individual profile (e.g., community-based assessment information, types of supports, functional resumé).	• Communicate regularly with school, supported employment, and other adult service agency representatives.	
• Share information with adult services.	• Refer individual for supported employment services.	
• Find a job before the individual leaves school.	• Arrange employment-related services and supports.	
• Provide technical assistance at the job site.	• Monitor quality and effectiveness of supported employment services and related supports.	
	• Advocate on behalf of the consumer.	

It is important to learn as much as possible about the service delivery system and about any agencies that could potentially provide assistance. This can be accomplished by calling and visiting an organization, asking a representative to come and speak to a group of interested people, interviewing service providers, talking with people receiving services, and requesting to observe the activities of different agencies. Other valuable sources of information can be informal networking with other individuals with disabilities who have sought employment and their parents, participating in an interagency planning meeting (e.g., individualized education program, individualized written rehabilitation program, individualized transition plan, individualized habilitation plan), attending workshops and conferences that emphasize topics of interest, reviewing consumer and professional materials and publications, and accessing computerized resources such as the Internet and World Wide Web pages.

After deciding on goals and discovering the types of supports that could be available, the next step is to communicate these preferences to the appropriate professionals. If the professionals do not try to elicit the consumer's goals, it is sometimes necessary for the individual and his or her stakeholders to initiate this communication. A consumer who is encouraged to specify his or her personal preferences has a higher likelihood of receiving the type and amount of assistance needed. The amount of time and effort spent gathering information and exploring the consumer's personal preferences is a key to gaining fulfilling supported employment; the stakeholders can and should play important roles in this process. Table 2 provides a listing of the activities and responsibilities that individuals and their family members or friends

Table 2.   Role of the consumer and family members in supported employment

- Determine your expectations.
- Explore career opportunities.
- Participate in a variety of experiences.
- Learn what adult and community services have to offer.
- Find out information about supported employment.
- Talk with other parents and individuals.
- Ask questions and persevere until you receive needed information.
- Participate in all individualized planning meetings (e.g., IEP, ITP, IWRP).
- Share your ideas and preferences with school, adult service, and supported employment professionals.
- Actively participate in decisions.
- Advocate for yourself or on behalf of your son, daughter, or relative.
- Don't give up.

can undertake to make the journey to successful supported employment a little easier.

HOW CAN SOMEONE BECOME A SKILLED SELF-ADVOCATE?

A crucial step in becoming a successful self-advocate or an advocate for a person with disabilities is to remember that the "customer is always right." These words often ring hollow when individuals with disabilities seek the supports they need to live self-defined lives of quality. For this phrase to have meaning in the disability field, the service delivery system needs to respond to requests for services as though individuals with disabilities were customers (Turner, 1994b). Furthermore, agency personnel and individuals with disabilities need to recognize the rights of people with disabilities as mandated under various legislation (e.g., Rehabilitation Act Amendments of 1992 [PL 102-569], the Americans with Disabilities Act [ADA] of 1990 [PL 101-336], the Individuals with Disabilities Education Act of 1990 [PL 101-476], the Individuals with Disabilities Education Act Amendments [IDEA] of 1997 [PL 105-17]). The most significant general "right" is the right to choose services that the individual believes to be the most appropriate for his or her individual needs (Turner, 1994b).

In the business world, in general, customer satisfaction is extremely important and is used to measure the success of those selling goods and services (see Chapter 6). That has typically not been true in the disability field. Traditionally, customers with disabilities who seek supported employment services have found themselves in the position of either having to accept what they are given or receiving no services. It has been only through long, difficult, and vigilant systems change advocacy efforts that individuals with disabilities have begun to see themselves as customers and to demand that services system personnel do so as well. As customers, individuals with disabilities must realize they have the right to expect services of the highest quality and tailored to their specific needs (Turner, 1994b). The following section describes some important tips that can help individuals with disabilities become satisfied customers. Self-advocacy is one influential strategy for accomplishing that goal.

The most powerful self-advocacy training tool is self-confidence. People who have self-confidence 1) are sure of themselves, 2) feel comfortable with themselves, 3) believe in their own abilities, 4) present a positive image of themselves, and 5) know what they want and ask for it (Turner, 1994a). Many individuals with disabilities, unfortunately, have learned to be passive because they are overwhelmed by parents and professionals telling them what they can or cannot do. For example, doctors and therapists may set limits on activities because a person has a disability, overprotective parents may instill fear by cautioning their children to play carefully, psychologists may cite test results that discourage learning, or guidance or vocational counselors may give limited career options based on types of disabilities (Turner, 1994a). As a result, many individuals often are limited in the knowledge and experiences to which they have been exposed, which affects their confidence and ability to advocate for themselves. Table 3 illustrates the importance of self-confidence and its impact on self-advocacy (Turner, 1994a).

Several key factors are associated with successfully advocating for the services and supports to assist an individual in all aspects of his or her life including employment, independent living, education, and personal assistance. The "Six B's of Self-Advocacy" are as follows: 1) Be self-confident, 2) Be informed, 3) Be assertive, 4) Become a proficient self-advocate, 5) Be persistent, and 6) Be familiar with the chain of command (Turner, 1995). Table 4 provides examples of each "B" for use in advocating for vocational services and supported employment. Table 5 offers strategies for becoming a self-advocate, for building self-advocacy skills, and for helping others develop self-advocacy skills.

CONCLUSION

The power and impact of self-advocacy by people with disabilities is enhanced by several key factors at the individual, local, state, and national levels. First, individuals with disabilities are the experts and need to be viewed as such. Seasoned self-advocates readily acknowledge that they are not professionals in the field of disability. In fact, they quickly add that they do not desire to be a professional or professionalized.

Table 3. Reasons why self-confidence is so powerful

Self-confidence allows individuals to
- Ask questions without fear
- Set agendas so that their issues will be addressed
- Speak up for themselves
- Be assertive, but not aggressive
- Not be intimidated by authority figures
- Be self-assured when meeting with others
- Project confidence through their body language
- Believe what they have to say is important
- Be unafraid to ask as many questions as it takes to understand an issue
- Know when they are right
- Keep calm but be firm in confrontational situations

Table 4. The "Six B's of self advocacy"

1. Be self-confident.
   - Act like a customer shopping for a service.
   - Don't be intimidated.
   - Keep eye contact at all times.
2. Be informed.
   - Become familiar with the service requested.
   - Learn the eligibility requirements.
   - Ask follow-up questions to be sure you understand.
3. Be assertive.
   - Set timelines when you expect to get answers about services.
   - If timelines are not met, call again.
   - Be courteous but serious.
4. Become a proficient self-advocate.
   - Know what you want.
   - Establish a reputation of one who usually gets what he or she goes after.
   - Learn how to negotiate so you will always get your bottom line.
5. Be persistent.
   - Keep calling or asking until they answer your requests for services.
   - If "no" is the answer, ask why.
   - Never take "no" the first time.
6. Be familiar with the chain of command.
   - If not satisfied with the counselor's responses, ask for the supervisor.
   - If not satisfied with the supervisor's answer, ask to speak with their supervisor and keep moving up.

Reprinted from *Journal of Vocational Rehabilitation*, 5, Turner, E., Self-advocacy: A key to Self-determination, 334, copyright 1995, with kind permission from Elsevier Science Ireland Ltd., Bay 15K, Shannon Industrial Estate, Co. Clare, Ireland.

What they do want and demand is the recognition and respect they deserve as *experts* on their disabilities, the impact of disability on their lives, and the supports they need so they can live how they want.

Second, agencies need to adopt new management and service delivery styles that are based on consumer-directed policies and procedures. Recommended practices in supporting people with disabilities come from service providers who follow the principles of customer choice, customer control, full societal and community inclusion, community–business partnerships and supports, total quality management, and person-centered planning (Brooke et al. 1995).

Third, professionals and more experienced self-advocates must support training designed to prepare individuals with disabilities as self-advocates. This includes, but is not limited to, asking people what their training needs are, asking people who best to support training opportunities, locating training, working with trainers to develop more self-advocacy training, and supporting people to attend workshops and training sessions.

Table 5. Strategies for becoming a skilled self-advocate

Pair up with someone who has been through it before.

Establish informal networks with individuals who want the same things.

Participate in trainings, workshops, and conferences aimed at consumers and/or professionals.

Attend leadership institutes and self-advocacy training seminars.

Join and become actively involved in other self-advocacy groups.

Link up with a seasoned mentor to provide on-going guidance and assistance.

Contact a Center for Independent Living for information, resources, and support.

Learn as much as you can by gathering information from as many sources as possible.

Become affiliated with professional organizations.

Practice, practice, practice!

Fourth, the development of newer self-advocates as leaders needs to be promoted and supported by professionals and by more experienced self-advocates. Examples of strategies for accomplishing this are to encourage new self-advocates to participate in public forums in which they express their views and share their ideas, to invite beginner self-advocates to be on boards and committees (Note: It is important to make sure individuals have the necessary supports to be full participating members), to develop leadership training curriculums and opportunities, to disseminate information on available leadership curriculums and training sessions, to provide leadership training sessions, and to network with self-advocates on projects (e.g., policy position papers, lobbying efforts, fact sheets, grant writing, program development and evaluation).

TAMMY: THE POWER OF SELF-ADVOCACY

Before attending the Rehabilitation Research and Training Center on Supported Employment's Self Advocacy Leadership Institute, I had great difficulty in finding a job of my choice.

During the Institute, I learned about my employment rights under the Americans with Disabilities Act and my right to select vocational services that would best lead me to a job. I also learned about self-advocacy skills in order to take full advantage of those rights. I learned how to be assertive enough to speak up for myself and how to let my vocational counselor know that I had the right to choose a job close to my home and that I needed to learn how to drive.

Shortly after the Institute, I heard of a job opening in the food services division of a nursing home close to my home. I applied and got the job. Now my vocational counselor is assisting me to obtain training so that I will be able to drive to and from work.

I am very excited about my job and about what I learned at the Institute, I am a member of my local people-first chapter, and I am teaching others about how to use self-advocacy to make things happen in their lives. Knowing how to use self-advocacy has made a difference in my life, and it can do the same for you.

REFERENCES

Americans with Disabilities Act (ADA) of 1990, PL 101-336, 42 U.S.C. §§ 12101 et seq.

Brooke, V., Barcus, J.M., & Inge, K. (Eds.). (1992). Consumer advocacy and supported employment: A vision for the future. Richmond: Virginia Commonwealth University, Rehabilitation Research and Training Center.

Brooke, V., Inge, K., Armstrong, A., & Wehman, P. (1997). Supported employment handbook: A customer-driven approach for persons with significant disabilities. Richmond: Virginia Commonwealth University, Rehabilitation Research and Training Center.

Brooke, V., Wehman, P., Inge, K., & Parent, W. (1995). Toward a customer-driven approach of supported employment. Education and Training Mental Retardation and Developmental Disabilities, 30(4), 308–320.

Carabello, B.J., & Siegel, J.F. (1996). Self-advocacy at the crossroads. In G. Dydwad & H. Bersani, Jr. (Eds.), New voices self-advocacy by people with disabilities (pp. 237–239). Cambridge, MA: Brookline Books.

Harris, L., & Associates. (1994). The National Organization on Disability/Harris Survey on Employment of People with Disabilities. New York: Author.

Hoffman, M. (1992). Leadership plus. Tulsa, OK: Tulsa Arc.

Individuals with Disabilities Education Act (IDEA) Amendments of 1997, PL 105-17, 20 U.S.C. §§ 1400 et seq.

Individuals with Disabilities Education Act (IDEA) of 1990, PL 101-476, 20 U.S.C. §§ 1400 et seq.

Job Training Partnership Act of 1982, PL 97-300, 29 U.S.C. §§ 1501 et seq.

Johnson, J. (1996). Self-advocates speak out during APSE's pre-conference self-advocacy workshop. The Advance, 6(4), 10–11.

Moon, M.S., Inge, K.J., Wehman, P., Brooke, V., & Barcus, J.M. (1990). Helping persons with severe mental retardation get and keep employment: Supported employment strategies and outcomes. Baltimore: Paul H. Brookes Publishing Co.

Nelis, T. (1994). Self-advocacy: Realizing a dream. Impact, 7(1), 1.

Nietupski, J., Verstegen, D., & Petty, D.M. (1995). The job development handbook: A guide for facilitating employer decisions to hire people with disabilities. Knoxville: University of Tennessee.

Parent, W. (1996). Consumer choice and satisfaction in supported employment. Journal of Vocational Rehabilitation, 6(1), 23–30.

Parent, W., Unger, D., Gibson, K., & Clements, C. (1994). The role of the job coach: Orchestrating community and workplace supports. American Rehabilitation, 20(3), 2–11.

People First of Washington (no date-a). Self advocacy is. Tacoma, WA: Author.

People First of Washington (no date-b). A community where self-advocacy grows. Clarkston, WA: Author.

Rehabilitation Act Amendments of 1992, PL 102-569, 29 U.S.C. §§ 701 et seq.

Self-Advocates Becoming Empowered. (1994). *Taking place.* Tulsa, OK: People First of Oklahoma.

Turner, E. (1994a). *A self advocacy training tool: Self confidence.* Presented at the Self-Advocacy Leadership Institute, Virginia Commonwealth University, Rehabilitation Research and Training Center on Supported Employment, Richmond.

Turner, E. (1994b). The customer is right! *The Customer Is Right, 1*(1), 1–2.

Turner, E. (1995). Self-advocacy: A key to self determination. *Journal of Vocational Rehabilitation, 5,* 329–336.

Unger, D., Parent, W., Gibson, K., & Kane, K. (1997). *Natural supports in supported employment: An employment specialist's guide for maximizing community and workplace supports.* Richmond: Virginia Commonwealth University, Rehabilitation Research and Training Center.

Virginia Commonwealth University, Rehabilitation Research and Training Center. (1996). *National marketing initiative fact sheet: Part two.* Richmond: Author.

Virginia Department of Rehabilitative Services. (1994). *Virginia guide to supported employment and job coach training services.* Richmond: Author.

Wehman, P. (1992). Consumer advocacy and supported employment. In V. Brooke, M. Barcus, & K. Inge (Eds.), *Consumer advocacy and supported employment: A vision for the future* (pp. 1–12). Richmond: Virginia Commonwealth University, Rehabilitation Research and Training Center.

Wehman, P., & Kregel, J. (1985). A supported work approach to competitive employment of individuals with moderate and severe handicaps. In P. Wehman & J.W. Hill (Eds.), *Competitive employment for persons with mental retardation: From research to practice.* (Monograph, Vol. 1). Richmond: Virginia Commonwealth University, Rehabilitation Research and Training Center.

Wehman, P., & Melia, R. (1985). The job coach: Function in transitional and supported employment. *American Rehabilitation, 11*(2), 4–7.

Wehman, P., Sale, P., & Parent, W.S. (Eds.). (1992). *Supported employment: Strategies for integration of workers with disabilities.* Boston, MA: Andover.

West, M.D., Barcus, J.M., Brooke, V., & Rayfield, R.G. (1995). An exploratory analysis of self-determination of persons with disabilities. *Journal of Vocational Rehabilitation, 5*(4), 357–364.

West, M.D., & Parent, W.S. (1992). Consumer choice and empowerment in supported employment services: Issues and strategies. *Journal of The Association for Persons with Severe Handicaps, 17*(1), 47–52.

Williams, P., & Shoultz, B. (1982). *We can speak for ourselves.* Bloomington: Indiana University Press.

APPENDIX A

Individual Supports
Assessment Form

Individual Supports Assessment Form

Date _____   Provider ID _____

Consumer's Name _____ SS# _____

Employment Specialist _____ ID Code _____

Address _____

Initial Assessment _____ Ongoing Assessment _____

Please answer each question regarding the consumer's current goals, preferences, and experiences. Information needed to respond to each question
should be obtained from the consumer during a face-to-face interview prior to
placement into employment or while working if a change in employment situation is desired.

I. VOCATIONAL GOALS AND EXPERIENCES

1. **What are your career and life goals?** (Describe the job or position you
    would like to have and any other goals that you would like to pursue
    [e.g., school, independent living].)

2. **Where might you like to work?** (Check all that apply.)

    _____   1) restaurant
    _____   2) grocery store
    _____   3) retail store
    _____   4) hospital/nursing home
    _____   5) office building
    _____   6) hotel/motel
    _____   7) university/school
    _____   8) child care facility
    _____   9) factory
    _____   10) service provider/agency (e.g., church, park)
    _____   11) don't know
    _____   99) other (describe: _____)

Developed by the Rehabilitation and Training Center on Supported Employment, Virginia Commonwealth University, Natural Supports Transition Project (1994).

3a. What type of job might you like to have? (Check all that apply.)

    ___   1) dishwasher/kitchen utility worker
    ___   2) food preparation person
    ___   3) food server
    ___   4) busperson/lobby attendant
    ___   5) janitor/housekeeper
    ___   6) laborer
    ___   7) assembler
    ___   8) laundry worker
    ___   9) stock clerk/bagger/warehouse worker
    ___   10) machine operator
    ___   11) clerical/office worker
    ___   12) groundskeeper/landscaper
    ___   13) human service worker
    ___   14) don't know
    ___   99) other (describe: _____)

b. Is there anyone that you know who works in the places or in a position that you might like to have and that you wouldn't mind us contacting?

Name	Relationship	Phone #	Employment
1.			
2.			
3.			
4.			

4. What types of things might be important to you in working in the position of your choice? (Check all that apply.)

    ___   1) hours
    ___   2) benefits (e.g., paid vacations, sick leave, employee discount)
    ___   3) health insurance
    ___   4) wages
    ___   5) location of business
    ___   6) co-workers
    ___   7) work environment
    ___   8) nothing/don't know
    ___   99) other (describe: _____)

5. Have you ever been employed in a paid job before?

___ 1) yes
___ 2) no

a. If yes, where did you work, and what was your job title?

1. _____

2. _____

3. _____

6. Have you participated in any other work experiences (e.g., volunteer work, vocational training)?

___ 1) yes
___ 2) no

a. If yes, describe the work that you did.

_____

_____

7. Who might you like to assist you in finding a job? (Check all that apply.)

___ 1) parents
___ 2) siblings
___ 3) relatives
___ 4) girlfriend/boyfriend/spouse
___ 5) friends
___ 6) community member (describe: _____)
___ 7) professional (describe: _____)
___ 8) no one/don't know
___ 99) other (describe: _____)

8. In what ways would you be willing to help with finding a job? (Check all that apply.)

___ 1) identify job leads
___ 2) look in the newspaper
___ 3) contact employers
___ 4) pick up job applications
___ 5) develop a resume
___ 6) none/don't know
___ 99) other (describe: _____)

9. **What means of transportation would you be willing to use to get to and from work?** (Check all that apply.)

    ___   1) drive self
    ___   2) friend or family member transport
    ___   3) walk
    ___   4) ride a bicycle
    ___   5) ride a bus
    ___   6) use a taxi
    ___   7) carpool
    ___   8) ride with co-workers
    ___   9) use specialized transportation
    ___   10) none/don't know
    ___   99) other (describe: _____)

II. INTERESTS

10. **What do you do during your free time?** (Check all that apply.)

    ___   1) watch television
    ___   2) shop/go to mall
    ___   3) participate in organized recreational or sporting activities
    ___   4) go to sporting events
    ___   5) go bowling
    ___   6) roller skate/in-line skate/ice skate
    ___   7) read books or magazines
    ___   8) go to movies
    ___   9) listen to music
    ___   10) go to concerts
    ___   11) hang out with friends
    ___   12) go dancing
    ___   13) talk on the telephone
    ___   14) engage in hobbies
    ___   15) do arts and crafts
    ___   16) do nothing/don't know
    ___   99) other (describe: _____)

11. **Are there other things you would like to do during your free time?**

    ___   1) yes
    ___   2) no

a. **If yes, what kinds of things would you like to do?** (Check all that apply.)

    ___   1) watch television
    ___   2) shop/go to mall
    ___   3) participate in organized recreational or sporting activities

___ 4) go to sporting events
___ 5) go bowling
___ 6) roller skate/in-line skate/ice skate
___ 7) read books or magazines
___ 8) go to movies
___ 9) listen to music
___ 10) go to concerts
___ 11) hang out with friends
___ 12) go dancing
___ 13) talk on the telephone
___ 14) engage in hobbies
___ 15) do arts and crafts
___ 99) other (describe: _____)

12. With whom do you usually spend your free time? (Check all that apply.)

___ 1) friends
___ 2) girlfriend/boyfriend/spouse
___ 3) parents
___ 4) siblings
___ 5) relatives
___ 6) neighbors
___ 7) peers (e.g., students, workshop participants)
___ 8) general public
___ 9) no one
___ 99) other (describe: _____)

13. Do you participate in any clubs or organizations? (Check all that apply.)

___ 1) 4-H clubs
___ 2) church/synagogue
___ 3) health/fitness club
___ 4) hobby clubs (e.g., card or stamp collecting, bingo)
___ 5) community recreational programs
___ 6) sports teams
___ 7) school clubs/groups
___ 8) YMCA/YWCA
___ 9) civic organizations (describe: _____)
___ 10) special interest group (describe: _____)
___ 11) none/don't know
___ 99) other (describe: _____)

14. Are there any clubs or organizations to which you would like to belong or in which you would like to participate?

___ 1) yes
___ 2) no

a. **If yes, with which clubs or organizations would you like to become involved?** (Check all that apply.)

_____ 1) 4-H clubs
_____ 2) church/synagogue
_____ 3) health/fitness club
_____ 4) hobby clubs (e.g., card or stamp collecting, bingo)
_____ 5) community recreational programs
_____ 6) sports teams
_____ 7) school clubs/groups
_____ 8) YMCA/YWCA
_____ 9) civic organizations (describe: _____)
_____ 10) special interest group (describe: _____)
_____ 99) other (describe: _____)

15a. **Does a family member or friend belong to or participate in any of the following clubs or activities?** (Check all that apply.)

_____ 1) American Association of Retired Persons
_____ 2) American Red Cross
_____ 3) Big Brothers/Big Sisters
_____ 4) Chamber of Commerce
_____ 5) church/synagogue
_____ 6) Civitans
_____ 7) community or neighborhood association
_____ 8) Elks Club
_____ 9) hobby clubs
_____ 10) Jaycees
_____ 11) Junior League
_____ 12) Junior Women's Club
_____ 13) Kiwanas
_____ 14) Knights of Columbus
_____ 15) Lions
_____ 16) Masonic Temple
_____ 17) Mocha Temple
_____ 18) Moose Club
_____ 19) recreation and parks department
_____ 20) Shriners
_____ 21) sports team (describe: _____)
_____ 22) special interest group (describe: _____)
_____ 23) union (e.g., Teamsters, AFL-CIO)
_____ 24) United Way
_____ 25) volunteer work (describe: _____)
_____ 26) none/don't know
_____ 99) other (describe: _____)

b. **Are there any individuals who belong to the above clubs or organizations who you wouldn't mind us contacting?**

Name	Relationship	Phone #	Employment

1.

2.

3.

4.

III. POTENTIAL SUPPORT OPTIONS/SUPPORT NEEDS

16. **With whom do you live?** (Check all that apply.)

_____ 1) no one
_____ 2) parents
_____ 3) girlfriend/boyfriend/spouse
_____ 4) siblings
_____ 5) relatives
_____ 6) friends
_____ 7) roommates
_____ 8) personal assistant
_____ 9) professionals/paid staff
_____ 10) residents
_____ 99) other (describe: _____)

17. **Who usually assists you when you need something or have a problem?** (Check all that apply.)

_____ 1) parent/guardian
_____ 2) siblings
_____ 3) girlfriend/boyfriend/spouse
_____ 4) relatives
_____ 5) friends
_____ 6) community members
_____ 7) neighbors
_____ 8) teacher
_____ 9) rehabilitation counselor
_____ 10) service coordinator
_____ 11) no one
_____ 99) other (describe: _____)

18. When you want to go somewhere, how do you usually get there?
(Check all that apply.)

_____   1) drive
_____   2) friend or family member transports
_____   3) walk
_____   4) ride a bicycle
_____   5) ride a bus
_____   6) take a taxi
_____   7) use specialized transportation
_____   99) other (describe: _____)

19a. Do you receive Social Security benefits (e.g., SSI, SSDI)?

_____   1) yes
_____   2) no

b. If yes, is the potential loss of Social Security benefits due to future employment a concern?

_____   1) yes
_____   2) no

20a. Are there any types of services or supports that you would like or are in need of and are not receiving?

_____   1) yes
_____   2) no

b. If yes, identify the type of assistance you would like.

_____

_____

APPENDIX

B

Developing a
Functional Resumé

Functional Resumé Worksheet

Name _____ Phone _____

Address _____

I. Career objective (optional)
    To _____

II. Education

    Degree _____ Major/program _____ School _____

    Location of School _____ Graduation date _____

III. Skills

    Skill _____

    Accomplishment _____

    Skill _____

    Accomplishment _____

IV. Experience (most recent)

    Job title _____ Employer _____

    City _____ State _____ Dates _____

    Job title _____ Employer _____

    City _____ State _____ Dates _____

    Job title _____ Employer _____

    City _____ State _____ Dates _____

V. Interests

    Interests/hobbies _____

VI. References (available upon request)

Suggested Responses for the Resumé Worksheet

Directions: The lists in each category are suggestions to help you recognize the experience, skills, interests, and so forth that you possess. Please list all information that is applicable to you. It is better to have too much information than to not have enough. The resumé worksheet is merely a guide; please use additional space to complete your answers.

I. Career objective (optional)
    • To perform work that is meaningful to me in the area of _____
    • To give me the opportunity to learn new things
    • To earn an income and be a productive citizen
    • To help others
    • To meet and work with others

II. Education
    • List all schools
    • List training centers
    • List college courses
    • List other courses (e.g., leisure, living skills)

III. Skills
    • Include household chores
    • List any tasks performed at home, school, church, or other location
    • Remember, all skills are important (e.g., using the telephone, operating electrical appliances)

IV. Experience
    • List specific school duties (e.g., dishroom, cafeteria, office)
    • List volunteer work and experience
    • List community services (e.g., child care, lawn care)
    • List work experience, whether paid or unpaid

V. Interests
    List all interests and hobbies because there may be a job that can match this area. Remember to include responsibilities of each category under the Skills section.

    • Music   • Gardening, flowers, plants
    • Television   • Cooking
    • Video games   • Talking with friends
    • Sports (list types)   • Reading
    • Animals   • Art, drawing

VI. References
    Identify three people who can provide references for you. Usually, you should know the individual for at least 1 year. Collect addresses and telephone numbers, and get permission from each person so that he or she will be prepared to provide employers with information.

<NAME>
<ADDRESS>

CAREER OBJECTIVE To be employed in a position that will utilize my skills and develop my interests

EDUCATION **Nelson Community College**
Richmond, Virginia (1994–present)

Modeling Program
Richmond, Virginia (completed 1992)

Middletown High School
Richmond, Virginia (Diploma, June 1990)

SKILLS Ability to work independently
Desire to perform well
Ability to get along well with others
Good personality, sociable, likable
Strong communication skills
Knowledge of entertainment facts and trivia

EXPERIENCE **Activities Volunteer**
Roseville Convalescent Center, Richmond, Virginia (January 1993–present)
Assisted activities coordinator with activities, assisted residents with participating in activities, transported residents to activities and meals

Dietary Aide
Piedmont Nursing Home, Richmond, Virginia (June 1991–December 1992)
Prepared food trays from select menu, served trays to residents, responded to residents' needs, bussed tables, cleaned dishes, prepared food and beverages, performed other assigned cleaning duties

Lobby Attendant
Burger King, Richmond, Virginia (1990–1991)
Cleaned tables and trays, greeted customers, performed other assigned duties

HOBBIES/INTERESTS Listening to music, watching movies, socializing

REFERENCES Available upon request

CHAPTER

Maximizing Community and Workplace Supports

Defining the Role of the Employment Specialist

Darlene D. Unger, Wendy S. Parent,
Karen E. Gibson, and Kelly Kane-Johnston

The concept of using natural supports as a service delivery practice to assist individuals with severe disabilities in becoming competitively employed has gained increasing popularity since its introduction in the late 1980s (Nisbet & Hagner, 1988). The idea underlying this approach is simple: Maximize the use of employer and co-worker supports already present in the workplace to enable workers with disabilities to function in a manner similar to other employees in the company. The assumption was that utilizing natural supports would improve employment outcomes and social integration while reducing reliance on job coaches and other human services supports (DiLeo, Luecking, & Hathaway, 1995). Following the successes of supported employment (Wehman, Revell, & Kregel, 1997), the established practice of relying on co-worker advocates for assistance on the job (Wehman, 1981), and the use of new technologies to support workers with severe disabilities (Flippo, Inge, & Barcus, 1995), the expansion of using natural supports within the existing supported employment model became the next step in the evolution of community-based employment for individuals with disabilities.

In the years since the introduction of the concept of natural supports, several definitions and strategies for using natural supports to assist individuals with disabilities in obtaining and maintaining competitive employment have emerged in the professional literature (e.g., Butterworth, Whitney-Thomas, & Shaw, 1997; DiLeo et al., 1995; Hagner, Butterworth & Keith, 1995). In general, *natural supports* are considered to be

> any assistance, relationships, or interactions that allow a person to secure, maintain, and advance in a community job of his or her choosing in ways that correspond to the typical work routines and social actions of other employees and that enhance the individual's social relationships. (Rogan, Hagner, & Murphy, 1993, p. 295)

Storey and Certo proposed the idea that natural supports refer to

> people who are not disability services providers, who provide assistance, feedback, contact, or companionship, to enable people with disabilities to participate independently, or partially independently, in integrated employment or other community settings. Individuals providing natural supports, typically, receive assistance and consultative support from disability services providers, and provide natural supports with or without compensation, depending on the situation. (1996, pp. 4–5)

In general, proposed definitions of natural supports appearing in the professional literature share certain commonalities, including the following: Assistance or support is provided predominantly by people other than human services personnel (Nisbet & Hagner, 1988); greater emphasis is placed on workplace personnel as means of support (DiLeo et al., 1995); and the type of support provided should simulate typical assistance or support existing or available in the work environment (Mank, Cioffi, & Yovanoff, 1997; Rogan et al., 1993).

Numerous definitions of natural supports or the idea of using natural supports exist in the professional literature. The lack of consensus on what constitutes a natural support and when and how natural supports should be used contributes to much discourse on what the role and level of involvement of the employment specialist should be when natural supports are utilized. Several strategies for using natural supports and the types of natural supports have been documented (e.g., Butterworth et al., 1997; Hagner et al., 1995; Hagner & Faris, 1994; West & Parent, 1995). However, descriptions of the role of the employment specialist in using natural supports during supported employment have been limited. Many professionals in the field of supported employment and rehabilitation believe that the employment specialist should function more in a consultative role both to the individual with a disability and to the employer (e.g., Butterworth et al, 1997; DiLeo et al., 1995; Luecking, 1996; Rogan et al., 1993). Thus, the employment specialist should be more of a *facilitator* of services and supports as opposed to the *primary provider* of services and supports to the individual as well as to the employer. This chapter describes the type of support provided by the employment specialist utilizing a natural support strategy during the provision of supported employment services.

NATURAL SUPPORTS TRANSITION PROJECTS

A specific natural support strategy was developed and implemented by the Natural Supports Transition Projects (referred to in this chapter as the Projects) at Virginia Commonwealth University's Rehabilitation Research and Training Center on Supported Employment (VCU-RRTC). The seven-step approach relies on supports that exist or might be available in community or workplace environments to assist people with disabilities in achieving their vocational and career goals. The model promotes the ideas of individual choice and self-determination in assisting individuals with identifying their support needs and career preferences. In keeping with the "best practices in supported employment" noted by Brooke and colleagues (Brooke, Inge, Armstrong, & Wehman, 1997), the Community and Workplace Support Model was developed to promote consumer choice in supported employment by ensuring that all individuals are presented with a variety of experiences, options, and supports to assist them in achieving their career goals. The ideas of self-determination and control are also inherent in the model because individuals can accept or deny specific types of services and supports. A frequently cited shortcoming of supported employment is that although it has afforded an increasing number of individuals with significant disabilities an opportunity to compete in the labor force, supported employment falls short in addressing career advancement or career changes for people placed into competitive employment (Pumpian, Fisher, Certo, & Smalley, 1997). The Community and Workplace Support Model addresses this concern through the identification and development of ongoing support people to assist an individual in pursuing his or her unique vocational endeavors.

A description of each step in the Community and Workplace Support Model follows in the case study about Tim, a dietary aide at a nursing home. Tim's story illustrates how each step in the model maximizes the use of natural supports and shows how the model can be implemented for an identified support need during the supported employment process.

1. Determine Individual Needs and Preferences

A critical first step in the model is the identification of the type and amount of assistance that an individual needs or would like to receive to obtain, learn, and maintain a job of his or her choosing. It is anticipated that a variety of support needs will be identified for each individual, which will vary across individuals and during each individual's life. Table 1 presents just a small sample of the many support needs that were identified for young adults with a variety of disabilities who were referred to the Projects for supported employment services.

TIM

Tim has difficulty attending to his personal hygiene and often leaves his home without bathing, shaving, brushing his teeth, or combing his hair. He does not recognize when his clothes are dirty, and he forgets to change them. Tim was recently hired as a dietary aide in a nursing home. His new job's dress code requires him to wear a uniform and to be well groomed. Tim desperately wants this job, but he and his father are concerned that he will lose his job because of his poor hygiene skills.

2. Brainstorm Potential Options

The identification of potential support options, Step 2, involves a collaborative effort among the individual with a disability; his or her

Table 1. Examples of possible support needs

- Determining job choices
- Finding a job
- Remembering how to do the job
- Participating in social activities during work hours
- Arranging work schedule/hours
- Calling in sick or late
- Taking lunch and/or breaks
- Getting along with co-workers
- Picking up/cashing a paycheck
- Handling SSI or SSDI
- Making ride arrangements (e.g., co-worker, friend, family members)
- Developing a resumé
- Learning how to do the job
- Orienting around the workplace
- Being able to perform infrequent duties associated with the position
- Signing in and out at work
- Attending company meetings
- Receiving a raise or increased benefits
- Developing friendships
- Finding transportation to and from work
- Getting a learner's permit or a driver's license
- Learning how to use public transportation (e.g., taxi, bus, subway)

designated support people such as family members, friends and/or advocates, the employment specialist and other human services personnel, and the employer. Each person should explore all of the potential supports that they know of and share his or her ideas with the individual. The unique suggestions that each party contributes to the identification of support options, based on his or her knowledge of the individual with a disability or the community and workplace, will significantly expand and diversify the number and type of supports that are identified. The idea is to generate as many potential support options to meet the needs of the individual so that he or she can choose the support that best meets his or her needs. By providing the individual with a variety of potential support alternatives, one promotes the individual choice component underlying the Community and Workplace Support Model.

Resources should not be limited to traditional supports provided by people or agencies that specifically provide services to individuals with disabilities. All potential supports with any agency, organization, or employer should be investigated. For example, perhaps the individual's church, neighbors, or a club to which a family member belongs will provide assistance in identifying job leads, providing transportation, accompanying the individual on social outings, or purchasing a desired item. In addition, if an employer, agency, or organization has not provided a specific type of assistance in the past, it does not necessarily mean that it should be immediately dismissed as a potential support option. Oftentimes, employment specialists can creatively negotiate for the supports to be provided if they are knowledgeable about the services offered by organizations and individuals in the community and workplace.

At this phase in the Community and Workplace Support Model, it is imperative to think about everything that might be available to the individual no matter how remote or unlikely the support resource might be. Decisions based on what is available and what the individual would like will be made later from the extensive list of options identified during this brainstorming period. Furthermore, the individual with a disability is the person who has ultimate control over what type of support he or she will decide to use.

Tim, his father, and other significant people in his life met and thought of the following things to help him comply with the dress code: Use a checklist, make an audio cassette of tasks to play when getting ready, use a programmed talking alarm that could remind him of tasks, have his father help him, have a neighbor help him, have his residential counselor prompt him, call a co-worker who could remind him of what to do, keep a travel bag at work that includes personal hygiene products and a spare change of clothes, hire a personal assistant, or take grooming classes at the local Center for Independent Living (CIL).

3. Assess Job and Community Supports

At Step 3 in the Community and Workplace Support Model, a clear and detailed explanation of what a particular support option would entail is discussed with the individual. The employment specialist and individual will explore the availability of the support options and identify the pros and cons of each. The individual then can make an informed decision about the support(s) he or she could use. Discussing the individual's employment and community support preferences will help the employment specialist by providing a direction for pursuing supported employment activities. For example, one individual who was in need of transportation had the choice among riding the bus, taking a taxi, carpooling with co-workers, or riding her bicycle. However, she refused to ride the bus, found the taxi costly, and could ride her bicycle only within a 2-mile radius of her home. She, therefore, required specific job development emphasizing a close location or assistance with identifying other co-workers with whom to ride.

The employment specialist's role is to communicate to the individual what is involved in implementing each of the identified support options (identified during Step 2). The individual could then make an informed decision based on the information gathered by the employment specialist and other people involved. When assessing job and community supports, the employment specialist describes how the supports could be used, what they have to offer, and the type of assistance that could be received so that each individual can select the job and support resources that best meet his or her needs and preferences.

Tim assisted his job coach in determining which support options were available, and they found that most of them were available. They discussed the ways the supports could be implemented, and Tim tried out a few of them to see if he would like them. For example, Tim's residential counselor was available to prompt Tim to get ready for work. As an option for pursuing supports for his personal hygiene needs, they identified grooming classes, which were offered by the CIL on several evenings each month. Although the grooming classes offered at the CIL did not address Tim's immediate support need, the classes were still included as a potential option.

4. Identify Individual Choices

Without sufficient information presented in a meaningful manner, individuals with disabilities often have difficulty selecting the job they would like to have and the supports they would like to use. Some individuals may not know which options are available; others may not have identified their preferences; and others may lack the skills to make choices among the alternatives. The employment specialist provides whatever assistance is needed to ensure that the consumer has information about the support resources in a way that he or she understands, such as verbal presentation, written format, and/or hands-on experience. For example, having the consumer accompany the employment specialist when initiating employer contacts during job development is often an effective strategy. Not only does this strategy allow the individual to directly look at the job and assess the job's desirability, it also provides an opportunity to get his or her foot in the door and make that critical first impression with the employer.

To make choices about whether a particular support will be utilized or whether it will be optimal, the employment specialist assists the individual with talking to or visiting the person or organization who would provide the support. The consumer can also try the support firsthand to determine its effectiveness.

Tim determined which supports he wanted to use by first trying each one. Tim selected the following supports, listed in order of his preference: use a checklist, use a programmed talking alarm that could remind him of tasks, keep a travel bag at work that included personal hygiene products and a spare change of clothes, call a co-worker who could remind him of what to do, take grooming classes at the CIL, and have his residential counselor prompt him. He made his choices in this order primarily because of his preference for independence. The checklist provided him steps that, if followed, would ensure proper grooming; he could see his mistakes readily if an item were not checked off. He choose the alarm clock because it eliminated the need for support from someone else. The third support, the travel bag, was a "safety net" to assure him that even if he made it to work without being properly groomed, he would be able to remedy his error on arrival. Tim agreed that his last two choices—taking classes at the CIL and having his residential counselor prompt him—would be used only if necessary because these were his less favored options.

5. Develop Strategies for Gaining Access to Supports

Even though a community or workplace support is available does not necessarily ensure that an individual interested in using it will automatically have access to it. A formal, systematic process for gaining access to supports must be initiated. With the Community and Workplace Support Model, the person with a disability either contacts the support resource and makes the specific arrangements for its use or designates someone (e.g., employment specialist, family member, friend, teacher) to contact the support resource and make the arrangements. Strategies that have been found to be effective include giving the individual specific steps to follow, guiding him or her through the process, and accompanying him or her during the initial meeting or use of the support. For example, asking the individual to pick up job applications or to contact any interesting employers about a job opening may not be as productive as having him or her come to the employment specialist's office, decide on specific employers to call, and be provided with a telephone to actually make the calls. Similarly, an individual employed by a company that offers a co-worker mentor may need help in linking up with that co-worker, expressing his or her support needs, learning how to communicate with the co-worker, and indicating his or her preferences if a more compatible co-worker is desired.

Tim's job coach developed a laminated picture and a simple word checklist to keep in the bathroom for daily use. Tim's father purchased a talking alarm, which was programmed to sound to list his tasks in sequential order, allowing 5–10 minutes between each task. So that he could perform his hygiene when needed, Tim's employer allowed him to keep a travel bag at work, which included his personal hygiene products and a spare change of clothes. His employer also suggested that the front receptionist keep a list of Tim's tasks and to have Tim call her daily so that she could monitor the tasks he had completed and remind him of others to do. Tim's vocational rehabilitation counselor referred him for personal grooming classes at the CIL. His residential counselor agreed to monitor, oversee scheduling, and arrange transportation for the classes. His residential counselor included hygiene assistance in Tim's program.

6. Evaluate Support Effectiveness

Once a support has been arranged and implemented, it is imperative that the support be monitored to ensure that it is successful in addressing the needs of the individual. Evaluation procedures should be implemented by the employment specialist to determine the support's effectiveness at meeting the individual's needs. Receiving the desired assistance alone does not ensure that the intended outcome has been achieved. Rather, the employment specialist should obtain multiple measures of the quality, stability, and desirability of the support from all stakeholders potentially affected including the individual, employer, co-workers, family, and members of the community.

To determine if a support is effective, it is critical to consider a variety of factors. These factors include making sure that the individual is satisfied with the arrangement and that the individual's needs are being met, and making sure that the employer is satisfied and that company standards are being maintained. In addition, it is important to determine whether the presence of the support affects the individual's wages, work hours, and level of social integration. Developing support systems with the individual's input, frequently asking how he or she likes the support option, and asking how it can be modified to better satisfy his or her needs is the best way to ensure success.

Once Tim was at work, he needed assistance with clocking in and out. He first chose to have a designated co-worker who worked during the same hours enter his Social Security number in the computer. On several occasions, however, Tim never clocked in for work because he could not locate the designated employee. Tim's father notified the employment specialist that his son's paycheck did not reflect the hours that he actually worked. The employment specialist intervened and worked with Tim to select another support option. He decided to carry a laminated card with his Social Security number on it so that he could hand the card to any available employee to make sure that he was clocked in for work. The best evaluation of the effectiveness of the supports selected will be if Tim arrives at work every day groomed properly. Stakeholders will monitor and observe Tim and will use telephone contact to ensure that breakdowns in a support strategy are determined immediately and that other support options are developed and implemented. Tim's father, employer, designated co-worker, and residential counselor also will be contacted regularly.

7. Arrange Provisions for Ongoing Monitoring

The stability and dependability of community and workplace supports on an ongoing basis are essential issues affecting employment success. With the help of the employment specialist, an individual can proactively address the idea of the ongoing maintenance of the support. A multitude of factors can influence the reliability of an ongoing support, such as a change in the needs and preferences of the individual, coworker and supervisor turnover on the jobsite, a modification in work procedures or job duty responsibilities, a geographical change in the individual's living situation, or a desire by a community volunteer to terminate the previously arranged support relationship. In some instances, these issues or concerns can be foreshadowed; but typically, when a support breaks down, it is often due to unforeseen circumstances. Therefore, it is essential to have multiple layers of support for the ongoing maintenance of support. Because Steps 2, 3, and 4 of the Community and Workplace Support Model emphasize a thorough identification and development of support options, the identification of alternative supports usually requires minimal effort. Therefore, if altering supports is necessary, it can be accomplished with minimal intrusion.

Tim's father will be the primary person responsible for ensuring that the system of supports is working effectively. Tim selected his father for this role because he is the only person in Tim's life who is involved in all aspects of his day-to-day activities. His father will be readily able to identify a support's effectiveness, and in the event of a problem, he will serve as the point of contact. Furthermore, his father has regular contact with Tim's employer and will contact the job coach when an issue arises that requires additional assistance.

The employment specialist oversees the support and employment situation by guaranteeing that a stable point of contact is available in case a change or breakdown in the support occurs. This is accomplished by making regular visits to the jobsite, maintaining ongoing communication with the individual and employer, conducting periodic assessments of individual and supervisor satisfaction, and collecting data aimed at monitoring work performance. For example, one consumer's follow-along support was provided by the supervisor and mother, who communicated weekly regarding his performance. The mother and individual contacted the job coach twice a month to relay information regarding the work situation and the availability of the supports provided by worksite personnel. Infrequent and random visits were made by the job coach to monitor the situation and address problems as they occurred, such as advocating for more hours, facilitating co-worker training on a new job task, and assisting with arranging new transportation on the individual's request. The employment specialist coordinated activities among all people affected by the support through the dissemination of important information in written form including monitoring activities, frequency of ongoing assistance, the roles of key people, and the names and contact information for all involved.

WHEN IS THE COMMUNITY AND WORKPLACE SUPPORT MODEL UTILIZED?

The Community and Workplace Support Model is not a replacement or substitute for an employment specialist or separate from the existing supported employment model. Instead, the seven-step process should be used for each and every support need that arises during the provision of supported employment services. The employment specialist is still ultimately responsible for gathering assessment information, identifying jobs in the community, making good job matches based on the individual's preferences, training an individual with a severe disability, and providing follow-along services.

With the use of supports that exist within the individual's community and workplace combined with this seven-step process, however, the employment specialist's role evolves from one of a *provider* of services to more of a *facilitator* of services. The level of direct support provided by the employment specialist will ultimately depend on the identification and development of supports and the desire of the individual with a disability to use the natural support. The individual may choose an employment specialist, a co-worker mentor, or a volunteer such as a college student intern to provide the support. Paramount to the success of this process is that the decision to utilize a support rests with the individual with a disability and his or her family or advocate and that the support is systematically arranged, implemented, and monitored. The Community and Workplace Support Model offers a means for maximizing the use of employer, co-worker, community, and family supports to enable an individual to work, live, and participate in the community and work environments of his or her choice.

DEFINING THE ROLE OF THE EMPLOYMENT SPECIALIST

The following section helps to define the role of the employment specialist in the Community and Workplace Support Model. Whereas this chapter provides a specific model for implementing community and workplace supports during supported employment, Chapter 7 explores the many roles that the employment specialist plays during the job search and attainment process.

Performing Consumer Assessment

It is critical to gather as much relevant information as possible on the consumer's abilities, preferences, and support needs. The information should be gathered from a variety of sources—primarily, from the individual with a disability and key stakeholders in his or her life. Information from psychological evaluations and vocational evaluations are useful, but typically, more pertinent information can be gathered from the individual by spending time with him or her and by communicating with people in the individual's life.

By talking with the individual and his or her family, the employment specialist can facilitate a discussion of the individual's likes and dislikes and his or her desires and expectations, as well as identify potential support options. For example, the job coach should obtain information on employment-related preferences such as work hours desired, preference for working at a slow- or fast-paced job or business, and preferences for types and kinds of businesses. Oftentimes, individuals may not be able to communicate their job or support preferences because of a variety of factors. These factors may include insufficient exposure to job or career opportunities, limited work experience, and the severity of one's disability. It is important for the employment specialist to share information with the individual and observe the individual in a variety of settings that provide the individual with an opportunity to demonstrate his or her likes or preferences and support needs. As stated previously, all individuals, regardless of the nature of their disabilities, can communicate their needs, preferences, and desires in some manner. By observing the individual in multiple environments and by communicating with his or her support people, the employment specialist will also be able to validate the information, which may be communicated to him or her by the individual through direct observation of the individual's actions. For example, an individual said that he wanted a job that required physical labor and at which he could work outside. After the employment specialist asked him if extremely hot weather would bother him, he responded, "No." The individual, however, was subsequently observed in a work environment that was characterized by extremely warm conditions and somewhat physically intensive labor: a large laundry room in a busy hotel. The individual quickly communicated to the employment specialist that he did not enjoy working in the extremely warm temperatures. Even though he said he liked the work, he demonstrated his discomfort with the working conditions to the employment specialist by continuously asking for a break, fanning himself with his hands and saying, "I'm hot" repeatedly. The employment specialist should constantly be on the lookout for subtle or nonverbal clues concerning the individual's likes and preferences.

Community and situational assessments are two methods by which the employment specialist can maximize opportunities to assess an individual's functioning level, support needs, and job preferences. More important, the individual will be provided with an opportunity to make informed choices regarding the type of career he or she might like to pursue. The community assessment gives the individual an opportunity to demonstrate and communicate to the employment specialist the places that he or she frequents in his or her community and the things that are important to him or her. In a community assessment, the consumer provides the employment specialist with a "tour" of his or her community, pointing out where his or her family shops or does business and showing where friends or a favorite neighbor may live. In addition, the community assessment gives the employment specialist a chance to scout out the area and explore types of businesses that are located within the individual's community as well as the types of agencies or organizations that might be available to provide support to the individual. The goal of a community assessment is twofold: 1) to aid in determining the individual's likes and dislikes and 2) to identify potential employment options and supports existing within the community.

Situational assessments are also a useful means for gathering information regarding the individual's employment and support needs and preferences. A situational assessment allows the individual to perform real work in a real job within a business in the community (Moon, Inge, Wehman, Brooke, & Barcus, 1990). The situational assessment is typically a 4-hour, nonpaid trial work experience in a position within a business setting in which the employment specialist accompanies the consumer into the business and works with the individual performing the job. The situational assessment sites are usually prearranged by the employment specialist based on the individual's preferences. The assessment allows the employment specialist to observe the individual performing job-related tasks in addition to exposing the individual to specific jobs available in his or her locality. Maximizing opportunities for the individual to observe or try out many different types of jobs will greatly assist the individual in determining what type of job he or she might prefer as well as with deciding the types of business and environmental characteristics that are important to him or her. Situational assessments also give the employment specialist an opportunity to develop a rapport with the individual with a disability.

Frequent, effective, and open communication among the individual with a disability, his or her family, and the employment specialist will increase the likelihood of identifying employment and support options that are successful. Community and situational assessments are useful means for the employment specialist to observe the individual across many employment or community settings with diverse environmental characteristics. Working with the employment specialist, the individual can begin to identify preferred commonalities across job settings. The information may not always dictate the exact type of work but rather the characteristics that the job should entail. Sometimes it may not be possible to locate the individual's first choice or ideal employment; nonetheless, the specific characteristics of the job that are important to the individual should be included in the pursuit of the individual's alternative job and career choices. For instance, one woman had a school work experience reshelving books in a library and wanted to work in a similar job. When it was not feasible to obtain that specific job, she accepted a job in merchandise returns, which required her to reshelve merchandise in a department store. Other characteristics of the individual's identified ideal job, which may not be present in the job he or she ultimately chooses, should be incorporated into the individual's life as social or recreational supports, which may serve as work reinforcers. The woman in this example chose to regularly visit the library in her community.

The assessment process assists in the identification of individual support needs, the type of career the individual wishes to pursue, and potential community and business resources that may provide some type of support to the individual. The ability of the employment specialist to uncover and develop potential support resources and identify individual support needs and preferences may significantly contribute to the effective implementation of natural supports and of the Community and Workplace Support Model throughout the remaining components of supported employment services delivery.

Assisting with Job Development

The individual with a disability, other people identified by the individual (e.g., family members, friends, teachers), and the employment specialist should work collaboratively to develop a job search strategy. Critical components of the strategy include the individual's career goals; the type of job to pursue; the types of businesses to target; and the geographical location to search. The job search strategy also should include the specific roles and job development activities of each of the parties involved, as designated by the individual. For example, an individual may choose to contact employers independently or with someone such as a family member or a friend. A parent may choose to contact employers alone or with their son or daughter to explore job openings. In both situations, guidance and assistance will be required as part of the methodology. Participants in the job search process may need a verbal or written reminder of key information to gather from potential employers to obtain a company business card, employment application and written job description from potential employers. Figure 1 contains a form that the individual or person assisting the individual can use to remind themselves of the type of information to be gathered from prospective employers. This information will assist the employment specialist in following up on job leads and will greatly expedite the search process. It is important that the specific strategy chosen be feasible for the individual to use. For example, if the individual is unable to write, he or she could use a pocket-sized tape recorder to gather the information, or he or she may request that the employer write the information down. Encouraging the individual with a disability to gather job-related information will demonstrate to employers that the individual has positive characteristics, such as initiation, motivation to work, and determination. Also, encouraging the individual's participation helps to foster a sense of pride, ownership, and control in his or her job search.

Natural Support Provider Job Development Questionnaire

Name of business: _____

Location of business: _____

Telephone number: _____

Person contacted: _____

Follow-up person: _____

Best time to contact: _____

Positions available: _____

Hours available: _____

Figure 1. Job development form to be completed for each natural support provider.

When using the Community and Workplace Support Model, the individual chooses who he or she would like to assist with job development activities. The professional literature indicates that family members, friends, and personal connections frequently are used in the job search process (e.g., Hagner et al., 1995; Hagner, Cotton, Goodall, & Nisbet, 1992; Rogan et al., 1993). It is useful for individuals to have a resumé, which can be given to employers by natural support providers when conducting job development. If the individual desires, he or she can attach the employment specialist's business card to the resumé and leave the resumé with employers of interest. Several agencies (e.g., state employment office), organizations (e.g., local Adult Literacy Council, career planning and development offices at colleges and universities), or individuals (e.g., high school guidance counselors) exist within one's community that can assist the individual with developing a resumé. The resumé development form included in Chapter 7 is a useful tool for assisting the individual or support provider in gathering the information to include on a resumé.

The employment specialist may be called on to perform a variety of job development activities. The employment specialist may be required to secure an interview for the individual, negotiate with the employer to create a new position or modify an existing position, and educate the employer regarding supported employment or outside resources available to the company and the individual (e.g., rehabilitation engineering, assistive technology, compensatory strategies). When an individual expresses a desire to work at a specific business (e.g., video and tape store), and the type of job is secondary to the type of business, the employment specialist may have to use job carving as the job development strategy. Job carving involves analyzing work duties at a job location and identifying specific tasks that might be assigned to an employee with severe disabilities (Griffin, 1996). In some instances, the employment specialist also may create a position within a business that does not presently have the particular position that the individual is seeking or that represents specific, preferred job duties.

If the individual desires, it may be beneficial for the individual to accompany the employment specialist when job development is being conducted. Self-advocacy and self-representation demonstrate enthusiasm and a strong desire to work, and gives the individual an opportunity to witness the job being performed. Information regarding the position should be presented in a manner that is understandable, and it is critical that the individual know exactly what the job entails to ensure that it is the job that he or she prefers.

Using the Community and Workplace Support Model, the individual can designate the role(s) of each person who will assist him or her in locating employment. The greater the number of people who are aware of the individual's employment needs and desires and who are willing to assist in the specific job search, the more crucial the role of the employment specialist will be in managing and responding to support providers. Table 2 outlines strategies that the individual, natural support providers, and the employment specialist can use in identifying employment opportunities.

Assisting with Job Placement

In planning for the individual's first day of work, all support people identified during the assessment or job development components of supported employment may be utilized to address some of the individual's pre-employment concerns. For example, an individual may need assistance in notifying Social Security of a change in employment status as well as with reporting the use of work incentives. In addition, the individual and the employment specialist may work together to identify someone who will help the individual complete all the necessary pre-employment paperwork such as Internal Revenue tax forms and the Federal I-9 immigration/naturalization forms. The employment specialist can facilitate the identification of co-workers, neighbors, or members of the individual's church to assist in getting the individual to and from work. It may be helpful for the employment

Table 2. Strategies to use in identifying potential employers

Conduct a community analysis.
- Drive around the consumer's community to locate different types of businesses.
- Target those businesses that match the skills and desires expressed by the individual.

Determine local labor market trends.
- Read business magazines and newspapers.
- Track businesses coming into and leaving the community.
- Network with other job coaches for leads and for their experiences with specific employers.

Get to know different jobs and position requirements.
- Talk with different employers about the jobs for which they hire.
- Tour businesses to see the positions available.
- Complete job analysis for specific positions.
- Chat casually with consumer's neighbors about places and types of jobs.
- Collect information about family acquaintances because these people could provide job leads later.

Explore personal contacts and those of family, friends, and neighbors.
- Ask where they work and whether they have any useful contacts.
- Get parents, friends, and siblings involved with job development activities. Have them watch for signs and ads; have them fill out applications then give you the information for follow up.

Utilize existing employment resources.
- Connect with Chamber of Commerce groups, local state-funded employment centers, and job fairs.
- Network with current employers.
- Search classified ads, job hotlines, mailing lists of large employers, and state-managed employment opportunities databases, which are available at local employment commissions or at the Department of Motor Vehicles.

Develop business contacts.
- Cold call employers who have been identified as matches.
- Connect with referred employers.

---

specialist to refer back to the responses contained on the *Individual Supports Assessment Form* (see Chapter 7) to identify potential support providers, such as a club to which a parent belongs. For example, to find transportation the parent could post a "Ride Needed" sign at the place where the club meets or could advertise in the club newsletter.

In addition, ensuring that the individual has the appropriate work attire is also a need that could potentially arise during job placement (see the previous discussion of Tim's case). For each of the needs, the seven-step Community and Workplace Support Model should be implemented, and a variety of supports should be identified. The continued identification and development of additional support resources should assist in building the multiple layers of support to ensure that the needed assistance will be ongoing.

Prior to the individual's first day of employment, the employment specialist should confirm with the individual with a disability and the employer the specific training strategy that will be implemented and the level and type of direct support to be provided by the employment specialist. This may mean that the employment specialist will have to review with the supervisor the specific job duties that have been negotiated with the employer during job development to ensure that all individuals are clear on each person's responsibilities and expectations.

Assisting with Jobsite Training

In implementing the Community and Workplace Support Model during job placement and jobsite training, the employment specialist and the individual with a disability should work with the employer to develop the most efficient and effective means to train the new employee. Table 3 outlines the role of the employment specialist during jobsite training. At this point in the supported employment process, the job coach will already be aware of the individual's strengths, weaknesses, preferences, and learning styles. In developing a specific jobsite training strategy, it is important for the job coach to assess these character-

Table 3. Employment specialist's role in jobsite training using a natural supports approach: How to implement the job training strategy

Know the individual's:
- Strengths
- Weaknesses
- Preferences
- Learning style

Identify all training options:
- Co-worker mentor
- Videotape training
- Supervisor training
- Student volunteer/intern
- Former employees

Allow the individual to select his or her preferred training option.

Arrange and monitor the training:
- Negotiate with the employer
- Provide assistance
- Get feedback
- Make modifications

istics in relation to the individual's job duties and the available training options. Effective communication with the employer and with co-workers will assist in identifying all available training options. Communicating with the employer and co-workers also affords the employment specialist an excellent opportunity to continue to foster the relationship among the employer, the new employee, and his or her co-workers.

In exploring training options with the employer and the individual with a disability, the job coach should compare the individual's needs and preferences with options offered by the employer. Information gathered during job development should assist the employment specialist in identifying and developing supports that might be available in the employment setting to train the individual or to provide ongoing support if needed or desired by the new employee. The business may offer a co-worker mentor to the new employee, who would typically be a senior employee who knows the business. Other natural support options may include the following: company-sponsored videotape training; training performed by the supervisor; using an intern or college student as a volunteer; or using former employees of the company for training purposes (see Table 4). The employment specialist can assist the employer with identifying company training aides or resources that the employer already possesses that might be beneficial to the individual with a disability. For example, most companies, especially those that are a national chain or franchise, have very systematic and standardized training methodologies. These training programs might include such things as checklists of job duties for specific positions, picture cues of the procedures that should be followed in performing a specific task, or colored pictorial displays.

Training aides often can be modified to match the learning style of a new employee. In addition, the employment specialist can also help to train the individual to perform the job (see Chapter 7). The amount of support the employment specialist actually provides will be dictated by the preferences of the individual, the supports available from the employer, and the needs of the business. When the employment specialist is not involved in the actual training, he or she should observe the training and be prepared to provide support to the trainer or to train as the need arises. It is crucial that the individual with a disability and the job coach have a back-up strategy available if the initial training strategy does not meet the needs of the individual with a disability or the employer.

To the greatest extent possible, the employment specialist should carve, create, restructure, extend, and customize the training strategy to meet the needs and desires of the individual. The job coach may

Table 4. Community and workplace support options for jobsite training

Co-worker mentor
- Is typically a senior employee who is assigned to train any new employees
- May assist the individual with integrating into the workplace culture
- May be on-going relationship after the new employee is trained

Videotaped training
- Is available during a new employee's orientation session
- Explains company history and mission
- Provides detailed descriptions of the individual's job duties, customer service, sexual harassment policies, employee safety, and employee benefits
- Can be used to refresh the employee's memory about job

Supervisor trainer
- May provide initial training to all new employees
- Works one-to-one with all new employees to familiarize the employees with job and work environments

Student volunteer/interns
- May be secondary school or college students interested in either earning course credit or volunteering their time (often in pursuit of degrees in rehabilitation counseling, education, or supported employment)
- Provides training or support to new employee just as an employment specialist would
- May form on-going relationship or relationship may end after the individual is trained to perform the job

Former employees
- May be individuals who have previously been employed by the business or organization who know the routines and expectations of the business or organization

Retirees
- May be individuals who are familiar with the individual and who also reside in the same community
- Provide training and support to the individual with a disability and often establish on-going relationships

Systematic instruction
- Uses a task analysis training method (e.g., method of least prompts, combines principles of behavior modification)
- Can be used by human services employee (e.g., employment specialist, transition specialist, educator) to train or instruct a person with a disability (Snell, 1993)

have to educate the employer as to what strategies work best in teaching the individual to do the job or identify the individual's preferred mode of learning. The employment specialist should inform the employer of his or her availability to assist in any of the training should the need arise. Also, the job duties should be task analyzed so that the job coach can provide the most effective guidance to the person performing the training, whether it be a co-worker, retired company employee, student volunteer, paid assistant, or the employment specialist him- or herself.

Establishing Extended Services

Once the individual has learned to do the job and the employment situation is stable, the individual makes the transition into the ongoing follow-along component of supported employment. This phase, known as extended services, is one of the critical elements of supported employment that significantly distinguishes it from other vocational rehabilitation models (see Chapter 7). At this time, a major shift in agency responsibility typically occurs involving funding resources, services providers, or both.

Expanding the concept of extended services to include a variety of traditional as well as new and creative support options has major implications for supported employment. The addition of natural supports as an extended services option within the Rehabilitation Act Amendments of 1992 (PL 102-569) opens the door to supported employment for anyone who could potentially be a candidate for services. Not only does this allow individuals who previously had no extended services options to gain access to time-limited services, but all people, regardless of extended services eligibility, can choose how and by whom ongoing support services will be delivered.

Utilizing natural supports during extended services is a process that is initiated during the employment specialist's first contact with the individual. Every need that has previously been addressed and every resource that has been used throughout the supported employment process lays the foundation as others prepare for their roles as extended services providers. Examples such as providing the supervisor or co-worker mentor with skills to provide jobsite training during the training phase or teaching a family member to assist with arranging scheduling, are roles that will continue long into the employment relationship during extended services.

Finding a job and learning how to perform the job are essential to gainful employment. Equally important, however, is keeping one's job or responding to job changes, career advancement, and job mobility issues as they arise. During follow-along, periodic assessments, on-site visits, frequent communication, and data collection are implemented as proactive mechanisms for addressing an individual's support needs. Beginning the first day of employment, planning and provisions regarding an individual's services and support needs should be considered not only for initial employment but throughout his or her employment tenure.

When preparing for follow-along services, it is imperative that the job coach remain proactive in addressing the individual's support needs as well as in assisting the individual in developing an ongoing support plan. The ongoing support plan is an extremely effective document used to delineate the responsibilities of people providing long-term support to the individual. The ongoing support plan is a comprehensive written document that addresses the following areas: the individual's past, present, and future support needs; an array of potential supports for every identified support need; the individual's preferred support(s) options for a specific need; the contact person, telephone number, and responsibilities for both primary and alternate supports; and additional support resources. A completed ongoing support plan is included in Appendix A.

Based on the comprehensiveness of the ongoing support plan, it is imperative that the employment specialist work together with the individual with a disability and with significant people in his or her life to develop the ongoing support plan. When preparing for long-term supports on the jobsite, the employment specialist should work collaboratively with the individual, the employer, and the workplace support people to address current support needs as well as to anticipate support needs that may arise in the future. Together, these individuals should be able to identify which supports may be effective in meeting the employee's support needs on a day-to-day basis. All potential supports should be explored with the employer and employee as well as the extent and level of supports to be provided.

In designing the ongoing support plan it is important for the employment specialist and the individual to address future needs that may arise in the employment setting, such as the individual's desire to change jobs and pursue career advancement opportunities or the desire to change some aspect of the job. The ongoing support plan provides an opportunity for key people to assist the individual with thinking about career planning and advancement. For example, an individual who aspired to be a model wanted a job that included a great deal of walking and physical activity so she could maintain her weight. She also desired to work in an environment that afforded an opportunity for recognition and socialization. Even though the individual and her support people were unable to secure a job as a model, employment was located in a business that allowed her to be physically active by communicating with a large number of individuals in an adult retirement community. In addressing this individual's career goals in her ongoing support plan, support needs were identified and developed that would assist her in working toward her career goal as a model. The individual's desire to participate in modeling classes and attend aerobics at the local YMCA or at her community association's recreational program to help her maintain her figure were included in her plan, along with the names and telephone numbers of people to contact. Support needs and steps that could be taken for this individual to pursue her career goals were clearly outlined in her ongoing support plan.

Although each support need may have numerous people providing support either consecutively or concurrently, the overall monitoring of the entire plan is conducted by a person that the individual has chosen, who is usually involved in some way in every aspect of the individual's life. This person has the responsibility for ensuring that the individual is receiving the type and level of support that he or she desires.

The following case study is provided to illustrate how the Community and Workplace Support Model can be incorporated into existing supported employment services delivery systems. By no means is the Community and Workplace Support Model intended to replace or significantly modify supported employment, an already proven effective model for improving the employment outcomes of people with disabilities. Rather, the strategies and procedures are suggested as additional support resources, which are designed to enhance supported employment to be even more responsive to the many individuals with disabilities who desire competitive employment and who wish to choose and be able to use any type of support that they believe would work for them. The accompanying table (Table 5) provides a comprehensive list of support needs that were identified throughout the supported employment process.

JACOB: UTILIZING THE COMMUNITY AND WORKPLACE SUPPORT MODEL

Jacob is 24 years old, resides with his parents, and has been employed for the past year as a soft lines processor at a national retail store, earning $6.00 an hour. In this position, Jacob is responsible for removing the plastic shipping wrap from clothing. Jacob sustained an acquired brain injury at age 18 from a car accident. At that time, he was a full-time student preparing for graduation. Jacob returned to school as a part-time student and gradually worked his way back to full-time status. Effects from his brain injury included loss of speech, contracture of the right side, spasticity of the limbs, limited range of motion, severe long- and short-term memory impairments, and low-level functioning of intelligence in all areas. Jacob had sleep disturbances and severe explosive behavior outbursts for unknown reasons; he was not able to remember what upset him before his outbursts. He frequently responded to these outbursts with statements of profanity relating to instinctual familiar behaviors such as "I'm hungry" or "I have to go to the bathroom." Although Jacob had limited verbal communication, he could proficiently use a portable augmented communication device that gives a printed message tape. He preferred, however, to express himself through verbal responses and gestures. He exhibited the ability to understand what was going on around him and understood directions that were given to him. Following the accident, he used a wheelchair and required help with self-care, but by age 22 he was ambulatory without physical aids, although he experiences difficulties with stairs and uneven surfaces.

Jacob was referred by his vocational rehabilitation counselor to the Projects for supported employment services. Initial assessment activities to collect information from Jacob to determine his preferred job choices included conducting a home visit. It was learned at this meeting that Jacob was supported by numerous relatives and an interdisciplinary team at his school. He was assigned a full-time aide while in school who accompanied him to and from school on the bus, provided assistance with self-care needs, and provided training and assistance with all daily structured activities. Jacob's school team included Jacob, his mother, an instructional specialist, the personal aide, a case manager, a speech therapist, a physical therapist, an occupational therapist, a State Vocational Rehabilitation Counselor, and a Rehabilitation Engineer. It was determined that the school system would be an ideal avenue of support in assisting with assessment activities. For example, the team met bi-weekly to review Jacob's progress on his tasks, stamina, preferences, needs, and any issues that arose.

The job coach, who became a member of the team, informed the group of information collected during his community assessment and situational assessments. During his school day, the team incorporated tasks that had marketable and transferable skills that were beneficial to Jacob in formulating a resumé of his vocational experiences. The team worked together to modify the tasks and to make accommodations so that Jacob could better perform them. Throughout Jacob's assessment period with his job coach, the theme of fishing kept reoccurring. During his community assessment, he went directly to the sporting goods department at a local retail store and began handling the fishing rods. As the information from the home visit was reviewed, it was noted that there was a brief mention that fishing was one of Jacob's hobbies. When this was explored with his parents, it was reported that Jacob was an avid fisherman before his accident and had planned to join the professional fishing circuit after his graduation. Other assessments also focused around his interest in fishing. As part of a situational assessment, Jacob was taken to a sporting goods section of a department store and was assessed in his ability to identify fishing equipment and to perform stocking duties such as hanging hooks, bobbers, and lures. Another assessment activity included taking Jacob fishing for an hour at a local park near his home. From these assessments, Jacob had retained only minimal knowledge of the activity or equipment involved but still expressed an interest in the sport. The following table outlines Jacob's support needs and his choices of support to address his needs that arose during the individual assessment component of supported employment. Table 5 provides a comprehensive list of Jacob's identified needs, primary choices for support, and alternative or backup supports. The first section of Table 5 lists Jacob's needs that were identified during the assessment process.

Because job development activities were focused around Jacob's interest, positions in a sporting goods department at a retail store or at a bait and tackle shop would be targeted. While touring a large local retail store, it was determined that Jacob did not have the ability to provide customer services even with significant prompting and support from the employment specialist. At the specific businesses in which the employment specialist was targeting, it was necessary that Jacob be able to respond to customer questions or to direct the customer to other associates who might be able to help. After observing Jacob on several occasions and by communicating with Jacob and significant people in his life, the employment specialist determined that positions in which Jacob would have to communicate with customers should be eliminated from the job search.

Non–customer service positions then were explored by the employment specialist as well as by the people on Jacob's school team. Due to Jacob's limited physical ability, many positions were ruled out. While walking through the warehouse section of a larger retail store, the job coach observed workers removing articles of clothing from boxes, removing plastic wrapping, and hanging the clothing on racks to be taken to the sales floor. This was only one component of the position of soft line processor, which also included taking the clothes to the sales floor and assisting customers while straightening items on the floor. This position was also initially ruled out.

Through negotiation, however, the employment specialist was able to get the human resources manager at the retail store to interview Jacob for a possible carved position. Prior to the interview, the employment specialist spent a great deal of time preparing the employer for the interview. Even though one could see that Jacob had a significant disability, full disclosure of the extent of Jacob's disability was necessary in an effort to make the necessary accommodations available for the interview. This included scheduling an individual appointment as opposed to the store's mass interviewing process that typically lasted approximately 15 minutes. The human resources manager agreed to set the appointment for a minimum of 1 hour to be sure to get to know Jacob during the interview. The employer was prepared as to what to expect regarding Jacob's limitations, which included, but were not

Table 5. Establishing support priorities for Jacob

Identified need	Primary choice of support	Alternative or backup support
	ASSESSMENT	
Determining job choices	Interdisciplinary team	Situational assessments, community assessments, review of records.
	JOB DEVELOPMENT	
Finding a job	Employment specialist	Parents, teacher, VR counselor
Addressing communication issues	Prompt to use communication device	Arranging opportunity to express self through performance Educating the employer
Interviewing	Arrange for increased time allowance	Preparing the employer Using communication device
	JOB PLACEMENT	
Negotiating duties	Let Jacob decide and supervisor determine	Assistance from employment specialist
Arranging work schedule	Supervisor should determine	Assistance from parent or employment specialist
Finding transportation to and from work	Parents	Other family member, friend, co-worker, pay a neighbor
Completing company and pre-employment paperwork	Send paperwork home for parents to complete	Bring information for employer to copy onto paperwork, parents or employment specialist assist in completing the paperwork during orientation
Handling Supplemental Security Income (SSI) issues	Parents	Hire an independent consultant, use Social Security Administration outreach office
Getting up and ready for work	Parents	Other family member, friend, or hire an assistant
Addressing fatigue and stamina issues	Allow scheduled breaks	Arrange schedule for work to occur during peak performance times

Table 5. *(continued)*

Identified need	Primary choice of support	Alternative or backup support
	JOBSITE TRAINING	
Learning how to do the job	Co-worker	Employment specialist, volunteer, peer mentor
Remembering how to do the job	Employer to build new workstation designed to prompt task completion	Multiple co-workers stagger prompts, supervisor prompts
Orienting around the work place	Parents	Friend, paid assistant, alternate co-workers (1–5)
Completing all regular duties	Rehabilitation engineer to redevelop workstation	Occupational therapist, employment specialist, co-workers, supervisor
Performing infrequent duties associated with work	Co-workers prompt	Team with co-workers
Signing in and out	Co-workers assist	Supervisor assists, compensatory strategy
Getting along with co-workers	Role-play appropriate interactions	Employment specialist educates co-workers to redirect undesired behaviors and conversations
Picking up and cashing a pay check	Obtain direct deposit	Employer cashes check, parents assist with banking, co-worker assists
Changing something about the job	Jacob determines	Employer determines, co-worker teaches, employment specialist teaches
Taking care of personal hygiene and grooming at work	Arrange work schedule around bathroom schedule	Hire outside personal assistant, hire interested co-worker to assist, modify bathroom with appropriate accommodations
Dealing with aggressive, disruptive, and problem behaviors	Parents discuss with significant people how to address challenging behaviors	Doctor, medication, educate employer, develop behavior modification plan
Requesting time off from work	Parents assist with communicating with the supervisor	Siblings assist
Addressing and monitoring medical and medication issues	Parents	Other family members, friend

(continued)

Table 5. *(continued)*

Identified need	Primary choice of support	Alternative or backup support
	FOLLOW ALONG	
Monitoring work performance	Supervisor and co-workers	Parents, employment specialist
Learning independent living skills	Center for Independent Living combined with adult education courses through community college	Take course through recreation and parks department
Participating in recreational or volunteer programs and activities offered by community and civic organizations	Family members and employment specialist identify opportunities and resources that provide information and activities	Employment specialist
Pursuing career advancement	Employer reviews opportunities with Jacob and parents at evaluation time	Jacob requests change when desired
Finding a different or second job	Family members and Jacob use newspaper ads, employment commission, networking with friends to identify opportunities	Contact employment specialist and former teacher to assist
Arranging connection with disability support groups	Family members work with Jacob to identify organizations Jacob likes, and they link Jacob to times and locations of meetings	
Connecting with agency for case management services	Employment specialist works with family members to identify public and private agencies. Share information with Jacob, and discuss which services to pursue	
Identifying personal assistance supports	Specific co-worker to provide assistance at work	Parent, volunteer, or paid assistant to provide the support

limited to speech, strength and lifting, walking, memory loss, and awkwardness. It was reiterated to the employer that Jacob was a striving and determined young man who would be a good employee, if she could see past his limitations and get to know him better.

The human resources manager had multiple levels of staff present during Jacob's interview. Following the interview, the employment specialist recommended that Jacob see the job to find out if he was interested in the position and that he be given the opportunity to attempt to perform the essential duty of removing the plastic from the clothing to provide Jacob with concrete information in making his decision. This was arranged, and Jacob was able to independently devise his own strategy to remove the plastic, which was not the method demonstrated to him by an employee. The manager was so impressed that she hired him immediately. (See the Job Development category in Table 5 for the support needs that were identified during the job development phase of supported employment as well as for the supports that were arranged to address Jacob's needs.)

Once Jacob was hired, he was required to complete company paperwork and to attend the orientation session. The company was willing to provide accommodations to assist him. His parents had concerns regarding Social Security issues and had fears that Jacob would lose his Social Security benefits. In addition, they were worried about his transportation to work and concerned that he would become too tired to work. Their greatest concern, however, was in regard to Jacob's behaviors that were threatening to others and how his co-workers would react to these behaviors. It took a great deal of time and effort to meet these needs. Fortunately, everyone involved was willing to do their best to assist Jacob in succeeding at his job. (See Job Placement in Table 5 for a summary of Jacob's needs that were identified and addressed during the Job placement process.)

Through negotiation and information sharing, the employment specialist was able to build an effective relationship with Jacob's employer. Jacob was involved during the majority of contacts with the employer, which promoted his desire and determination to be a valuable employee. Jacob's initial training was conducted according to the company's general practice of utilizing a co-worker. This training period was observed by the job coach, who also provided training to the co-worker to assist with effective training strategies to meet Jacob's needs. Numerous issues and support needs became apparent during jobsite training. For example, his parents were the first to notice that Jacob was leaning severely to one side when they picked him up from work. When they questioned Jacob in front of his supervisor and the job coach as to why he was leaning, his mother readily identified that it was due to spasticity from standing. It was identified that Jacob's work station needed to be modified to accommodate his physical impairments. Jacob demonstrated the need for the change and communicated to his supervisor, in the presence of his employment specialist, that he needed to sit down.

This was the first incident of many that prompted responsive change to Jacob's work station. Jacob's co-workers, supervisor, parents, school, and professional teams involved worked collaboratively to assist Jacob with meeting his identified support needs. (See Jobsite Training in Table 5 for the needs that were identified for or by Jacob during the jobsite training process.)

At the point that Jacob had been employed for more than a year, he and his parents expressed an interest in increasing the number of hours per week that he works as well as in increasing Jacob's participation in community activities. Jacob expressed that if his employer were unable to increase his hours, he would be interested in working at a second job on days that he was not scheduled to work.

The last section in Table 5 identifies Jacob's support needs that were addressed during the ongoing, follow-along phase of supported employment. Incidentally, these support needs would also become part of Jacob's ongoing support plan developed by Jacob, the employment specialist, his family members, employer, and other key people in Jacob's life.

CHANGING ROLE OF THE EMPLOYMENT SPECIALIST

In facilitating consumer choice in supported employment using a natural supports approach, an employment specialist must be open to trying new ideas and utilizing new supports instead of always being the support provider. The process of incorporating a community and workplace support model into the supported employment process involves the willingness of the employment specialist to take a step back from the traditional "do-it-all" method and implement new, alternative approaches to providing support for any identified employment-related need, if the individual so desires. At first, it may be difficult for a seasoned employment specialist to change his or her way of thinking when it pertains to supporting a person with a disability in the job of his or her choice. The employment specialist may be apprehensive about approaching potential support providers. The identification and development of nontraditional support providers, however, involves the use of similar communication, negotiation, and marketing techniques expended during job development. One should approach potential support providers with the same furor and determination that he or she approaches employers in job development.

How does an employment specialist make the transition from the old way of providing support to the new? Customarily, employment specialists may have believed it is easier to provide the support themselves than to spend the initial time up front developing an array of supports that a person with a disability might potentially use. It is imperative that the job coach start from the initial meeting with the consumer in identifying potential support options. This will expedite the process of developing and gaining access to community and workplace supports during later phases of the supported employment process, such as in the development of the individual's ongoing support plan.

It is also crucial that the employment specialist keep a broad focus and explore all potential support options, regardless of how feasible they might seem to him or her. It is not the employment specialist's function to rule out any of the identified supports; this is left to the individual and significant people in his or her life. The employment specialist must approach each and every support need with the idea that there are endless supports available to a person with a disability. The role of the job coach is to assist the individual in identifying, developing, and gaining access to the support; the employment specialist does not ultimately choose the support for the individual.

In exploring all potential community and workplace supports, the employment specialist should identify and utilize all available resources. The employment specialist must collaborate with the individual with a disability and "key stakeholders" in the individual's life in identifying and using all available resources within the community and workplace. The job coach should enlist the assistance and expertise of the employer, co-workers, parents, family members, neighbors, and other rehabilitation providers. Also, the employment specialist should investigate the community agencies and businesses that were identified during the individual's community assessment, for the possibility of the support they could provide. For example, the individual's support need is transportation and, prior to the community assessment, the individual's parent shared with the job coach the name of a church member who lived in the neighborhood who might be willing to provide transportation. The job coach would discuss with the parent the best method for using the neighbor as a transportation support and how to go about enlisting the community member's assistance.

In utilizing supports that exist in the community and workplace, the job coach should present to the consumer, in an organized and systematic manner, all support options that have been identified and that are readily available to the individual to access. This may involve meeting with the individual and his or her parents or advocate to describe exactly what using each identified support will entail, such as availability, cost, and advantages and disadvantages of each. The more resources that have been identified and developed, the more proficient the job coach will be at providing individualized support options and subsequently fostering consumer choice in the supported employment process. Using community and workplace supports does not mean that the job coach will never have to provide any direct support or that supports have been haphazardly identified and developed. The employment specialist should always be available to provide whatever support is necessary, if the individual so desires or the need is warranted. The adaptation of the Community and Workplace Support Model into the existing supported employment services delivery model is a systematic process that uses methods inherent in the approach for monitoring supports to increase the likelihood of its success and increase the satisfaction of all parties involved.

CONCLUSION

The use of supports that exist within the workplace or community environments to assist a person with a disability in working in the job of his or her choice has contributed to the change in role of the employment specialist in providing supported employment services. Using the Community and Workplace Support Model, the employment specialist is both a facilitator of services and a provider of services. The employment specialist's ability to identify, develop, coordinate, and arrange a variety of support possibilities, as well as to provide the support him- or herself, will greatly enhance the choices presented to the individual as well as assist in achieving successful employment outcomes. It is purported that the use of natural supports in the provision of supported employment services may improve the social integration and employment outcomes of people with disabilities. Though minimal research presently exists pertaining to the efficacy of natural supports in supported employment, preliminary studies by Mank and colleagues (1996, 1997) indicated that the more typical the employment of people with disabilities (i.e., extent experiences of people with disabilities mirror typical employment conditions compared with people without disabilities), the more likely they are to realize better wage and social interaction outcomes.

As more individuals with disabilities exercise choice and control in the types of services and supports they receive, and are presented with a variety of potential support options, the idea of using supports that exist in the community and workplace will continue to evolve. This will enable an increasing number of individuals with significant disabilities to enjoy career opportunities that their peers without disabilities presently receive, such as the opportunity to pursue and obtain employment that one desires, the ability to change jobs and pursue other employment endeavors if one so chooses, and the ability to advance in one's chosen career.

REFERENCES

Brooke, V., Inge, K.J., Armstrong, A.J., & Wehman, P. (1997). *Supported employment handbook: A customer-driven approach for persons with significant disabilities.* Richmond: Virginia Commonwealth University, Rehabilitation Research and Training Center on Supported Employment.

Butterworth, J., Whitney-Thomas, J., & Shaw, D. (1997). The changing role of community based instruction: Strategies for facilitating workplace supports. *Journal of Vocational Rehabilitation, 8,* 9–20.

DiLeo, D., Luecking, R., & Hathaway, S. (1995). *Natural supports in action: Strategies to facilitate employer supports of workers with disabilities.* St. Augustine, FL: Training Resource Network.

Flippo, K.F., Inge, K.J., & Barcus, J.M. (1995). *Assistive technology: A resource for school, work, and community.* Baltimore: Paul H. Brookes Publishing Co.

Griffin, C. (1996). Job carving as a job development strategy. In D. DiLeo & D. Langton (Eds.), *Facing the future: Best practices in supported employment* (pp. 36–37). St. Augustine, FL: Training Resource Network.

Hagner, D., Butterworth, J., & Keith, G. (1995). Strategies and barriers in facilitating natural supports for employment of adults with severe disabilities. *Journal of The Association for Persons with Severe Handicaps, 20*(2), 110–120.

Hagner, D., & Faris, S. (1994, December). *Inclusion and support in the workplace, naturally.* Paper presented at the annual conference of The Association for Persons with Severe Disabilities, Atlanta.

Hagner, D.C., Cotton, P., Goodall, S., & Nisbet, J. (1992). The perspectives of supportive coworkers: Nothing special. In J. Nisbet (Ed.), *Natural supports in school, at work, and in the community for people with severe disabilities* (pp. 241–256). Baltimore: Paul H. Brookes Publishing Co.

Luecking, R. (1996). The job coach as an employment consultant. In D. DiLeo & D. Langton (Eds.), *Facing the future: Best practices in supported employment* (pp. 87–88). St. Augustine, FL: Training Resource Network.

Mank, D., Cioffi, A., & Yovanoff, P. (1996). *Patterns of support for employees with severe disabilities.* Unpublished manuscript.

Mank, D., Cioffi, A., & Yovanoff, P. (1997). Analysis of the typicalness of supported employment jobs, natural supports, and wage and integration outcomes. *Mental Retardation, 35*(3), 185–197.

Moon, M.S., Inge, K.J., Wehman, P., Brooke, V., & Barcus, M.J. (1990). *Helping persons with severe mental retardation get and keep employment: Supported employment strategies and outcomes.* Baltimore: Paul H. Brookes Publishing Co.

Nisbet, J., & Hagner, D. (1988). Natural supports in the workplace: A reexamination of supported employment. *Journal of The Association for Persons with Severe Handicaps, 13,* 260–267.

Pumpian, I., Fisher, D., Certo, N.J., & Smalley, K.A. (1997). Changing jobs: An essential part of career development. *Mental Retardation, 35*(1), 39–48.

Rehabilitation Act Amendments of 1992, PL 102-569, 29 U.S.C. §§ 701 et seq.

Rogan, P., Hagner, D., & Murphy, S. (1993). Naturals supports: Reconceptualizing job coach roles. *Journal of The Association for Persons with Severe Handicaps, 18*(4), 275–281.

Snell, M. (1993). *Instruction of students with severe disabilities.* New York: Macmillan.

Storey, K., & Certo, N. (1996). Natural supports for increasing integration in the workplace for people with disabilities: A review of the literature and guidelines for implementation. *Rehabilitation Counseling Bulletin, 40*(1), 62–76.

Wehman, P. (1981). *Competitive employment: New horizons for severely disabled individuals.* Baltimore: Paul H. Brookes Publishing Co.

Wehman, P., Revell, G., & Kregel, J. (1997). Supported employment: A decade of rapid growth and impact. In P. Wehman, J. Kregel, & M. West (Eds.), *Supported employment research: Expanding competitive employment opportunities for persons with significant disabilities* (pp. 1–18). Richmond: Virginia Commonwealth University, Rehabilitation Research and Training Center on Supported Employment.

West, M., & Parent, W. (1995). Community and workplace supports for individuals with severe mental illness in supported employment. *Psychosocial Rehabilitation Journal, 18*(4), 13–24.

APPENDIX

Ongoing Support Plan

Ongoing Support Plan

**Person with Overall
Monitoring Responsibilities:** Leslie Hanson   **Date Completed:** 8/27/96

Name: Brad Hanson   **Telephone #:** 344-1081
SS#: 222-33-5555

Address: 14803 Riverside Dr.
Richmond, VA 22233

Employer: Burger King   **Telephone #:** 344-2220
Supervisor: Dave Jones

Address: 14803 Riverside Dr.
Richmond, VA 22233

Hire Date: 2/23/96

Rehabilitation Counselor: Referral to Susan Bilns   **Telephone #:** 672-5555

Service Coordinator: Tia Small   **Telephone #:** 788-8609

Employment Specialist: Carol Gilman   **Telephone #:** 277-5640

School Personnel: _____   **Telephone #:** _____

Other: Karen Filman   **Telephone #:** 829-7864

Identified need: (Describe)	Status: (Indicate past, present, future need)	Potential options: (Brainstorm and list all possible support options)	Consumer's preferences: (Rank order the individual's preferred support options)
A. Social/ recreational/ leisure	Present, Future	Chester Jaycees (784-9115) Chesterfield Co. Parks & Recreation Contact: Kathy Smart (784-5561) YMCA	County Parks & Recreation YMCA Jaycees
B. Health insurance/ medical benefits	Present, Future	Purchase through Burger King Apply for Medicaid Apply for Medicare	Apply for Medicaid Burger King Blue Cross— Trigon

Primary support: (Include the name of support person, contact information, responsibilities, and monitoring activities)	Back-up support: (Include the name of support person, contact information, responsibilities, and monitoring activities)	Other resources: (Include the name and contact information for any other support resources chosen)
Chesterfield Parks & Recreation Kathy Smart (784-5561)	YMCA—Midlothian Branch Coalfield Rd. (937-8665)	Chester Jaycees (784-9115)
Apply to Medicaid— service coordinator to provide assistance	Purchase through Burger King—Talk to Dave—work average of 30 hrs. to be eligible	Contact Trigon—Blue Cross (344-7000)

(continued)

Identified need: (Describe)	Status: (Indicate past, present, future need)	Potential options: (Brainstorm and list all possible support options)	Consumer's preferences: (Rank order the individual's preferred support options)
C. Work performance (e.g., attendance, appearance, performance)	Past, Present, Future	Supervisor Monitor Co-workers support Parents communicate with supervisor	Supervisor/ co-workers monitor and assist Parents keep contact with supervisor Utilize job coach to monitor and provide assistance
D. Residential services/housing/ independent living skills	Future	Stay at home Explore options through CSB Request DRS refer to CIL	Request DRS refer to CIL—talk to Laura Hill (647-2553) Explore options with CSB—talk to Tia Small
E. Referral to VR (DRS) Services	Future	Self-refer to Chesterfield VR Job Coach refers to VR Service coordinator refers	Job coach make referral to VR—Laura Hill (647-2553)
F. Transportation	Past, Present, Future	Mother/Father CES Van Friend Co-worker carpool	CES—van Mother/father Friend
G. Driver's license	Future	Get learner's permit through DMV—take test orally Advertise for a tutor to study for test	Will wait to decide what to use

Primary support: (Include the name of support person, contact information, responsibilities, and monitoring activities)	Back-up support: (Include the name of support person, contact information, responsibilities, and monitoring activities)	Other resources: (Include the name and contact information for any other support resources chosen)
Supervisors: Dave and Donna monitor and assist Co-workers provide routine assistance	Parents communicate with supervisor weekly to request time off, manage schedule and pay, inquire about job performance at that time	Job coach—CES provides assistance as needed and monitoring at least twice monthly: Contact VR for training hours if needed
Explore options—CSB: Tia Small (788-7889)	Laura Hill (647-2553) refer to CIL Call CIL to self-refer (353-6305)	
Job coach—CES assist Brad and family in understanding referral and financial eligibility	Service coordinator— Tia Small provides assistance as needed	
Mother/father Friend Retired person Cab	CES—Van (have arranged)	

(continued)

Identified need: (Describe)	Status: (Indicate past, present, future need)	Potential options: (Brainstorm and list all possible support options)	Consumer's preferences: (Rank order the individual's preferred support options)
H. Career advancement	Future	Company offer at evaluation period Parents assist with pursuing opportunities presented Job Coach assist	Job coach assists Company manager assists Use DRS
I. Social Security Issues and reporting	Present, Future	Service coordinator assists Use private consultant Follow directions given in form letter	Service coordinator assists Use private consultants Joanne Davis (626-1772)
J. Respite care	Present, Future	Use counselor through CSB Hire a paid companion Arrange weekend away with friends/family	Counselor/CSB Friends/family Interview private person to hire as companion

Primary support: (Include the name of support person, contact information, responsibilities, and monitoring activities)	Back-up support: (Include the name of support person, contact information, responsibilities, and monitoring activities)	Other resources: (Include the name and contact information for any other support resources chosen)
Employer offer Job coach assists DRS assists	Parents contact: Virginia Employment Commission, check newspaper classified ads, network of family/friends	
Service co-ordinator/private consultants	Local office representative (447-2207)	
Respite counselor—CSB	Use friends/family Interview private person to hire as companion	

Assistive Technology from a User's Perspective

Amy J. Armstrong and Mary R. Wilkinson

TOBIAS

Tobias is a user of assistive technology (AT). He uses technology daily to perform basic tasks that many individuals may take for granted. Tobias is 38 years old and has experienced multiple sclerosis for 7 years. He uses a wheelchair because of progressive muscle weakness, and he wears a brace on his right hand and wrist for support. Visual aid devices support him in the performance of his job.

Tobias believes that *everyone*, with or without disability, uses AT. He states, "It is a matter of convenience for all of us. Anything that makes life and life's activities easier or more convenient is assistive technology." A kitchen amenity that makes it easier to prepare food, a television remote control that makes it easier to become a couch potato, and a computer that makes it easier to do a job are all examples of AT. In Tobias' mind, although use of technology by all is a matter of convenience, there are degrees of convenience. Without technology, as with many of his co-workers, Tobias would not be able to work as productively as he does; without technology, however, Tobias may not be able to work at all.

IMPACT OF ASSISTIVE TECHNOLOGY ON QUALITY OF LIFE

What may be convenience for many is essential for others. With a television remote control, one can change channels without getting up from the chair. Most people who do not have a disability can get up, walk across the room, and change the channel. It is inconvenient but possible. An environmental control unit, which is a small technological advance from the television remote control, allows a person with limited use of his or her extremities to control a television, lights, temperature, computer, photocopier, or other electrical device.

To the individual without a disability, the absence of technology becomes a nuisance that can affect his or her *perceived* quality of life. And to an individual with a disability, the absence of technology can act as a deterrent to one's quality of life, which can increase dependence. Thus the acquisition of appropriate AT by a person with a disability increases independence, inclusion, and employability. AT includes the following: seating, mobility, transportation, computer accommodations, augmentative communication devices, social-recreational equipment and devices, rehabilitation engineering and worksite modifications (Gordon, 1995).

There is a distinction of convenience that becomes apparent when speaking of AT and individuals with disabilities (users). It is *not* convenience in the sense of comforts and amenities but convenience in the sense of freedom and accessibility. AT, although perhaps not completely leveling the playing field for many users, may close the gap between people with disabilities and those without by increasing quality of life possibilities. Users typically experience greater physical mobility, communication, dexterity, and accessibility to integrated employment.

AT is used in all aspects of an individual's life: home, work, social, and recreational; and the availability of AT in all aspects of living influences the success of the individual. For example, adaptive driving equipment on a van can make transportation to the workplace possible. Mobility equipment, such as a power scooter, can make employment a reality. Devices that assist in daily living skills such as with food preparation and hygiene have an impact on independent living. Using assistive devices to maximize independent living is a necessary first step to community inclusion and employability.

With this interdependence between AT and independent living acknowledged, this chapter focuses on AT from the user's perspective in the employment arena. The chapter highlights elements or aspects that professionals should consider when working with individuals to acquire AT. In the past, many chapters have been written on AT; this chapter, however, is different. Consider this a brief introduction to technology through the mind set of someone who uses technology in an attempt to level the playing field.

Maximizing Independence in All Aspects

Before being used to enhance employment opportunities, AT first may be used by the person with disabilities to maximize independent living. The user needs to be comfortable with his or her activities in the home and community before exploring job opportunities. AT can be an important part of the daily living routine of a person with a disability or his or her attendant. In simple terms, housing, food, hygiene, medical care, and transportation needs have to be addressed first. Many times, optimal independent living can be achieved by resolving these needs with AT services.

Examples of AT devices used for independent living are bathing and dressing aids; food preparation aids; lifts; augmentative communication devices; wheelchairs; and low-tech items such as reachers, rubber jar openers, grips, and so forth. Individuals also may require home modifications and specialized transportation.

Addressing independent living issues first will contribute to success in the employment arena. (Not all individuals with disabilities, however, may need to address independent living on the same level.) Devices used in other areas of life may be used on the jobsite as well.

EMPLOYMENT AND TECHNOLOGY

The availability of and access to AT is often a primary barrier to becoming and staying employed for people with disabilities. In terms of integration and production at the worksite, AT strives to "equalize" the individual with disabilities with his or her co-workers who do not have disabilities. Although technology usually has a positive impact on work performance, Inge (1997) contended that it may not always provide solutions for challenges faced by the user. For example, if the individual is not employed and is looking for employment, he or she may want to carefully analyze a job. A position that requires a high production rate could still present a barrier even with the use of technology.

The user of AT must constantly represent his or her respective needs and make suggestions for possible worksite solutions. To be effective in this process, an individual must become familiar with legislation, advocacy skills, and available technology options and use a team approach.

Legislation

It is critical for the user of technology or the respective advocate to become as knowledgeable as possible about issues affecting technology use. Knowledge is an important step toward empowerment. Few users can afford to skip over this step if they truly wish to direct personal technology decisions. There are several pieces of legislation that address technology. Becoming familiar with the legislative definitions and mandates will serve the individual well.

According to the Technology-Related Assistance for Individuals with Disabilities Act of 1988 (Tech Act, PL 100-407), *assistive technology* refers to any device or service that supports an individual with a disability in achieving greater independence in the pursuit of life goals. That is, AT is any device—whether it is off the shelf, commercially produced, or creatively developed—that increases an individual's level of functioning and participation in the community (Wallace, Flippo, Barcus, & Behrmann, 1995). Devices may be used for home, work, school, or recreation.

The Tech Act also defines *assistive technology services* as any service provided that assists an individual to choose, acquire, and use a device. This legislation is comprehensive in its commitment to furthering the community integration and independence of individuals with disabilities.

The reauthorization of the Tech Act (by the Technology Related Assistance for Individuals with Disabilities Act of 1994, PL 103-218) addresses the development of state policies and practices and coordinates state agency activities. It acknowledges the barriers that individuals face in acquiring technology such as gaining access, funding, and outreach. Thus, it takes a further step from the individual's perspective and places it within a larger context of a system. In other words, the Tech Act of 1994 looks at how individuals interact with organizations and agencies to identify and acquire needed services and devices. This act defined the term *consumer responsive* while focusing on empowering people with disabilities as they determine their technology needs. The Tech Act of 1994 also addresses advocacy and systems change, emphasizing inclusion of users in the process of systems change and recognizing the user's active involvement and satisfaction in the services received.

In 1990, a substantial piece of civil rights legislation, the Americans with Disabilities Act (ADA) of 1990 (PL 101-336), was passed. The ADA attempts to end discrimination directed toward individuals with disabilities. The ADA states that an employer must provide reasonable accommodations; however, it does not dictate how accommodations should be made but relies on the individuals involved to make this determination (Wallace et al., 1995). When providing accommodations, employers also must determine what constitutes an "undue hardship" *to the employer*. Nonetheless, the ADA may have an impact on the use of AT within the workplace in terms of procuring and modifying equipment and the worksite.

In 1992, the Rehabilitation Act Amendments (PL 102-569) mandated state plans, which delineated the use of rehabilitation technology. These amendments also address the individualized written rehabilitation program (IWRP) and how rehabilitation technology will be provided within the plan. (The IWRP contains vocational and related goals, timelines, and objectives to accomplish the identified goals.)

The Individuals with Disabilities Education Act (IDEA) of 1990 (PL 101-476), in part, relates to the use of AT by school-age youth. It identifies the school system as being responsible for providing AT, if the identified technology devices and services are considered to be necessary to achieve a free and appropriate public education.

These legislative examples represent an acknowledgment that AT and access to technology is a critical component of an individual's ability to be an integrated member of a community. By delineating definitions associated with users, system delivery, civil rights, devices, and services, a national stance that enhances the integration of individuals with disabilities becomes very much a potential reality. The challenge, however, is to transform the legislation into practice or practical application. Technology users must carry the knowledge of supportive legislation with them as they procure devices and services. Such an awareness of the laws will enhance the leading role users must play in the technology process.

Role of Self-Advocacy

There was a time when a traditional model of AT assessment consisted of a professional spending a brief amount of time with the person, making a decision about what was needed ("assessment"), placing an order, and finally delivering a device without training or follow-up. Fortunately, that practice is now outdated, although some effects of it still linger. Sanctioned dependency instituted by professionals in the guise of protection, accepted by people with disabilities for lack of experience or another option, is no longer acceptable or the preferred method. Instead, in the late 1990s, individual choice and advocacy should empower the AT attainment process.

Often, in the technology attainment process, the individual may not know how to advocate for him- or herself because he or she has not had the opportunity or experience, or the individual may allow professionals to make the final determination. Allowing others to make the critical decisions often has been a lifelong learned behavior. This has been the usual, status quo professional–patient relationship for decades. Professionals can encourage and teach leadership skills to individuals who do not possess self-advocacy skills. It often has been the case that a user will abandon technology that he or she did not have a central role in choosing. This is a costly occurrence in many respects and is discussed later in the chapter.

In order for a person with a disability to learn to take control of the technology process, reciprocation—a combination of the professional teaching the user and the user teaching the professional—is necessary. The professional's role is to facilitate opportunities for decision making and assertive communication. Professional mentoring may include teaching the user how to gather information; communicate effectively; make decisions based on data, preference, and need; navigate the system; and choose a support network.

In kind, within the process of developing self-advocacy skills, the user may provide the professional with beneficial information and experience. This may include but not be limited to providing the following: feedback on the professional's ability to teach self-advocacy skills, individualized insights on specific needs and preferences, local community contacts known to them, the opportunity for a true team effort, and the opportunity for professional growth. If the individual has difficulty communicating or has a cognitive disability, the role of the mentor/advocate is especially critical. This role may be filled by a professional or a community or family member as long as the individual selects his or her own mentor/advocate.

IDENTIFYING ASSISTIVE TECHNOLOGY

The definition of AT offered in the previous section can be developed further to refer to low- and high-tech devices and related services that support an individual with a disability, thereby increasing independence. Low-tech devices are simple, usually inexpensive solutions that can be easily identified and are easily accessible (Mann & Lane, 1991). Examples include using a rubber grip for opening jars, inserting the handle of a toothbrush into a tennis ball to create a larger gripping area, using tools that come with enlarged handles, and using flat levers rather than doorknobs to open doors. Modified equipment or homemade solutions often meet an accessibility need. The use of switches, Velcro, or grips on existing items often solve accessibility obstacles. These low-end solutions usually fit well into the work environment and do not cause stigma. Creativity and brainstorming are the keys to simple, low-tech solutions.

High-tech devices usually are associated with power or electronics and inevitably are expensive, and they often are made specially and are more complicated to use and maintain (Anson, 1993). Language synthesizers, environmental control units, power wheelchairs, and computers are examples of high-end technology.

One must keep in mind that high-tech solutions may not always be needed. That is, when problem solving, look to the low-tech, simple solutions before moving on to the more involved or elaborate solutions. This strategy, of course, is dependent on the individual and his or her respective needs. If, for instance, communication or mobility is the issue of concern, one may require a higher-end device such as a Liberator for communication or a powered wheelchair for mobility.

Identifying appropriate worksite solutions is paramount. Solutions may include but are not limited to the following:

- Worksite/environmental modifications such as raising a desk or table for a worker using a power wheelchair; modifying space, access, and handrails; or changing auditory signals such as a fire alarm to a visual cue (e.g., flashing light) or a tactual cue (e.g., vibration)
- Equipment modifications such as adjusting the slant of a computer keyboard, adding a guiding mechanism on to the paper tray of a copier or adding braille next to the copier buttons, making modifications to a telephone, or adding a keyboard guide (which makes it easier for a person to push the correct key)
- Equipment creation such as a grounded desktop stamper with a lever for dating invoices received, jigs used for counting items, or a carrying unit for supplies
- Existing equipment usage such as a head pointer to type or a writing splint, a lap board to carry supplies, print magnification devices, a telecommunications device, or a shoulder phone rest
- Purchases from a vendor or use of available electronic equipment or other high-tech devices

These solutions vary in terms of cost; however, most AT scenarios are inexpensive, depending on the individual's need. Katharine's experience demonstrates a creative, low-tech solution to an accessibility-related challenge in the workplace.

KATHARINE

Katharine is a young woman with spina bifida. She uses a wheelchair and has limited use of her hands. Katharine enjoys coffee throughout the work day. Although this is not a task specifically related to performance of her work, it is an activity engaged in by many of her co-workers. Katharine used to use a reacher to get her coffee mug from the shelf on which she stores it. Most of the time, the mug would move down the shelf and slide out before she could get a good grip on it. A team member suggested that she put a latex, nonskid lining on the shelf. This was available at a local store for a little more than $2.00. It worked. Another possible solution to the same situation may have been to just lower the shelf or to rig a support to keep the mug from moving.

Another example of a creative, low-cost solution is evident in Joseph's experience. Again, as with Katharine, the activity that presented difficulty is not a work task; however, it is work-related and has an impact on Joseph's successful employment. Conrad provides an example of a core work task accommodation.

JOSEPH

Joseph works at a restaurant. As a result of a brain injury, he could not read or remember his work schedule and was in danger of losing his job. He frequently was late to work. His rehabilitation counselor contacted the Assistive Technology System Project within the Department of Vocational Rehabilitation. The Department suggested a memo minder, which costs about $20.00. Joseph's supervisor records his daily and weekly schedule on the memo minder. Joseph plays it at night and sets his alarm clock accordingly. Joseph has been on time ever since.

CONRAD

Conrad is a 42-year-old male who lives in a small town. As a result of an automobile accident, he has right-side hemiplegia. He was referred to a supported employment program, and he located a job as a beverage can crusher at a recycling company that had just opened in town. The volume of cans was such that Conrad would do this activity for the majority of his shift, along with one other co-worker. Co-workers would crush the cans with their hands, wearing gloves, and then toss them into a bin. A fellow employee rigged a device in which Conrad places a can on the bottom holder of the rig, pulls a lever, and the can is crushed. With this device, Conrad's production is almost as high as his co-workers. Conrad's experience is a good example of creating a device using a "tinkerer" within the community. Not all devices or modifications need to be developed by professional experts. Users can educate themselves as to who in their communities may be helpful with AT solutions.

THE TEAM APPROACH

The strategy proffered most readily in identifying and acquiring AT, especially high-tech devices, is the team approach. Within this approach, the user of technology is the central driving force, leading the process. It is his or her input and opinion that determine the final solution. After all, it is the individual who will develop an intimate relationship with the device(s) chosen. Self-advocacy skills, as mentioned previously, used within a team approach, are necessary to ensure the user's active participation.

Empowerment, Effectiveness, and Efficiency

In a team approach, individuals from a variety of backgrounds and experiences come together to assist the individual in evaluating and identifying the most useful solution. Team members vary depending on the individual and information needs. A team approach highlights the three "E's": empowerment, effectiveness, and efficiency.

- Professionals ascribe a role of consultant, providing practical and competent suggestions. With professionals as consultants, the user actively participates and influences the direction of the process. This is *empowerment.*
- The team approach strategy is *effective,* contributing a multitude of expertise and knowledge. Communication and activities are clear, constructive, and outcome-oriented.
- Team members may have delineated responsibilities, which decreases the likelihood of duplication and incompletion and increases the likelihood of procurement in a timely manner. This strategy is *efficient.*

As the following case demonstrates, technology abandonment is a typical outcome for a group who does not incorporate the strategy of a team and the three E's.

JASON

Jason is a 27-year-old computer programmer who has experienced diabetes for most of his life; as a result of diabetic retinopathy, his vision has gradually deteriorated. Jason contacted his rehabilitation counselor to request equipment that would assist him in reading the data he enters into the computer. He is also having difficulty reading interoffice memos, mail, and other documents. The counselor suggested a familiar device that enlarges print. This device was previously purchased for somebody else but was no longer being used. Jason made several attempts to incorporate the device into his work tasks. Jason, however, never received any training on how to use the device; hence, it seemed cumbersome, and he became frustrated. He also could not read the computer screen once he entered the data, and the new device did not seem to address this need. Jason decided not to use the device.

Jason's experience is an example of what can happen in the absence of the three E's, which were not implemented in his AT process. Jason did not feel empowered and did not pursue issues to rectify his concerns about the device. The device was procured without the input and assistance from other expert team members, which could include the employer, vendors, or a vision adaptive equipment representative. Thus, the process was inefficient and ineffective, as was the item itself. This left Jason without resolution of his specific needs.

The next case discusses a technology user, Nolanda, who identified a work task need and conducted her own research to prepare for determining an appropriate solution with her team. The case illustrates how the three E's can assist with resolving work task needs.

NOLANDA

Nolanda is an elementary school teacher with severe arthritis, which has limited her use of her hands. Nolanda expressed an interest in using a computer to help her with lesson plans and other written work. She is exploring all possibilities including modified computer keyboards, software that assists with simultaneous keystrokes, wrist supports, and voice recognition systems. With this information, she expects to obtain a complete computer evaluation before deciding which AT products work best for her (i.e., demonstrating effectiveness). To help achieve her goal, she will chair the team, having identified her need and many possible solutions (i.e., demonstrating empowerment). Other team members include her physician, an occupational therapist, a computer consultant/evaluator, her employer, and a vendor.

The constellation of professionals enhances the effectiveness of Nolanda's effort to acquire the appropriate AT. Once a decision is made on the best device, team members are assigned tasks to procure the item (i.e., demonstrating efficiency).

Roles of a Team

There are many roles on a team in a consumer-driven approach to technology assistance. Team members can include the user of the technology, his or her family, and members from many different professions.

User's Role   As stated previously, the user has center stage as the "expert" based on his or her needs, comfort level, and preferences. With a consumer-driven approach, teams will *always* include the individual with a disability. The user must be involved in the development of his or her own team or support network. Professionals may assist in the development of the team or support network, if requested to do so or if the individual requires assistance. The user should be careful not to rely on a single profession for technological solutions and should encourage ideas from different sources.

The team is in place to support and consult with the individual. The rapport with the team should be open, direct, and encourage brainstorming. As the word "team" implies, members work in concert for the common goal of community inclusion for the individual by providing maximum accessibility to all opportunities offered.

To determine whether a team is maximizing its potential, the AT user can ask him- or herself the following questions: (Note: If the user has a mentor, the user and the mentor are one unit and may ask these questions in tandem.)

- Did I assist in the selection of team members?
- Do I have decision-making responsibilities? Am I willing and ready to take on this role?
- Do I have input into the direction of my AT needs and preferences?
- Do I have or want a mentor who can assist me with developing advocacy skills or advocating on my behalf?

Other Team Members' Roles   Human services professionals have been used for many years as "experts" in their respective fields. Which of these professions are represented depends on the individual and specific needs. Besides the user, a basic, skeleton team probably will consist of a rehabilitation counselor and an occupational or physical therapist. This team, ideally, will be complemented by several other members including but not limited to family members, a physician, various therapists, vendors, an employment specialist, a rehabilitation engineer, educators, employers, a speech-language pathologist, and a social worker or service coordinator. The standard role of each of these members in the attainment of AT is represented in Table 1. When using AT on the job, the user and team identify the essential functions of the job and barriers to accomplishing those tasks. Through this method of isolating needs, creative solutions may arise.

Often, there may be a distinction between a team and a support network. The team's primary role is to assist in the identification and acquisition of technology. The support network's primary role occurs once the technology is acquired. The support network assists with the successful implementation and use of the equipment or device. The support network may be an ongoing entity and may consist of only a few, specific team members and family members. Whatever the composition of the team and support network, it is essential that the stakeholders communicate effectively with one another.

Finding a Common Language

Professional jargon or language associated with AT can be confusing for a prospective user. Terms such as "lay-back," "eye-gaze," "modified," "adaptive," "functional assessment," and the technical names for

Table 1. Team members and roles

Team member	Role
Employment specialist	Assists with job accommodation needs to enhance job performance; may assist with funding issues
Vendors	Offer knowledge on available technology, services, and repairs (usually high-end technology)
Rehabilitation engineer	Assists in development or modification of devices, accommodations, and job redesign
Occupational therapist	Assesses performance in daily living tasks, positioning, and mobility. Recommends activities, devices, and adaptations to environment
Recreational therapist	Identifies and assesses social/recreational needs and preferences
Physical therapist	Assesses work capacity: physical strengths and limitations, and analysis of work station. Recommends mobility needs, work station design, and modifications
Employer	May assist with job accommodation needs, input, and approval of work station modifications
Speech-language pathologist	Assesses language and speech capabilities and recommends specialized communication aids
Educator	Shares knowledge of individual based on experience within school system and community-based instruction sites. Provides insight into matching assistive technology to continuing education, which may enhance long-term employment opportunities and advancement
Family members	Share knowledge of individual and environments; advocates on user's behalf. Demonstrates willingness to acquire knowledge of the device to provide in-home support, which adds to probability of user success
Rehabilitation counselor	Assists with funding issues and logistics of services to be provided in effort to reduce barriers to employment
Physician	Provides input on medical issues and on cognitive and physical abilities of individual. Addresses health concerns and provides prescriptions and letters of medical necessity when needed for evaluations and durable medical equipment
Social worker/service coordinator	May act as coordinator of holistic/community services
Computer consultant	Evaluates computer needs and recommends adaptive computer equipment and training.

Adapted from Tanchak and Sawyer (1995).

higher-end devices can be intimidating. Funding options, such as Plans for Achieving Self Support (PASS) or Impairment Related Work Expense (IRWE), and specific professional language of team members also may be intimidating. The user and/or his or her advocate should ask for explanations in lay terms if something is not understood. They can ask questions such as the following: What are the benefits? What does this device do? Can you show me how I can use this? What is your role? How will you assist me? For a user to make an informed decision concerning a new technology, it is essential that team members use consistent and comprehensible language.

Team Evaluation

Part of the team process is to continually evaluate the team's success. Are outcomes being realized? Are team members contributing equally? Additional questions concern follow-up and follow-through. Once a device or service has been identified, do team members follow up to make sure it is acquired in a timely manner? Is the AT being applied correctly? Is it working? Are team members following through with commitments in a timely manner? Constant evaluation and re-evaluation will ensure an effective team experience. If weaknesses are discovered, the team should resolve these to get back on track by brainstorming possible strategies for overcoming barriers to effectiveness, efficiency, and empowerment.

DETERMINING THE PREFERRED TECHNOLOGY

From the user's perspective, it is imperative that the AT being considered is discussed, researched, and evaluated. Several strategies assist in determining the most preferred device and services, including the following: looking at the environment in which the technology will be used; trying out the device, equipment, or modification; and brainstorming a variety of possibilities. The bottom line is, "Use it before you choose it."

Choice Based on Need and Preference

An individual easily can become lost in the maze of rehabilitation technology. There are so many possibilities in terms of individual needs, preferences, and potential options. Any acquisition of AT is preceded by a need—a person with a disability wants to be able to perform a specific task, but his or her disability may prohibit or limit him or her from doing so. The individual, family members, and/or professionals begin to brainstorm about devices that would assist the individual in performing the task. The specific task may be something as simple as getting a cup off of a shelf or as complex as using a computer to perform job functions. Regardless of whether a device or equipment is low or high tech, choice and effectiveness remain central concerns. The user must be comfortable with the AT, and it must satisfy the need.

When a user is excluded from the process, or his or her input is minimized, the longevity and usefulness of the intended solution is in jeopardy. A user must be vested in the technology and must be trained on how to use the technology; if not, the new technology will be destined to collect dust in a closet. Choosing technology based on individual need or preference is intertwined with self-advocacy and a team approach.

Try It Out, Get Training, Use It   If an individual is seeking employment, the individual and the professionals he or she is working with may have a tentative concept of needed technology or supports. That is, needs can be anticipated at some level. As a cautionary note, however, it is critical to apply potential technology solutions within the specific task or environment in which it will be used. Technology may seem to be appropriate, but when actually used may not be comfortable for the user or may not result in the anticipated outcome.

Recognizing and anticipating a potential need for AT—and developing possible solutions—are especially useful when an individual is first considering filling a specific job. In such a situation, AT may level the playing field and may enhance the individual's expected performance, which can help ensure success in the position. But before a final solution can be implemented, the applicant should actually perform the work in the real environment while using the device. If, however, the individual is currently employed, he or she can problem solve based on immediate needs and preferences. Because the individual already knows the job requirements, the team can apply technology devices or services immediately.

After discussing appropriate primary and secondary environments in which to use the device, the team can perform a functional evaluation (i.e., actually trying out the AT within the environment). Questions to ask include the following: What is the function, role, or purpose of the device? Will it be used in a variety of environments or solely at work? Consider the fact that most people would not dream of buying a car without the opportunity to drive it down the street, kick the tires, and haggle with the salesperson. Yet, people with disabilities often have both high- and low-tech devices chosen for them, without an opportunity to try them out in the environment. If an individual is unable to try a new device and receive instruction about the device, the result can be very discouraging and, ultimately, expensive. It is also important to note that a device that worked for one person may, in fact, be a horrendous solution for another person. Individualized services and devices will be furthered by trying out the proposed solution.

If at all possible, the user should borrow or rent the device, and use it at home, at work, or in the community before making a purchasing commitment. The device can be tested for its capabilities, limitations, and comfort. The device should look good, feel good, and create a greater feeling of self-esteem or capability. One user ordered a chair that she believed was big, black, and bulky when she received it. The chair did not make her feel good, even though it was functional. She did not want to use the chair. Another individual, who uses forearm crutches, has several pairs that represent different functions and settings: bright neon for informal days, a classy bronze for business days, and so forth. These are typical examples of user acceptance or non-acceptance of specific devices or equipment. Clara, a woman with postpolio syndrome, was very pleased with her modified office appearance, which had a positive impact on her job performance. If the user of AT feels good about her or his ownership of the device, he or she uses it to its fullest. It makes the individual more independent, so it is the right equipment to own.

Another key element is to provide training for proper use of the selected equipment. Most likely, the user will have a close, personal, long-term relationship with the device. Replacements are sometimes very hard or impossible to get if an unwise choice is made. An opportunity to try out the device and insistence on training for appropriate use, as well as for available features, can mean the difference between successful application or failure.

The reality of procurement and funding issues or policies, however, may impede this device try out process. The user and/or the team can negotiate this process with a vendor and/or funding source.

Looking at the Environment   It is critical to examine the environment into which the device or modification will be introduced. The device or modification must fit with the environment, the employer, and the intended user. The ideal strategy is to select the technology that is the least intrusive. To ensure that the optimal fit occurs, the team brainstorming approach is valuable. Again, the user and the employer provide primary input in the direction of this process. Depending on the location, user's needs, and job requirements, team members may differ; but the user always has significant input, which maximizes the probability of success.

The following case demonstrates an example of a user, Clara, who successfully implemented modifications to her entire work station.

CLARA

Clara is 53 years old and works part time as an information and referral specialist. Clara experiences postpolio syndrome, with muscle weakness, fatigue, and pain. She uses a power wheelchair and has difficulty reaching objects. A rehabilitation engineer evaluated Clara's work environment and proposed several changes to increase access and function. Her employer was very supportive. Clara's desk was reconfigured as an L-shaped counter top, attached to the wall. This space houses a computer, a telephone, and file holders. Open-ended file folder organizers were mounted, within her reach, on the wall. A file cabinet was purchased that had drawers that could be lifted open and slid back, so that they are always open. A reacher is used to gain access to files on a higher shelf. Clara's power wheelchair also raises and lowers electronically so that she can reach files from her chair. Clara believes the new design is functional, simple, and professional looking. Her work environment suits her needs and preferences as does her power wheelchair.

As mentioned previously, functional analysis, or actually using the device or new design within the environment, will help to ensure satisfactory outcomes. Clara was involved in the development of her new office design and was greatly satisfied with the results.

SELECTING A VENDOR

Another aspect of technology selection is the selection of a vendor. An informed user can make a case for using a specific vendor. Although choosing the ideal product is a critical component, vendor selection should not be solely based on the product or device chosen. The vendor's relationship with the user and the device is only beginning; it is important for the user to "look down the road" because there may come a day when the equipment or device needs repairs. An inoperative device can be a user's worst nightmare, depending on the function that the device serves in the user's life. High-end technology such as power wheelchairs and augmentative communication may be difficult to live without, no matter how temporary.

The following are questions that can be asked of a potential vendor:

- What services do you offer?
- Do you provide a try out or trial period?
- What will you do for me if this device breaks down (e.g., lend equipment)?
- What is your turn around time for repairs?
- How much do you charge for services and repairs?

Service costs can be enormous. As in any business, customer responsiveness and satisfaction should be a priority for the vendor. A quality vendor will offer to lend a comparable device in event of malfunction and will ensure rapid repair service.

Training may be a part of the vendor agreement, and the purchase can be made contingent on receiving immediate and quality training. If a vendor lists services in promotional materials, the user should look for training, repair, and temporary replacements as indicators of whether he or she should do business with the respective vendor.

The loan aspect is critical to the user who would not have mobility, communication, accessibility, or integration otherwise. Being proactive with anticipated needs and repairs will serve the user well in selecting a vendor. With high-end technology, the user, vendor, and device may have a relationship for life. As with all relationships, it should not be entered into lightly.

Funding Issues

Anyone who uses AT knows that funding is often a challenge and a barrier to access. Most work accommodations, however, cost very little. As suggested by the Job Accommodation Network (1997), 80% of work accommodations cost less than $500.00. As with identifying technology solutions, creativity and perseverance may be the keys to success. An individual may be able to make use of a variety of funding options. Traditional sources include the Department of Rehabilitation Services, Medicaid, Department of Education, private insurance, Social Security Administration (e.g., PASS, IRWE), Veterans Administration, and Centers for Independent Living. Each of these sources has eligibility requirements and specific procedures. Nontraditional sources may include service, civic, or religious organizations (Wallace, 1995).

It is often possible to blend funding sources: that is, to use different sources for different devices and services or to use a variety of sources to fund one device or service. Before selecting a funding source, the user can gain a "leg up" in the acquisition of AT by becoming informed about all available funding sources and their respective stipulations.

According to Wallace and Neal (1993), several steps are involved in locating funding. The user must

- Be prepared
- Prove a need
- Match the need with the device or service
- Research prices, providers, and alternatives
- Choose and contact funding sources (i.e., identify a specific contact person)

- Be determined and persistent
- Do all of the necessary paperwork
- Keep detailed, written records
- If denied, appeal
- If denied again, move on to another funding option

The ADA has created another potential funding option in cases in which the solution is deemed a reasonable accommodation: employers. Acquiring funding is a tedious process, one which requires preparation, organization, and perseverance. The user must go in with the attitude that this may take patience, thought, and time.

KEEPING UP WITH AVAILABLE TECHNOLOGY

Needs change, technology changes, and goals change. The user must be a visionary to anticipate physical, medical, and/or career changes. Low-tech solutions—because they are creative, simple, and often inexpensive—do not necessarily require a prophetic approach. High-end devices, however, because of funding issues and expense, will require a future-oriented vision. Funding sources may have time frames in which, once a device is acquired, they will not pay for another similar device or equipment for a certain period. Thus, it is important for the user to know what insurance coverage he or she has.

The team approach will assist an individual with planning for the future. Turner et al. (1995) suggested that the user must get information about the longevity of a device, about how it can be adapted or exchanged in the future, and about data on quantity of sales and satisfaction with a specific product.

Strategies for Staying Informed

Awareness and knowledge are power. Waitley in his book, *Empires of the Mind: Lessons to Lead and Succeed in a Knowledge-Based World*, stated, "The new power will be in the ability to adapt, to assume responsibility, to have a shared vision, to empower others, to negotiate successful results, and to assume control of your behavior and your life. Knowledge is power" (1996, p. 11). The power to make one's own decisions and the power to be an active member in one's own life are achieved by staying informed. It is incumbent on the user of technology and/or the user's advocate to keep abreast of legislative, technological, and advocacy issues that may have an impact on AT and its use. This, perhaps, may be one of the greater challenges for the individual with a disability. It is imperative that users maintain knowledge of the latest technology available.

If the user is unable to stay informed, a member (e.g., family member, team member) of his or her respective network can perform this role. Advocacy has two faces: self-advocacy in which the individual performs activities that result in a desired outcome and advocacy performed by others on behalf of another. Each can be equally effective depending on the individual and the team or support network in place.

Computer and Database Resources With an ever-exploding market of AT devices and services, users can often find several devices that will fill a need. Sorting through them can be frustrating. There are, however, databases such as AbleData, Job Accommodation Network, and numerous catalogs that can be utilized. In addition, many states offer Assistive Technology Information and Referral Systems to help customers find options. These resources may be accessed by both users and services providers or professionals. Users who have as much information as possible have the best chances of getting the right devices.

Accessing the Internet is a highly effective and helpful source to gather information. The Internet is a giant information and referral Rolodex. A challenge for the Internet "surfer" is locating relevant information. Users may conduct a web search by simply using a search engine, typing in the term or phrase he or she seeks information on such as "assistive technology," "assistive listening devices," or "headphones." One also may join listservs or newsgroups to get specific information and updates on technology. In the late 1990s, many organizations, agencies, and businesses have created home pages describing their services and available resources.

One may also find peers through e-mail or discussion groups. Sharing insights and similar experiences regarding AT is not only informative but empowering as well. Griffin and Wehman (1996) stated that the ability to communicate with others having similar disabilities, to share strategies and horror stories, and to find resources makes access to the Internet a prime vehicle for promoting informed choices in rehabilitation services and more.

Newsletters and Magazines Newsletters and magazines that are dedicated to disability-related issues also provide valuable information. These resources may be written by and may focus on individuals with disabilities, or they may have professional affiliations.

Local and State Agencies Other sources for staying current on new assistive devices include local and state agencies and disability-specific nonprofit groups such as the Multiple Sclerosis Society or the Muscular Distrophy Association. The Easter Seals Society and local centers for independent living provide information and referral services. State agencies may include the Department of Rehabilitation Services, Department for the Visually Handicapped, Department for the Deaf and Hard of Hearing, Community Services Boards, or other departments and offices with similar names.

Personal Support Networks   Users can create their own personal networks of resources and supports. Creating support groups or gaining access to available support groups or peer groups is a good avenue for information and insights based on personal experience.

Conferences and Workshops   Often national, state, or regional conferences and workshops are sponsored by a variety of special interest groups, organizations, and agencies. Attending these events provides a wealth of current information on AT and specific applications.

Whatever strategy or combination of strategies one pursues, maintaining current information is an ongoing activity, which requires persistence and energy. The antithesis of this (i.e., not staying informed), however, serves to reinforce a services model, which may stigmatize one's self-determination and personal life satisfaction. Lack of knowledge also may have an impact on a national phenomenon known as technology abandonment.

TECHNOLOGY ABANDONMENT

As mentioned previously in this chapter, if a solution does not work for the individual, a device most likely will be abandoned. The results of this abandonment are two-fold, and neither is desirable. First, the situation the intended user is attempting to alter is not changed. For example, if an augmentative communication device is purchased but is discarded because it is too cumbersome on the job, the person is still without alternative speech. Second, inappropriate devices can be costly. No one wins when the device is abandoned—neither the person with the disability nor the payer.

Devices are abandoned simply because they just do not work for the respective user (Phillips, 1993). Abandonment happens for a variety of reasons: no evaluation period, incompetent evaluation, little or no user input, and no training or support.

There also are other, rarely recognized, reasons for abandonment. Timing and acceptance by the user together are one such reason. A person with a disability must be ready to accept the need and the usage of the device, otherwise, he or she may reject the device or find excuses for not using it. Funding is another reason for technology abandonment. For example, third-party payers frequently will pay for a manual wheelchair but not for a power chair. So, the user gets the manual chair and is unable to propel it adequately. The chair goes into the closet to gather dust, while the person with the mobility difficulties either stays at home or waits a very long time for funding of the wheelchair that he or she needed in the first place.

Devices that end up in the "AT closet" present a challenge. They need to be recycled, but there is little funding. Third-party payers rarely pay for a used item. In the future, some method of consistent redistribution needs to be developed to assist in combating technology abandonment.

CONCLUSION

AT can close the gap between inaccessibility and accessibility. Technology at the worksite continues to be an exciting, integrating opportunity for many individuals with disabilities. The user must, often in concert with a mentor, be as prepared, as relentless, and as questioning as possible to arrive at appropriate solutions. Technology continues to advance and change at a rapid pace, with all members of society becoming dependent on, and benefiting from the use of some form of technological assistance. Individual advocacy and research in procuring AT at the worksite as well as in other areas of daily living will continue to increase the independence of individuals with disabilities.

Identifying and acquiring appropriate technology, however, takes planning and diligence. This process incorporates the policies and procedures of a variety of service providers and professionals. It is a process that is interdependent with many who may have their own personal agendas. Funding issues abound and often are perplexing to some degree. Perhaps, the information and strategies addressed in this chapter appear to be ideal; albeit, as a user or a potential user, one must be prepared to advocate for the best possible outcome(s) to further one's positive life experience. If an individual can be successful in approximating some level of empowerment, he or she will achieve greater benefits from the application of AT within the work place as a matter of convenience in terms of freedom and quality of life.

REFERENCES

Americans with Disabilities Act (ADA) of 1990, PL 101-336, 42 U.S.C. §§ 12101 et seq.

Anson, D. (1993). *Rehabilitation 487: Course syllabus*. Seattle: University of Washington, Division of Occupational Therapy.

Flippo, K.F., Inge, K.J., & Barcus, J.M. (Eds.). (1995). *Assistive technology: A resource for school, work, and community*. Baltimore: Paul H. Brookes Publishing Co.

Gordon, R. (Presenter). (1995, July 26). *Learning from the winners* [Live teleconference]. Richmond: Virginia Department of Information Technology.

Griffin, S.L., & Wehman, P. (1996). Applications for youth with sensory impairments. In P. Wehman (Ed.), *Life beyond the classroom: Transition strategies for young people with disabilities* (2nd ed., pp. 303–336). Baltimore: Paul H. Brookes Publishing Co.

Individuals with Disabilities Education Act (IDEA) of 1990, PL 101-476, 20 U.S.C. §§ 1400 et seq.

Inge, K.J. (1997). Job site training. In V. Brooke, K.J. Inge, A.J. Armstrong, & P. Wehman (Eds.), *Supported employment handbook: A customer-driven approach for persons with significant disabilities* (pp. 159–197). Richmond: Virginia Commonwealth University, Rehabilitation Research & Training Center on Supported Employment.

Job Accommodation Network. (1997). Discover the facts about job accommodations. [On-line]. Available: http://janweb.icdi.wvu.edu./english/affects. htm.

Mann, W.C., & Lane, J.P. (1991). *Assistive technology for persons with disabilities: The role of occupational therapy.* Rockville, MD: American Occupational Therapy Association.

Phillips, B. (1993). Technology abandonment from the consumer point of view. *NARIC Quarterly, 3*(2,3), 4–91.

Rehabilitation Act Amendments of 1992, PL 102-569, 29 U.S.C. §§ 701 et seq.

Tanchak, T.L., & Sawyer, C. (1995). Augmentative communication. In K.F. Flippo, K.J. Inge, & J.M. Barcus (Eds.), *Assistive technology: A resource for school, work, and community* (pp. 57–79). Baltimore: Paul H. Brookes Publishing Co.

Technology-Related Assistance for Individuals with Disabilities Act of 1988, PL 100-407, 29 U.S.C. §§ 2201 et seq.

Technology-Related Assistance for Individuals with Disabilities Act of 1994, PL 103-218, 29 U.S.C. §§ 2201 et seq.

Turner, E., Barrett, C., Cutshall, A., Lacy, B.K., Keiningham, J., & Webster, M.K. (1995). The user's perspective of assistive technology. In K.F. Flippo, K.J. Inge, & J.M. Barcus (Eds.), *Assistive technology: A resource for school, work, and community* (pp. 283–290). Baltimore: Paul H. Brookes Publishing Co.

Waitley, D. (1996). *Empires of the mind: Lessons to lead and succeed in a knowledge-based world.* New York: Quill-William Morrow.

Wallace, J. [Presenter]. [1995, September]. *Learning from the winners* [Live teleconference]. Richmond: Virginia Department of Information Technology.

Wallace, J., & Neal, S. (1993). *Special topic report: Funding assistive technology.* Richmond: Virginia Assistive Technology System.

Wallace, J.F., Flippo, K.F., Barcus, J.M., & Behrmann, M.M. (1995). Legislative foundation of assistive technology policy in the United States. In K.F. Flippo, K.J. Inge, & J.M. Barcus (Eds.), *Assistive technology: A resource for school, work, and community* (pp. 3–21). Baltimore: Paul H. Brookes Publishing Co.

Related Issues

Section III addresses employment- and career-related issues for people with disabilities. This section focuses on the fact that the path to securing a satisfying career is rarely straight or obvious for anyone. For example, the transition from school to adult life is a major life challenge for all individuals—both those with and without disabilities. Because individuals with disabilities face the additional challenge of *disabilities*, this transition may be complicated by low self-esteem, mobility problems, communication difficulties, or other types of physical and/or health discomforts. Ms. Izzo and her colleagues look at transition in the context of work and career development with a special perspective from a young adult with a disability. The themes from Ms. Izzo's chapter permeate Section III and provide the necessary framework for the remaining chapters in the book.

Dr. West and colleagues wrestle with the difficulties of assessing transportation needs, finding necessary resources, and locating the ideal transportation supports, highlighting the perspectives of an individual with a disability who has experienced firsthand the difficulties associated with transportation. Other important, and often overlooked, issues are making friends, building relationships, and engendering appropriate social skills within the workplace. The Gilsons discuss the reasons that friendships exist and the creation of friendship bonds; and more important, because many people have difficulty with developing friendships, they detail ways to help people with disabilities make and maintain relationships. Many people are unable to get employed or stay employed because of poor relationship abilities, and, therefore, this chapter reminds the reader to look at the whole person and not just at the job in which he or she works.

The final chapter ties together many of the themes found in the book. Written from the perspective of three individuals who use wheelchairs, this chapter addresses gaining access to the community. It is no secret that barriers to people with disabilities still remain in the community, even since the passage of the Americans with Disabilities Act in 1990. In this chapter, Mr. Turner and his colleagues identify self-determination as paramount to successful community access.

CHAPTER

10

Transition from School to Adult Life

New Roles for Educators

Margo Vreeburg Izzo, John R. Johnson,
Mitchell Levitz, and Jennifer H. Aaron

MITCHELL

Mitchell was born in 1971 with Down syndrome, a disability that has presented him with some significant challenges. Mitchell graduated with a Regents diploma from Walter Panas High School in New York in 1991. He is the co-author with his classmate and best friend, Jason Kingsley, of *Count Us In: Growing Up with Down Syndrome*. This widely known book describes many of his experiences while growing up and addresses issues related to self-advocacy, empowerment, and self-determination of people with disabilities. Mitchell's story is taken in part from this book and from interviews conducted for the writing of this chapter.

Mitchell lives independently and is employed full time as the self-advocacy coordinator at Capabilities Unlimited in Cincinnati, Ohio. The

The first author would like to thank colleagues of the transition system change grants, especially Bob Stodden, Joan Mazzoli, Teresa Grossi, Katrina Karoulis, Bob Baer, Lawrence Dennis, and Judy Reichle. Many of the insights incorporated into the chapter emerged through discussions with these and other members of the state and local transition committees of California and Ohio.

following excerpts, taken from Mitchell's book, summarize discussions about his high school and postsecondary experiences and his initial years of employment.

In the following excerpt, Mitchell discusses his final year of high school and his plans for the future:

> I am planning on college, planning on being independent. . . . I have to take responsibility for myself. And the hardest part (is) to make the right decisions and the right judgments. I will study more about government and politics. How the government works and how my skills will get better—my reading skills and writing skills. I probably would get a job working in a government office and to learn the same skills and do what I'm doing now in Assemblyman George Pataki's office. . . . I work one day a week after school. . . . I do the mail, filing, and also straightening things out in the office. . . . This is a voluntary job. This is influencing my future goals, where I'm going. (Kingsley & Levitz, 1994, p. 162)

In this personal conversation, Mitchell discusses his middle school and high school individualized education programs (IEPs):

> I requested to be part of my own IEP meeting. It really helped me to speak up for myself, to make my own decisions and choices. That is all a part of growing up—and part of learning the responsibility to become a young adult. I had both regular education and special education, and I learned a lot of things. One, I learned to be able to develop my own style. In mainstream, I took, business courses, a computer course, and a theater course. It was a decision I made through my guidance counselor and my parents. It was my interest to be in the field where I am today, because I have a strong interest in politics and government. . . . I felt it was important for me to be (at my IEP meeting) so I could speak my mind, and really to make my own choices and decisions. And I felt the people there were very supportive, and they understood what exactly I was talking about. It's something that many people with disabilities should be doing in the future. We will become the next generation of leaders. And if we are given the chance to participate in our own meetings, then we can participate on local, state, and national organizations and committees, because we are proving ourselves—that we can speak up for ourselves. (Students should start going to their IEP meetings) . . . early—like in the middle school years. Because I have seen and noticed that in middle school, they're primarily the hardest years for many students . . . that's where most of the kids will make fun of you, tease you and laugh at you. And sometimes they will even take advantage of you because you have a disability. What I have learned from that experience, is that I am able to develop my own style, and to develop and identify my own strengths, instead of being popular or being with the cool gang. (M. Levitz, personal communication, 1996)

In April 1991, Mitchell was preparing to graduate within the following 2 months. He had taken and passed the New York State Regents Exams, which one must pass to be awarded a Regents high school diploma. Mitchell's discussion of this period follows:

The way I feel is instead of going to college it's better to look for the opportunities where the people can help you, people with disabilities, help you to live on your own. . . . The reason why I decided not to go to college (is) because I feel it would be more difficult and tougher and the courses would be harder, too. . . . I feel that I do not want to repeat courses again and the pressure on me to do it again without the help from my parents.

I see in my future . . . being able to work in government, in an office, being able to continue my skills by joining a residence program. . . Now I am on a waiting list until an apartment is open and when I am accepted to move in, I am able to continue on with my future. . . . And they will give me some knowledge . . . such as cooking, cleaning, shopping . . . to be able to hold your money and to be able to use a budget that is useful to do all I want. The other part is with jobs . . . (is) to find a job that is fit for you and you go into that job . . . and get paid for the job, for my knowledge. After work, they may have dances, they will go to basketball games or down into the city. (Kingsley & Levitz, 1994, pp. 166, 168)

After graduation from high school, Mitchell reflects on his accomplishments:

The graduation felt very important to me. It meant that I achieved a lot. With a lot of support and guidance from my family and friends. . . . When I received the diploma and the awards, . . . I was recognized as a student . . . The graduation ceremony . . . helped me recognize that I have a future. A future that will build to a dream. (Kingsley & Levitz, 1994, p. 50)

Following graduation, in March 1993, Mitchell had been at a local independent living and employment program for people with disabilities for a year and a half. His comments below suggest his acknowledgment of his potential and of the contributions he can make to others with disabilities:

The first thing is to have a job. . . . What I was thinking of is having one job—like working in an office complex . . . instead of sitting at a desk all day; I'd rather go out and go to meetings or meet with clients, like helping people out. I don't want to be in one place. I want to move around. . . . The main key is to be productive. (Kingsley & Levitz, 1994, p. 170)

Helping people with disabilities is of major importance. Being an advocate, speaking out, talking to other people with disabilities, seeing what they have to say, speaking to new families, I do want to have a major contribution toward this. (Kingsley & Levitz, 1994, p. 172).

Jennifer Aaron was identified as having a significant learning disability while she was in grade school. In 1991, she graduated from Ohio University. The following story is based on a personal interview conducted for the writing of this chapter.

JENNIFER

I am a 1991 graduate of Ohio University with a bachelor of arts degree in communications. I was diagnosed as having a learning disability in grade school. I have always used tutoring services for students with learning disabilities to support me in mainstream classes. I explain my disability as "an across-the-board" dyslexic. It means my disability affects every academic area possible. My success comes from understanding my disability at a young age and learning to communicate my needs, as well as my strengths to others. When you find out you have a disability, you have to just deal with it and go on. It's not anybody's fault. I'm 29 now, and I finally understand who I am. I have had to learn time management skills and how to set realistic goals. The learning disability has taught me to give myself permission to make mistakes. And stay focused on what I can do—and not focus on what I can't do.

I offer workshops, which are geared to parents of children with learning disabilities, secondary education students, teachers, and potential employers. My workshops deal with various subjects such as lack of sensitivity and awareness, communicating with teachers, professors, and employers. I also cover accepting and understanding the disability; seeking and accepting help; working with strengths and weaknesses; adaptation for particular needs; and responsibilities of the students, teachers and employers. I conduct exercises that help participants experience firsthand what it is like having a disability. I also have techniques, which I will explain and demonstrate, which will help aid in the frustration often experienced in everyday life.

Always being the "round peg in the square hole," I've still managed to own and operate my own catering business and be a national speaker for alcohol and drug abuse prevention programs. I was also a speaker for Ohio University's Students' Senate and vice-commissioner of minority affairs. I also worked with the students in the education department on what it's like having a learning disability. I spoke to teaching assistants on different learning styles and made a videotape for the university about learning disabilities. (J. Aaron, personal communication, 1996)

The following are Jennifer's comments on self-esteem and self-worth:

A child with a disability needs to understand (his or her) personal self-worth very early—this needs to be the focus early in school. The foundation can be sabotaged by excusing the disability—using the disability as a crutch or becoming overly sensitive or overly protective of the child. The best way to empower the student and family is to keep an open line of communication and to give responsibility to the parent, the students, and the teachers. For example, parents may agree to help with homework. The student will complete homework using good time management skills. Students need to have short-term goals that teach time management. Natural consequences need to be enforced.

Tests and scores are measurements of ability and potential success, but there is no measurement for desire, tenacity, and determination. Everyone misjudged my willingness to pursue what I wanted—an education. The high school counselor told my mom that I'd never make it through college. When I went to college, I had to take charge of my own life. If I didn't go to tutoring . . . the tutor got paid, but I didn't get the help I needed. I took all my tests orally. If I didn't ask for those services, I didn't succeed. I accepted that I needed services. I majored in public and human relations with an emphasis on special populations in order to earn a communications degree. I wanted to be an exercise physiologist because I ran my own aerobics classes and had my own catering company. But I couldn't succeed in logic, physics, and chemistry. My talents are in my people skills. I needed to revise my major to build on my strengths—what I can do.

In our society, today, people will have much more of a chance to succeed, but the need for more awareness is a must for all of us. Life is a series of challenges. I have found that I must focus on my strengths and not on my weaknesses. After all it's not where you start, it's where you finish. (J. Aaron, personal communication, 1996)

THE TRANSITION-PLANNING PROCESS

Mitchell and Jennifer present a number of points to seriously consider during the transition-planning process. The literature has addressed transition from the perspective of professionals with extensive experience studying the transition of students with disabilities from school to adult life. Although these perspectives are important and are intended to assist people with disabilities to achieve success as adults, the importance of both the student and the family perspective in the transition process may have been understated. In fact, Mitchell and Jennifer both mentioned that the *primary* support for their successful transition to adulthood came from their families. Neither mentioned nor addressed concerns near and dear to the hearts of those published in the field such as collaboration, recommended practices, or systems change. Maybe these are important issues to Mitchell and Jennifer; maybe they are not well understood, so they were not even addressed; and maybe they do not even care about these issues. Both Mitchell and Jennifer stated in no uncertain terms that they wanted the lead role in determining their own destinies. Both Mitchell and Jennifer focused on their accomplishments, their responsibilities, their goals, and their perspectives of what they needed to do to get where they wanted to go. They got involved with their IEP planning because it was theirs and their family's—not the school's. They set goals; and as they achieved goals, they set some more. Developing a sense of personal identity and self-determination was not merely a nice psychotherapeutic intervention or extracurricular activity but an essential ingredient of their successful transition. Understanding one's disability was not part of the disability but part of life; that is, understanding one's personal limitations and needs in a healthy balance with a sense of what one can and wants to do. More important, this balance is not taught or structured through formal or informal assessments of needs and strengths. Inferring from Mitchell and Jennifer's comments, achieving a healthy balance is a function of direct experience—at least it was for them.

The reader might not consider either of these stories as typical. Both Mitchell and Jennifer experienced a tremendous amount of parental support and guidance through their transition processes. Some might argue that such family support is unusual, and if their families had not provided this support, Mitchell and Jennifer may have not experienced successful transitions. In addition, it also might be argued that they would not have the self-esteem and confidence in their abilities that they have demonstrated as adults were it not for their families. Although these arguments have merit, they miss the point. The point is that Mitchell and Jennifer were supported not led. Mitchell and Jennifer took the lead role in achieving a successful transition from school to adulthood. They learned that planning begins and really never ends, that achieving one set of goals leads to setting others, and that to achieve goals one must face challenges and work through those challenges sometimes with and sometimes without support. They learned to depend on their own resources and their own skills while acquiring and using resources that were made available to them. Mitchell and Jennifer now realize that they are responsible for their own lives, and they also know how to get what they want. In short, Mitchell and Jennifer suggested that their successful transition could be almost exclusively attributed to their self-determination.

SELF-DETERMINATION:
THE FUNDAMENTAL TRANSITION EXPERIENCE

The stories of Mitchell, Jennifer, and a host of other adults with disabilities who have successfully achieved the transition from school to adulthood make a strong case for concluding that the emergence from adolescence to adulthood may be fundamentally characterized as a quest for self-determination. *In essence, self-determination is **the** transition experience for the adolescent emerging into adulthood.* Employment, independent living, access to the community, and social integration are important and valued outcomes; but in the mind of the teenager, these authors would argue that they are only as important as they are determined and directed by the person achieving them. Those of us who are parents of teenagers do not need research or systems change projects to tell us this. Therefore, the most important lesson learned is from the perspective of the student for whom transition is a true-life experience: A student- or family-directed (also known as consumer-driven) approach to transition from school to adulthood must incorporate self-determination as *the* priority.

Self-Determination Defined

Ward took the first step to define *self-determination* as "the attitudes [that] lead people to define goals for themselves and their ability to take the initiative to achieve these goals." Ward also noted the "importance of people taking control, without undue external influence, over what affects their lives" (1988, p. 2). Wehmeyer described self-determination with respect to "the attitudes and abilities required to act as the primary causal agent in one's life and to make choices and decisions free from undue external influence and interference" (1992, p. 302). Powers et al. referred to self-determination as the "personal attitudes and abilities that facilitate an individual's identification and pursuit of goals." Powers et al. also noted that "the expression of self-determination is reflected in personal attitudes of empowerment, active participation in decision making, and self-directed action to achieve personally valued goals" (1996, p. 292). Attributes associated with self-determination include self-awareness, self-advocacy, self-efficacy, self-regulation, decision making, autonomy, goal setting, assertiveness, and control over what affects one's life (Field & Hoffman, 1996b; Martin, Marshall, Maxson, & Jerman, 1995; Wehmeyer, 1992; Wehmeyer & Kelchner, 1995; Wehmeyer & Lawrence, 1995).

Need for Transition Services that are Student Driven

A generation of students with disabilities completed their entire educational program in 1987 under the provisions of the Education for All Handicapped Children Act of 1975 (PL 94-142), which was amended by the Individuals with Disabilities Education Act (IDEA) of 1990 (PL 101-476) and amended again by the Individuals with Disabilities Education Act Amendments of 1997 (PL 105-17). Follow-up studies conducted in selected states indicated that graduates with disabilities were experiencing poor adjustments to adult life, as evidenced by low employment rates, low wages, and low rates of participation in postsecondary education (Hasazi, Gordon, & Roe, 1985; Mithaug & Horiuchi, 1983). Also in 1987, under a contract with the Office of Special Education Programs, SRI International initiated the National Longitudinal Transition Study of Special Education Students (NLTS) to examine the educational progress of a nationally representative sample of students with disabilities while in special education and to study their occupational, educational, and independent living status after graduating from secondary school (U.S. Department of Education, 1995). Preliminary results of the NLTS study indicated that students with disabilities drop out of school at higher rates and are employed and/or attending postsecondary education programs at significantly lower rates than their peers without disabilities (Wagner, 1989). The first comprehensive report from SRI International, entitled *Youth with Disabilities: How are They Doing?* (1991), indicated the following:

- Approximately one third of students with disabilities dropped out of school (32%), and an additional 4% were expelled or suspended, as compared with 20% of their peers without disabilities. The dropout rate was highest for youth with serious emotional disturbances (50%).
- Among out-of-school youth, approximately 46% were reported to be employed, a rate markedly lower than their peers without disabilities. Among those employed, 40% worked part time.
- Enrollment in occupationally oriented vocational education, receipt of tutoring assistance, and personal counseling were significantly related to a lower probability of dropping out of school.

Policy makers responded to these poor postschool outcomes by focusing renewed attention on the student's role in preparing for successful transitions to adult life through legislation for both school and agency personnel. An expanded role for students/families is specifically addressed in IDEA of 1990, the Rehabilitation Act Amendments of 1992 (PL 102-569), and the School-to-Work Opportunities Act (STWOA) of 1994 (PL 103-329). School-to-work transitions became a national priority for *all* students as the United States began to acknowledge the role that students must embrace to improve employment and adult life outcomes. A new surge of student-focused empowerment philosophies emerged such as self-determination, self-directed IEPs, and person-centered planning. It suddenly became trendy and politically correct to implement student-focused and person-centered planning processes. These student-driven practices cannot be implemented unless educators and other services providers assume a new role—one that empowers students to take control of their lives. Educators and other human services providers must assume a cooperative, supportive, and assistive role that promotes people with disabilities and their families in determining how they want to live, work, and play as adults.

KEY LEGISLATION

The following section presents an overview of key legislation related to transitions made by people with disabilities.

IDEA of 1990

In 1990, IDEA added new obligations, through the IEP process, for school systems to include a focus on planning for adult life after the secondary school years. A statement of the needed transition services must be included within the IEP as well as, if appropriate, a statement of each participating agency's responsibilities or linkages, or both, before the student leaves the school setting. Therefore, schools are obligated to coordinate the referral process to ensure that students gain services that they may need and that they may be eligible to receive to be successful in their adult roles.

Transition is defined in IDEA as a

coordinated set of activities for a student, designed within an outcome-oriented process, that promotes movement from school to post-school activities, including post-secondary education, vocational training, integrated employment (including supported employment), continuing adult education, adult services, independent living or community participation. The coordinated set of activities . . . must be based upon the individual student's needs, taking into account student's preferences and interest; and include instruction, community experiences, the development of employment and other post-school adult living objectives, and, if appropriate, acquisition of daily living skills and functional vocational evaluation. (1990, 34 C.F.R. §300.18)

The definition of transition introduces four components of transition planning that IEP planning teams must consider: Plans must 1) have a coordinated set of activities, which includes instruction, community experiences, and the development of employment and other postschool adult living objectives; 2) be designed within an outcome-oriented process; 3) be based on the individual's needs; and 4) promote movement to other postschool activities such as employment, adult education, adult services, and independent living.

The coordinated set of activities should connect instruction (or school-based learning) with the community experiences (or work-based learning) through objectives that address employment and other postschool adult living competencies. Activities also should be coordinated across academic settings. The general, special, and/or vocational educators can coordinate their lessons to maximize the impact that their educational objectives have on the student. These integrated activities may assist the student to connect subject matter across curricula as well as within the world of work through work-based community experiences. The IEP also should document services provided by school and adult services agencies so that strategies that work and the progress that the student makes can be reinforced.

To effectively design services using an outcome-oriented process, IEP teams must initiate transition planning with the student's long-range goals for employment and independent living. If these long-term plans require college course work, then the IEP team should plan to meet postsecondary prerequisites such as a given number of credits dispersed across math, science, and English. If the student's vision encompasses supported employment and supported living outcomes (i.e., intended outcomes), however, the IEP team should assess the knowledge, skills, and attitudes (i.e., needed transition services) to teach to the student to assist him or her with postschool goals. In essence, the transition planning process drives the educational program for youth with disabilities (Izzo & Shumate, 1992; Virginia Department of Education, 1995; Wehman, 1995).

Whereas, traditionally, the IEP team planned annual goals and objectives for a 1-year period, IDEA of 1990 required the IEP team to include a statement of the needed transition services for each student by age 16 (and younger, if appropriate), which ultimately promotes movement to postschool outcomes such as employment. Therefore, the focus of the educational program is not simply to assist students to earn credits toward graduation but to promote movement to employment and independent living outcomes. Systems change and educational reform are needed by both secondary and adult services programs to implement quality transition services for youth with disabilities.

IDEA Amendments of 1997

The IDEA Amendments were signed by President Clinton on June 4, 1997. Although the definition of transition services remains the same, two changes concerning the implementation of transitions were made:

> 1) Beginning when a student is 14, and annually thereafter, the student's IEP must contain a statement of his or her transition service needs under the various components of the IEP that focus upon the student's courses of study (such as participation in advance-placement courses or a vocational education program); and 2) beginning at least one year before the student reaches the age of majority under State law, the IEP must contain a statement that the student has been informed of the rights under the law that will transfer to him or her upon reaching the age of majority. (1997, §614[d][1])

The IDEA Amendments of 1997 require the IEP to focus on transition planning from age 14, and annually thereafter, and on the delivery of services from age 16, and annually thereafter. The emphasis on transition planning beginning at age 14 brings increased attention to the need for planning appropriate transition services within the context of the secondary education program and the potential adult services programs. The IEP team needs to involve the student to determine what his or her desired postschool outcomes are, and then focus attention on how the student's educational program can be planned to assist the student in making a successful transition to postschool goals.

In addition to the transition services requirements, IDEA states that if the purpose of the meeting is the consideration of transition services, the school must invite the student. If the student does not attend, the school must take other steps to ensure that the student's preferences and interests are taken into account. Parents, too, must be informed that the student and any other agency representatives have been invited to the meeting.

The intent of IDEA is evident: Students with disabilities must be invited to become active participants whose interests, preferences, and needs drive the IEP process. As Mitchell Levitz testified:

> I requested to be part of my own IEP meeting. It really helped me to speak up for myself . . . to make my own decisions and choices. It's something that many persons with disabilities should be doing in the future. We will become the next generation of leaders. (M. Levitz, personal communication, 1996)

Rehabilitation Act Amendments of 1992

The Rehabilitation Act Amendments of 1992 also include changes related to the role of rehabilitation services in making transitions. The amendments include the same definition of transition that is presented in IDEA of 1990. Section 103 of the Rehabilitation Act Amendments promotes the attainment of long-term rehabilitation goals and intermediate rehabilitation objectives to the scope of rehabilitation services. The Rehab Act requires states to outline how "they will facilitate the development and accomplishment of long-term rehabilitation goals, intermediate rehabilitation objectives, and goals and objectives related to enabling a student to live independently before the student leaves a school setting" (Barcus, 1995, p. 2). This act requires each state rehabilitation program to specify within its state plan how transition services will be coordinated with the educational agencies. The plan must address policies that will be implemented to ensure that students who require rehabilitation services receive those services with no break as the students exit school (Barcus, 1995).

Students with disabilities must be active participants in their own rehabilitation programs, including making meaningful and informed choices about the selection of their vocational goals and objectives and the vocational rehabilitation services that they receive, as indicated on their individualized written rehabilitation programs. The act clearly states that disability is a natural part of the human experience and in no way diminishes the right of individuals to live independently, to enjoy self-determination, to make choices, and ultimately, to contribute to society.

School-to-Work Opportunities Act of 1994

The STWOA was passed May 4, 1994. Congress recognized in the STWOA that improving employment outcomes for all students would require a fundamental restructuring of the educational services system (Benz & Kochhar, 1996). By recognizing the relationship among schooling and the broader issues of work force development, this joint initiative between the U.S. Departments of Education and Labor calls on states to improve the knowledge and skills of all students by integrating academic and occupational learning, by integrating school-based and work-based learning, and by building the connection between school environments and such postschool environments as postsecondary education and employment. With specific references to students with disabilities and other minority students, this act recognizes the need to create a high-quality school-to-work transition system that enables all students to successfully enter the workplace and participate fully in their communities (Norman & Bourexis, 1995).

The National School-to-Work Office provides an overview of STWOA:

> This law provides seed money to states and local partnerships of business, labor, government, education, and community organizations to develop school-to-work (STW) systems. This law doesn't create a new program. It allows states and their partners to bring together efforts at education reform, worker preparation and economic development to create a system—A system to prepare youth for the high wage, high skill careers of today's and tomorrow's global economy.
>
> Using federal seed money, states and their partnerships design the school-to-work system that makes the most sense for them. There is no single model. While these systems are different from state to state, each provides every American student with:
>
> - Relevant education—allowing students to explore different careers and see what skills are required in their working environment;
> - Skills—obtained from structured training and work-based learning experiences, including necessary skills of a particular career as demonstrated in a working environment; and
> - Valued credentials—establishing industry-standard benchmarks and developing education and training standards [that] ensure that proper education is received for each career. (School-to-Work Web Page, 1997)

The goals of STWOA include the following:

- Establishing the framework within which all states can create school-to-work systems that are part of comprehensive education reform

- Helping students achieve high-level academic and occupational skills
- Widening opportunities for all students to participate in postsecondary education and advanced training and to move into high-wage, high-skill careers
- Providing enriched learning experiences for low-achieving youth, school dropouts, and youth with disabilities; and assisting them in obtaining good jobs and pursuing postsecondary education
- Increasing opportunities for minorities, women, and people with disabilities by enabling them to prepare for careers from which they traditionally have been excluded and utilizing workplaces as active learning environments in the educational process.

Two components described in the preceding list include systems-building and an emphasis on *all* students. The latter is of particular importance and interest to the National School-to-Work Office, particularly as it applies to students with disabilities.

As of 1997, a total of 37 states have been awarded implementation grants, and all 50 states, the District of Columbia, and 7 U.S. territories had received noncompetitive development grants totaling $24.3 million in 1994. Since the passage of STWOA, $245 million was appropriated in fiscal year 1995, and $350 million was appropriated in fiscal year 1996 (Riley & Reich, 1996). These grants were awarded to design statewide School-to-Work systems and may be renewed until a state is ready to compete for, and be awarded, a School-to-Work implementation grant. The STWOA identifies three core components that compose a school-to-work system. They include school-based learning, work-based learning, and connecting activities. These components are described in further detail in a subsequent section of this chapter.

Enforcing the Transition Requirements: News from the Courts

The transition requirements undoubtedly impose new and expanded duties on already-strapped public school districts (Hakola, 1996). IDEA requires a coordinated set of activities including instruction, community experiences, and employment and other postschool adult objectives, and when appropriate, acquisition of daily living skills and functional vocational evaluation (34 C.F.R. §300.18). Clearly such activities can involve a broad range of services—including vocational training, curriculum beyond the standard offerings of public high schools, and community-based instruction. Congress' sweeping language indicates a legislative intent for an expansive and flexible range of services that, in part, need to be delivered beyond the walls of the school building. Hakola commented that as with special education in general, the touchstone will be individualization and appropriateness. Services must be tailored to the particular needs of the individual student and schools should be wary of falling into a "one size fits all" approach, even, for example, when the school's career preparation program is outstanding. (1996, p. 2)

Hakola reported that "as of October 1996, the *Individuals with Disabilities Education Law Report* indicated that there have been about 10 disputed cases involving the merits of transition services which have been decided by hearing officers" (1996, p. 3). Of these decisions, seven favored the student/parent position, and three favored the school district. The following are summaries of key cases involving transition services (Hakola, 1996):

- In *Mason City Community School District*, a district's transition efforts were determined to be inadequate when a 19-year-old student with mental retardation requiring intermittent support was slated for graduation because he had met the requisite number of credit hours under the district graduation policy. Although the transition plan indicated that the vocational rehabilitation agency would be contacted at the time of the student's graduation, the hearing officer ruled that the transition plan was inadequate because it did not detail the specific responsibilities of the school and vocational rehabilitation agency and did not include instruction, community experiences, and the development of employment and other postschool objectives. The hearing officer also faulted the school for not establishing individualized graduation criteria for the student.
- In another case involving a different 19-year-old student, "a hearing officer found that a school policy of graduation once a certain number of credit hours were reached violated the IDEA with respect to students with more severe disabilities who do not simply participate in the general curriculum but instead require significant alterations in teaching methods and expected outcomes... For such students, termination of services must be based on attainment of individualized criteria for graduation. Further, the individualized graduation criteria must be determined in a manner which includes parent and student participation" (Hakola, 1996, p. 4). Another hearing officer commented that the use of a checklist approach to transition planning was woefully inadequate.
- In *Chuhran v. Warren Consolidated Schools*, "the federal courts upheld a hearing officer's decisions that the failure to have a written transition plan was a harmless error, finding that despite the lack of written transition plans, the school had contracted vocational rehabilitation on a timely basis and had made coordinated efforts to

plan for the student's departure from high school" (Hakola, 1996, p. 4).

- In *Yankton School District v. Schramm*, the courts found fault with the school transition planning process and stated that "simply telling the student and her family about other community agencies and leaving it up to the family to follow through is inadequate. . . . The federal court examined the legislative history and found that Congress intended that schools 'familiarize themselves with the post-school opportunities and services available for students with disabilities in their communities,' and 'take responsibility for developing and implementing interagency participation' rather than leave such tasks up to the family or an 'already heavily-burdened teacher' " (Hakola, 1996, p. 4).

Hakola (1996) commented that these cases highlight some critical areas in which schools are at risk of inappropriate planning. He offered the following practical approaches to increase the quality of transition plans and to minimize legal risks:

1. Examine the interrelationship between graduation requirements and transition planning; graduation termination decisions must be addressed by the IEP team rather than by general district policy.
2. Involve vocational rehabilitation and other agency personnel on a timely basis, well in advance of the termination of special education services.
3. Involve the student and his or her family in a meaningful and productive manner.
4. Ensure that all specific activities—instruction, community experiences, and employment and adult living objectives—are documented by the school district. The IEP must indicate when and how these services are coordinated or indicate why the IEP team decided that these services are not needed by the student at this time.
5. Special education staff members should work closely with their peers in community agencies to develop expertise in the services and roles of these other agencies. The special education staff should meet regularly with representatives from these other agencies to systematically explore ways of adapting traditional services to meet individualized needs.

If the schools in these cases had implemented a family-/student-driven process to develop an IEP that resulted in a transition to post-school environments based on the students' interests, abilities, and special needs, it is doubtful that the families would have taken legal actions. The student-focused process would have resulted in an IEP that would have deviated significantly from the districts' general graduation policies. More important, if the students were engaged in postschool environments of their choosing before graduation—such as jobs based on the students' interests and abilities—then the students would have successfully made the transition to their adult lives.

THE GRADUATION DILEMMA

A common theme throughout Hakola's (1996) report is the relationship between transition planning and graduation requirements. The National Transition Network (NTN) first addressed this dilemma in a 1993 Parent Brief entitled "Students and the Graduation Dilemma" (NTN, 1993). The Parent Brief stated that

> for many students with disabilities, a high school diploma (and when to accept it) is sometimes a dilemma. Rather than being a celebration of a job well done, a high school diploma can be an end to the special education services and supports a student has been entitled to under the law. (NTN, 1993, p. 1)

The Parent Brief asked the U.S. Department of Education if school systems can continue to provide transition services after graduation. The Department commented as follows:

> The IDEA neither requires nor prohibits the provision of services to a student after the student has completed the state's graduation requirements. Thus, if the student is still within the eligible age range for free and appropriate public education (FAPE) within the state, the state at its discretion could continue to provide needed transition services to the student and use funds under the IDEA to pay for the transition services or contribute to the cost of those services through a shared cost arrangement with another agency—provided that all applicable requirements of this part are met. (NTN, 1993, p. 1)

Clearly, IDEA permits states to continue providing services after graduation, as long as the student is within the age requirements.

Deferred Graduation

Some districts across Ohio have addressed the issue of continuing services by implementing a policy of "deferred graduation" (Rutkowski, 1996). Deferred graduation is a district-level policy and/or procedure that allows students with disabilities the opportunity to go through the graduation ceremony when they have earned all the necessary credits for graduation. The diploma is held with the school district, and the student can continue with his or her education at the local school or at the vocational school until he or she completes the school year of his or her 22nd birthday. If the educational program is completed before that time and/or the IEP team decides that the student is ready to leave the educational system, the student can accept the diploma and end services from the school district (Rutkowski, 1996).

There are many benefits to deferring graduation for students with disabilities. First, it allows students who have earned the required credits for graduation to participate in the graduation ceremony with their peers, but because they decline to accept the diploma, they can continue to gain additional vocational and transitional services. Second, even though students with disabilities are chronologically the same age as their peers, frequently they are developmentally delayed. Remaining in school allows students additional time to learn necessary daily living skills, vocational competencies, basic academics, and any other skills necessary to be successful as they make the transition from school to adult life. Third, there are many resources and services available for students while they are in a school setting that are not available or are costly after graduation. Fourth, students can participate in a vocational training program to gain skills for competitive employment. This can be seen by students and their families as a postsecondary experience. Students could participate in the vocational program half day and then gain work experience in a related job on a part-time basis. The job placement services of the vocational program would benefit the student as he or she makes the transition from school to work (Rutkowski, 1996).

There also are merits for the school district that adopts the deferred graduation policy. First, the policy demonstrates the district's commitment to the transition-planning process. Second, the district could continue to count the youth as a student and gain the federal and state flow-through dollars. Third, the student and school personnel would have additional time to complete the transition goals. And finally, the district's Business Advisory Council as well as the local business/industry community would support deferred graduation because it would better prepare students for the work force (Rutkowski, 1996).

Preferred Consumer-Driven Transition Practices

Table 1 outlines both traditional transition practices and recommended practices to shift service providers' perspectives from "systems thinking" to "consumer-focused thinking." Based on historical and more recent follow-up studies of what happens to youth with disabilities after high school as well as on court decisions, it appears clear that in the late 1990s there is inadequate transition preparation of students with disabilities. The common practice of graduation on completion of the students required number of Carneigie Units does not meet the intent, nor the spirit, of IDEA. The intent of IDEA promotes

Table 1. Traditional and proposed consumer-directed transition practices

Traditional transition practices/concepts	Proposed consumer-directed transition practices/concepts
Underlying assumptions	
• Students graduate from school once they have earned the Carneigie Units required by district policies	• Students graduate after they are enrolled in postsecondary or adult services programs and/or are employed in jobs of their choice
• Agency representatives who could provide necessary services and supports not involved in IEP meeting	• Student's vision for employment and adult living drives IEP
• Focus on satisfying agency documentation requirement rather than on addressing individual's needs	• Student writes his or her own goals/objectives
• Delayed employment and reduced independence	• IEP integrates instruction; significant community experiences based on student's interests and needs
• Wasted staff time and resources; confused and frustrated students and families	• Agency representatives intricately involved in transition planning
• IEP written by professionals with minimal student/family input	• Services jointly planned and funded by numerous agencies
• IEP written to complete school requirements for graduation, not to provide skills needed for transition to adult life	• Students and families develop, manage, and evaluate individualized plans (Gillespie & Turnbull, 1983)
Single-service coordination process	
• Many potential service coordinators exist (e.g., work-study coordinators, counselors, case managers, probation officers)	• Service coordination process consistent across agencies, and all utilize basic person-centered principles that empower the student/family through active involvement in all decisions
• Service coordinators do not have clear understanding of different agencies' eligibility criteria or services	• Student/family selects preferred service coordinator from their IEP team participants
• Existing service coordinators place students in programs rather than customizing individualized services and supports for student	• Selected service coordinator builds a relationship with and serves the student/family over a period of years and interacts with service providers across programs/agencies to ensure that a quality transition process occurs without gaps
• Each agency prefers to have its own separate meeting and requires its own planning document	
• Often confusion among individuals with disabilities and their families	

Assessment, eligibility, and referral process

- Focus on past or current impairments of student, instead of on desired results
- Families, consumers, and service providers unduly burdened with multiple layers of assessment, eligibility, and referral requirements
- School personnel not aware of all potential services that may be available and therefore do not gain access to community or adult services in a timely manner
- Students do not receive necessary services or supports and/or are placed on waiting lists

- Assessments completed to determine strengths, interests, preferences, and special needs using a consumer profile/mapping process that clarifies consumer choices
- Assessment results implemented by one agency are accepted by other agencies to reduce the number of assessments that students must complete
- Common intake and referral forms used by multiple agencies, reducing the amount of paperwork to process
- A common release of information form used and accepted by all human services agencies

Single planning process and document

- Separate planning forms, processes and meetings
- Lack of involvement of people who can help the youth move toward desired future goals
- Focus on agency documentation requirements rather than on consumer choices
- Repetitive information on separate plans, requiring wasted time on service providers and families to sort-through
- Goals/objectives/services duplicated by several programs, and gaps in services not addressed

- Develop a single planning process and document that coordinates services across multiple agencies
- Involve relevant people in all planning meetings to help reduce duplication and/or gaps in services
- Empower consumer to take responsibility for his or her plan
- Focus on the strengths, interests, preferences, and life goals of student
- Standardize information across agencies to reduce time engaged in gathering information

Cross-training

- Training activities fragmented, uncoordinated, redundant in some areas but missing in others
- Training resources and programs for service providers and families not delivered in a timely manner
- Training programs and supports targeted to families not adequate to meet the needs
- Most training programs are delivered by professionals for professionals—families/consumers are not involved in the planning or delivery of training

- Cross-training initiatives that are jointly coordinated and funded by multiple agencies that target service providers across those agencies and families/consumers
- Cross-training planned and implemented by families and service providers
- Cross-training includes student perspectives delivered by students
- Cross-training results in consistent knowledge across families, school, and agency personnel

(continued)

Table 1. (continued)

Traditional transition practices/concepts	Proposed consumer-directed transition practices/concepts
Empowerment strategies	
• Families and students do not feel empowered, therefore, are not active participants • Lack of family and student input to the transition process • Lack of sensitivity to cultural values and barriers • Lack of early transition planning by families, students, and service providers	• Students empowered to lead their own IEP meetings • Students take responsibility for their own plans • Students and families advocate for customized services and supports • Students and families have the freedom to plan their lives with necessary supports rather than purchase programs • Students and families have authority to control a certain sum of dollars to purchase supports • Educators will implement self-determination curricula (Field & Hoffman, 1996; Wehmeyer & Kelchner, 1995) • Educators will structure opportunities for students to develop relationships with adult mentors who will support their self-determination • Listen to lessons learned from adults with disabilities who have made successful transitions

the concept of students successfully moving into adult life once a carefully sequenced transition-planning process has been implemented that is based on the students' visions for employment and adult living and includes instruction, community experiences, employment and adult living objectives, and interagency linkages and supports. Ideally, the students are engaged in their postschool environments prior to graduation from secondary education programs. If not actively engaged, the student has clear plans for entering a postsecondary program, for gaining employment, or for gaining services from an adult services agency.

During the final years of a student's educational program, the transition plan—namely the intended postschool outcomes in employment, postsecondary education, adult living, and community participation—must drive the IEP. These postschool outcomes must be based on the student's interests, preferences, and desires. Discussions concerning outcomes need to occur frequently during the final years of a student's secondary education program and should not be limited to an annual IEP meeting. Table 1 provides traditional "systems thinking" transition practices and recommended "consumer-focused" practices across seven areas: underlying assumptions; single-service coordination; assessment, eligibility and referral process; single planning process; cross-training; and empowerment strategies.

COORDINATING TRANSITION SERVICES THROUGH A SINGLE PLANNING PROCESS

As of the late 1990s, eight agencies use agency-specific planning documents to plan services (Ohio Department of Education, 1996). Each of these planning documents contains similar information related to the consumer and his or her services such as the following:

- Demographic data such as name, address, birth date, and so forth
- Case numbers or Social Security numbers
- Dates—placement, initiation/duration of services, and review dates
- Assessment data—current levels of performance and identification of strengths and needs
- Services information—agency names, service coordinators, and so forth
- Goals and objectives—academic, employment, independent living and/or treatment (with evaluation procedures), criteria, and support services needed
- Signature information—signatures for the agency representative, the consumer, and/or family members

The planning process results in the development of a planning document, which is designed to coordinate services for the individual within a particular agency but not necessarily with other agencies also providing services. Planning documents are generally completed by a teacher, service coordinator, vocational rehabilitation counselor, social worker, therapist, or advisor in conjunction with consumer, family, and adjunct personnel (i.e., clinical staff, advocates, other agency personnel) through a face-to-face meeting. The amount of time for participants to meet and complete the document ranges from 1 to 4 hours with an average of approximately 2 hours (California School to Work Interagency Transition Partnership [STWITP], 1995). Participants may become overwhelmed with volumes of paperwork and too many meetings rather than focusing on outcomes for the youth with a disability. The following results can occur when a consumer in transition receives services from more than one agency (California STWITP, 1996; Ohio Department of Education, 1996):

- Separate planning forms, processes, and meetings
- Lack of involvement of people who can help the youth move toward his or her desired future goals
- Focus on past or current impairments of the consumer instead of on desired results
- Focus on agency documentation requirements rather than on the consumer
- Confusion and frustration among consumers, their families, and other planning participants
- Delay of services to assist the consumer reach goals
- Waste of staff resources
- Magnification of costs in terms of staff and consumer time

Transition planning involves the development of multiple plans describing goals, objectives, and services that may result in fragmentation of services that ultimately disempowers the consumer, his or her family, and services providers. The next section discusses an interagency, consumer-driven planning process as a solution to the disjointed services delivery process.

Proposed Interagency Consumer-Driven Planning and Process

Some advocates have proposed to replace the separate agency planning process with a single planning document/process to be shared by all agencies that share mutual consumers with disabilities. The proposed system would have the youth and family meet with interagency services providers and community representatives in a mutual planning and service coordination effort, resulting in one coordinated planning document and one transition service coordinator being responsible for overseeing the implementation of the plan.

The following parameters are provided to guide the development of a single planning document/process:

- Actively involve the student and his or her family members in the planning process. Use person-centered planning to ensure consumer choice and empowerment.
- Provide an orientation to participants of the person-centered planning process, including the purpose of the plan and the roles and responsibilities of staff, parents/guardians, student, other agency personnel, and others as appropriate.
- Establish a shared vision with the student and participants beyond school in the areas of employment, postsecondary education, postschool adult living and community participation.
- Explore with the student and family information about all service options and community supports that assist the student now and in the future, in the areas of independent living, community participation, employment, education, and if appropriate, activities of daily living and functional vocational evaluation.
- Assist the student and family to determine who will serve as the services coordinator, with the planning team actively involved.
- Maintain communication among the student, family, teachers, service providers, advocates, and friends to monitor the progress that the student is making toward the long-term goal(s) and the delivery of services.
- Develop an integrated plan that indicates roles, responsibilities, timelines, individualized outcomes, the single services coordinator, and future meeting dates. Ensure that all people involved in the development of the plan are aware of and agree to the commitments identified on the plan.
- Address issues of confidentiality and release of information during plan development.

A multiagency transition planning document and process are expected to result in more effective transition planning. For the family and the student, this process is expected to result in fewer meetings, a focus on strengths, interests, preferences, and life goals and outcomes rather than agency documentation requirements.

MODELS OF CAREER DEVELOPMENT

The early conceptualization of the transition of youth with disabilities from school to adulthood did not significantly deviate from typical developmental models addressing transition from adolescence to adulthood. Traditional developmental stages typically describe stages from early infancy through late adulthood (Capuzzi & Gross, 1995), including infancy (through age 5 years), later childhood (ages 6–12), adolescence through early adulthood (ages 12–24), early adulthood (ages 21–40), middle adulthood (ages 40–60), and late adulthood (ages 60+). Developmental approaches typically include descriptors of physical, intellectual, emotional, social, and sexual attributes and functioning. Counseling and psychotherapeutic approaches tend to examine developmental stages in terms of presenting problems that may be attributed to change occurring during developmental stages. Although Levinson's (1978) work focused exclusively on adult male development, he suggested that the process of transition begins at around age 17 and continues until around age 33. He also suggested that it takes about 15 years to emerge from adolescence into stable adult life. Ianacone and Stodden conceptualized transition for youth with disabilities as the "process of movement through life phases, or the methodology associated with the life development process of persons as they move from the structure of one social institution or services delivery system to that of another" (1987, p. 3).

In addition to developmental theories through various stages are theories of career development and the development of a work personality. (See Hershenson & Szymanski, 1992, for a comprehensive overview and description of the potential application of theories and models of career development to people with disabilities. Specifically, Hershenson and Szymanski provide an overview of each model, their key elements, basic propositions, common applications, and special concerns for people with disabilities.)

Traditional developmental models have a number of limitations when used to address the issues confronting youth with disabilities. First, traditional developmental models did not account for the significant barriers that youth and adults with disabilities confronted to achieving typical postsecondary outcomes. Issues that often require intensive planning, training, and/or support services are dropout prevention; social isolation; educational segregation; employment discrimination; the need for ongoing supports to achieve employment; accommodations required for successful postsecondary education and training; limited opportunities for postsecondary education and training; employment and independent living; and issues related to communication, transportation, and accessibility. Second, although there was an assumed relationship between school-based experiences and postsecondary experiences, developmental models emphasized psychosocial and emotional milestones and processes. Based on the results of longitudinal and follow-up/follow-along studies of adolescents and adults with disabilities who exited school, it became obvious that the successful transition of youth with disabilities was not simply a developmental process but would require a more systematic approach for achieving desired goals on leaving high school. A third problem involved definition and scope. Developmental models tended to focus on psychosocial characteristics of a mature adult to define the successful transition from adolescence to adulthood. For people with disabilities, transition was defined initially as achieving employment on exiting school and was quickly expanded to include a variety of typical adult experiences including but not limited to employment, independent living, development of social support networks, and postsecondary education and training experiences.

MODELS OF TRANSITION FROM SCHOOL TO ADULTHOOD FOR STUDENTS WITH DISABILITIES

A number of conceptual models have been proposed that suggest the degree, type, duration, and range of services and supports necessary for students with disabilities to successfully exit school and to be successful as adults. Some of the most widely disseminated models are discussed in the following sections (for a comprehensive summary, see Gajar, Goodman, & McAfee, 1993; Wehman, 1996).

Bridges from School to Work

In 1984, Madeleine Will released a policy paper for the U.S. Department of Education, Office of Special Education and Rehabilitative Services (OSERS) in her capacity as Assistant Secretary, proposing a model of transition from school to work for students with disabilities. This model included three bridges from school to work representing her conceptualization of the degree and duration of supports students might need. These supports included no support, time-limited support, and ongoing support. The focus of Ms. Will's proposed model was on the successful employment of students with disabilities on exiting school. This focus continues to be a major influence in subsequently proposed models of transition.

Community Adjustment Model

Halpern (1985) proposed a model of transition for students with disabilities that focused on community adjustment defined in terms of residential environment (or independent living), employment, and social and interpersonal networks. His model expanded on Will's (1984) model by incorporating the degree and duration of services and supports (i.e., generic, time-limited, and ongoing) included in her model. This model continues to receive widespread support in the education and research communities. In 1993, Halpern revised his model to argue for the application of quality of life outcomes as a conceptual framework for delivering and evaluating transition services.

Vocational Transition Model

Wehman, Kregel, and Barcus (1985) suggested a model of transition focused on vocational services. They proposed three stages that address the types of services that would be provided in secondary vocational special education programs. These stages included the delivery of 1) functional curricula, integrated school environments, and community-based services; 2) an individualized program planning process that includes interagency cooperation and direct involvement and participation by the student and parent; and 3) achievement of a vocational outcome related to competitive employment, work crew placement, or other specialized arrangements. Again, employment continued to be a critical focus for this model.

Life-Centered Career Education Model

Brolin and Kokaska (1979) proposed one of the earliest career/ vocational education and transition models for students with disabilities. This model addresses the major components of the school experience including competencies necessary for successful transition. The model involves the family, the school, and community experiences to facilitate learning across four stages of career development 1) awareness, 2) exploration, 3) preparation, and 4) placement/follow-up. Competencies developed for this model are organized into three major curricular areas including daily living skills, personal-social skills, and occupational guidance and preparation. Competencies were designed to be integrated within the general education curriculum.

National School-To-Work Opportunities Model

As indicated earlier, the three components of the transition from school to work envisioned through STWOA included school-based learning, work-based learning, and connecting activities. Each are described in detail.

School-Based Learning As might be expected, school-based activities focus on those activities directly related to school-based planning, learning, and collaboration that promote a successful transition from school to work. School-based learning component may include but are not limited to the following activities:

- Curriculum and instruction that meets academic standards each state has established for all students

- Hands-on learning experiences
- Integration of applied academics and workplace learning
- Employer input that provides real-life applications that are project and problem-based
- New schedules and teaching approaches
- Established career clusters

Work-Based Learning Work-based learning focuses on the interface and interaction between school and the business community, which promotes vocational/career development, work skills and attitudes, and building relationships with the business and labor communities in private and public sectors. Work-based learning components may include job shadowing, internships, services learning, paid work experiences, youth apprenticeships, cooperative work experiences, and school-based enterprises. Work-based learning for teachers, often called teacher externships, also are encouraged. During these experiences teachers spend time within employment settings to learn how to apply academics to workplace tasks and demands.

Connecting Activities Connecting activities emphasize the integration of school-based and work-based activities and collaborative relationships among schools, communities, employers, families, and students. Connecting activities require the development of active participatory partnerships among all relevant stakeholders including K–12 education, higher education, business and industry, organized labor, community-based organization, human services, parents, and students. Connecting activities of a comprehensive school-to-work system encourages the active involvement of all stakeholders to establish a greater understanding of the school setting and the work setting by all parties and may include the following:

- Providing professional development to teachers, administrators, and counselors
- Training worksite mentors
- Providing technical assistance to help teachers integrate work-based learning in their curriculum and instruction
- Providing teachers, students, and parents with information about work-based learning opportunities available in their communities
- Matching students with appropriate worksite experiences

Preparation, Linkage, Connection/ Reception: The Common Denominators

Three elements common to models of transition that have emerged for youth with disabilities are preparation, linkage, and connection/ reception (Ianacone & Stodden, 1987). *Preparation* refers to school-based experiences and activities that promote the skills, knowledge, and mastery necessary to achieve adult-based goals. In addition, preparation involves comprehensive planning focused on identifying adult-referenced goals and lifestyles and determining the experiences and services necessary to achieve those goals. Examples of transition activities and components that may be categorized as preparation include the application of curricular and instructional systems such as Life Centered Career Education, emphasis on work-based experiences, and person-centered planning approaches. *Linkage* refers to those activities that include the involvement of non–school-based agencies and organizations (e.g., vocational rehabilitation, mental health) and personnel to plan, develop, and implement services intended to assist students with exiting school and achieving postsecondary outcomes such as employment, independent living, or enrollment in postsecondary education or training programs. In addition, services may be provided by agencies in a number of other areas deemed appropriate for achieving successful transition to adult life.

Connection/reception involves the actual movement from high school into adult life and postsecondary environments. Connection/reception activities directly result in employment, independent living, enrollment and completion postsecondary education, and training programs and participation in typical adult-based and community environments.

OSERS-Sponsored Initiatives

OSERS has been directly involved with promoting the successful transition of youth with disabilities from school to adult life since the early 1980s. The Education of the Handicapped Act Amendments of 1983 (PL 98-199) authorized more than $5,000,000 for fiscal years 1984 through 1986 to implement Section 625 of the "Postsecondary Education Programs" and more than $6,000,000 for grants authorized by Section 626, "Secondary Education and Transitional Services for Handicapped Youth" (Rusch, Kohler, & Hughes, 1992). These sections, and the associated fiscal allocation, are an indication of the increased attention to the relationship between school-based experiences of youth with disabilities and their early adult experiences on graduation or exiting school. Since 1983, OSERS has continued to be directly involved with promoting the successful transition of youth with disabilities using discretionary monies to fund projects that involve research, systems change, technical assistance, training, demonstration, and dissemination of products and materials related to transition. The Transition Research Institute reported in their 1995 Compendium of Transition Model Demonstration Programs that OSERS has funded 393 programs to facilitate a wide range of service delivery models to promote the successful transition of youth and adults with disabilities from secondary education to higher education, employment, independent living and into their local communities (Gajar et al., 1993; Harmon, Wallace, Grayson, & Leach, 1995).

National Transition Network The NTN provides technical assistance and evaluation services to states with grants for Transition Systems Change and School-to-Work Implementation and Development. The general mission of NTN is to strengthen the capacity of individual states to effectively improve transition and school-to-work policies, programs, and practices as they relate to youth with disabilities. In addition to direct technical assistance to states with projects, NTN develops and disseminates a variety of policy publications and other networking activities (NTN World Wide Web site, http://www.mail.ici.coled.umn.edu/ntn/).

National Transition Alliance In 1995, the National Transition Alliance (NTA) was formed and includes six key collaborating partners to expand existing efforts with a focus on efforts to involve youth with disabilities in state school-to-work activities supported through development and implementation grants funded by authority of the School-to-Work Opportunities Act. In addition to the Transition Research Institute and the NTN, four additional partners are members of the NTA: the Academy for Educational Development, the Council for Chief State School Officers, the National Alliance of Business, and the National Association of State Directors of Special Education. This alliance is funded collaboratively through OSERS, the National School-to-Work Office (Department of Labor and Department of Education), and the National Institute on Disability Rehabilitation and Research (NIDRR). Although the particular focus and interest of the NTA is clearly the involvement of youth with disabilities in school-to-work activities, the NTA also works in close cooperation with local and state school-to-work partnerships to promote effective school-to-work policy and practices for *all* students. Partners of the alliance continue to conduct training, provide technical assistance, evaluate the effectiveness and impact of the federal transition initiative as it relates to school-to-work activities, conduct research specific to transition and school-to-work practices, and disseminate materials and information related to the involvement of school-age youth involved in school-to-work activities.

EMERGING RECOMMENDED PRACTICES

Although theories and conceptual models establish a basis and framework for the study of transition from adolescence and school to adulthood, questions have emerged about the effectiveness of specific practices and strategies. Although numerous transition practices have been strongly recommended, there continues to be a need for evidence supporting their presumed effectiveness (Johnson & Rusch, 1993; Kohler, 1993; Kohler, DeStefano, Wermuth, Grayson, & McGinty, 1994; Rusch et al., 1992). Johnson and Rusch (1993) reviewed federally funded project reports and the literature to identify those elements in the school experience and transition process that increase the probability of successful adult outcomes. The elements that repeatedly appear are 1) early intervention, 2) interagency collaboration, 3) systematic interdisciplinary individualized education planning, 4) appropriate integration, 5) community-based life and work skills curricula, 6) staff development, and 7) program evaluation.

Recommended Transition Practices

Kohler (1993) conducted a literature review to identify which transition practices have been identified or supported in the literature as having a positive impact on student outcomes. After a review of 18 follow-up documents and 11 theory-based or opinion articles, 21 transition services emerged as recommended practices (see Table 2). Among those practices cited, vocational training, parent involvement, interagency collaboration/services delivery, social skills training, paid work experience, and individualized plans were the six most frequently cited practices. Three practices—vocational training, parent involvement, and interagency collaboration/services delivery—were cited as recommended practices in more than 50% of the documents reviewed.

Table 2. Recommended transition practices

Vocational training	Interagency agreements
Social skills training	Integration/LRE/mainstreaming
Interagency collaboration and service delivery	Daily living skills training
	Career education curricula
Parent involvement	Community-based instruction
Paid work experience	Vocational assessment
Employability work skills training	Identification of vocational, residential, and social outcomes
Follow-up employment services	
Employer input	Early transition planning
Individualized transition plans and planning	IEP reflects transition
	Community-referenced curricula
Interdisciplinary transition teams	Academic skill training

From Kohler, P.D. (1993). Best practices in transition: Substantiated or implied? *Career Development for Exceptional Individuals, 16,* 115; reprinted by permission.

Validated Employment Outcomes

Concurrent research by Kohler and Rusch (1994) focused on identifying and validating employment outcomes, indicators, and activities for youth and adults with disabilities. Using a Delphi approach, these researchers asked respondents to rate 22 employment-related outcomes and 65 associated activities. All outcomes and activities were organized using a systems-level analytic approach. This approach employs four levels of analysis including 1) the student and family, 2) the program or services entity, 3) the organization that typically delivers program services, and 4) the community in which all prior entities operate. Subsequent research by these same authors expanded the focus to identify employment indicators that might be appropriate measures of employment outcomes achieved (Kohler & Rusch, 1994). Table 3 identifies the level of analysis and the 16 employment outcome statements under which employment was categorized by Kohler and Rusch (1994).

Taxonomy for Transition Programming

Peters and Heron (1993) proposed five criteria for identifying recommended practices. The transition processes should be 1) well-grounded in theory, 2) supported empirically through studies that are internally and externally valid, 3) based or supported by existing literature, 4) associated with meaningful outcomes, and 5) considered socially valid. In a rigorous effort to empirically apply these criteria, Kohler (1996) employed concept mapping methodology to identify, to categorize, and to socially validate transition practices considered to be recommended practices. The result has been the development of a taxonomy of transition practices clustered into these five areas: 1) student development, 2) student-focused planning, 3) interagency collaboration, 4) family involvement, and 5) program structure and attributes. (Kohler, 1996). Figure 1 provides an overview of the taxonomy for transition programming.

Self-determination principles are embedded within the taxonomy in four of the five categories. For example, within the Student Development category, it is recommended that Life Skills Instruction competencies be delivered to the student. Suggested Life Skills Instruction competencies include the following: self-determination skill training, including goal setting and decision making; self-advocacy training; and rights and responsibilities training.

THE BIG PICTURE: THINKING BEYOND ANNUAL GOALS

Since the 1970s, educational planning for students with disabilities has been driven by the IEP. Through annual IEP meetings, educators, par-

Table 3. Systems-level employment outcomes

INDIVIDUAL/FAMILY EMPLOYMENT OUTCOMES

Model transition-to-employment projects must
- Place students into competitive, integrated employment (including supported employment)
- Provide job placement services
- Work with adult service agencies to ensure job placement
- Provide job exploration and job training opportunities as part of the school curriculum to prepare students for competitive employment
- Provide job support services
- Provide technical assistance to adult service agencies to provide job placement and job support services

PROGRAM-LEVEL EMPLOYMENT OUTCOMES

Model transition projects should
- Utilize individualized transition planning for students with disabilities
- Develop strong cooperative linkages with vocational rehabilitation services to develop the IEPs

ORGANIZATIONAL-LEVEL EMPLOYMENT OUTCOMES

Transition-to-employment projects should
- Develop and document a cooperative service delivery model when more than one agency is providing consumer services
- Articulate the roles of all associate agencies
- Employ personnel whose role is to coordinate project activities
- Document services provided by cooperating agencies

COMMUNITY-LEVEL EMPLOYMENT OUTCOMES

Model transition-to-employment projects should
- Demonstrate improved work opportunities for youths with disabilities
- Evaluate and document effective job placement and maintenance activities
- Research job trends and business requirements
- Work cooperatively with community agencies to conduct longitudinal studies

From Kohler, P.D., & Rusch, F.R. (1994). *Employment of youths with disabilities: Outcomes, activities, and indicators.* Champaign: University of Illinois, Urbana-Champaign, Transition Research Institute, pp. 108–115; adapted by permission.

ents, and other team members have discussed present levels of performance, determined areas of need, and written annual goals and short-term objectives to address those stated needs. In many school programs, the goals generated by this process encompassed the core curricular areas such as reading, writing, math, and science. As indicated previously in this chapter, however, follow-up studies have reported that many students with disabilities experience poor outcomes in employment and independent living domains after completing their educational program (Hasazi et al., 1985; Kohler, 1993; Mithaug,

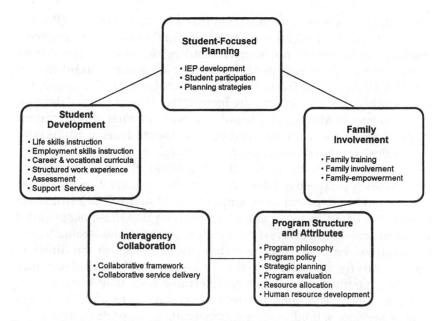

Figure 1. Taxonomy for transition programming. (From Kohler, P.D. (1996). *Taxonomy for transition programming: Linking research and practice*, p.118. Champaign: University of Illinois at Urbana-Champaign, Transition Research Institute; adapted by permission.)

Horiuchi, & Fanning 1985; SRI International, 1991; Wagner, 1991; Wehman et al., 1985).

Both the 1990 amendments (PL 101-476) and 1997 amendments (PL 105-17) to the Education for All Handicapped Children Act of 1975 emphasized the need to improve secondary special education and transition services so that youth with disabilities would have the skills, knowledge, and attitudes to make the transition to employment and independent living. However, Ward and Halloran (1993) stated that despite the emphasis on equality, integration, and independence as intended by both the 1983 and 1990 legislative amendments, significant numbers of students in special education leaving public education are not successfully achieving desired goals.

It is clear that educators must examine how schools can better prepare students for adult life. The literature has addressed how students with disabilities might be better prepared for adult life almost exclusively from the point of view of educators and other human services professionals. A significant piece missing from the "professional" literature is the perspective of adults with disabilities who have actually made a successful transition from school to adult life, although emphasis has increased on promoting the self-determination and empowerment of students with disabilities and their families (Powers et al. 1996; Sands & Wehmeyer, 1996). A number of researchers have emphasized the importance of understanding the lessons learned from adults with disabilities who have achieved a successful transition to adult life (Devlieger & Trach, 1996; Powers et al., 1996). To this end, the stories of Mitchell and Jennifer are instructive. The purpose of describing the stories of Mitchell and Jennifer is two-fold. First, it is important for professionals to learn from and become the students of adults with disabilities who have been and are successful, as they define success. Second, it is absolutely critical that transition efforts move from a systems-level perspective based on what professional experts appear to know and understand to an empowerment and self-determination perspective based on the fundamental premise that those people most vested in achieving a successful transition are those undergoing transition and will be those who ultimately should establish the direction and policies for transition practice. In short, people with disabilities and their families will ultimately determine how they want to live, work, and play as adults. The role of education, rehabilitation, and human services should assume a cooperating, supporting, and assistive role and relinquish the lead role they assert.

FINAL WORDS FROM MITCHELL

The following excerpt is taken from a conversation with Mitchell in November 1996:

If I'm given the opportunity and a chance to go to the board of education, I will tell them one thing and that is the sole purpose of education is to do what's best for the students . . . for all students—people with disabilities and people without disabilities. I think a key factor is that they should look beyond just their disabilities. I think they should look at what they can do and how we can develop programs to help the students. They are playing politics, and if you play politics, then the family, the parents will not be happy—they will be caught in the process and that will not be fair for the child, for the student.

I would like to see them working together. If they work together they can get more things done, and more students will get the education. . . . If people pay less attention to power—who takes control over whom—we will get more things accomplished. However, there are people who think by working together they lose power and give up control. . . . Sometimes people have major egos, saying that they want things . . . one way . . . (if they don't get what they want they make sure) the idea fails—that is not compromising.

ADVICE FOR TEACHERS

My advice to teachers is to really encourage the students, to give them the opportunities to be more active and also to be more included in mainstream or regular education, so that they can have an education and also make friends. . . . I believe strongly that (teachers) need to learn how to teach students to speak up for themselves. The formula that I see is this: I think all students with and *without* disabilities should belong in any class. I think what is unique, each person, each student, has a separate ability. . . . What I'm trying to say is clear to me—being included means giving a person a chance to be able to be involved in their school. . . . If we have diversity, any person can have an education, can be able to make friends, and most importantly, have acceptance from others.

REFERENCES

Barcus, M.J. (1995). *School-to-work transition utilization of multimedia computer based instruction* [Prepared as conference handout]. Richmond: Virginia Commonwealth University, Rehabilitation Research Training Center.

Benz, M.R., & Kochhar, C.A. (1996). School-to-work opportunities for all students: A position statement of the division of career development and transition. *Career Development for Exceptional Individuals, 19*, 31–48.

Brolin, D.E., & Kokaska, C.J. (1979). *Career education for handicapped children and youth.* Columbus, OH: Charles E. Merrill.

California School to Work Interagency Transition Partnership (STWITP). (1996). *Memorandum of understanding.* Sacramento, CA: Author.

Capuzzi, D., & Gross, D.R. (1995). *Counseling and psychotherapy: Theories and interventions.* Englewood Cliffs, NJ: Prentice Hall.

Devlieger, P.J., & Trach, J.S. (1996). *Ethnographic study of transition: On the threshold of adult life.* Champaign: University of Illinois at Urbana-Champaign, Transition Research Institute.

Education for All Handicapped Children Act of 1975, PL 94-142, 20 U.S.C. §§ 1400 *et seq.*

Education of the Handicapped Act Amendments of 1983, PL 98-199, 20 U.S.C. §§ 1400 *et seq.*

Field, S., & Hoffman, A. (1996a). Increasing the ability of educators to support youth self-determination. In L.E. Powers, G.H.S. Singer, & J. Sowers (Eds.), *On the road to autonomy: Promoting self-competence in children and youth with disabilities* (pp. 171–187). Baltimore: Paul H. Brookes Publishing Co.

Field, S., & Hoffman, A. (1996b). *Steps to self-determination.* Austin, TX: PRO-ED.

Gajar, A., Goodman, L., & McAfee, J. (1993). *Secondary schools and beyond: Transition of individuals with mild disabilities.* New York: Macmillan.

Gillespie, G.B., & Turnbull, A.P. (1983). It's my IEP. Involving students in the planning process. *Teaching Exceptional Children, 29*, 27–29.

Hakola, S.R. (1996). *Transitioning students: Your guide to successful strategies.* Horsham, PA: LRP Publications.

Halpern, A.S. (1985). Transition: A look at the foundations. *Exceptional Children,* 51, 479–486.

Halpern, A.S. (1993). Quality of life as a conceptual framework for evaluating transition outcomes. *Exceptional Children,* 59, 486–498.

Harmon, A.S., Wallace, B.F., Grayson, T.E., & Leach, L.N. (1995). *Compendium of transition model demonstration programs, 1995.* Champaign: University of Illinois at Urbana-Champaign, Transition Research Institute.

Hasazi, S.B., Gordon, L.R., & Roe, C.A. (1985). Factors associated with the employment status of handicapped youth exiting high school from 1979–1983. *Exceptional Children,* 51, 455–469.

Hershenson, D.B., & Szymanski, E.M. (1992). Career development of people with disabilities. In R.M. Parker & E.M. Szymanski (Eds.), *Rehabilitation counseling: Basics and beyond* (2nd ed., pp. 273–303). Austin, TX: PRO-ED.

Ianacone, R.N., & Stodden, R.A. (1987). *Transition issues and directions.* Reston, VA: Council for Exceptional Children.

Individuals with Disabilities Education Act (IDEA) of 1990, PL 101-476, 20 U.S.C. §§ 1400 *et seq.*

Individuals with Disabilities Education Act Amendments of 1997, PL 105-17, 20 U.S.C. §§ 1400 *et seq.*

Izzo, M.V., & Shumate, K. (1992). *Network for effective transitions to work: A transition coordinator's handbook.* Columbus: Ohio State University, Center on Education and Training for Employment.

Johnson, J.R., & Rusch, F.R. (1993). Secondary special education and transition services: Identification and recommendations for future research and demonstration. *Career Development for Exceptional Individuals,* 17, 1–18.

Kingsley, J., & Levitz, M. (1994). *Count us in: Growing up with Down syndrome.* Orlando, FL: Harcourt, Brace & Co.

Kohler, P.D. (1993). Best practices in transition: Substantiated or implied? *Career Development for Exceptional Individuals,* 16, 107–121.

Kohler, P.D. (1996). *Taxonomy for transition programming: Linking research and practice.* Champaign: University of Illinois at Urbana-Champaign, Transition Research Institute.

Kohler, P.D., DeStefano, L., Wermuth, T.R., Grayson, T.E., & McGinty, S. (1994). An analysis of exemplary transition programs: How and why are they selected? *Career Development of Exceptional Individuals,* 17, 187–202.

Kohler, P.D., & Rusch, F.R. (1994). *Employment of youths with disabilities: Outcomes, activities, and indicators.* Champaign: University of Illinois at Urbana-Champaign, Transition Research Institute.

Levinson, D.J. (1978). *The seasons of a man's life.* New York: Ballantine Books.

Martin, J.E., Marshall, L.H., Maxson, L., & Jerman, P. (1995). *Self-directed IEP.* Colorado Springs: University of Colorado at Colorado Springs, Special Education Program.

Mithaug, D.E., & Horiuchi, C.N. (1983). *Colorado statewide followup survey of special education students.* Denver: Colorado Department of Education.

Mithaug, D.E., Horiuchi, C.N., & Fanning, P. (1985). A report on the Colorado statewide follow-up survey of special education students. *Exceptional Children,* 51, 397–404.

National Transition Network (NTN). (1993). *Parent brief: Students and the graduation dilemma.* Minneapolis, MN: Author.

Norman, M.E., & Bourexis, P. (1995). *Including students with disabilities in school-to-work opportunities.* Washington, DC: Council of Chief State School Officers.

Ohio Department of Education. (1996). *Policy statement: Simple planning document/process.* Columbus: Author.

Peters, M.T., & Heron, T.E. (1993). When the best is not good enough: An examination of best practice. *The Journal of Special Education, 26,* 371–385.

Powers, L.E., Sowers, J., Turner, A., Nesbitt, M., Knowles, E., & Ellison, R. (1996). TAKE CHARGE: A model for promoting self-determination among adolescents with challenges. In L.E. Powers, G.H.S. Singer, & J. Sowers (Eds.), *On the road to autonomy: Promoting self-competence in children and youth with disabilities* (pp. 291–322). Baltimore: Paul H. Brookes Publishing Co.

Rehabilitation Act Amendments of 1992, PL 102-569, 29 U.S.C. §§ 701 *et seq.*

Riley, R.W., & Reich, R.B. (1996). *Implementation of the School-to-Work Opportunities Act of 1994: Report to the Congress.* Washington, DC: U.S. Department of Education and U.S. Department of Labor.

Rusch, F.R., Kohler, P.D., & Hughes, C. (1992). An analysis of OSERS-sponsored secondary special education and transitional services research. *Career Development for Exceptional Individuals, 15,* 121–143.

Rutkowski, S. (1996, May). *Extending transition services beyond graduation.* Paper presented at the biennial topical conference of Ohio's Division of Career Development and Transition, Columbus, OH.

Sands, D.J., & Wehmeyer, M.L. (Eds.). (1996). *Self-determination across the lifespan: Independence and choice for people with disabilities.* Baltimore: Paul H. Brookes Publishing Co.

School-to-Work Opportunities Act (STWOA) of 1994, PL 103-239, 20 U.S.C. §§ 6101 *et seq.*

School-to-Work Web Page. (1997). Internet location: http://www.stw.ed.gov.

SRI International. (1991). *Youth with disabilities: How are they doing? The first comprehensive report for the National Longitudinal Transition Study of Special Education Students.* Menlo Park, CA: Author.

U.S. Department of Education. (1995). To assure the free appropriate public education of all handicapped children: Seventeenth annual report to Congress on the implementation of the Education of the Handicapped Act. Washington, DC: U.S. Department of Education.

Virginia Department of Education. (1995). *A skydiver's training guide to IEP: Transition planning.* Richmond: Author.

Wagner, M. (1989). *Youth with disabilities during transition: An overview of descriptive findings from the National Longitudinal Transition Study.* Menlo Park: CA: SRI International.

Wagner, M. (1991). *The benefits of secondary vocational education for young people with disabilities.* Menlo Park, CA: SRI International.

Ward, M.J. (1988). The many facets of self-determination. *Transition Summary, 5,* 2–3.

Ward, M.J., & Halloran, W.D. (1993). Transition issues for the 1990s. *OSERS News in Print, 6*(1), 4–5.

Wehman, P. (1995). *Individual transition plans: The teacher's curriculum guide for helping youth with special needs.* Austin, TX: PRO-ED.

Wehman, P. (1996). *Life beyond the classroom: Transition strategies for young people with disabilities* (2nd ed.). Baltimore: Paul H. Brookes Publishing Co.

Wehman, P., Kregel, J., & Barcus, J.M. (1985). From school to work: A vocational model for handicapped students. *Exceptional Children, 51,* 25–37.

Wehmeyer, M.L. (1992). Self-determination: Critical skills for outcome-oriented transition services: Steps in transition that lead to self-determination. *The Journal for Vocational Special Needs Education, 15,* 3–7.

Wehmeyer, M.L., & Kelchner, K. (1995). *Whose future is it anyway? A student directed transition planning program.* Arlington, TX: The Arc.

Wehmeyer, M.L., & Lawrence, M. (1995). Whose future is it anyway? Promoting student involvement in transition planning. *Career Development of Exceptional Individuals, 18*(2), 69–83.

Will, M. (1984). *OSERS programming for the transition of youth with disabilities: Bridges from school to work.* Washington, DC: U.S. Department of Education, Office of Special Education and Rehabilitative Services.

CHAPTER 11

Getting to Work

Personal and Public Transportation

Michael West, Thomas Hock,
Katherine Mullaney Wittig, and Victoria Z. Dowdy

KIRK

Kirk is a 16-year-old student with emotional disturbance and mental retardation requiring intermittent support. He has only recently been reenrolled in a public school after completing a year of court-ordered therapy in a private rehabilitation setting for his outbursts of anger. Academically, Kirk reads on about a beginning third-grade level and does math at the fourth-grade level. He has visual perceptual impairments and experiences great difficulty in reading charts, schedules, or graphs.

Kirk has experienced many failures in his prior educational programs. On his return from his out-of-school placement, he was anxious to begin a job training program. The school's Education for Employment (EFE) teacher helped Kirk locate a job training program at a local restaurant. The restaurant manager participated as a member on Kirk's individualized education program (IEP) team, along with Kirk's parents, the EFE teacher, a vocational rehabilitation counselor, Kirk's probation officer, and Kirk.

Kirk's duties at the restaurant include making coffee and cleaning. He has mastered the basic skills, likes his job, and is well-liked by his fellow workers. The primary obstacle has been transportation to and from work. Initially, the EFE instructor provided transportation, but this arrangement could not continue indefinitely. The IEP team convened to resolve the problem. After considering several possibilities and the limitations that each posed, the team arrived at a workable plan:

- Kirk's supervisor would fix Kirk's work schedule at 5 days a week, 7:00 A.M.–2:00 P.M., to limit transportation difficulties.
- Kirk would carpool with the manager of a video store next door to the restaurant.
- Kirk would require training to walk independently from his home to the carpool pickup point approximately three blocks away.
- The EFE teacher and Kirk's mother would collaborate on this training, gradually fading their presence as Kirk showed that he could walk to the pickup point safely.
- His stepfather's work schedule enabled him to pick up Kirk at the end of his work shift to take him home.

This orchestration of transportation training and family supports has enabled Kirk to hold the job that he wants at a workplace that wants him.

TRANSPORTATION AND EMPLOYMENT OF INDIVIDUALS WITH DISABILITIES

Transportation to and from work is a critical issue in job exploration and placement for people with virtually every type of disability (President's Committee on Employment, 1992). It is obvious that individuals cannot hold jobs that they cannot reach. Therefore, reliable and affordable transportation is essential for bringing more individuals with disabilities into the work force.

Yet for many people with disabilities, this essential component is beyond their control. Most workers without disabilities drive themselves to and from work and therefore have options for the businesses and organizations from which they can seek employment. For many people with disabilities (e.g., epilepsy, visual impairments), driving is restricted by law; for people with other types of disabilities (e.g., cerebral palsy, mental retardation, psychosocial impairment), driving is restricted by functional or economic limitations. For both groups, the result is the same—many individuals with disabilities must rely on family members, public transportation, or other alternative modes of transportation.

The Americans with Disabilities Act (ADA) of 1990 (PL 101-336) requires that public transportation facilities and vehicles (e.g., bus, rail) be accessible to people with disabilities (Architectural and Transportation Barriers Compliance Board, 1994). Although much progress has been made in improving transportation systems since the passage of the ADA, many individuals with disabilities have not seen improvements in the availability of accessible transportation. This may be due to a number of reasons, including the following: lack of voluntary compliance by some public transportation systems; cutbacks or discontinuation of public transportation routes rather than making them accessible to riders with disabilities; and general lack of public transportation in suburban areas, smaller cities and towns, or rural areas (National Council on Disability, 1995a, 1995b; Weller, 1994).

Mobility within the community is necessary for employment as well as for social and recreational activities and for use of community resources and accommodations. Transportation is therefore a prerequisite to self-determination for individuals with disabilities. Self-determination refers to the degree to which individuals are able to exercise choice and control over both immediate and long-term decisions regarding their lives (Ward, 1989; Wehmeyer & Kelchner, 1995).

In a study of adults with disabilities conducted by West, Barcus, Brooke, and Rayfield (1995), available means of transportation and independent mobility in the community were believed to be a major factor in perceived levels of choice and control. Having a means of gaining access to different environments increased the range of options that were attainable in the areas of work, socialization, recreation, and housing. Being mobile also enabled those individuals to exercise control, allowing them to decide where and how they lived, rather than relinquishing that control to service agencies, family members, or others. The development of self-determination skills has been shown to increase the likelihood of youth with disabilities becoming successful adults (Gerber, Ginsberg, & Reiff, 1992; West et al., 1995).

Transportation is an important consideration in educational programs as well, particularly as the student approaches the transition to adult life. Students with disabilities who are dependent on family or social services agencies for transportation will be functionally limited in the postschool options that are feasible for them in the areas of work, housing, postsecondary education and training, and leisure.

The following account from Thomas, a computer programmer at Virginia Commonwealth University in Richmond, is illustrative of the link between transportation and self-determination.

THOMAS

Transportation could be a huge barrier for people with disabilities to be employed. I know because I have a disability (cerebral palsy), and I am employed. Over many years of working, I have had to use several methods to get to my jobs. When I began working, my father took me to work every day. We lived about 10 minutes from my job, and he was retired and did not mind giving me a ride. After his health declined and he could not drive any more, I had to find other transportation to work.

I use a walker and need assistance getting into and out of cars. I did not want to use the local paratransportation company because I knew it was not very good. For 3 years, I was lucky enough to be able to ride with several people who work with me. The first person was a woman who rode by my neighborhood. She would pick me up and drop me off at night. It worked out just fine, and I paid her $20.00 per week. After a year, she decided that she could not do it anymore.

After trying to use the paratransportation company for a couple of weeks, I found it very unsatisfactory. The driver got upset with me because I asked her to let me out on the right side of the alley leading to my office. So that I would not have to walk so far across the graveled alley, my mother helped me ask the driver if she could come in from another direction so that the door of the van would be next to the door of the building. The driver told me that nobody was going to tell her how to drive. Although she would help me across the rocks, it would have been easier for both of us to do it the way that I had suggested.

I got very upset, so a friend at work offered to give me a ride every day. Although it was out of his way, he would not take any money. He took me to work for about a year and a half until I moved to the other side of the city.

I was very lucky again to have another person at work who lived near me and who was willing to give me a ride. I paid the tolls, but she would not take any payment. After about 8 months, she decided she could not do it anymore. Nobody at work could give me a ride anymore, and I had to find another way.

There are several companies that provide transportation to people with disabilities. After calling them, I found that the cost was too high. They primarily take people to medical appointments, and insurance pays $50.00 each way. That is too much money for people who need transportation to work. I had no choice but to use public specialized transportation. The city transit company contracts with a company to provide paratransportation, and riders pay only the regular rate. Maybe I am lucky to have a way to get to the office, but it is far from excellent.

As a computer programmer who uses paratransportation to get to work and return home again, I know what it is like to be dependent on specialized public transportation. It is not like driving your own car or like riding the regular bus. Most people can decide when they have to leave from home to get to the office in time and to get home at a reasonable hour. It would take me about half an hour to get to work in a car, but the specialized van has to pick me up 1 hour before work and take me around the city to pick up other riders. It is right to have more than one rider on the van at one time, but it makes me get up earlier than I would like to so that I am ready for the van. People who use public transportation might have to leave home earlier than if they were driving, but they usually have a choice of times to catch the bus. The paratransportation company tells me what time to be ready.

I am lucky because most mornings they pick me up on time, but in the afternoon it is a different story. My working day ends at 4:30 P.M., and my pickup is scheduled for 4:45 P.M. But the van picks me up after 5:00 P.M. most days. After working all day long, everybody wants to go home, not wait for a ride. If the van is going to be late by 5 minutes or so, it would be understandable. But it is very unsatisfying to be picked up more than 15 minutes late every day.

It is bad for the company to be late all of the time for a couple of reasons. First, it makes my day much longer. Many nights I get home almost an hour and a half after work. After getting up early to catch the bus and working all day, anybody would be tired, especially a person with a disability. Second, my office is in a bad area of town, and I don't feel safe by myself. A person with a disability such as mine could not protect him- or herself or call for help. Many times, people in my office work late, and sometimes a co-worker will wait with me so that I am not alone. But other times I am by myself and don't feel comfortable. Finally, it is bad because when a company provides a service to customers, the company should want to provide the best service.

Thomas's account exemplifies the difficulties and exasperation that many individuals with disabilities experience with obtaining reliable transportation to work. The remainder of this chapter addresses, first, assessment of transportation needs and resources for either students or adults with disabilities who are making transitions and, second, two options for addressing transportation needs: instruction of transportation skills and locating transportation supports.

Assessment of Transportation Needs and Resources

Assessment of transportation needs and resources requires a functional approach. This approach involves, first, identifying the environments that students or adults with disabilities want or need to reach, such as workplaces, restaurants, grocery stores, movie theaters, and so on. Then, an assessment of the students' capacities and resources will help determine if the necessary skills can be taught or if support options are more appropriate (McGregor, 1995). It would be a waste of precious instructional time to teach an individual to use public transportation if he or she does not live in an area with bus service. These situations underscore the need for the instruction of functional mobility and transportation within *natural environments* and *ecological assessment* of mobility needs and resources (Bailey & Head, 1993; Everson, 1993).

Natural environments are those environments in which the individual currently engages or is likely to engage in the future. In a secondary school, use of natural environments could include community-based training, such as work experience and job training programs, training in shopping and money-handling skills, home-based instruction, and the like. Following exit from school, students will enter diverse work, social, and residential environments. No two people will have identical needs and solutions during any of these stages. The most effective means of identifying transportation needs is through an individualized assessment of the mobility requirements of the environments into which the individual functions or is expected to function (e.g., ecological assessment) and matching those requirements to training, adaptation, or support options that are available (Bailey & Head, 1993). A process such as person-centered planning is useful for targeting potential work and social environments for students and adults with disabilities who are making transitions (Mount, 1991).

Instruction in Transportation Skills

Once the available needs and resources are identified, consideration should be given to which modes of transportation can be most readily attained through instruction and adaptation. Through instruction and adaptation, individuals with disabilities can achieve maximal independence within their communities. Some transportation methods that can be instructed and/or adapted are as follows:

- Reaching specific destinations using primary mobility mode (e.g., ambulation, wheelchair)
- Using mass transit (e.g., bus, subway, commuter train)
- Instructing in operation of personal automobile
- Instructing in reaching destinations by bicycle
- Using taxi services

In many cases, it is likely that an individual will require multiple methods of reaching a destination. For example, instruction may be needed in how to walk to the nearest bus stop safely, as well as instruction in using the bus service (i.e., reading schedules, paying fares, using transfers). For individuals with learning difficulties, task analysis is often a helpful strategy. This involves breaking the major task into smaller, more easily mastered steps or objectives. These steps then are instructed through verbal cues, modeling, manual prompting, or other strategies, until the learner is able to complete the full process. A couple of examples will help to clarify both the use of multiple methods and use of task analysis.

MOLLY

Molly is a 16-year-old student enrolled in a suburban high school near a large metropolitan area. She lives at home with her parents. She has mental retardation requiring limited support, a mild anxiety disorder, and mild nerve palsy in her lower right leg for which she wears an orthopedic brace for support. Molly has just completed her second year in a community-based supported employment preparation program and has been referred to her school's transition team for assistance with transportation training.

Molly has a strong desire to work at a large amusement park located 18 miles from her home. Molly worked there the previous summer in a school-sponsored food services training program and received high recommendations from the managers. Molly has been hired for summer employment contingent on obtaining transportation.

Assessment and Planning

A shuttle bus is operated by the amusement park. To catch the shuttle bus, Molly must walk four blocks from her home to a pickup point located at a nearby community college. Molly, her parents, and her orthopedic doctor participated in a planning meeting, at which Molly's mother expressed her concerns for Molly's safety while en route to the bus stop. She lamented that her work schedule afforded no flexibility to provide Molly with transportation. Other options were considered including locating carpools, changing the mother's work schedule, and not allowing Molly to work at the amusement park over the summer. Molly's father was supportive of the team's willingness to assist her in reaching the bus stop independently. Molly's doctor recommended the daily walk to the bus stop as additional therapy for her damaged leg muscles. Molly insisted she was ready for additional independence.

A decision was made to teach Molly to walk to and from the shuttle pickup point before school ended for the summer. Tim, Molly's teacher, would be paid by the school system for up to 24 hours of follow-along instruction during the summer.

Individualized Education Program/
Individualized Transition Plan Goals and Objectives

Table 1 presents the goals that were placed into Molly's IEP and her individualized transition plan (ITP). Because the shuttle bus made only one drop-off at the amusement park, no further instruction was needed once Molly boarded the bus in the morning. If the bus had made several stops, her teacher could have ridden with her and taught her how to recognize her stop by focusing on either the sequence of stops or on unique landmarks such as rides or buildings.

Outcomes

Molly was able to achieve 100% independence with both goals by the beginning of summer. Molly initially displayed some trepidation about crossing the highway but became more confident with each training session. She went from holding Tim's sleeve to ambulating ahead of him. By the completion of training, Molly would meet Tim at the college parking lot.

Table 1.   Molly's IEP/ITP transportation goals and objectives

Goal #1:   Molly will walk from her home to the designated bus Monday through Friday at 9:00 A.M.

Related objectives:

1. Using a map and assigned cues, Molly will walk three blocks to Parham Road.
2. After pushing the crosswalk button and using visible cues (flashing WALK signal, cars stopped both ways), Molly will cross Parham Road at the designated crosswalk independently.
3. After crossing the highway, Molly will proceed to Parking Lot A to the busstop sign.
4. Molly will board her bus there.

Goal #2:   At 5:00 P.M. on Monday through Friday, Molly will ride her shuttle bus and walk home.

Related objectives:

1. Molly will locate and board her bus next to the Human Resources office in the employee parking lot.
2. Molly will exit the bus and walk from Parking Lot A to the crosswalk on Parham Road.
3. After pushing the crosswalk button and using visible cues (flashing WALK signal, cars stopped both ways), Molly will cross Parham Road at the designated crosswalk independently.
4. Molly will walk home independently.

MARK

Mark is a 19-year-old student who lives in a suburban area with his parents and younger brother. He has mental retardation requiring intermittent support and a psychiatric disorder.

Mark has had a variety of community-based work experiences and has expressed a desire to become a cook. Prior to the end of the school year, Mark obtained a part-time summer job as a bus boy in a restaurant at which he had previously worked as a member of a small work crew during the school year. Mark was very excited about the job, and his parents were very supportive.

Assessment and Planning

At the IEP/ITP meeting, various options were considered for assisting Mark to get to his desired job. Public transportation was not available in Mark's area, and his position required him to work evenings, which conflicted with his parents' work schedules. Some of the options discussed included rearranging his parents' schedules, using a paratransportation company, carpooling with other employees, and using a taxi. Each of these had disadvantages of cost or convenience. After much discussion of the available options, the team decided that Mark's mother would take him to work, which fit within her current work schedule; and Mark would take a taxi home after work.

IEP/ITP Goals and Objectives

Table 2 shows goals and objectives that were included in Mark's IEP and ITP for independent use of a taxi service. Because his mother drove him to work, no instruction was necessary for that component. As Table 2 shows, the second objective required the instructor to make an adaptation for Mark and teach him to use it as substeps to completing the objective. The "cue card" that was made for Mark had the number for the taxi service and instructions that he could read to the dispatcher regarding the requested pickup time and location.

Outcomes

Mark was able to call the cab service independently. He had no difficulty communicating his needs to the driver. He has a good sense of direction and could clearly articulate his address. At first, he had some difficulty returning to task after making the call to the cab service. Two employees at the restaurant took it on themselves to assist Mark with this problem. They reassured him that they would help him watch for the cab and would call him when it arrived.

Locating Transportation Supports

It is important to understand that instruction in independent transportation is only one option. Many people with disabilities can be taught to drive or to ride a bicycle, to use public transportation, to cross streets safely, and to achieve other mobility and transportation needs independently. If individuals can learn to accomplish these skills inde-

Table 2. Mark's IEP/ITP transportation goal and objectives

Goal: Mark will independently obtain a taxi to get home from work.
Related objectives:
1. Mark will determine the correct time to call the taxi.
2. Mark will call the taxi service.
   a. Remove card with phone number from wallet.
   b. Courteously make request of hostess to use phone.
   c. Dial correct number.
   d. Using cue card, give complete information to taxi dispatcher.
   e. Return to work until shift end.
   f. Watch for taxi at end of shift.
   g. Identify taxi upon arrival and board.
   h. Give taxi driver correct address.
3. Mark will independently pay his taxi fare.

pendently or with adaptations, then they should be taught to do so. But there are individuals who are not able to move among environments independently because of either their limitations (e.g., physical or cognitive impairments) or the nature of their communities (e.g., lack of public transportation). In these cases, transportation supports can be developed to assist them in meeting their transportation needs.

Personal Support Options Personal support options involve the assistance of another person (e.g., family members, friends, neighbors, co-workers, paid personal assistants). For example, a friend or family member can be asked to assist with transportation to work or to other community environments. For individuals with physical or health impairments, paid personal assistants often are used for activities of daily living, and these assistants also can be used as providers of transportation. Personal assistants often are funded through state vocational rehabilitation or medical/health services funding agencies.

Ride-Sharing Options Ride sharing is common in many workplaces and other community organizations. Ride-sharing options involve locating other workers within an employment setting or, in the case of recreational outings, people with similar interests with whom the individual can ride. In ride-sharing arrangements for people without disabilities, as with other ride-sharing arrangements, an agreement can be reached regarding reimbursement for expenses based on mileage, tolls, and so on. This reimbursement also might take into account other factors, such as assistance required for moving from the individual's doorway to the automobile, transferring from a wheelchair to the car seat, storing a wheelchair, and so on.

If a support person cannot be located within the workplace, advertisement through other means can be tried. For example, many apartment complexes have bulletin boards for posting articles for sale, neighborhood events, and other items of interest; and the individual with a disability can be assisted with writing an advertisement and displaying it. Other means of advertising could include newspapers, public service announcements, community access cable television channels, electronic bulletin boards and support groups, community service groups, and state or local agencies promoting volunteerism.

Targeted Job Placement Job development activities can be targeted to the available transportation and mobility resources of the consumer. For example, if an individual is dependent on public transportation, then only those workplaces on or close to bus routes can be targeted. If an individual is capable of walking or riding a bicycle, then businesses that are accessible to him or her by those means can be targeted, with follow-up training as needed for street-crossing and other safety skills.

Many workplaces in which staff attendance is critical, such as nursing facilities and hospitals, offer transportation assistance to their employees for minimal or no cost. This is a mutually beneficial and cost-effective arrangement. Using vehicles the facility already owns ensures adequate staff coverage despite inclement weather, lack of public transportation, and any problems that employees have with their own vehicles. Employees, particularly those in lower pay levels, have an affordable means to reach their job, perhaps while saving for their own automobile. Employment service agencies can make calls to identify workplaces in their consumers' communities that offer transportation assistance and target those workplaces for their consumers as well.

The ultimate example of targeted job placement is home-based employment. Examples include self-employment in such areas as accounting, bookkeeping, child care, or sales. Other jobs can be accomplished primarily through telecommuting, such as remote data entry, computer programming, writing or editing, database research, and so on. Although both self-employment and telecommuting options are steadily growing in use and popularity with workers without disabilities, they often are disregarded for individuals with disabilities who are seeking employment.

Using a targeted job development strategy for transportation purposes is likely to require a trade-off for the consumer. Perhaps the jobs that are most accessible to the consumer do not fit with his or her career plans or do not offer the desired level of pay and benefits. Home-based employment may be beneficial from a transportation standpoint, but it offers few or no opportunities for the consumer to develop friendships with co-workers. Telecommuting may be attractive to the consumer but may require additional education or training.

The consumer and his or her family will need to weigh all these factors in deciding whether to pursue a specific job. The role of job development and placement staff is to ensure that the consumer and his or her family have all the information needed to fully understand the options before them, including the advantages and disadvantages of each option, in order to make informed choices.

Transportation Cooperatives In most communities, a number of vehicles provide transportation services at any given time. They may be transporting people to senior recreation services, medical appointments, employment training or day support programs, church programs, or to many other activities. Transportation cooperatives take advantage of all available vehicles to assist people with disabilities who do not have readily available transportation. For example, a Red Cross van transporting individuals to a hospital for medical appointments also can sell available seats to riders who are employed at the hospital, provided the schedules are compatible, the riders' homes are within a reasonable distance from the Red Cross route, and there is space available. Cost to the riders can be negotiated based on typical costs plus charges for travel from the regular route to the riders' homes, needed assistance, and other factors.

A number of cities and communities have centralized transportation cooperatives, with one agency serving as coordinator and/or dispatcher. Each participating agency submits its routes to the coordinating agency, serving such functions as 1) locating the most appropriate provider based on route and scheduling; 2) negotiating fees to riders; 3) providing training to drivers who are unfamiliar with the needs of people with disabilities; and 4) ensuring liability coverage for riders, drivers, and vehicles involved in the co-op.

A centralized system works well when there are existing cooperative relationships between services agencies and an agency willing to coordinate the day-to-day operations. But transportation co-ops need not be centralized and formal. An employment agency for people with disabilities can reach informal agreements with other community services agencies to provide transportation to their consumers. Many agencies would likely be open to the idea, particularly for routes or schedules that are not cost-effective for them because of small numbers of riders.

When using support options for transportation needs, teachers and employment service staff should identify both main support options and backup options (Parent, Unger, Gibson, & Clements, 1994). If, for example, an individual utilizes a ride-share to get to work, there will be days when the co-worker will be unable to drive to work because of illness, vacations, car problems, or time conflicts. Having the consumer totally dependent on one co-worker would mean that both would be absent or late those days, which would reflect poorly on the consumer.

CONCLUSION

This chapter has examined mobility and transportation skills within the context of increasing consumer success and self-determination and, ultimately, increasing the quality of an individual's adult life. Instruction in mobility and transportation can be most effectively conducted in natural environments, guided by ecological assessment of individualized abilities and mobility needs. Instruction in mobility and transportation is but one option; transportation supports can be used when a consumer is unlikely to be able to attain independence through instruction.

REFERENCES

Americans with Disabilities Act (ADA) of 1990, PL 101-336, 42 U.S.C. §§ 12101 et seq.

Architectural and Transportation Barriers Compliance Board. (1994). *Americans with Disabilities Act: Accessibility guidelines for buildings and facilities, transportation facilities, and transportation vehicles.* Washington, DC: Author.

Bailey, B.R., & Head, D.N. (1993). Providing O&M services to children and youth with severe multiple disabilities. *RE:view, 25,* 57–66.

Everson, J.M. (1993). *Youth with disabilities: Strategies for interagency transition programs.* Boston: Andover Medical Publishers.

Gerber, P.J., Ginsberg, R., & Reiff, H.B. (1992). Identifying alterable patterns in employment success for highly successful adults with learning disabilities. *Journal of Learning Disabilities, 25,* 475–487.

McGregor, M.L. (1995). *Orientation and mobility for students with multiple severe disabilities.* Paper presented at the 73rd annual International Convention of the Council for Exceptional Children, April 5–9, 1995, Indianapolis, IN.

Mount, B. (1991). *Person-centered planning: A sourcebook of values, ideals, and methods to encourage person-centered development.* New York: Graphic Futures.

National Council on Disability (1995a). *The Americans with Disabilities Act: Ensuring equal access to the American dream.* Washington, DC: Author.

National Council on Disability (1995b). *Voices of freedom: America speaks out on the ADA: A report to the President and Congress.* Washington, DC: Author.

Parent, W., Unger, D., Gibson, K., & Clements, C. (1994). The role of the job coach: Orchestrating community and workplace supports. *American Rehabilitation, 20*(3), 2–11.

President's Committee on Employment of People with Disabilities and Arkansas Research and Training Center on Vocational Rehabilitation. (1992). *Employment priorities for the '90s for people with disabilities.* Washington, DC: Author.

Ward, M.J. (1989). The many facets of self-determination. *National Information Center for Children and Youth with Handicaps: Transition Summary, 5,* 2–3.

Wehmeyer, M., & Kelchner, K. (1995). *Whose future is it anyway? A student-directed transition planning process.* Arlington, TX: The Arc.

Weller, D. (1994). Unmet needs for developmental disabilities services. *Population and Environment: A Journal of Interdisciplinary Services, 15*(4), 279–302.

West, M., Barcus, J.M., Brooke, V., & Rayfield, R.G. (1995). An exploratory analysis of self-determination of persons with disabilities. *Journal of Vocational Rehabilitation, 5,* 357–364.

CHAPTER

Making Friends and Building Relationships

Beth Bader Gilson and Stephen French Gilson

MARTHA AND JENNY

Martha and Jenny have work stations next to each other. They are both in their 20s, are very particular in the way that they dress, and have personal mementos decorating the space around their computers. Both have been hired part time to do data entry. During break-time conversations, the two women have found that they share a passion for finding bargains when shopping for clothes, and both are waiting for Mr. Right to come into their lives. On Saturdays, Martha and Jenny often meet at the mall, shop for a few hours, and then eat lunch at the food court. Jenny then goes home to her apartment, which she shares with a roommate and two cats. Martha goes home to a building that she shares with 99 other people who have varying degrees of physical, sensory, and cognitive disabilities. When Martha and Jenny were asked who they consider their friends to be, both, without hesitation, named each other first.

WHY FRIENDSHIPS EXIST

Most of us consider having friends to be an essential part of our lives. "Friendships help ensure a person's well being and health, and they

301

help to protect people from exploitation, abuse and neglect" (Strully & Strully, 1992, p. 165). Friendships also provide us with comfort, re-assurance, and support. We share our hopes, dreams, and fears with friends. We go to the movies with friends, we attend the weddings of our friends, and we share a cup of coffee or tea with friends. Sometimes we tend to our friends; sometimes they pay attention to us. We can spend time with some friends every day, some once a month, and others only once a year. Some people have many friends; others have one or two people who they consider to be their friends. We may have known one of our friends since childhood, but we may have known someone else, who is just as important a friend, for only a few months. We may meet someone who becomes a friend through a mutual ac-quaintance or quite by chance, such as being assigned bunk mates at camp. Friends may be of the same age, or there may be quite a few years' age difference. Our friends may be of similar cultural and racial backgrounds, or they may have been raised very differently from us. A friend may be what we consider a soul mate with whom we share everything in common; or he or she may be someone who has nothing in common with us. Some of our friends may look like us, or they may be very different in appearance. Friendships may be invisible to every-one except those who consider themselves to be friends (O'Brien & O'Brien, 1993). And there are many of us, both with and without dis-abilities, who have friends with disabilities.

This chapter reinforces the fact that there are more similarities than differences in the ways that friendships and relationships de-velop between people with disabilities and those without. The need for friends in our lives is universal, but people with disabilities may have fewer opportunities to meet people who would be potential friends and may not have the resources to maintain their friendships. This chapter discusses the essential components that allow friendships to happen. The chapter also discusses why people with disabilities may choose to have friends who also have disabilities and why consumer–staff friendships exist. This chapter describes the role of a relationship coach who can set the stage and increase opportunities for people with disabilities to meet and interact with other people and discusses some of the social skills that may need to be taught to someone who has never experienced being a friend. Finally, this chapter presents issues that affect relationships between people who have disabilities and those who do not have disabilities. Having a disability is important to consider when making friends and building relationships, but the dis-ability and the issues that accompany it should be of importance only to the individuals who are friends and not to professionals and other outsiders.

FRIENDSHIPS CANNOT BE FORCED

Despite the best of intentions of disability services professionals, it is important to understand that friendships cannot be forced, neither with people with disabilities nor with those without (Stainback & Stainback, 1990). Because many people with disabilities have been educated, have lived, and have worked in artificial or constructed environments (e.g., group homes, sheltered workshops), it has been mistakenly assumed that setting up equally artificial recreational and social opportunities would or should lead to making friends. No person with or without a disability should be forced to support or to make friends with any other person or group of people (Zygmunt, Larson, & Tilson, 1994). Providing opportunities in which free choice and personal preference can occur requires "hard work" (Strully & Strully, 1993), especially for people with severe disabilities. For many people with disabilities and their families, however, it is the maintenance of friendships that is the hard work, the extra cost, and the required expenditure of energy, not necessarily the implementation of social skills training programs.

ESSENTIAL COMPONENTS OF FRIENDSHIPS

For a friendship to occur, there must be at least two essential components in place: proximity (Stainback & Stainback, 1990) and shared commonality (O'Brien & O'Brien, 1993). *Proximity* usually means being in the same place at the same time, but many friendships have developed via letters. Today, with the advent of electronic mail (e-mail) and the Internet, friendships exist without face-to-face contact. The questions that might arise, however, are whether these electronic friendships are true friendships, and whether both parties can really know if commonality exists. Commonality can be thought of as similarity in experience or, perhaps, in terms of a shared circumstance. O'Brien and O'Brien stated that commonality, along with "equality, mutuality, and comprehension are best understood from the perspective of the friends themselves, rather than according to the measurements of a detached observer" (1993, p. 20). E-mail and the Internet can provide wonderful opportunities for people with disabilities to be in control of when, with whom, and how they create associations and develop relationships.

The technological era brings with it risks as well as opportunities for all people. We are in the beginning stages of creating, working through, and understanding the rules and etiquette associated with use of the Internet—an electronic medium that allows people with disabilities to directly connect with each other without an intermediary.

TERESA

Teresa has had a muscular disorder since early childhood and has lived with her parents all of her life. Her parents are now in their late 70s and do not drive at night and rarely go out of the house except for grocery shopping and to attend church. Teresa depends on public paratransit services to get to and from work and to other appointments, but this service is available only during weekdays. As a form of recreation and to keep in contact with friends, Teresa is a frequent user of the Internet. She can play games, have discussions about current events, and get advice regarding disability-related issues daily with friends that she has had since high school and with friends that she has never met face to face. The Internet affords people with disabilities the chance to communicate with others without regard to distance, issues of accommodation or access, or time.

The friendship discussed in the opening case between Martha and Jenny has both face-to-face proximity and commonality. They work in the same place of business and have adjoining workspaces. Because both of them take their breaks at their desks, it was only natural that they began to talk together. What is not usual in this situation is that Martha's speech is very difficult to understand, and it took quite a while and a lot of repeating for Jenny to begin to understand anything that Martha was saying. Conversations between the two women were quite limited at first, but the more Martha talked and the more Jenny listened, they became quite used to their conversational style, and, in fact, Martha often asks Jenny to translate for her when their supervisor is asking her questions. By spending time together, both Jenny and Martha began to realize that they had similar tastes in many things and shared many of the same dreams. When they began to meet outside of work and go clothes shopping—the commonality component—it was not with the idea that Jenny, who does not have a disability, would be helping Martha, who has the disability, pick out or purchase clothing. Both women are capable of shopping alone, but Jenny can more easily try on an outfit to see what it looks like, and Martha can more easily carry the packages in the bag attached to the back of her wheelchair. More important, Jenny and Martha enjoy being with each other. Although it was the work situation that provided the proximity, Martha and Jenny like to think that they would have met sooner or later at the mall.

Being in the same place at the same time is conducive to the development of a friendship as well as is having common experiences, but there are additional ingredients that need to be present. It is possible to meet someone for the first time, and after being with them for only a short time, have a sense that you will be friends. A friendship may last for a very short time or be lifelong (Strully & Strully, 1992). More often, friendships develop only after finding something that is valued by both individuals. Strully and Strully stated that "all individuals must be valued for their gifts" (1992, p. 168). What gifts or talents the individual brings into the relationship have to be of importance only to the other person. People need to like each other and to develop a degree of mutual respect for friendships to be able to exist.

MAC AND DAVE: THE SHARED DISABILITY EXPERIENCE

Mac and Dave live 2,000 miles apart: Mac on the east coast and Dave on the west coast. They met a few years ago at a conference focusing on disability issues and found that they both shared the same wry sense of humor and sarcasm concerning a number of the speakers at the conference. Mac and Dave found that they had many of the same experiences in coming to terms with their acquired disabilities but currently share few similar day-to-day interests. Yet, they spend at least an hour each week talking together on the telephone, and there are many e-mail messages crossing the continent between calls. They frequently talk about each other to their other friends. Not only do they consider each other to be close friends, but they also list each other as important members of their personal support systems.

Mac and Dave share more of a friendship of spirit than a friendship requiring proximity. Although they met at a time when they were in the same place, since then they have had few face-to-face meetings. Their shared experience is their disability, which provides them with a similar perspective on life. They can look at a situation and see the same things, whereas people without disabilities may see something completely different.

Professionals without disabilities who are involved in the disability field have long been promoting the need for people with disabilities to have friends who do not have disabilities. Much emphasis has been placed on integration and inclusion in all aspects of an individual's life, especially socially. Special curricula have been developed for teaching social skills for individuals with disabilities from the time they are young children with the specific goal of being able to interact with people without disabilities. What may have been forgotten, or at least de-emphasized, is the development of skills and the promotion of friendships among people with disabilities. Also lost or unrecognized is the value and support that people with disabilities experience when they spend time together (Gilson, 1996). For many people with disabilities, the experience of disability community and culture is a positive affirmation of their lives (Hahn, 1994). There exists a sentiment among many people with disabilities that they can share things with others with disabilities and be more comfortable than they can with people who do not have disabilities. This experience and sense of comfort is very similar to that of other communities with minority status (e.g., women, African Americans, Native Americans). It often has been found that human services and health care professionals who do not have disabilities, by acting under presumptions of "recommended practices," have determined that the quality of life for a person with a disability can be measured by the amount of time spent in inclusive settings. Unfortunately for many people with disabilities, inclusion may translate into an experience of exclusion and isolation from other people with disabilities, from their community, and from their culture (Gilson, 1996). Two fundamental issues exist here for the professional without disabilities: 1) There is the need to truly appreciate the disability community and the value that people with disabilities may bring to any relationship; and 2) people with disabilities must be afforded the opportunity to choose how and with whom they wish to spend their time, where and how they choose to live, where and how they choose to recreate, and where and how they choose to work.

ROB AND SAM: FRIENDSHIPS DON'T JUST HAPPEN

Rob and Sam have work stations next to each other. They are both in their 20s, but unlike many of their age peers, they are not into making a personal statement by the way they dress. Jeans and tee-shirts are their preferred clothing style. Because they work in a sheltered workshop, there is no space available for them to personalize their work stations, but both are very particular about having a neat and orderly space around them. Both men work the same hours, ride the same van, and share a two-bedroom townhouse. Supported living staff take the two men shopping together every Friday evening, and then they stop for pizza and beer before returning home. When Sam and Rob were asked who they considered their friends to be, both listed the staff who provide periodic supervision, and neither listed each other. In fact, when questioned specifically whether he considered Sam his friend, Rob said, "No, I don't even like him."

At some point in time, someone decided that Rob and Sam would make good roommates and assumed that they could be friends. The decision was probably made by a well-meaning staff person who deals on a day-to-day basis with a large waiting list of individuals with disabilities who are in need of residential services. Often the reason that people with disabilities become roommates is because of similar skills, because of a need for the same level of assistance or supervision, or because of funding source availability. Too often a bed becomes available and the next person on the waiting list moves into that slot. This is likely what happened with Sam and Rob. Although roommates do not have to be friends, it was assumed that Sam and Rob were friends because they were always seen together doing common things. Neither man is very assertive, and neither has complained about doing everything together nor have they exhibited any behavior that would indicate that they were not friends. The reader should be careful not to blame Rob or Sam for not developing skills of being assertive. Unfortunately, for many people with disabilities, medical, educational, and vocational settings reinforce capitulation and acquiescence. Although self-advocacy organizations provide a sense of the right to choice, self-determination, and empowerment, for some individuals with disabilities these behaviors and approaches to life must be learned. This also may require an unlearning, or rejecting, of what was taught earlier in their lives.

It is important to also consider that Rob and Sam are visited frequently by staff members, and it was those same staff members whom the men consider to be their friends. So perhaps having these people around them makes living, working, and having coffee together enjoyable for these two men. Too often, well-meaning supervisors and administrators have cautioned against friendships developing between consumers and staff. Staff members have been told to keep consumers at a distance from their personal lives outside of work. Luckily, for many people with disabilities who were isolated from community life, staff members who worked with them found ways around these written or unwritten agency policies. Being taken to a staff member's home for an afternoon visit or going to a neighborhood picnic was the only time away from the routine of the residential setting for many individuals with disabilities. When a friendship exists between paid staff and a consumer, there is typically "a reversal of the official or public roles that the two people are expected to play" (Lutfiyya, 1993, p. 101). The staff person is not in charge, and the consumer does not have to perform according to a program. What does occur is a mutual sharing of whatever talents each brings to the relationship.

CIRCLES OF FRIENDS

When *Circles of Friends* (Perske, 1988) was first published, it confirmed to many professionals without disabilities what people with disabilities (Zola, 1993) have been writing about and saying for many years: Individuals with disabilities can live successfully in various community settings if there is a sharing of talents and a commitment by individuals with and without disabilities who considered themselves to be friends. The term *circle of friends* was actually created by Judith Snow, a person with a severe disability, and her friend Marsha Forest as a result of their experiences with the Joshua Committee created to support Judith (Forest & Pearpoint, 1992). The Joshua Committee was the name given to the people who provided personal care, services, and friendship to Judith before the term "circle" began to be used. Circle of friends is based on the concept that everyone has "layers of relationships, like concentric circles, with different levels of intensity in the relationships" (Forest & Pearpoint, 1992, p. 79). The inner circles are reserved for those who are our supportive family members, our close friends, and for the people with whom we are intimate.

Many people with disabilities do not have people in their inner circles. These are the people with disabilities who many times slip through the cracks (i.e., are not offered social support opportunities), either because they are not noticed or because their behavior causes too much notice. They are often the people who are the last to be considered for community living, the last to be considered for employment options, and the last to be included in social settings in which there is opportunity for friendships to develop. If we assume that quality in one's life can be measured in part by the friendships he or she has, then a person's life can be improved if we fill up his or her "inner circle" (Forest & Pearpoint, 1992).

SHONDA: CREATING A "CIRCLE"

After living for 10 years in a nursing home, Shonda was finally able to move into an accessible apartment that provided 24-hour personal assistance services. Although her family visited her several times each year in the nursing home, they could not afford all of the medical care that she needed nor did they live in a home that could be made accessible for a wheelchair and the other equipment that Shonda needs. Shonda does not speak, but through an eye gaze augmentative communication system, she is able to communicate quickly and effectively. It is clear that she is a very intelligent young woman. After a few weeks of settling into her new home, Shonda was connected with an employment service for people with disabilities and assigned a job coach. Within a matter of weeks, her job coach heard about a new defense contract that a local company had received. The company had a job opportunity that was appropriate for Shonda if she were provided with adapted computer software and if she were able to use her own personal assistive devices. Shonda began to work part time 5 days per week, spending the rest of the time at home.

Everything was going smoothly until Shonda's personal assistance services were reduced to 16 hours a day. Because she cannot feed herself or take care of her personal hygiene needs, she needs the availability of an attendant at all hours of the day and for safety, at night. One of Shonda's personal attendants shared her outrage at the prospect of her having no other alternative than to return to the nursing home and advocated strongly that there be full 24-hour coverage. All efforts to get the 8 hours reinstated were to no avail. Shonda notified her job coach of the impending crisis, and the job coach, also outraged, decided that there must be another way to solve the problem. The job coach met with Shonda and the attendant, and together they decided to take the dilemma to Shonda's supervisor at work. A "circle" began to evolve when Shonda's employer mentioned the situation to two of Shonda's co-workers, and Shonda, using her adapted telephone system, called her sister. Within days, this group of seven people began to brainstorm about what could be done that would allow Shonda to continue to live in her apartment and continue to work. Shonda's "circle" came up with the vision that if she used her 16 hours of personal assistance services at home, then co-workers could feed her lunch. Her supervisor offered to make arrangements with the nurse in charge of the company's employee wellness office to check on Shonda's daily personal hygiene needs. The supervisor, the job coach, and Shonda went to the head of the company and requested that Shonda's hours be increased to 6 each day, which meant that with the 2 hours of transportation and the 6 hours at her place of employment, Shonda could manage to continue to live in her apartment.

Weekends remained a problem. Shonda's recently widowed sister, with whom she had never been close, began to spend Saturday and Sunday nights at the apartment. At first, it was just to sleep, but gradually, her sister began to come over a little earlier in the evening so that they could go out to dinner or go to a movie. And then the two sisters began to do things with the personal care attendant who did not work on weekends. Shonda's inner circle began to fill. It continued to fill with people who Shonda was able to meet when she went out on those weekend evenings, people who began to laugh with Shonda, share secrets with her, and value her ability to really think before "speaking."

"A circle of friends is both a process and an outcome. . . . To build that process and to reach that outcome takes energy, creativity, and a deep belief that different kinds of people can be friends. . . . Support circles do not and will not happen spontaneously" (Forest & Pearpoint, 1992, p. 76). It is striking to note that many of the friends without disabilities who participated in circles of support when they first began to be called "circles" (Perske, 1988) were current or former staff members who had cared for the person with the disability, as with Shonda and her former personal care attendant. In fact, Shonda's job coach, a paid services provider, was the one who began to assemble people who thought it unfair that an impersonal decision made for fiscal reasons would cause Shonda to lose her home. People who worked with Shonda, both in her home and at work, cared about her enough to take time out of their lives to make her vision a reality. In doing this, they began to get to know her better, share her frustrations, and celebrate successes with her. This certainly happened with the evolving relationship with her sister. A relationship that existed only because of blood ties, over a period of time, became a friendship, and this friendship created opportunities for other friendships and for gaining access to new relationships (Amado, 1993). This provided Shonda with the opportunity to have a number of people to whom she could turn for support. No one had to carry the full burden of supporting Shonda all of the time. When a circle of friends is working well, no one person feels that he or she has to carry more responsibility than any other circle member.

SARA: SOME OF US NEED A RELATIONSHIP COACH

Sara is at risk of losing her job—not because she does not possess the skills to perform her work or because she is not punctual or dependable. Sara constantly talks to anyone who is around her, and productivity is markedly reduced in her department. Recently, a number of Sara's co-workers, in response to being told that the department's productivity has decreased, went to their mutual supervisor to complain that Sara talks about the intimate details of her life to the extent that it interferes with them getting their own jobs done. For example, Sara describes in great detail what she and her boyfriend did the night before, with such embellishments that her story is not believable. The supervisor has met with Sara's job coach and explained what he considers to be Sara's disruptive behavior. After speaking with Sara and others, her job coach determined that the majority of what Sara is telling her co-workers is false information or, at a minimum, gross exaggerations of the truth but that she was being encouraged to provide more and more details by many of the people around her. When the job coach talked to Sara about this, Sara explained that she was only "talking girl talk with her friends, just like they do on television." She had no idea that her co-workers were egging her on, and in fact, were encouraging the exaggerations. Sara did not realize that her co-workers were laughing at her and were really not her friends.

There are people like Sara who have never had the experiences or opportunities to develop mutual friendships. For many people with disabilities, education primarily has focused on acquiring skills and mastering tasks; little time has been allotted to or allowed for the development of social skills and social relationships. What is striking in Sara's situation is that she is the only person who has been identified as having a disability among her co-workers, which makes her inappropriate conversations a "problem" rather than just a nuisance. Rather than just confront Sara and tell her that she is interfering, her co-workers requested that someone else—their supervisor—do something. This is the first clue that the people who Sara thinks are her friends are really not. If these people were Sara's friends, they would not want to see her embarrassed and would speak to her directly. A friend might also confront the other co-workers who make fun of Sara, and a friend might come to her defense. It also suggests that Sara's job coach may not have conducted a full evaluation of the work environment, including looking for attitudinal barriers that may be present that would need to be addressed to increase Sara's opportunity for success.

Sara uses television relationships as her guide as to what constitutes a friendship. This is not directly due to her disability but rather to her lack of experience in interacting with a number of people on many different levels of association. Tied to Sara's disability are the attitudes that some people hold about and toward individuals with disabilities, as exemplified by the reluctance of her co-workers to take up the interference issue directly with Sara. Besides work skills, Sara needs to have the opportunity to acquire social skills to "fit in" and be included in her current, and perhaps any future, work environments.

WHAT RELATIONSHIP COACHES DO

One of the ways that Sara can learn what friendship is all about and learn different ways to interact with people is with a coach (Stainback & Stainback, 1990), sometimes also referred to as an integration facilitator (Strully & Strully, 1993). A coach is someone who will role play and model for Sara in actual situations as she learns appropriate conversational skills and body language. In reality, professionals cannot program friendships, but they can build connections to foster and support friendships between individuals with and without disabilities (Grenot-Scheyer, Coots, & Falvey, 1989). The relationship coach provides the feedback that we all require as we develop, extend, and expand our social relationships. Sara needs a coach to make introductions, find opportunities so that people can really get to know her, and perhaps even represent her (Strully & Strully, 1993). Grenot-Scheyer et al. (1989) considered the following social skills and actions that are often expressed by friends, capable of being shaped, modeled and/or coached:

- Displays a positive interaction style
- Gets the message across
- Is reinforcing to others
- Initiates thoughtful actions
- Is a good listener
- Shares belongings and feelings
- Has similar likes and dislikes
- Takes the perspective of others
- Is trustworthy and loyal

For example, for someone who is nonverbal, a smile or special eye gaze as a greeting conveys a message and is a skill that can be easily reinforced. Individuals with varying types of disabilities can be taught to initiate thoughtful actions such as sending a greeting card or telephoning someone just to say hello and knowing when to keep a secret when it is entrusted by a friend (Grenot-Scheyer et al., 1989). Active listening is a communication skill that can be taught that can improve both listening and expression of wants and desires.

With Sara, a relationship coach definitely would want to work with her on increasing her listening skills. When she is with her co-workers, she does all of the talking, always about things happening to her. Learning to ask other people questions about themselves and then listening and giving the other person her full attention would provide an opportunity for a more mutual interaction. The coach working with Sara might have to role play and rehearse conversations in the beginning, but Sara would soon be able to take this skill to the workplace. The coach also could help Sara identify things that she could do for others, such as asking others if there is anything she can do to help when she finishes her own work. Or, Sara could find out her co-workers' birthdays and send them cards or bake something and take it to work to share on special occasions. These are all things Sara could do that would allow people to see her as a potential friend rather than just as a co-worker with a disability.

Another way for Sara to learn about friendship is by joining a peer support group or peer disability organization through which she may have the opportunity to develop natural friendships based on shared or similar experiences. A peer support group is different from a formalized friendship or support circle. The more formal situation has the potential of placing an "overemphasis in the 'helper–helpee' relationship, [which] can easily skew the delicate balance of giving and receiving that is the precursor of true friendship" (Van der Klift & Kunc, 1994, p. 393). For Sara, learning about friendships among peers, rather than with people who do not have disabilities, may be an easier and more positive experience than learning from professional intervention. Whereas Shonda's peers can tell her, in very concrete terms, how they make friends at work, a professional also can make suggestions. But those ideas come from the perspective of someone who does not have a disability and who does not have the same experiences.

BILL AND JANET: DISABILITY DOES MAKE A DIFFERENCE WITHIN A RELATIONSHIP

Bill and Janet met at work on Bill's first day on the job. They started flirting with each other from the day that they met. Within a month Janet asked Bill out on a date, the first of many during a 3-month courtship that gradually changed into a sexually intimate partnership. Their romantic relationship never interfered with their professional responsibilities, and both believed that they had the support of their co-workers and employer. Janet and Bill took each other home to meet their respective families; spent holidays with each family; and after a year, announced that they were going to marry. It was only when Janet's family questioned whether she knew what she was getting herself into was there any true acknowledgment that Bill's physical disability had and would have an effect on their relationship.

When one or both partners in a relationship or a friendship has a disability that relationship is different than if neither had a disability. This fact is sometimes forgotten when developing programs that include individuals with disabilities with people without disabilities with the hope of developing mutual relationships. It is also sometimes forgotten in situations in which well-meaning friends play Cupid and match a friend with a disability with an acquaintance without a disability in the hope of a future romantic liaison.

In any relationship, one person may have strengths that make up for the limitations of the other; but in a relationship in which one partner has a disability, limitations may require an unequal distribution of responsibility. This unequal distribution may be with very apparent things such as one partner always having to carry the luggage or in smaller, more subtle ways that few people realize. For example, Bill cannot bend to tie his shoes and requires someone to do this for him. On those days when Bill wears tennis shoes, Janet must be there to tie them or he runs the risk of tripping over the laces until he finds someone else to tie them. One might think that this is insignificant because Bill can always choose to wear different shoes, but Bill really likes to wear tennis shoes. Janet knows that she must stay to tie the shoes, but gets very impatient on the days she knows that it will make her late to work. This example is only one of a number of daily accommodations that Bill and Janet must make. Before they married, they had no idea of the extent of the accommodations that they would be making, and it is only after a period of a few years that they are becoming comfortable with the roles of their relationship.

ISSUES THAT ACCOMPANY INTIMATE RELATIONSHIPS

Relationships between partners with and without disabilities may also pose very unique issues in terms of personal care issues and the maintenance of sexual intimacy. Because of the nature of Bill's disability, there are occasions when Janet must assist Bill with cleanup following bowel care. Such cleanup or hygiene care may be more commonly performed by a personal assistant. For individuals for whom such requirements are only episodic or may be beyond budget capabilities, the spouse or partner must necessarily provide such care. Such role switches, between that of intimate sexual partner and that of personal care assistant, can place discomfort and unease within the relationship. For people without disabilities, such experiences may be so rare as to be virtually nonexistent. But for many people with disabilities, the experiences are much more common, as they are with Janet and Bill. In addition, for couples who live in both a nondisability world, in which independence and autonomy are hallmarks of success and achievement, and a disability world, in which personal assistance is more commonplace, it is likely that both partners will, at times, feel out of sync with one or both worlds. Janet and Bill then are confronted with needing to adapt to both worlds because neither can be fully a part of the other world.

Intimate relationships between some people with and without disabilities can be very much like intimate relationships in which each partner is of a different religious faith, different race, or different ethnicity. As those people with disabilities increasingly identify with the disability community, natural tensions may emerge with partners without disabilities. These are tensions and ways of thinking and being that can be worked through with dialogue and effort. Among the many points that are important to consider is that the experience of disability, for many, is an experience that affects people to the very core of their identities. As such, it must be a part of the dialogue and conversation of the relationship. Many people with disabilities experience the world differently than partners or mates without disabilities. The partners share in the experiences of discrimination, lack of access and accommodation, and disenfranchisement. People with disabilities may never be able to truly grasp the feelings of their partners without disabilities when they see their partners with disabilities turned away from events or being unable to complete tasks or enter buildings because the necessary accommodations are not available. They will never experience the personal disappointment of not being able to attend an event because an interpreter has not been supplied or because an art gallery is on the third floor of a building and there is no elevator. Understanding, acknowledging, and accepting that the experiences of people with disabilities may be quite different is essential to the development and growth of intimate relationships.

DISCUSSION

Seven different cases are presented in this chapter, each providing a different glimpse of friendships and/or relationships experienced by people with disabilities. There are many different ways that friendships develop, but all require some mechanism (i.e., proximity) that allows people to meet each other. Also required is a common interest or issue. Although some friendships occur naturally, such as those between Martha and Jenny and Mac and Dave, other friendships require someone else to set the stage so that friendships can evolve. For example, Sara may need a relationship coach to help her learn the social skills that can facilitate the development of friendships between her and some of her co-workers. Without help, Sara's excessive and inappropriate talking will probably continue and will interfere with her social life and also with her employment.

What is shared and what it takes to attract people to become friends should be of importance primarily to the friends themselves and not to those outside of the relationship. Professionals sometimes make the mistake of putting people together who they think would make great friends and then fail to check whether this is so. Rob and Sam do everything together only because staff take them both together everywhere they go. Rob and Sam do not consider themselves to be friends, but they do consider some of the staff that work with them and take them places to be their friends. Friendships that exist between staff members and people with disabilities are not frowned on in this chapter, because often individuals with disabilities have the opportunity to get into the community and meet other people through staff interactions. In this way, staff members serve as the facilitators for other relationships that develop.

Friendships and relationships exist between people with disabilities, between people without disabilities, and between people with and without disabilities. Shonda and her circle of friends is a good example of friendships among someone with a disability and others without. In response to a crisis in Shonda's life, people who worked with her "circled" about her to support her and to prevent another nursing home placement. Friendships developed because there was an opportunity to get to know Shonda and to share similar interests. The more Shonda is able to get out in the community, the more opportunity she will have to acquire friends of her choosing.

The relationship between Bill and Janet is different from the other cases because their relationship is more than a friendship—it involves intimacy. Their relationship reinforces the fact that having a disability is sometimes irrelevant to forming friendships and relationships. The issues that develop when a friend, partner, or spouse has a disability, however, should not be ignored. Having a disability may or may not make it more difficult to initially make friends or to enter into a relationship, but it certainly makes it more difficult to maintain.

Barriers to transportation and the extra costs involved may make it difficult to maintain a face-to-face relationship. This is why many people with disabilities such as Teresa are turning to the Internet and to other electronic technology for regular communications with their current friends, as well as using it to meet other people. No matter whether we interact with our friends face-to-face on a regular basis or depend on long-distance communication, friendships are an essential part of our lives.

CONCLUSION

There is no difference in the importance that friendship plays in the lives of people with or without disabilities. Friends can be very similar to each other or very different. Friendships can exist when one person has a disability and the other does not, when both have disabilities, or when neither has a disability. This chapter has shown differing ways that friendships develop when the necessary components of proximity and commonality are present. The extent to which these components exist, and the form they take, is primarily important to the people involved in a relationship, and it is not a matter for professional judgment. The authors acknowledge that we have only touched the surface of the many different types of relationships that exist and have discussed only a few of the ways that friendships develop for people with disabilities.

Although people with and without disabilities share many of the same joys, problems, satisfactions, and frustrations in their relationships, the presence of a disability provides a different dimension. Having a disability might mean that some skills must be learned and some beliefs unlearned before close and meaningful relationships can occur with other people or might mean that coaching is needed to open the door for the possibility of a relationship to exist. The presence of a disability may require an unequal distribution of tasks or responsibilities within a relationship. The relationships or friendships that someone with a disability might have may be only with paid caregivers until one gains access to increased opportunities for meeting people. Or someone with lack of access to his or her community because of a mobility impairment may choose to maintain or even develop meaningful relationships through the technology of the Internet and have only minimal face-to-face proximity with his or her friends. In every friendship and relationship there is a sharing of talents and gifts, which no matter how simple or complex, how equal or unequal, or how long the friendship or relationship lasts, affects the quality of life of the people involved.

REFERENCES

Amado, A.N. (1993). Working on friendships. In A.N. Amado (Ed.), *Friendships and community connections between people with and without developmental disabilities* (pp. 279–298). Baltimore: Paul H. Brookes Publishing Co.

Forest, M., & Pearpoint, J. (1992). Families, friends, and circles. In J. Nisbet (Ed.), *Natural supports in school, at work, and in the community for people with severe disabilities* (pp. 65–86). Baltimore: Paul H. Brookes Publishing Co.

Gilson, S.F. (1996). Students with disabilities: An increasing voice and presence on college campuses. *Journal of Vocational Rehabilitation, 6*, 263–272.

Grenot-Scheyer, M., Coots, J., & Falvey, M.A. (1989). Developing and fostering friendships. In M.A. Falvey (Ed.), *Community-based curriculum: Instructional strategies for students with severe handicaps* (2nd ed., pp. 345–358). Baltimore: Paul H. Brookes Publishing Co.

Hahn, H. (1994). The minority group model of disability: Implications for medical sociology. *Research in Sociology of Health Care, 11*, 3–24.

Lutfiyya, Z.M. (1993). When "staff" and "consumers" become friends. In A.N. Amado (Ed.), *Friendships and community connections between people with and without developmental disabilities* (pp. 97–108). Baltimore: Paul H. Brookes Publishing Co.

O'Brien, J., & O'Brien, C.L. (1993). Unlikely alliances: Friendships and people with developmental disabilities. In A.N. Amado (Ed.), *Friendships and community connections between people with and without developmental disabilities* (pp. 9–39). Baltimore: Paul H. Brookes Publishing Co.

Perske, R. (1988). *Circles of friends: People with disabilities and their friends enrich the lives of one another.* Nashville, TN: Abingdon Press.

Stainback, W., & Stainback, S. (1990). Facilitating peer supports and friendships. In W. Stainback & S. Stainback (Eds.), *Support networks for inclusive schooling: Interdependence integrated education* (pp. 51–63). Baltimore: Paul H. Brookes Publishing Co.

Strully, J.L., & Strully, C.F. (1992). The struggle toward inclusion and the fulfillment of friendship. In J. Nisbet (Ed.), *Natural supports in school, at work, and in the community for people with severe disabilities* (pp. 165–177). Baltimore: Paul H. Brookes Publishing Co.

Strully, J.L., & Strully, C.F. (1993). That which binds us: Friendship as a safe harbor in a storm. In A.N. Amado (Ed.), *Friendships and community connections between people with and without disabilities* (pp. 213–225). Baltimore: Paul H. Brookes Publishing Co.

Van der Klift, E., & Kunc, N. (1994). Beyond benevolence: Friendship and the politics of help. In J.S. Thousand, R.A. Villa, & A.I. Nevin (Eds.), *Creative and collaborative learning: A practical guide to empowering students and teachers* (pp. 391–401). Baltimore: Paul H. Brookes Publishing Co.

Zola, I.K. (1993). Self, identity and the naming question: Reflections on the language of disability. In M. Nagler (Ed.), *Perspectives on disability* (2nd ed., pp. 15–23). Palo Alto, CA: Health Markets Research.

Zygmunt, L.L., Larson, M.S., & Tilson, G.P., Jr. (1994). Disability awareness training and social networking. In M.S. Moon (Ed.), *Making school and community recreation fun for everyone: Places and ways to integrate* (pp. 209–219). Baltimore: Paul H. Brookes Publishing Co.

Gaining Access
to the Community

Ed Turner, John C. Barrett,
and Mary-Kay Webster

Since the early 1970s, Congress has passed many laws to enable people
with disabilities to more easily become active members of their communities. The enactment of these laws began with the reauthorization
of the Rehabilitation Act of 1973 (PL 93-112), which was followed by
the passage of a landmark special education law, the Education for All
Handicapped Children Act of 1975 (PL 94-142). That Act was followed
by the passage of the Americans with Disabilities Act (ADA) of 1990
(PL 101-336). Despite these and other legislative milestones, many individuals with disabilities continue to live in institutions or with their
families and remain isolated from their communities. Although laws
have been passed giving people with disabilities the right to gain access to their communities, paternalistic attitudes of disability services
providers, legislators, professionals, and the general public still exist.
These attitudes remain a considerable barrier for people with disabilities in their quest to gain access to their communities. This chapter
reviews barriers to the community, illustrates how barriers have been

The authors wish to thank Valerie (Vicki) Brooke, our friend and Associate Director
of Training at the Virginia Commonwealth University Rehabilitation Research and
Training Center on Supported Employment, for her assistance in the preparation of this
chapter.

reduced, and describes strategies designed to create accessible communities that can be used by people with and without disabilities.

Any attempt to discuss barriers to employment must be accompanied by an explanation of difficulties people with disabilities face when trying to gain access to the community. The road to employment is as bumpy as the road to living successfully in the community. Many of the same community access strategies described in this chapter can be applied to employment.

There are many parallels between gaining access to the community and gaining access to employment opportunities. Laws against discrimination do not remedy barriers to employment or to the community. For example, the ADA prohibits discrimination on the basis of disability in the employment field, and the Fair Housing Amendments of 1988 (Federal Housing Amendment, 1989) prohibits discrimination in housing on the basis of disability. But despite the laws, unemployment remains high among individuals with disabilities, and the availability of accessible housing has not increased. In other words, laws do not stop employers and landlords from continuing to doubt the abilities of people with disabilities to work and live in the community.

The essential ingredient for both successful employment outcomes and for community living is how people with disabilities use self-advocacy and self-determination to make laws and services work best for them. How this can be accomplished to enable people with disabilities to become involved in their communities has broad implications for successful employment outcomes.

BARRIERS

Significant barriers still exist that contribute to people with disabilities being forced to live in isolation. The most serious and pervasive barrier is related to public attitudes and misconceptions regarding disability issues. Foremost among these misconceptions is the belief that people with disabilities need to be raised in seclusion and live in protective environments *for their own good*. These negative attitudes or public misconceptions continue to be part of the general public's belief system. Evidence of this can be found in the structure of many of the newer disability rights laws. Although federal funds typically are tied to new specific public laws and/or projects when new regulations represent a major shift in policy, the ADA, for example, was structured in a manner that did not include federal funding to promote and/or change old practices and to create critical new community practices, even though it represented a major shift in public policy. Therefore, it appears that although lawmakers were supportive of the ADA, they still had sufficient lingering doubts that resulted in a lack of federal funds to support this major shift in national policy.

Further evidence of the public's misconceptions that people with disabilities need to remain in seclusion and/or protective environments can be found in the division of the federal budget. In the late 1990s, the bulk of federal funds to support people with disabilities goes directly to facility-based programs. These funds are not designed to flow down to the individual; rather, these funds support the services of institution-based programs. The facility managers of these disability services programs make extremely strong arguments supporting the notion that facilities can efficiently care for people with disabilities in group settings such as residential facilities, sheltered workshops, and day treatment programs. Yet, these programs are not designed to meet the individual needs of people with disabilities. Efficiency is achieved by meeting group demands and administrative convenience. Therefore, concepts such as people with disabilities exerting choice and/or control over the services that they receive do not occur in these environments.

The first time that these beliefs of segregation and protection underwent serious public questioning was in the 1960s. It was not surprising that these long-held beliefs would start being questioned during this time when so many other social changes were occurring in the United States. Also many movements were underway that were giving birth and life to the disability rights movement, including the parent-motivated deinstitutionalization movement, the civil rights movement, DeJong's nonmedical model movement, and a variety of self-help movements. This atmosphere of changing social values and attitudes caused individuals with disabilities living in nursing homes to assert their right to integrated lives in their communities (McDonald & Oxford, 1996). By the 1970s, the outcry from this very large and diverse constituency group and their supporters was loud enough to cause the then–U.S. President Jimmy Carter to call for the first White House Conference on Disability, which forever changed the world for people with disabilities.

Many of the recommendations that came out of the White House Conference on Disability formed the basis of the historic legislation that is highlighted in the opening of this chapter. More important, many of the people with disabilities attending this momentous conference became the leaders in the emerging disability rights movement. These leaders became the driving force that turned revolutionary recommendations into laws that have become more than words on paper. Many of these leaders not only played a key role in getting these historic laws passed, but also served as role models by encouraging the disability community to fight for the implementation of those laws.

DISABILITY RIGHTS MOVEMENT
CRACKS THE DOOR TO THE COMMUNITY

Certainly there were great leaders before the 1970s who made tremendous contributions to opening the door to the community for individuals with disabilities. Most notable among these leaders was Helen Keller (Sullivan, 1953). Her personal fight for equality as a person with a visual impairment, earlier in the 20th century, inspired many people across many different disabilities to become active members of their communities. Helen Keller's life and work advanced the rights of people with visual impairments to a level far beyond those of other disability groups. She nullified many long-held misconceptions about people who are blind and increased public awareness of this particular disability and demonstrated how people with this disability could actively participate and contribute to their own communities.

Despite the leadership efforts of pioneers such as Helen Keller, it was not until the 1970s that an organized effort was initiated to open the entire community to all people, regardless of disability. The White House Conference on Disability seemed to motivate people with disabilities to take charge of their own destinies. This was an important era in the disability rights movement.

Several important national leaders have emerged since the 1970s to breathe life into the disability movement. Each of these leaders has done a great deal to shape much of the disability-related public policies in the United States. There are three leaders who are particularly noteworthy because of their responsibility in starting a national and, in some cases, international movements to promote the rights of people with disabilities. In addition to providing leadership to a national crusade, each of the individuals presented here has made significant contributions to U.S. society by developing tools that promote and increase community access. These three leaders serve as role models for all Americans and include the late Ed Roberts, Judy Heumann, and Justin Dart. Their work has permanently changed the lives of hundreds of thousands of people with disabilities.

While living in a residential care facility, Ed Roberts (died March 14, 1995), a noted advocate, recognized the need for flexible independent living services. He often spoke of his nursing care experience and how his daily needs were met according to a staff's schedule rather than according to what he needed or wanted. Ed was determined that he and other individuals with disabilities would have the same rights to community access as people without disabilities. His determination led to the establishment of the independent living movement, which began with 30 Centers for Independent Living (CILs). The number of

CILs has grown, and there are more than 350 Centers nationally (Michaels, 1996). Ed Roberts' list of accomplishments is long and inspiring, having served as the Commissioner of the California Department of Rehabilitative Services and as the Director of the World Institute on Disability. Yet, Ed Roberts will be remembered best as the father of the national independent living (IL) movement.

The IL movement that Ed helped to establish provides life-changing services that enabled individuals with disabilities to actively participate as vital members of their communities. The IL movement is unique in the disability community. The IL movement has had a formidable impact on the lives of many people, both with and without disabilities.

Judy Heumann, another great advocate, in her effort to open doors to the community, has had an extremely powerful influence on the lives of millions of people with disabilities. Judy became nationally recognized for her work at the World Institute on Disability where, under her leadership, research was conducted that demonstrated the effectiveness of consumer-directed personal assistance services (PAS). This research, which has been documented in a monograph entitled *Attending to America* (Levatt, Heumann, & Zukas, 1978), has led to many states establishing models for personal assistance programs that are consumer-directed. These programs enable thousands of former nursing home residents to live, work, and recreate in their communities.

The work that Judy started in the early 1990s is continuing because of compelling data that continues to document the cost-effectiveness of a consumer-directed PAS program. In fact, this database is becoming so compelling that many national political figures have considered endorsing the consumer-directed personal assistance movement.

As of 1997, Judy works in federal services with a presidential appointment as the Assistant Secretary of Education, but she continues to be a strong advocate for services that are consumer directed and consumer controlled. Her strong voice advocating for the rights of people with disabilities is well respected among her colleagues in Washington, D.C. Judy Heumann has surrounded herself with other qualified individuals with disabilities, such as the Honorable Howard Moses, who serve on her staff and provide a constant national reminder that employees with a disabilities can work at all levels of government.

In the late 1980s, Justin Dart was appointed Chairperson of the President's Committee for the Employment of People with Disabilities by President George Bush. From the first day of his appointment, Justin's burning passion became advocating for the enactment of the ADA. He knew that the ADA would be a key factor in helping people with disabilities to gain access to the community at all levels. After the

ADA was enacted, Justin Dart turned the President's Committee on Employment of People with Disabilities into a clearinghouse for information on the ADA. This singular act gave people with disabilities an opportunity to provide their thoughts and ideas into the writing of the regulations for all five of the ADA's titles.

Justin Dart has traveled across the country urging people with disabilities to accept nothing less than full compliance with the ADA. What is more impressive about Justin's leadership is, after resigning as Chairperson of the President's Committee on Employment of People with Disabilities, he continued urging people with disabilities to insist on ADA enforcement using his own resources to cover travel expenses.

In addition to his leadership on the enactment and compliance with the ADA, Justin Dart has became a leading advocate on health care for people with disabilities. This in turn led him to be one of the founders of Justice For All, an organization that promotes the rights of citizens with disabilities. In the beginning, the primary mission of Justice For All was to advocate for PAS and other important health benefit issues to be included in national health care legislation. When national health care did not secure a favorable score in Congress, Justin and the Justice for All organization turned their attention to maintaining federal disability programs that appear to be threatened by Congress. As of the mid-1990s, Justin Dart has become involved in teaching to people with disabilities the importance of becoming involved in the political process at all levels. As Justin moves across the country he shares advice from his father, as well as some of his own sage advice: "Get involved in politics as if your life depended on it. Because for many of us it does."

Each of these disability rights pioneers have contributed to paving the bumpy road to community access. Their collective accomplishments have created real and lasting change for the disability community and for the entire United States. These leaders have become examples for people with disabilities to follow as they work to become fully integrated into the fabric of their communities.

KEYS TO GAINING ACCESS TO THE COMMUNITY

Developing open and accessible communities remains a large and daunting task. Some communities are further along in this process than others. The following section offers seven key strategies for success.

1. Gaining Knowledge of Disability Rights

A knowledge of disability rights is essential to gaining access to the community. It is empowering to know that federal laws require our

communities to meet certain accessibility requirements. Without specific knowledge about these laws and subsequent violations of the
laws, however, change cannot occur. The old adage of "knowledge is
power" is particularly important when the goal is to create positive
and effective change.

Although it is hard to believe, many people with disabilities have
never heard of the ADA. The powerful titles of the ADA give people
with disabilities the right to employment and the right to gain access to
local government services and in addition give people with speech and
hearing impairments the right to understand and to be understood.
These rights are all relatively new concepts to people living in institutional care facilities or in isolated situations with family members. A
vivid reminder of this lack of information occurs repeatedly during the
self-advocacy training seminars conducted at the Virginia Commonwealth University Rehabilitation Research and Training Center on Supported Employment (VCU-RRTC), a training seminar developed by
people with disabilities for people with disabilities. During each seminar, participants are asked if they have heard of the ADA, and in the
majority of the cases individuals respond with a negative reply. These
experiences are constant reminders that there are still many people
with disabilities who have never heard about the monumental piece of
legislation that gives them the right to be a part of their communities.

2. Putting the Customer in Charge of Services

Large residential care facilities and generic service agencies—not
customer-controlled, community-based services—receive the majority
of federal funds. For example, funding for PAS is often relegated to
home health agencies that give consumers little or no control over the
very intimate services that a personal assistant provides. These agencies continue to thrive despite the growing body of evidence that documents lower operating cost and higher customer satisfaction ratings
for community-based services (Russell, Toy, & Malone, 1996). As a result, there is a struggle developing between small services organizations and the larger facilities. Although customers are voicing their desire for change, there appears to be to a strong interest in maintaining
the system in the 1990s. This struggle is most evident in the statewide
controversy concerning PAS in California. In particular, Californian
decision makers are attempting to resolve whether home health agencies or consumers should be in charge of personal assistants. If the state
finds that the customer should be in charge, then individuals will have
the right to hire; supervise; train; and, if necessary, release paraprofes-
sionals under their supervision. Many states are watching to see how
California will resolve this controversy. In addition, procedures and

guidelines that are developed by the state of California will have an impact on the design of a national PAS program.

3. Being Determined

Gaining access to the community takes more than having knowledge about disability rights and legislation or being able to obtain and direct services. It requires knowing which services are available in the community and having the tools and determination to obtain what is needed. People with disabilities and other community members must truly recognize that diversity builds a strong and effective community and that nothing short of that goal is acceptable.

As was true with the civil rights movement of the 1950s and with the women's rights movement of the 1970s, it takes more than knowing one's rights to ensure equal access. People with disabilities must learn to exercise their right to self-determination as did African Americans and women. Only when a large majority of individuals with disabilities exercise their rights though self-determination and through the use of self-avocacy skills will the promises of laws like the ADA be fully realized and full access to the community be achieved.

4. Supporting and Encouraging

People who have lived in isolated situations, in closed communities made up of family members, or in a residential care facility will need support to obtain important community access goals. Isolation has made many individuals fear the community, and, as a result, these individuals may need support and encouragement to take the important first steps to community involvement. Sometimes fear of the unknown can be a barrier to an individual attempting to gain access to new environments. The following is a case example of how one CIL assisted people with disabilities to overcome their fear of full community participation.

NORFOLK ENDEPENDENCE CENTER

In the early 1980s, the Norfolk Endependence Center recognized the vast number of barriers that people with disabilities confront when attempting to gain access to the community. These barriers were prioritized in terms of significance. The top three barriers included the following: 1) personal fear when attempting to gain access to the community, 2) limited opportunity to use accessible transportation services because of limited service hours, and 3) high costs of leisure and entertainment. Member of the Endependence Center approached these barriers by enlisting the support of the Center's governing board.

One of the Center's governing board members was employed as the executive director of Cultural Experiences Unlimited (CEU). This agency distributed free tickets to local cultural or entertainment events. CEU agreed to donate 20 tickets to the center each month, thereby giving interested participants an opportunity to select community events based on their interest level. Events included college basketball games, live theater, movies, and musical concerts. The center then developed a contract with the local transportation services provider to ensure that CIL members physically could reach these community events. A center staff person, usually a peer counselor, was assigned to accompany participants on these community outings. This would give the peer counselor an opportunity to work with a participant as he or she was attempting to confront community access situations, fears, and concerns.

This approach to community access had many positive and long-term outcomes. The CIL members obtained a taste of the fun and excitement that waited for them once they moved out into the community. Peer counselors acquired new insights into how participants deal with their fears and what types of interventions or supports would be effective and necessary. Parents of participants experienced the excitement of their adult children after participating in a cultural event. Furthermore, the local transportation services provider saw a need for expanding service hours to include weekends and evenings to meet the demands of this new customer base.

The staff at the center redesigned their services to include the new effective techniques that they had learned for assisting people with disabilities with their entry into the community life. Greater emphasis was placed on socialization goals, which had been demonstrated to be a powerful motivator for CIL participants. CIL participants demonstrated incredible determination to achieve independent living goals following the community outings. These experiences became so powerful that the center expanded these outings to include plaza shopping, trips to the mall, visits to museums, local resort vacations, and visits to other sites throughout the community. CIL staff who accompanied participants on these outings stayed in the background so that the participants could practice their independent living goals. Staff would be visible only if there was a demonstrated need to provide support or assistance.

Perhaps one of the most important outcomes of the community access project was that all of the participants became engaged in an organized advocacy effort to expand accessible transportation services. This advocacy effort was in effect for almost 3 years. CIL members wrote letters, made telephone calls, and demonstrated as they demanded evening service operating hours. At the end of this 3-year advocacy campaign, the services provider agreed to offer longer operating hours.

This case demonstrates that people with disabilities may need support to feel comfortable in the community, perhaps from a peer counselor, a friend, or a neighbor. Regardless of the source of support, the goal remains the same: to assist the individual in gaining confidence and to build a personal comfort level with gaining access to the community. This case demonstrates the importance of making the individual with a disability feel at home in the environment in which he or she intends to live or work.

5. Finding the Right Assistive Technology

Assistive technology (AT) remains an important issue for people with disabilities accessing the community (see Chapter 9). From such simple devices as pencil grips to sophisticated driving equipment, AT has revolutionized the lives of individuals with disabilities. The appropriate AT can and will make almost anything possible in every facet of a person's life. AT can increase the employment possibilities of the person with disabilities, as well as make living independently a realistic goal.

For people with disabilities to benefit from AT, they must have legislative information and know how to gain access to the best information and services. Most states have AT systems change projects created by funding provided through the Technology-Related Assistance for Individuals with Disabilities Act of 1988 (PL 100-407). These projects are charged with informing people with disabilities about AT options and how to obtain funding.

6. Having the Right Information

Since the mid-1990s, participants of VCU-RRTC self-advocacy training seminars have cited the lack of information about goods and services as a major barrier to employment. It stands to reason that when someone does not know where or how to gain access to critical information regarding vital community services, there will be a delay in obtaining employment and other independent living goals. Sometimes the delay is so long that apathy begins to set in on the part of people with disabilities and contributes to a loss of desire to become an active part of the community.

CILs have recognized that having accessible and reliable information is necessary for participants to reach their goals. This is why information and referral is a mandated core service of all CILs (Title 7 of the Rehabilitation Act of 1973 [PL 102-569]). Most centers have staffed their agencies with an information and referral specialist who is responsible for maintaining information files on local providers who specialize in goods and services for people with disabilities. These goods and services cover a broad range of items, from wheelchair repair services to vendors that sell medical supplies or hearing aids. In addition, information is available on a variety of community services ranging from accessible housing to vehicle modifications. These specialists are responsible for maintaining information for people with disabilities that will ultimately enable them to fully participate in their community.

Table 1 presents a list of tips for gaining access to information. These tips and/or strategies were developed during a VCU-RRTC Self-Advocacy Leadership Institute for mentors. The tips in Table 1 are designed to increase access to critical information. It should be noted that all of the items have proven to be effective in obtaining services (RRTC Self-Advocacy Leadership Institute, 1996).

7. Being an Effective Self-Advocate

Knowledge of disability laws and rights is not enough to become an active participant in the community. Once a strong knowledge base has been built, then proficiency must be established at using self-advocacy skills to bring change. As all civil rights movements have demonstrated, societal and attitudinal changes do not occur with the mere passage of legislation. Those of us who have worked in the disability rights field since the 1960s have discovered the same is true in the struggle for equality for people with disabilities (Turner, 1994). Despite

Table 1.   Techniques for obtaining information

- Call organizations and/or agencies and ask for a service description brochure. Use the telephone book, library, and personal referrals to obtain contact numbers.
- Ask to be placed on mailing lists.
- When calling organizations and/or agencies, ask the receptionist for a name, position title, and extension number of the person you are interested in contacting.
- Obtain information from magazines that offer consumer report information related to services and merchandise.
- When obtaining equipment, obtain three separate bids with the name of the company, contact person, location, description of equipment and/or service, and price.
- Obtain written documents from doctors and occupational and physical therapists when acquiring needed equipment.
- Work at home until available work outside the home is reached (e.g., tutoring, typing, making telephone sales, selling crafts/hobbies).
- Volunteer at local organizations and agencies. It may lead to a competitive job.
- Obtain information regarding problems/complaints from Medicaid/Medicare assistance board when using home health care agency.
- Talk with people who are working in the area of your career interest. They can give an insider's view of their work, a forecast of the future, and strategies for breaking into the field.

From Chumbley Co., & Turner, E. (1996, May). *Identifying community resources.* Paper presented at Virginia Assistive Technology Conference, Arlington, VA; adapted by permission.

the many enlightened disability rights laws, paternalistic attitudes and prejudices remain that prevent people with disabilities from becoming active members of their communities. These attitudes and prejudices can be overcome by self-determined people with a knowledge of self-advocacy skills and the assertiveness to use them. (To achieve their goals, consumers can apply the techniques presented by the "Six B's of Self-Advocacy" listed in Chapter 7.)

For these tools to be effective, one must have the determination to apply them in real-life situations. They must be put into action by people who are determined to become active members of their communities.

SELF-DETERMINATION: A KEY TO COMMUNITY ACCESS

Following are two stories about individuals with disabilities: Mary-Kay, a woman from an urban setting who became disabled soon after graduating from college and beginning her professional career, and John, a man who was raised in a very rural setting and who became disabled at a very young age.

Although these two individuals came from different backgrounds and, consequently, present different issues and concerns, they share a similar belief that they belong in the community. Both of these individuals possessed a personal desire and determination to take the necessary steps to establish her and his rightful place in the community. Although their steps to community access differ, their will and determination are the same and the significant factor in their success. These cases, unlike many in this book, are not composites and are written by the individuals.

MARY-KAY: REZOOMS HER LIFE

Nineteen eighty-five was a very significant year for me in many ways. First, I was just getting comfortable in my field 3 years after receiving my bachelor of science degree in Accounting from Virginia Commonwealth University in Richmond. My employer, Chesapeake Corporation, had just promoted me from Cost Accountant to Cost Analyst, a position with more responsibility and with a direct impact on the company's earnings potential. Second, my self-image had just come full circle. I was confident in my abilities, comfortable with my introverted need to draw strength from solitude—the kind of solitude our society tends to view as antisocial—and generally was just happy to have survived teenage angst and the carefree madness of the college experience. Third, I was financially independent, unencumbered, and living life at 90 miles an hour: Traveling around the country and abroad, skiing, white water rafting, singing in a choir, and burning the candles at both ends. So, in

August 1985, when I broke my neck while vacationing at our family cabin in the spectacular Adirondack Mountains, my attitude was basically one of immediate acceptance. Acceptance from the standpoint that the first 25 years of my life had been pretty spectacular; so if the next 25 years were meant to be experienced in a chair, so be it. Never once did I think my lifestyle would change. I told Chesapeake I would return, although I was not sure exactly when, and they reassured me that it didn't matter when I returned because a job would be there for me. This became my lifeboat in what was to be a very exasperating journey back to independence.

Every spinal injury is unique. Mine was complicated by being injured 500 miles from my home. I spent 3 months in acute care just trying to stabilize a neck virtually destroyed from diving into 4 feet of water. Classified as a C/6 quadriplegic, I was transferred to what I fondly refer to as "baby rehab," a rehabilitation hospital close to my parents. From Day 1, I insisted that I would return to work in Virginia. Nobody actually said that this was an unrealistic goal, but many people doubted my ability. After 6 months in "baby rehab," I was transferred to Woodrow Wilson Rehabilitation Center in Fishersville, Virginia, a move on which I insisted. At least I was in the same state as my employer. Despite the distance, struggles with the rehabilitation process, and doubting parents, I was determined to resume my life.

Despite problems with rehabilitation, housing, personal assistance, and adaptive equipment, it was 1 year and 11 months before I returned to work. In total, I was hospitalized and in rehabilitation for 14 months. For a long time, I resented the amount of time it took to "REZOOM" my life (my license plate, "REZOOM," represents my philosophy—the emphasis should be to get someone back to as close a facsimile of their "pre-injury life" as possible).

Eleven years later, I am still employed by Chesapeake Corporation as a Systems Administrator. I manage personal attendants in my own home and still enjoy many of my "pre-injury" pleasures of traveling and singing (I did give up snow skiing, not out of necessity but out of personal preference). I serve on numerous local, state, and national committees attempting to simplify the path of others in similar situations.

Serving on the Mayor's Commission for the Disabled, a local Disabilities Services Board, and on the board of CIL allows me to share my experiences with people who are just starting their journeys. Having experienced firsthand and overcome difficult barriers and having nonetheless successfully re-entered the mainstream, I feel uniquely qualified to speak for consumers on advocacy issues in a variety of political forums.

JOHN: A RURAL MAN'S QUEST FOR INDEPENDENCE

I was born in rural southeast Virginia, and at 6 months of age I contracted whooping cough. This caused a high fever, which, in turn, caused cerebral palsy. My parents were told by several medical doctors that I would never be able to do anything for myself and that I would remain a "helpless vegetable" for the rest of my life. My parents took me to a chiropractor in Newport News, Virginia, as a last resort. Establishing regular visits of three or four times a week assisted me in developing the necessary strength to hold up my head and improve my health. My parents continued this medical routine for several years until we moved to Mineral Wells, Texas.

In Mineral Wells, I had a home-bound teacher to begin my early education. I was very slow to learn, but after several years I mastered the necessary educational requirements. After a few years, I returned to Virginia and attended my first public school, albeit in a segregated school for "handicapped" children.

Within a couple years, my family and I moved to a very rural area of Virginia. It was in this rural setting that I attended general education classes from grade 5 to grade 8. This public school system did not have lift-equipped school buses or an accessible school building. To get around these barriers, my mother drove me to and from school each day and paid a fellow schoolmate to transfer me from the car to the school and to provide assistance throughout the school day. After graduating from elementary school, at the eighth-grade level, I was ready to make the transition to the local high school. Again, this building was not accessible, and there were no accessible transportation options. To overcome this problem, I took my high school classes by home-correspondence courses and, within 2 years, earned my high school diploma. Physical barriers were always in my way. I never had any psychological or emotional barriers except when I was exposed to people in the community who would talk "down" to me or patronize. I never paid any attention to people when they stared or talked about me because I always knew that I had a right to be out in the community just as they did.

While living in a remote country area, I began to feel "left out," so I joined the local Boy Scout troop and went on many camping trips, achieved overwhelming tasks, and made new friends. Like school, the Boy Scouts helped me to socialize with others and to build confidence.

As I was getting older, I began thinking about being out on my own and getting a job. I wanted to be on my own and to live independently from my family. I always wanted to have a job that paid well so that I would have the means to live my life the way that I wanted.

Rural community life did not offer many options for jobs or housing. I knew I had to move to the city if I wanted to fulfill my dreams of employment. While attending a disability conference, I discovered a unique training opportunity. I decided to register for the training course and to move to the beach, where I would be close to school and to the beach. The training course assisted me in developing skills of data entry, microfilming, and security monitoring. Having very supportive parents who knew the value of a good education, I was able to succeed in getting the education and training, which has been a tremendous asset in my career path.

Having several years of experience in the disability-rights movement as an administrative assistant and as an active participant I'm very familiar with the law. As an office services assistant at VCU-RRTC, I'm able to provide an individual with a disability with the PAS that he needs. Together, we are the owners of a private consulting business that provides training and technical assistance to the business and professional communities on the unique needs and abilities of individuals with disabilities.

CONCLUSION

This chapter has shared some of the issues and concerns related to gaining access to the community. Increasing community access requires knowledge, determination, and self-determination. A look back through history, from the 1970s to the present, reveals just how far people with disabilities have come in their quest for inclusion in the community. Education needs to occur at all level of community life and especially among policy makers regarding the need to re-allocate public funds from facility-based programs to community-based services. We must remember that "customers" have the right to direct quality services that enables them to have a vital role in community life. In addition, it will be necessary to confront paternalistic and negative attitudes by using strong doses of advocacy in firmly established open and accessible communities.

Colleagues, professionals, students, or concerned advocates with and without disabilities must play a role in paving the road to the community. Recognize the signs of over-protection and paternalism, and correct it when it occurs. Finally, remember that it is not the role of people without disabilities to lead people with disabilities down the road to employment and into the community. Rather, people with and without disabilities must be equal partners and together build a world community, full of opportunity that is accessible for all.

REFERENCES

Americans with Disabilities Act (ADA) of 1990, PL 101-336, 42 U.S.C. §§ 12101 *et seq.*

Chumbley, C., & Turner, E. (1996, May). *Identifying community resources.* Paper presented at Virginia Assistive Technology Conference, Arlington, VA.

Education for All Handicapped Children Act of 1975, PL 94-142, 20 U.S.C. §§ 1400 *et seq.*

Federal Housing Amendment of 1988. 24 C.F.R. Part 14 (January 23, 1989).

Levatt, S., Hueneman, J., & Zukas, H. (1987). *Attending to America* (Monograph). Berkeley, CA: World Institute on Disability.

McDonald, G., & Oxford, M. (1996). *Independent living movement.* Houston, TX: Research and Training Center on Independent Living.

Michaels, B. (1996). *National Council on Independent Living, Rehabilitation Act Committee report.* Washington, DC: U.S. Government Printing Office.

Rehabilitation Act of 1973, PL 93-112, 29 U.S.C. §§ 701 *et seq.*

Russell, M., Toy, A., & Malone, B.L. (1996, November). A community divided. *New Mobility Magazine, 7*(38) 38–47.

Sullivan, A.M. (1953). *Story of my life.* Garden City, NY: Doubleday.

Technology-Related Assistance for Individuals with Disabilities Act of 1988, PL 100-407, 29 U.S.C. §§ 2201 *et seq.*

Turner, E. (1994). Consumers and the Americans with Disabilities Act. *Journal of Vocational Rehabilitation, 4*(3) 202–210.

Index